ISHAM G. HARRIS
of TENNESSEE

SOUTHERN BIOGRAPHY SERIES
BERTRAM WYATT-BROWN, SERIES EDITOR

CONFEDERATE GOVERNOR
AND UNITED STATES SENATOR

ISHAM G. HARRIS
of TENNESSEE

SAM DAVIS ELLIOTT

LOUISIANA STATE UNIVERSITY PRESS

BATON ROUGE

Published with the assistance of the V. Ray Cardozier Fund

Published by Louisiana State University Press
Copyright © 2010 by Louisiana State University Press
All rights reserved
Manufactured in the United States of America
FIRST PRINTING

DESIGNER: Amanda McDonald Scallan
TYPEFACE: Whitman
TYPESETTER: J. Jarrett Engineering, Inc.
PRINTER AND BINDER: Thomson-Shore, Inc.

Frontispiece: Isham Green Harris as Governor.
Courtesy of Tennessee State Library and Archives

Library of Congress Cataloging-in-Publication Data

Elliott, Sam Davis, 1956–
    Isham G. Harris of Tennessee : Confederate governor and United States
senator / Sam Davis Elliott.
        p. cm. — (Southern biography series)
    Includes bibliographical references and index.
    ISBN 978-0-8071-3490-0 (cloth : alk. paper) 1. Harris, Isham G.
(Isham Green), 1818–1897. 2. United States. Congress. Senate—Biography.
3. Legislators—United States—Biography. 4. Governors—Tennessee—
Biography. 5. Tennessee—History—Civil War, 1861–1865 I. Title.
    E664.H31E55 2009
    973.7092—dc22
    [B]
                                                        2009013460

To Nathaniel Cheairs Hughes, Jr.

CONTENTS

PREFACE

"Tennessee will not furnish a single man for purposes of coercion but 50,000 if necessary for the defense of our rights and those of our southern brothers." With these defiant words written on April 17, 1861, in response to the U.S. government's call for troops, Governor Isham Green Harris of Tennessee gave notice that the state would be on the side of the Confederacy in the war started just days before at Fort Sumter. In the weeks that followed, Harris would apply his considerable intellect and talents to transitioning Tennessee into the Confederate States of America, energetically and in some cases ruthlessly attending to the political and military necessities of the state's "revolution" against the government of Abraham Lincoln in Washington. Indeed, the "popular, cynical witticism" of the time noted by historian Stanley Horn was substantially true: "Tennessee never seceded; Isham G. Harris seceded and carried Tennessee along with him."[1]

Isham Harris grew up on the frontier in Middle Tennessee, the youngest of his parents' large family. He left home as a teenager and found and lost a fortune in the boom and bust times in 1830s Mississippi and West Tennessee. Drawn by an older brother's example to the law, he was admitted to the bar in 1841 and enjoyed almost immediate success based on a quick intellect, a naturally aggressive nature, and a native ability to influence people. Raised in a family of small-slaveholders, he married into a family whose patriarch owned more than thirty slaves, cementing his views in favor of the "peculiar institution." He became a Democrat in the days when Andrew Jackson and James K. Polk were Tennessee heroes, and launched a political career in 1847 that lasted, with some interruption, for fifty years, never losing an election.

Harris served in the Tennessee state Senate, as a U.S. congressman, and as governor as America slowly slipped into the sectional crisis that became the Civil War. He was governor in the momentous year of 1861, and was conceded by many to be the driving force in Tennessee joining the Confederacy. He spared no effort

1. Stanley F. Horn, *The Army of Tennessee* (1941; reprint, Wilmington, N.C.: Broadfoot Publishing, 1987), 47.

to recruit Tennesseans for Confederate service, and energetically mobilized the state for war. As a volunteer aide, he served each of the Confederate Army of Tennessee's commanders on nearly every one of its famed battlefields. To many of the people of his day, he was the most prominent Tennessean in the Confederacy, and was even deemed a possible successor to Jefferson Davis if the new republic should survive the six years of Davis's single constitutional term as president.

Sophisticated students of the War Between the States recognize Harris's central role in raising the Provisional Army of Tennessee, which in turn became the core of the Confederate Army of Tennessee, and his early role in defense planning along the Tennessee–Kentucky border and the Mississippi River. More casual readers will recall that the distraught governor tended to the dying Albert Sidney Johnston at Shiloh. Those with the ability to simply run a computer search of the *Official Records* of the war will see a man intimately involved as an advisor to the Confederate government and the high command of the Army of Tennessee, never ceasing his efforts to employ the state's men and resources on behalf of the Confederate States.

With a price on his head, Harris fled from the vengeful Radical government of Tennessee when the Confederacy collapsed in 1865. In an epic journey across the Mississippi River, Arkansas, Texas, and northern Mexico, the fugitive governor ended up in Maximilian's Mexico, seeking with other ex-Confederates to establish a colony of Rebel refugees in a country that itself was in the throes of civil war. Eventually, Harris's fellow expatriates began drifting home, leaving him among the last to leave Maximilian's tottering empire. Harris was able to return to Tennessee in late 1867, after spending the better part of that year in Havana and Liverpool. Harris retained a great deal of influence among former secessionists and other conservatives, and quietly resumed involvement in state politics until 1876, when he mounted a successful effort to become one of Tennessee's U.S. senators.

As a U.S. senator, Harris stuck to his prewar philosophies of keeping tariffs low so that Southern consumers might benefit from Northern and foreign competition and strict construction of the Constitution, which usually meant limiting the influence of the Federal government on those of the states. Yet, in matters where the Constitution specifically provided that Congress had power, such as monetary policy or interstate commerce, Harris showed a lawyer's keen mind and a political boldness that sometimes belied his conservative image. He gained the respect of senators on both sides of the aisle, and was actually the preferred candidate of several Republicans for the office of president pro tem of the Senate at one point in his first term.

During his time in the Senate, he was Tennessee's predominant Democrat, and dedicated himself to the ascendancy of the party within the state and his personal ascendancy over the party machinery. To Harris, "the success of his party meant the greatest possible good for the country." It is a great irony of Harris's later life that even as he was considered the ultimate arbiter of party regularity in Tennessee, he came into conflict with the only Democratic president who served during Harris's time in the Senate, Grover Cleveland, over monetary and tariff policy. Indeed, the last of Harris's significant political acts was to help those who advocated a pro-silver monetary policy gain control of the Democratic Party for the presidential election of 1896. Upon Harris's death in July 1897 a newspaper editor observed: "Tennessee is still the State that produced 'Old Hickory'; still, it is not going too far to say that Senator Harris possessed a strength of will equal to that of any other Tennessean who ever lived, and his control of the politics of the State was probably stronger and continued for a longer time than that ever exercised by anyone else."[2]

The people of his day knew Harris was a remarkable man in many ways. His efforts in private business endeavors as a merchant and lawyer were as successful as his ability to gain office. He had political skill that was unmatched by any Tennessean of his time, and embodied a strange dichotomy of conservatism and revolutionary. Even as his political opponents condemned his riding roughshod over the state constitution in 1861, they acknowledged his intellect, frankness, ability, and courage.[3] Although best known for his role in the Civil War, his story is not only that of the "War Governor of Tennessee," but also that of a talented lawyer, highly partisan Democrat, successful politician, and gifted public servant.

In 1931, the *Nashville Banner* conducted a survey among its readership to determine the "Greatest Tennesseans" to that point. The newspaper received 1,000 votes, naming over 350 persons. Thirty-four years after his death, Isham G. Harris was 10th on the list, behind such famous Tennesseans as Andrew Jackson, James K. Polk, Andrew Johnson, John Sevier, James Robertson, Sam Houston, and Nathan Bedford Forrest. In 1976, to commemorate its centennial and the Bicentennial of the American Revolution, the *Banner* once more conducted the sur-

2. "The Dead Senator," *Nashville American*, July 9, 1897.

3. Oliver P. Temple, *Notable Men of Tennessee from 1833 to 1875: Their Times and Their Contemporaries* (New York: Cosmopolitan Press, 1912), 339.

vey. Those asked to respond were members of the Tennessee Historical Society residing in Middle Tennessee. Presumably, this was a more sophisticated group, and 451 persons responded, nominating 170 historical figures. Many of the same names were again prominent, Jackson, Polk and Johnson, Forrest and Houston, Sevier and Robertson. In this survey, Harris was glaringly absent, not only missing the top 10, but in fact the top 25.[4]

Harris's undeserved omission may be the result of fading memories and the death of the generation that knew him. In 1931, there were many with living memory of his personality and influence over Tennessee in the latter half of the nineteenth century. By 1976, such was not the case, and then, as now, Harris was simply the leader of the ultimately unsuccessful effort to escort the state out of the Union. If Harris is recalled at all by the general public today, it is likely as the attendant of the dying Albert Sidney Johnston. Thus, in our time, the preeminent Tennessean of the Confederacy takes a back seat in the public mind to the man he appointed to his first command, Nathan Bedford Forrest. Harris's omission is striking and undeserved. Among Tennesseans, his was the greatest, and indeed most decisive, influence on Tennessee's course during the watershed event of the Civil War, at least until Andrew Johnson was returned to power by the Federal successes in the state during the war. Although he was on the losing side, Harris's prestige among the people of Tennessee survived the war, and indeed seems to have been enhanced by it. His influence over the state, which first arose in antebellum times, continued to his dying day. The story of nineteenth-century Tennessee cannot be told without a complete understanding of Isham Green Harris.

Isham Harris was a highly visible public figure, and newspapers and other public papers are a rich resource to flesh out the politician, and to a lesser degree, the lawyer. His governors' papers are available at the Tennessee State Library and Archives, but contain little personal correspondence. Other correspondence of a personal and political nature is found in the papers of various personages of his time, but these provide but glimpses of his private life. Harris and his wife, Martha Travis Harris, were apart for large periods in their lives together, either as result of the war, his voluntary exile in Mexico and England, and her preference to remain in Paris, Tennessee, with her family, but any personal correspondence they may have had is either lost or unavailable. The same is true of likely correspondence between Harris and his sons, four of whom survived him. Therefore,

4. Sandy Seawright, "Ten 'Greatest Tennesseans'—A Reappraisal," *Tennessee Historical Quarterly* 35 (Summer 1976): 222–24.

while this book portrays facets of the private individual, the focus here is, by necessity, on his public life.

I am grateful for the assistance from the staffs of the various libraries and repositories where information relating to Harris and his times may be found. Just blocks from my office, the Local History Department of the Chattanooga–Hamilton County Bicentennial Library is always a fruitful place to research matters of Tennessee history, or to seek assistance in obtaining inter-library loans. A few blocks in the opposite direction, the Lupton Library at the University of Tennessee at Chattanooga proved to be an excellent place to locate harder to find secondary sources and access certain internet resources. Within an hour's drive, the library at my alma mater, the University of the South, Sewanee, Tennessee, provided internet access to a plethora of internet historic newspaper databases as well as a few harder to find books.

No subject involving Tennessee history can be considered complete without mining the resources available at the Tennessee State Library and Archives, and in every case I found the staff helpful and the resources easily accessed. Likewise, the Special Collections staff at the University of Tennessee, Knoxville, were accommodating in helping me locate both primary source documents and unpublished dissertations bearing on Harris. Other helpful repositories included the Peabody Library at Vanderbilt University; the Southern Historical Collection at the University of North Carolina; the Perkins Library at Duke University; the James E. Walker Library at Middle Tennessee State University; the Memphis Public Library; the Howard–Tilton Memorial Library at Tulane University; the Western Reserve Historical Society in Cleveland, Ohio; the University of Georgia Library; the W. G. Rhea Library in Paris, Tennessee; and the Library of Congress, Washington.

Helpful individuals associated with libraries, public offices, or historical sites include Richard A. Baker, historian, U.S. Senate Historical Office; John Coski at the Eleanor Brockenbrough Library at the Museum of the Confederacy; Lynda Crist, editor of the Papers of Jefferson Davis; Wanda Marsh, a historian of Callahan County, Texas; workers in the Clerk's offices of Callahan County and Red River County in Texas; David Currey, former curator at Traveler's Rest in Nashville; and Stephanie Tayloe, a genealogist and librarian in Martha Travis Harris's beloved Henry County, Tennessee.

In this modern era of computer-assisted communication, potential sources of information are in every internet discussion group or blog. Pleas for references or copies of articles were responded to by fellow members of the Civil War Discussion Group Jim Epperson and Harry Smeltzer. My friend, Vance Floyd of Tampa, Florida, has an amazing library of Civil War information, and was able to translate a vague recollection of an article somewhere into a tangible copy of that article. Although the discussion too often strays from the Civil War into modern politics, I also acknowledge my friends in the Forlorn Hope discussion group, who are too many to name individually.

I am fortunate living in the state of Tennessee to have made friends with historians across the state who themselves are researching areas that might overlap with my areas of interest. Among these are Greg Biggs of Clarksville, Rick Warwick of Franklin, Tim Smith of Adamsville, and Larry Daniel of Memphis, all of whom provided useful information or guidance. Rick Warwick also put me in contact with Irby Bright and his son, Matt. The Brights are direct descendants of Harris and provided a photograph of the family portrait of Martha Travis Harris that appears in this book.

Chattanooga, of course, was the central focus of almost two years of campaigning in the Civil War, and I am gratified that we have a community of historians here, or with links to here, that are willing to share their time, talents, and viewpoints on a project of this nature. Keith Bohannon of Carrollton, Georgia, no longer lives here, but we count him as part of our community. Keith is always combing primary sources, and he was kind enough to keep his eyes peeled for references to Governor Harris, a number of which are included in this book. Jim Ogden, the historian of the Chickamauga Chattanooga National Military Park, has immersed himself in a study that involves the various mobilizations of Tennessee troops in 1861 and 1862, and his insights and sources were of great help.

My previous work had centered largely on the Civil War in the West and especially the Army of Tennessee, which was certainly not Harris's entire story. Through my fellow member of the Tennessee Historical Commission, Calvin Dickinson, I made contact with Derek Frisby of Middle Tennessee State University, who has done significant work on Tennessee during the crisis of 1860–61. Derek read a number of my early chapters and made very cogent comments and suggestions that definitely improved the final version. In the course of working on this manuscript, I became acquainted with Christopher Losson of St. Joseph's, Missouri. Chris wrote one of the first modern Army of Tennessee biographies dealing with Frank Cheatham, and was kind enough to read chapters relating to the campaign into Tennessee, the end of the war, and the period in which Cheatham himself was politically active. Chris's views and insights were likewise of great assistance. Finally, I learned that the anonymous reader process employed by LSU Press resulted in the review of this book in manuscript form by Dr. Stephen Ash of the University of Tennessee. Dr. Ash's suggestions as to additions and changes to the manuscript have without a doubt improved the final product. I am indebted to all three of these historians. Any mistakes are mine alone.

As in the past, my law partners, Charlie Gearhiser, Wayne Peters, Bob Lockaby, Terry Cavett, Wade Cannon, Robin Miller, Chris Varner, Lee Ann Adams, Deborah Varner, and Beverly Edge were tolerant of my being occasionally diverted from our firm business. As always, my assistant, Margie Tricoglou, provided cheerful assistance where requested. The atmosphere of friendly collegiality in which we work makes even the days when the profession I love is not very kind enjoyable.

I also would like to lovingly acknowledge the role that my family has had in this book. My parents, Ruth and Gene Elliott, each read through the manuscript and made valuable comments geared to improve the book for the general reader. The support and encouragement I received from my wife, Karen, and my daughters, Mary Claire and Sarah Anne, was inexhaustible. They have now, for the third time, endured my shutting myself up with my computer, the odd timing of visits to libraries, and my general blathering about my subject with grace, love, and understanding.

While I received an excellent undergraduate education in history at the University of the South, my career path took me in a different direction, one that prepared me for research, investigation, and writing, but divergent from the skill set and knowledge necessary to write and publish history in an avocational sense. When I began my work on Alexander P. Stewart in 1995, Jim Ogden suggested that I contact Nathaniel Cheairs Hughes Jr. for suggestions, which turned out to be across the board guidance and mentorship on sources, writing, the publishing industry, and the current state of Civil War scholarship. Since that time, we have enjoyed a friendship that has been much more to my benefit than his. Nat took time to read this manuscript, and his insights and suggestions were a valuable addition to this work. It is therefore with the deepest admiration, appreciation, and friendship that I dedicate this book to him.

ABBREVIATIONS USED IN NOTES

IGH   Isham G. Harris

LC   Library of Congress, Washington, D.C.

NA   National Archives, Washington, D.C.

OR   *War of the Rebellion: A Compilation of the Official Records of the Union and Confederate Armies.* 128 vols. (Washington, D.C.: U.S. Government Printing Office, 1880–1901). OR citations are to Series I unless otherwise noted and take the following form: volume number (part number, where applicable), page number (s).

ORN   *Official Records of the Union and Confederate Navies in the War of the Rebellion.* 30 vols. (Washington, D.C.: U.S. Government Printing Office, 1884–1927). ORN citations here are to Series I.

ORS   *Supplement to the Official Records of the Union and Confederate Armies* (Wilmington, N.C.: Broadfoot Publishing Co., 1994–2004).

PAJ   LeRoy P. Graf, Ralph W. Haskins, and Paul H. Bergeron, eds. *The Papers of Andrew Johnson,* 16 vols. (Knoxville: University of Tennessee Press, 1967–2000).

PJD   Lynda Lasswell Crist, Mary Seaton Dix, Kenneth H. Williams, Peggy L. Dillard, and Barbara J. Rozek, eds. *The Papers of Jefferson Davis,* 12 vols. to date (Baton Rouge: Louisiana State University Press, 1971–2008).

SNMPA   Shiloh National Military Park Archives

TSLA   Tennessee State Library and Archives, Nashville

UNC   University of North Carolina

ISHAM G. HARRIS
of TENNESSEE

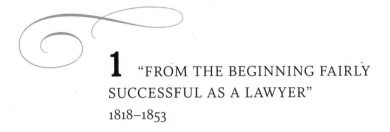

1 "FROM THE BEGINNING FAIRLY SUCCESSFUL AS A LAWYER"
1818–1853

For Isham Green Harris, the governor of Tennessee, April 6, 1862, dawned a bright, sunny day full of the promise of a great victory, one that would repel the blue-clad troops from the North who had, in the previous few weeks, invaded Tennessee. The Confederate army, gathered from all parts of the South, massed near Pittsburgh Landing on the banks of the Tennessee River expecting to crush the opposing force with a devastating surprise attack. The attack was launched, the enemy was driven back, and victory was in the balance. But things went horribly wrong. While pushed to the limit, the enemy was not destroyed. The Confederate commander, Albert Sidney Johnston, was mortally wounded. Acting as a volunteer civilian aide, Harris assisted the stricken commander from his horse and helplessly watched as he died. Later, the governor learned that the South's supreme effort not only cost the life of his commander, but also that of his brother and a nephew, as well as a number of friends. And the enemy remained on the field, to return to battle the following day reinforced and resurgent. Three years of internecine struggle would follow, ultimately concluding with Confederate defeat. It was a memory that Harris wanted to blot out.

He did not return to Pittsburgh Landing or the battlefield, known as Shiloh, until April 1896. Since those terrible two days thirty-four years before, Harris had seen the utter ruin of the Confederate cause, more than two bitter years of exile, nine years of political eclipse, and almost twenty years as a U.S. senator. At the request of the friends of the long-dead Johnston, Senator Harris, at age seventy-eight, finally returned to this field of sad memories in an effort to assist the park commission in locating the places where Johnston was wounded and bled to death. Showing remarkable recall, the old senator was able to fix those locations. The visit to Shiloh worked a sort of catharsis, and Harris, who to that point lacked enthusiasm for preserving the fields where so many bitter memories remained, changed his mind. There was indeed value in recalling the memories of the great War Between the States.[1]

Charles Todd Quintard, the Episcopal bishop of Tennessee, had reached the same conclusion more than a year before. Quintard decided to write a memoir of his experiences in the war, and sought information from a number of friends and acquaintances from those days that might be useful or help refresh his recollection. In December 1894, Quintard wrote Senator Harris, requesting information of a biographical nature as well as his recollection of certain events. In his reply, Harris declined to comment on the question relating to the war Quintard posed, deeming it an old sore that did not need reopening. But, in the space of a half hour, he wrote eight pages that outlined in the barest detail the story of his life over the space of more than seven and a half decades, tracing his career as a lawyer, state senator, and congressman. The old senator touched on his three successful elections as governor, and his service as a volunteer aide to the various commanders of the Confederate Army of Tennessee, and ultimately his election and subsequent reelections to the Senate. Notwithstanding the senator's eventful life and lengthy public service, the letter contained little embellishment of his accomplishments. The story of his life began in the simplest terms: "I was born on the waters of Blue Creek in the barrens of Franklin County about ten miles west of Winchester, on the 10th of Feby 1818."[2]

Isham Green Harris was the ninth child of Isham Green Harris and his wife, Lucy Davidson Harris. Young Green, as his family called him, carried not only the name of his father, but that of his grandfather as well. The elder Isham was born in North Carolina on November 24, 1770, Lucy on February 13, 1773, both from families that supported the American Revolution. The date of their marriage is not recorded, but since the first of nine children, George Washington, was born in 1802, it can be assumed that the union occurred around the turn of the century.[3]

1. D. W. Reed to Basil Duke, July 20, 1906, Series 1, Box 13, Folder 140, SNMPA; Timothy B. Smith, *This Great Battlefield of Shiloh* (Knoxville: University of Tennessee Press, 2004), 60–62.

2. IGH to C. T. Quintard, December 29, 1894, C. T. Quintard Papers, Duke University.

3. Robert E. Harris, comp., *From Essex England to the Sunny Southern U.S.A.: A Harris Family Journey* (Tucker, Ga.: Robert E. Harris, 1994), 83–84; "End of an Eventful Life," *Memphis Commercial Appeal,* July 9, 1897; Ila McLeary, "The Life of Isham G. Harris" (M.A. thesis, University of Tennessee, 1930), 1; George Wayne Watters, "Isham Green Harris, Civil War Governor and Senator from Tennessee, 1818–1897" (Ph.D. dissertation, Florida State University, 1977), 2; Gilbert R. Adkins, "Isham G. Harris, 'Faithful to the Truth as He Saw It,'" *Franklin County Historical Review* 16 (1985): 103.

It is difficult to characterize the senior Isham. Some considered him to be "a man of strong native intellect and a remarkably well balanced judgment, as well as of the highest sense of honor and of the strictest integrity of character." Another favorable account described him as having a "fair education" and "a very extensive library for the day and time." Other sources, however, indicate the future governor's father was deficient in thrift and discipline. Opinions of Lucy Davidson Harris were much less varied. Harris's mother was described as being a "most estimable woman and an exceedingly strong character." She was also considered "well read" and "interested in public affairs."[4]

The Harris family left North Carolina seeking to better their fortunes in "fresher fields" after an Indian treaty in 1806 opened up new land in Middle Tennessee. Although there is some indication the family first moved to a tract in the lowlands along the Duck River in Bedford County, the land they eventually settled was a thousand acres in Franklin County on the Blue Creek prong of Rock Creek about three miles from modern Tullahoma. The elder Isham built a "simple, unadorned and rough" log cabin for his family. He was a Methodist preacher, but owned about twelve slaves and worked his land with them; he initially prospered enough to send his sons, at least, to school at Carrick Academy in Winchester. As Harris later described, he was "sent to the neighborhood schools when a small boy and afterwards to the Academy in Winchester where I had to *unlearn* the little I had learned."[5]

The Harris land was not of the best quality, being in the "barrens" of Franklin County. By the time the boy was in his early teens, it became less productive. Not only was the land infertile, but labor may have been an issue as well. At that point, around 1831 or 1832, Green's two eldest brothers, George Washington Harris and William Roland Harris, had moved to West Tennessee, the former at the start of his own career as a Methodist minister, the latter as a lawyer. Even the next in age, Richmond Pickney Harris and James Trousdale Harris, were grown men and gone from home at that time. At that same point, it is possible that all four of the

4. "Grim Death Claims a Great Statesman," *Chattanooga Daily Times,* July 9, 1897; Adkins, "Isham G. Harris"; Joshua W. Caldwell, *Sketches of the Bench and Bar of Tennessee* (Knoxville: Ogden Bros., 1898), 336; "End of an Eventful Life" (estimable); McLeary, "The Life of Isham G. Harris," 1–2 (well read).

5. Watters, "Isham Green Harris," 2–5; "Senator Harris' Birthplace," *Washington Post,* January 26, 1883; Adkins, "Isham G. Harris," 103; Caldwell, *Sketches of the Bench and Bar of Tennessee,* 159, 336; IGH to Quintard, December 29, 1894, Quintard Papers.

family's girls, Martha, Nancy, Mary, and Lucy, were still at home. With no help from his older sons, the then over-sixty Isham senior likely had difficulty managing the farm and ensuring the productivity of the family slaves.[6]

Young Green attended Carrick Academy until age fourteen. Due to his father's failing prospects, he later recalled that he "decided to quit school and go out upon the world to earn a living." The elder Isham found it necessary to mortgage the farm while his youngest son was still at the academy. Green went to his father and proposed to leave school and go out into the world to make a living so he could assist his family. With the other sons gone, Green's father prevailed upon him to stay at the academy another year, at the end of which another mortgage was placed on the farm. According to one account, at this point the young man exclaimed: "Well, I don't care what you all say, I'm going anyway." As he began the preparations for his departure during the summer of 1832, the family's neighbors predicted he would soon be back, which increased the young man's determination. Anticipating making the journey on foot, he found on the day of his departure that his tearful parents were providing him with a horse. Thus mounted, he set off across the wilderness to join his brother William in Paris, Henry County, Tennessee.[7]

Although young Green Harris may have been planning to stop in Paris temporarily on the way farther west, perhaps as far as the Mississippi River, he ended up staying in the town, where his brother William was practicing law and overseeing a tract of their father's land. Seeking employment, Green contracted with merchant John Gibbs to serve him for a year for $100 and board. At the end of that year, Green considered renewing his journey westward, but was induced to stay by a raise to $350 a year, and in the subsequent year to $500. During the course of these three years, Green became quite proficient in the ways of commerce and business.[8]

6. IGH to Quintard, December 29, 1894, Quintard Papers; "End of an Eventful Life"; Caldwell, *Sketches of the Bench and Bar*, 159, 336; McLeary, "The Life of Isham G. Harris," 2; Harris, comp., *A Harris Family Journey*, 81; E. McLeod Johnson, *A History of Henry County, Tennessee: Descriptive, Pictorial Reproductions of Old Papers and Manuscripts* (n.p., 1958), 1:175; "Spirit of a Great Man Goes Over the River," *Nashville American*, July 9, 1897. It should be noted that the *Nashville American* article has been used with caution, as one anecdote, noted below, is demonstrably false.

7. IGH to Quintard, December 29, 1894, Quintard Papers; "Spirit of a Great Man"; Caldwell, *Sketches of the Bench and Bar*, 336; see also Watters, "Isham Green Harris," 6.

8. "Spirit of a Great Man"; IGH to Quintard, December 29, 1894, Quintard Papers. The article

Paris was a new town, laid out in 1823. It was named for the French capital in honor of the Marquis de Lafayette, who was visiting Tennessee at the time the name was chosen. By 1833, the population of the town numbered about eight hundred. Of these, there were "twelve lawyers, twelve physicians, two clergymen, five carpenters, four bricklayers, two cabinet makers, two hatters, eight tailors, two shoemakers, five blacksmiths, one silversmith, four tanners, two tinners, and seven saddlers." The structures in the town included a brick courthouse, one church, a printing office, an academy, "three schools, ten stores, two taverns, a cotton gin, and two factories." Notwithstanding its newness, Paris was "never a backwoods settlement, and the beaver hat soon outnumbered the coonskin hat."[9]

When Green was twenty, either his brother William, then a circuit judge, or his brother James Trousdale, the owner of the first cotton factory in West Tennessee, "proposed to furnish the capital and give [Green] half the profits if he would buy a stock of goods and manage the business." Accordingly, in 1838, Green departed for the North Mississippi town of Ripley, taking with him an African American blacksmith named Hubbard. The area had been acquired only two years before from the Chickasaw Indians and opened for white settlement, an area so rough that Harris later recalled that he and Hubbard were the best-dressed men there. While not dressed as if prosperous, a number of the land speculators and other settlers appear to have had money, and Harris was able to solicit their business, to the point that by the end of his first year in the Magnolia State, he was considered Tippah County's leading merchant.[10]

Notwithstanding his agreement to pursue the mercantile business in Ripley and his eventual success with the same, Green also determined to read law. Discussing his desire with William, the judge said, "Green, you are a merchant, and a successful one, and I would advise you to remain in that business rather than at-

---

in the *Nashville American* identifies Harris's employer as a Mr. Cooney, while Harris told Bishop Quintard the man's name was Gibbs, which is used here.

9. Edith Rucker Whitley, *Tennessee Genealogical Records: Henry County "Old Time Stuff"* (n.p., 1968), 5; Stephanie Routon Tayloe, *The Henry County, Tennessee Ancestor Series: Men of Distinction* (n.p., n.d.), 11–12, transcribing John S. Dunlap, "Paris—Historically Speaking," *The Parisian*, August 16, 1929.

10. IGH to Quintard, December 29, 1894, Quintard Papers; "End of an Eventful Life"; "Grim Death Claims a Great Statesman"; McLeary, "The Life of Isham G. Harris," 2; Watters, "Isham Green Harris," 9; "Spirit of a Great Man Goes Over the River."

tempt a profession." Not dissuaded by his brother, Harris later recalled that "from that time I devoted my time to the management of the business house through the day and read law until 11 or 12 o'clock every night."[11]

Green stayed in Ripley "a little less than three years." Over the protest of his brother, he sold his interest in the business, having cleared the enormous sum of $7,000 in the transaction, and deposited the money in the Union Bank of Mississippi. Returning to Paris, Green purchased a stylish wardrobe, and then set out for Franklin County, riding the same horse his father had given him on his departure from home, no doubt intending to impress the neighbors who had scoffed at him years before. With his earnings, he paid the mortgages on the farm. His parents then sold the farm, and the family journeyed to Henry County.[12]

Green had not given up his intention of practicing law. He stayed close to home, spending his time preparing to enter the legal profession. At one point, he spent time in Judge Andrew McCampbell's law office in Paris. One night, his brother, William, came out to visit the family place, and stayed up talking after dinner with Green and their mother, Lucy. The mother asked her older son, previously skeptical about Green's choice of a second career, to then and there examine the younger man on the law. He found that his brother had studied well, and pronounced him ready to start a practice. Green was not yet ready to do so, and ironically heard but a few days later of the failure of the "wild-cat" Union Bank and the loss of his large nest egg. He was effectively penniless again.[13]

Prior to his going to Mississippi, Green was approached by a local businessman, a Mr. Tharpe, known by the honorific "Colonel." Tharpe had offered to set Green up in business at that time, and the young man, now broke, went back to see if the offer was still open. It was agreed that Green would go to Philadelphia to purchase a stock of goods. Tharpe placed $12,000 at the young man's disposal. During the two-month trip to Philadelphia, Green pondered the means to get the goods back to Tennessee. The usual method was to have the goods transported to Pittsburgh, where they would be placed on a boat, shipped downriver a hundred

11. "End of an Eventful Life"; IGH to Quintard, December 29, 1894, Duke University.

12. IGH to Quintard, December 29, 1894, Duke University; "Spirit of a Great Man"; "End of an Eventful Life." There are slight variances in the accounts here, relative to the amount Green made in Mississippi and exactly when his family joined him in Paris. I have chosen those that seem the most logical.

13. "End of an Eventful Life."

miles or so, transferred to another boat for another leg, and so on until the goods reached Tennessee, causing lengthy delays and incurring transfer costs and commissions. Green bypassed this cumbersome procedure by chartering a boat all the way to Paducah, Kentucky, where the Tennessee River joins the Ohio. There, another boat was chartered to take the cargo to Paris Landing on the Tennessee near the town itself. In the end, Green reached Paris three months ahead of schedule, at half the transportation cost. With this head start, Green was able to engage in the joint venture with Colonel Tharpe for a year, when they agreed to sell the business. Green emerged from this, his last mercantile effort for about twenty-five years, again with a $7,000 profit.[14]

The minutes of the County Court of Henry County reflect that Harris appeared before the court on Monday, May 3, 1841, as a student at law. Having satisfied the judge that he was "of good moral character and twenty one years of age," and that he had resided in Henry County for twelve months, Harris received the certificate of good moral character necessary to practice law.[15] As Harris later related to Bishop Quintard, he was "from the beginning fairly successful as a lawyer." Harris told other friends as an old man that "he was much more successful for the first year in practicing than he had ever expected." Indeed, Harris's years as a businessman gave him unusual insight into commercial transactions, and his peers considered him "invincible" in property litigation. The records of the county court demonstrate the variety of Harris's practice at that time. In 1842, Harris was appointed "Solicitor General pro tem" to prosecute a bastardy case on the part of the state. A jury found the defendant, one Kendall V. Bumpass, the father of the child, although the minutes of the court showed he appealed that decision to the circuit court. Contemporaries considered Harris's "boldness of manner and audacity of statement in misdemeanors and cases of crime" attributes that "made him one of the best criminal lawyers in the State." Harris spent the next five years

14. "End of an Eventful Life"; "Spirit of a Great Man"; see also Caldwell, *Sketches of the Bench and Bar*, 337. Two versions of this incident exist, the first placing the trip to Philadelphia during Harris's first round of business in Paris, the second after the loss incurred by the failure of Union Bank. I have chosen the latter as it seems more consistent with the sequence set out in Harris's letter to Quintard. See McLeary, "The Life of Isham G. Harris," 7–8.

15. Works Progress Administration, *Transcription of the County Archives of Tennessee: Minutes of the County Court of Henry County, 1836–1849*, Part I (Nashville: Tennessee Historical Records Survey, 1942), 165.

building quite a lucrative practice, employing the "ardor and tireless energy" that he had previously shown in business affairs.[16]

With his professional affairs in order, Green Harris turned to matters of a more personal sort. Among the more prominent citizens of Paris was Major Edward Travis, a veteran of the War of 1812. Travis moved to Paris from Virginia in 1826 with his wife, her aunt, and the couple's ten children. Among the children was a daughter, Martha Mariah Travis, born January 15, 1822. Martha was nicknamed "Crockett," after the Tennessee hero of the same name, for her "skillful riding and daring deeds on horseback." Horse racing and gambling on such events was a favorite sport of the gentlemen of Henry County. An avid sportsman, Major Travis owned a number of racehorses, for which he built a mile race track on his large farm about five miles west of Paris.[17]

Among the blooded horses owned by Travis was Box, a mare that had taken a gold cup at New Orleans and set a time record that stood for over twenty years. One day, Travis invited Green Harris and other young men of the neighborhood to see his horses. Box's rider had left her saddled next to the entrance to the race track, and "Crockett," who had wanted to ride the horse for some time, saw her chance, mounted the animal, and turned her onto the track. Box took off, and raced around the track, with "Crockett" holding on for dear life, her skirts "flying about her head in voluminous masses of white and colors." Three times the horse flew around the track. Major Travis was terrified for his daughter's safety while the young men were amazed at the spectacle. Finally, the horse was exhausted, and "Crockett" fell off in a faint. Purportedly, Green believed that a young woman "who could ride like that must have other qualities desirable in a wife."

Green and Martha were married on July 6, 1843.[18] Martha bore Green seven sons: Eugene Travis was born in 1846, followed by George Ludson, James, Edward Kirby, Charles Henry, a fourth Isham Green, and Frank.[19] Like his father, Green

16. IGH to Quintard, December 29, 1894, Quintard Papers; "End of an Eventful Life"; Works Progress Administration, *Minutes*, 227–28; "Spirit of a Great Man."

17. "Spirit of a Great Man"; Roger Raymond Van Dyke, "Antebellum Henry County," *West Tennessee Historical Society Papers* 33 (1979): 48, 57; Paul W. and Joyce E. Jones, *Major Edward Travis* (n.p., 1993), at W. G. Rhea Public Library, Paris, Tennessee. A family correspondent related that Crockett's sobriquet came not from her horsemanship, but her expertise with a rifle. McLeary, "The Life of Isham Green Harris," 8.

18. "Spirit of a Great Man"; Jones, *Major Edward Travis*.

19. Eugene T. Harris Compiled Service Record, M-331, NA; Harris, comp., *A Harris Family Jour-*

seems to have waited to pass along his own name. By the end of the decade, the family had accumulated moderate wealth. Green owned close to three hundred acres of land and a town lot. The family farm produced mostly corn and wheat, and raised cattle and swine. The happiness and growth of Green's family was tempered with loss and sadness. In the mid-1840s, both the elder Isham and Lucy died, as well as Martha's father, Major Travis. County records show that Green was appointed the executor of his father-in-law's will in October 1846 as well as the guardian of his minor brother-in-law. The records reflect that the will was presented in January 1845, and was so certified and recorded, with George W. D. Harris and William R. Harris named the executors in the document.[20]

Travis's will made disposition of thirty-three slaves. Most were apportioned out to his many children in groups of two or three, although Martha's share included four slaves. For three slaves, Marilla, Randle, and Dick, Travis provided that when the youngest of them reached eighteen, if it were their desire, Harris as Travis's executor was to remove them to one of the free states and to "expend the sum of Five Hundred dollars in purchasing them a home and the necessities of life and liberate them and settle them there." Green was given two slaves, in compensation for anticipated expense relative to the liberation of three of Travis's slaves. If the three, or either of them, chose to stay in Tennessee, then they were to remain Green's property. Such apparently was the case with Randle, who was Harris's faithful servant for years to come.[21]

Travis's provision for the manumission of his slaves was not uncommon for the period. A number of slaves were freed by means of a deceased slaveholder's will, although during most of the interval from 1831 to 1861 the law provided that they, as contemplated by Travis for his three servants, be removed from the state upon manumission. Tennessee, and particularly East Tennessee, had a tradition of antislavery activities in the period before 1830, centered in the Methodist Episcopal Church, manumission societies, and abolitionist newspapers. There was even

---

ney, 85; "Mrs. Senator Harris' Funeral," *Memphis Commercial Appeal*, January 22, 1897. Eugene and George predeceased their parents. No information could be located relative to Frank.

20. Works Progress Administration, *Minutes*, Part II, 333, 343, 433–34, 438 (these records dispel an apocryphal account that the Harris brothers agreed to destroy Isham's will, which purportedly exclusively benefited Green, in favor of their four sisters); "Spirit of a Great Man"; Watters, "Isham Green Harris," 12; Jones, *Major Edward Travis*, 17–18.

21. Jones, *Major Edward Travis*, 17–18.

a project in West Tennessee near Memphis where slaves were brought to be edu-
cated and to work to earn their freedom. This endeavor, known as the Nashoba
experiment, flourished in the later half of the 1820s, surviving, for a while, even
a revelation of sexual experimentation among the participants. But in the 1830s,
the tone in West Tennessee changed, as the economic benefits of slavery, the fears
raised by the 1831 Nat Turner slave rebellion in Virginia, and the strident criticism
of abolitionists in the North hardened attitudes.

Only twelve years before Travis's death, antislavery delegates to Tennessee's
constitutional convention in 1834 barely missed defeating a provision that stated
that the legislature had no power to free slaves absent the permission of their
owners. The attitudes of the participants revealed that while many Tennesseans
viewed slavery as an unfortunate evil, the racial attitude was such that delegates
feared the social and economic impact of the freed slaves, ultimately contributing
to the defeat of the abolitionists' efforts. Subsequent efforts on behalf of the slaves
tended to be for colonization outside the United States rather than freedom within
them. In the end, there is no evidence that Travis was influenced by these trends.
As thirty of Travis's slaves remained in bondage after his death, his action on behalf of the three given the possibility of freedom was much more indicative of particular favor toward these three individuals, or their mother, than their deceased
owner's abolitionism.[22]

That Green Harris would be a supporter of slavery is not surprising. As noted
above, his father owned as many as twelve slaves, which was not an inconsider-
able number for that time period. Travis's will suggests that Harris already owned
slaves at the time the will was made in 1846, which, along with Travis's bequest,
would have given Green and Martha a significant personal stake in the institution. Certainly, the three hundred acres he owned outside of Paris indicates the

22. Durwood Dunn, *An Abolitionist in the Appalachian South: Ezekiel Birdseye on Slavery, Capitalism, and Separate Statehood in East Tennessee, 1841–1846* (Knoxville: University of Tennessee Press,
1997), 11–16, 72–73; Lester C. Lamon, *Blacks in Tennessee 1791–1970* (Knoxville: University of Tennessee Press, 1981), 6, 9, 13–14; Asa Earl Martin, "Anti-Slavery Activities of the Methodist Episcopal
Church in Tennessee," *Tennessee Historical Magazine* 2 (1916): 98–109; James W. Patton, "The Progress of Emancipation in Tennessee, 1796–1860," *Journal of Negro History* 17 (January 1932): 67, 82–
102; Bette B. Tilley, "The Spirit of Improvement: Reformism and Slavery in West Tennessee," *West
Tennessee Historical Society Papers* 28 (1974): 25, 28–42; Chase C. Mooney, "Some Institutional and
Statistical Aspects of Slavery in Tennessee," *Tennessee Historical Quarterly* 1 (September 1942): 195,
203–6; Chase C. Mooney, "The Question of Slavery and the Free Negro in the Tennessee Constitutional Convention of 1834," *Journal of Southern History* 12 (November 1946): 487–509.

necessity of slave labor, even though Harris did not grow the primary cash crops of tobacco and cotton. By the 1840s, slavery was well established in Henry County, and bondsmen constituted approximately a quarter of the total population of the county. In 1840, the total value of the slaves held in the county was calculated to be in excess of $3 million. Not only did the county's agricultural prosperity depend on slave labor, but there were industrial establishments in the county processing both tobacco and cotton. Harris's acceptance and support of slavery comported with the views of his fellow white Tennesseans as a whole. The social, economic, and political principles of the vast majority of the white citizens were based in large part on the existence of the institution. While most Tennesseans did not own slaves, many aspired to the economic status conferred by slave ownership, and indeed dreamed of producing a great cash crop that would allow them to join the ranks of the wealthy planters. In West Tennessee, which would be Green Harris's political power base, that cash crop was cotton, particularly suited for slave labor.[23]

For the most part, during Green Harris's formative years, Tennessee was squarely in the camp of the Democratic Party. Tennessee entered the Union in 1796 as a Jeffersonian Republican state, and Andrew Jackson's Democracy has been termed a "revival of Jeffersonianism." In Tennessee, many of the reforms that broadened the extent of democracy came at the instance of Governor William Carroll. Carroll's last term ended in 1835, at a time when, even in Tennessee, Jackson's popularity was wavering, thanks to his support of Martin Van Buren as a successor over fellow Tennessean Hugh Lawson White. By 1837, a Whig Party of equal strength to the Democracy was in place in Tennessee, a situation that remained in place for the next two decades.[24]

While the Whigs became established in other parts of the state, Henry County remained solidly in the Democratic camp. The two exceptions were the presidential election of 1836, when White won 56 percent of the vote against Van Buren,

23. Jones, *Major Edward Travis*, 17–18; Van Dyke, "Antebellum Henry County," 59–60, 72–73; Jonathan M. Atkins, *Parties, Politics, and the Sectional Conflict in Tennessee, 1832–1861* (Knoxville: University of Tennessee Press, 1997), 18–21; Blanche Henry Clark, *The Tennessee Yeomen, 1840–1860* (Nashville: Vanderbilt University Press, 1942), 12, 41, 109, 141.

24. Robert E. Corlew, *Tennessee: A Short History*, 2nd ed. (Knoxville: University of Tennessee Press, 1990), 159, 178–95; Jonathan M. Atkins, "Politicians, Parties, and Slavery: The Second Party System and the Decision for Disunion in Tennessee," *Tennessee Historical Quarterly* 55 (Spring 1996): 20, 23; Arthur M. Schlesinger Jr., *The Age of Jackson* (Boston: Little, Brown & Co., 1953), 306–8.

and the election for governor in 1837, when Governor Newton Cannon, at that point a Whig who blamed the Panic of 1837 on Jackson and Van Buren, defeated a weak Democratic candidate, General Robert Armstrong. In subsequent elections for governor and president, the Democrats approached or exceeded the 60 percent majority mark in the county.[25]

While these numbers would not have escaped a man as astute as Green Harris, the young lawyer, who would be later called by Senator James B. Beck of Kentucky the "best Democrat in the United States," had been "reared as a Democrat." The Whig Governor Cannon appointed William Harris a judge, likely because William supported White instead of Van Buren. But William was active on behalf of the 1844 Democratic presidential candidate, Tennessean James K. Polk, as he addressed a mass meeting of Democrats in neighboring Stewart County and Clarksville and wrote a lengthy letter to the Clarksville newspaper denouncing the Whigs. Likewise, George W. D. Harris penned a note to President-elect Polk in November, noting he was "both personally and politically your friend." Like his brothers, Green too supported Polk, campaigning in Paris and the surrounding area.[26]

Green proved to be quite adept at politics. Like a number of politicians before him, at some point he acquired an honorific military title, "General," a measure of respect in Southern society. As a young man, he made a "commanding appearance and knew all the tricks that make one a fine actor." Yet his speech was "brief, clear and compact." Green Harris was a strong speaker, recalled Senator Kenneth McKellar, who noted "he was never known to tell a story in a speech and he never indulged in the flowers and flights of oratory. Yet, he possessed a fine vocabulary and every word that he used bore straight on and direct on the point he was making."[27] As William Brimage Bate, Harris's future colleague in the U.S.

25. Corlew, *Tennessee: A Short History*, 193; Anne H. Hopkins and William Lyons, *Tennessee Votes, 1799–1976* (Knoxville: University of Tennessee Bureau of Public Administration, 1978), 18–34.

26. "End of an Eventful Life"; Kenneth McKellar, *Tennessee Senators: As Seen by One of Their Successors* (Kingsport: Southern Publishers, 1942), 394; Caldwell, *Sketches of the Bench and Bar of Tennessee*, 159; Wayne Cutler, ed., *Correspondence of James K. Polk* (Knoxville: University of Tennessee Press, 1993), 8:32, 358–59; "To the Democratic Committee at Clarksville," *Clarksville Jeffersonian*, November 2, 1844; Watters, "Isham Green Harris," 17; "Gen. Isham G. Harris," *Nashville Daily Union & American*, May 27, 1857.

27. John Hope Franklin, *The Militant South, 1800–1861* (Cambridge, Mass.: Belknap Press, 1956), 190–92; "End of an Eventful Life"; McKellar, *Tennessee Senators*, 403. Under Tennessee legal practice,

Senate, said, Harris's speeches were "plain, clear and cogent," as well as "sensible, strong, attractive" with the occasional touch of the "dramatic." Harris delivered his speeches earnestly and with force, using emphasis in his expressions and gestures. Bate recalled, "Indeed, this grew upon him with age until the emphatic seemed the dogmatic. In speaking he always had a definite point to drive to, and he let you know what it was, and generally got there in good time and in good order."[28]

Green's early success in business and legal ability suggested a keen intelligence. One admirer, Edward Ward Carmack, said that Harris's intellect was "robust, vigorous, direct, guided always by common sense." At Harris's death, a newspaper editor extolled his "strong intellect and great force of character," and observed that one of the secrets to his success was "his inexhaustible fund of sound, common sense." But Harris's record of success as a politician required more than mere intellect. After his death, his friends in Memphis held that his success was attributed to his "truthfulness, fidelity, integrity and force of character." Senator McKellar stated that Harris had "an overmastering personality and wonderful ability to draw men to him." Further, Harris "never had any doubt about any position he took." This strong conviction gave him an "indomitable will and an aggressiveness that balked at nothing." Even Judge Oliver P. Temple, a future antagonist, would acknowledge Harris's "ability, daring and exceeding aggressiveness."[29]

The Mexican War, and the political issues it raised, framed Harris's early political convictions. The acquisition of great territories in the Far West as a result of the war brought to a head the issue of whether the states organized from it would or would not allow slavery. Just before Congress adjourned in August 1846, Northern Democrat David Wilmot of Pennsylvania introduced an amendment to the appropriations bill for the Mexican War that any territory acquired as a result

---

attorney generals are also addressed as "general." It is possible Harris's temporary work as a prosecutor resulted in the title.

28. *Memorial Addresses on the Life and Character of Isham G. Harris Delivered in the Senate and House of Representatives* (Washington, D.C.: Government Printing Office, 1898), 18.

29. Ibid., 133; "The Dead Senator," *Nashville American*, July 9, 1897; "Isham G. Harris," *Memphis Commercial Appeal*, July 9, 1897; "End of an Eventful Life"; McKellar, *Tennessee Senators*, 404; Oliver P. Temple, *East Tennessee and the Civil War* (Freeport, N.Y.: Books for Libraries Press, 1971), 217. While a number of these accounts speak of Harris as an older politician, his early success indicates that his abilities as a younger man were much the same.

of the war would be free of slavery. The so-called Wilmot Proviso sharply defined the ensuing debate over the issue of slavery in the territories. Tennesseans and other Southerners saw the proviso and similar efforts at restricting slavery in the territories as limiting their rights, as citizens of the republic, to take their property wherever they desired. Opposing political camps were formed, not based on party affiliation, but on sectional interest.[30]

It was in this atmosphere, complicated by questions over the conduct of the Mexican War, that Green Harris, with all his formidable attributes, entered politics. In 1847, Henry County constituted a state senatorial district with Obion and Weakley counties. The district as a whole was "largely" Democratic, but two prominent party members threatened to dilute that strength when they announced themselves candidates in the election for the seat. With some Tennesseans weary of the Mexican War, and a credible Whig candidate, William Hubbard, as the opposition, the Democrats did not need a divided effort. Indeed, Whig control of the legislature would enable the election of a Whig to the U.S. Senate, a turn of events that would have national implications. Efforts were made to induce either of the Democrats running for the seat to withdraw for the good of the party, but neither would. In this "extremity," the party turned to Harris "as if by common consent."[31]

Committees and delegations hurried to Paris to induce Harris to take the field and reorganize the Democratic effort. Harris initially refused, "saying that he had adopted the law as the business of his life; that it was a jealous mistress; that his ambition and all of his prospects of success in life were bound up in it; that his tastes and inclinations were adverse to political life." Eventually, though, his resistance was worn down, and he entered the race. With the energy that he had earlier employed in business and as a lawyer, he challenged his opponents to meet him in appearances across the district, in which he castigated them for their infidelity to the party. To demonstrate his own loyalty and sincerity, Harris proclaimed that "he was a candidate against his inclinations," and that if one of the other two would be willing to abandon the race for the good of the party, he would walk off the stage as a candidate with that man, leaving the third to run

30. James McPherson, *Battle Cry of Freedom: The Civil War Era* (New York: Oxford University Press, 1988), 51–54; Atkins, *Parties, Politics and Sectional Conflict*, 21–22.

31. "Grim Death Claims a Great Statesman"; Watters, "Isham Green Harris," 18; Corlew, *Tennessee: A Short History*, 268.

the race against the Whigs. Neither would budge, but the effect on the electorate was "crushing and decisive" in Harris's favor.[32]

Harris showed equal shrewdness in dealing with his Whig opponent, although the Democratic Party organ *Nashville Daily Union* boasted "it is, however, the same as if he had none, as it regards the final election." The primary issues in the election were the conduct of the Mexican War and the challenge posed by the Wilmot Proviso. The Whig nominee for Congress for the district that included Henry County, Colonel William Haskell, criticized Polk's law partner, General Gideon Pillow, for his role in the war, and indeed, "regarded [the] war as inexpedient, unwise, unnecessary, and unconstitutional." Himself a wounded veteran of the Mexican War, Haskell argued that the only way to end the war favorably was to "rob the [Mexican] churches, plunder the houses, and burn the towns and fortifications." Haskell also seemed to insult American troops when he stated he would "call off the bloodhounds." Harris, sensing an advantage, called on his senatorial opponent, William Hubbard, to endorse Haskell's comments. Hubbard refused, and soon withdrew from the race. Only days from the election, the Whigs nominated a supporter of Haskell, Joseph P. G. Roerlhoe, who had little chance. Harris easily won the election over all three of his opponents, although the Democratic ticket statewide was "soundly and unmercifully thrashed."[33]

As a result of that "thrashing," Harris took a seat in a legislature controlled by the Whigs. Elected in large part for his stance against the Wilmot Proviso, Harris waited but one week into the first session before he introduced, on October 11, 1847, a resolution condemning the "twice repeated passage through the House of Representatives of the Congress of the United States, of what is termed the 'Wilmot Proviso,' and the combined affiliated resolutions" approving the proviso passed by other states' legislatures. Harris's proposal adopted anti-Proviso resolutions like those passed by the Virginia legislature, and declared that the Federal government "has no control, directly or indirectly, mediately or immediately, over the institution of slavery." Further, the resolution provided that the General Assembly would not recognize "any enactment of the Federal Government which

32. "Grim Death Claims a Great Statesman."

33. "The Canvass," *Nashville Daily Union,* July 15, 1847; Watters, "Isham Green Harris," 19–21; "Important to the Voters of the Jackson District," *Nashville Daily Union,* July 28, 1847; "Col. Haskell's Dresden Speech," *Nashville Daily Union,* August 4, 1847; "Grim Death Claims a Great Statesman"; "The Election," *Clarksville Jeffersonian,* August 21, 1847.

has for its object the prohibition of slavery in any territory to be acquired" south of the Missouri Compromise line, and that it was the "duty of every slave-holding State, and the citizens thereof . . . to take firm, united and concerted action in this emergency."[34]

As a member from slavery's stronghold in West Tennessee, Harris had the political luxury of being able to take solid, if not extreme, proslavery positions. But Harris's proposal was too fiery for the Whig-controlled Tennessee Senate, and was referred to the Committee on Federal Relations, which watered it down significantly. Reporting on January 20, 1848, the committee agreed with Harris that the proviso was undesirable, but declined to define the duties of the Federal government, "because those duties are already defined by the Constitution of the United States." It further deemed it "impolitic" for the legislature to declare that it would not recognize the acts of the Federal government, "because this would be nullification in advance." Harris and his supporters made a final effort to revise the committee's resolution, but the effort failed. Still, the affirmation that "no possible good" would come from the Wilmot Proviso was a something of a moral victory for Harris.[35]

Harris ran for state senator in order to bring order to the chaotic situation created by the rival candidates for the Democratic nomination. He intended to serve his term in the General Assembly and return to his law practice. During the legislature's session at Nashville, the state Democratic convention met on January 7–8, 1848. Harris assumed a prominent role, being one of a committee of nine appointed to "present a suitable preamble and resolutions for the action of the Convention." Harris's influence is suggested by the fact that, among the resolutions presented was one denouncing "every attempt . . . to clog and encumber by Congress, any cession of territory which Mexico may make, with provisos and prohibitions excluding any portion of the people of the United States from a full and fair participation in its benefits." When the convention selected the party's presidential electors for the coming campaign, Harris was unanimously selected the elector for the 9th Congressional District. Although he did not desire the post, Har-

---

34. Corlew, *Tennessee: A Short History*, 268; "Tennessee Legislature," *Nashville Daily Union*, October 12, 1847; *Senate Journal for the First Session of the Twenty-Seventh General Assembly of the State of Tennessee* (Nashville: J. G. Shepard, 1848), 56–57.

35. *Senate Journal for the First Session*, 508–9, 558–59; Atkins, *Parties, Politics and Sectional Conflict*, 21; Watters, "Isham Green Harris," 22–23; Stanley F. Horn, "Isham G. Harris in the Pre-War Years," *Tennessee Historical Quarterly* 19 (1960): 195, 197.

ris loyally undertook the position. Harris's selection was heartily approved by the *Clarksville Jeffersonian* as "the best selection . . . that could have been made."[36]

As elector, it was Harris's job to carry the standard of the Democratic candidate for president in the 1848 campaign, Lewis Cass of Michigan. The *Clarksville Jeffersonian* reported on a debate Harris had with a supporter of Zachary Taylor at Port Royal, Tennessee, in August 1848. Harris's opponent reportedly gave a speech "well calculated to draw the people off from the consideration of the important issues involved in the canvass." It was the pattern of the time in Tennessee that the adherents of the two parties would claim that the ascendancy of *his* party was the surest way to both protect slavery and preserve the Union. Harris therefore replied, denying that Cass was a former Federalist and reading from a letter by Cass unreservedly opposing the Wilmot Proviso. Harris then turned on Taylor, who was "unsound" on the issue of slavery, although a slaveholder himself. Harris also attacked Taylor's opposition to the exercise of the presidential veto power, which Harris viewed as ignoring the president's constitutional function as a check and balance on the actions of Congress. Another Whig, a certain Tyler, took the stump to rebut Harris, but, in the view of the Democratic *Jeffersonian*, "could not . . . touch [Harris's] arguments with a forty foot pole." The next day, at Clarksville, Harris engaged in a near six-hour marathon debate with his Whig opponent, Colonel Aaron Goodrich, and again was declared the victor by the *Jeffersonian*, who deemed the Democrats present "more than pleased with their champion, they were delighted." Although Cass was defeated in Tennessee by a "Taylor tornado," the Democrats maintained a majority in the 9th District, while Harris "added greatly to his reputation as an orator and debater."[37]

In January 1849, Congressman Lucian B. Chase announced to the people of the 9th District that he would not run for reelection that year. While Harris previously was a relative unknown outside of his senatorial district, "his gentlemanly bearing, thrilling eloquence, cogent and forcible reasoning, and true de-

36. "Grim Death Claims a Great Statesman"; "The State Convention," *Clarksville Jeffersonian*, January 12, 1848; "State Convention," *Clarksville Jeffersonian*, January 26, 1848; "Our Elector," *Clarksville Jeffersonian*, January 12, 1848. The newspapers of the time seem to have had difficulty printing the correct combination of Harris's first two initials.

37. "Grim Death Claims a Great Statesman"; IGH to Quintard, December 29, 1894, Quintard Papers; Atkins, "Politicians, Parties and Slavery," 20, 28; "The Contest in the 9th," *Clarksville Jeffersonian*, August 14, 1848; "Gen. Harris," *Clarksville Jeffersonian*, April 24, 1849; see generally Watters, "Isham Green Harris," 24.

mocracy" during the presidential election made him the front runner for the seat. The Democrats' 9th District congressional convention was held on April 14, 1849, during which Harris was nominated and unanimously approved as the party's candidate for Congress in the election. Harris's Whig opponent was a Mr. Morris, of whom little was known, "except that he is a minister of the Presbyterian denomination, lives in Stewart, and aspires to a seat in Congress. He is said to be a good speaker and very much a gentleman."[38]

Three years after it was first introduced, the Wilmot Proviso remained a point of contention in Tennessee. While the Whig gubernatorial candidate, Neill S. Brown, advocated resisting the passage of the proviso all the way to the Supreme Court, he promised to submit to the "action of the law." The Democrats, on the other hand, led by their candidate, William Trousdale, pledged to defend Southern rights "to the last extremity," a position that Brown deemed "unpatriotic and nullifying in character." While one of Harris's debates with Reverend Morris focused on tariffs and other issues of economic policy, clearly the Wilmot Proviso and the questions it raised were of substantial importance in the campaign, which saw twenty-five speeches and debates in the course of a month. Likely seeking to minimize a subject matter on which Harris had seized as a cornerstone of his political position, the incredulous *Jeffersonian* reported that Morris believed "that two thirds of the people in this district, have no interest in the Wilmot Proviso, and would not care if it was passed." The *Jeffersonian* questioned if the voters of the district wanted Morris to go off to Congress and tell the "northern abolitionists" that, "or would they hear the conduct of these fanatics rebuked, with scorn and indignation by a man jealous of the constitutional rights of his constituents. Such a man is General Harris."[39]

Harris won by a margin that was later claimed to be "the largest majority ever given before to any democrat in the district." He took office in December 1849, at a time when the sectional conflict over the issue of slavery threatened the continu-

---

38. "Hon. Lucien B. Chase," *Clarksville Jeffersonian*, January 23, 1849; "Gen. Harris," *Clarksville Jeffersonian*, April 24, 1849; "Congressional Convention," *Clarksville Jeffersonian*, April 17, 1849; "Movements of the Democracy," *Nashville Daily Union*, April 19, 1849; IGH to Quintard, December 29, 1894, Quintard Papers; "The Candidates," *Clarksville Jeffersonian*, May 29, 1849.

39. "Gov. Brown—The Proviso," *Clarksville Jeffersonian*, May 29, 1849; Atkins, "Politicians, Parties and Slavery," 28–29; "The Congressional Canvass" and "Congressional Appointments," *Clarksville Jeffersonian*, July 3, 1849; "Morris on the Proviso," *Clarksville Jeffersonian*, July 10, 1849.

ance of the Union. Immediately at issue were the questions of whether California and New Mexico should be admitted to the Union as free states, and compounding Southern irritation was the fact that President Taylor, himself a Southerner and slaveholder, was urging admission of the two potential states on a Free Soil basis. Heated rhetoric from both sides thundered in each house of the Congress, and threats of personal violence and actual physical conflict occurred in the halls of the Capitol. Harris spent much of his first days in the House participating in the sixty-three votes it took to elect a Speaker. Into that tense atmosphere stepped Henry Clay, who, on January 29, 1850, introduced eight resolutions "proposing an amicable arrangement of all questions in controversy between the Free and Slave States, growing out of the subject of Slavery." Clay's resolutions linked the admission of California with a guarantee that the rest of the Mexican cession would be organized "without the adoption of any restriction or condition on the subject of slavery." Other measures related to Texas's border with New Mexico and its public debt, slavery in the District of Columbia, and the need for a more "efficient" fugitive slave law. Finally, Clay proposed that Congress acknowledge it had no power over "the trade in slaves between the slaveholding states."[40]

Harris got the chance to speak on the compromise, and especially the issue of California, on April 9, 1850. Acknowledging himself as "inexperienced," "obscure," and "humble," he stated that he nonetheless was compelled to speak as his constituency had a "deep and abiding interest in the questions now agitating" Congress and the country. Harris's main theme was that Congress had no constitutional power to prohibit slavery in the territories. Arguing that previous legislation that limited the extension of slavery were not valid precedents, Harris posited that the Missouri Compromise was not an admission by the South of Congress's power to limit slavery above the compromise line, but was a concession laid down by the South "as a peace offering on the altar of the Union." From there, Harris proceeded to analyze the arguments of those who claimed the power to limit slavery existed, arguing various constitutional points in opposition. In lawyerly fashion, he argued that the U.S. Constitution's privileges and immunities clause allowed a slave owner to carry and hold "any and every description of property he owns" into the territories. Harris excoriated those who sought the "gratification of the sordid selfishness of fanaticism," noting that they were "rendering wider and deeper that gulf that, unfortunately, already exists between us."[41]

Because of Andrew Jackson's denunciation of nullification in 1832, the differing distribution of slavery across the state, and the narrowness of the divide between the Democrats and the Whigs in any given election year, Tennessee's political culture was not of the fire-eating Southern rights variety, although elements of the Democratic Party, including Harris, were aggressively proslavery.[42] Therefore, Harris recognized that his constituents wanted the compromise to work. Portraying the Northern abolitionists as the real threat to the Union and peace, Harris stated:

> I utter this in no spirit of threat or menace. I speak of facts as I understand them to exist. Sir, if we would restore peace and quietude to the country—if we would perpetuate the Union of these States, we must return, and in my opinion, return speedily too, to that spirit of concession, compromise and mutual respect for the rights, interests, and feelings of the people of each and every section of this Confederacy, that characterized the deliberations of our fathers who formed the Confederacy, and gave us this proudest monument of human wisdom—the American Constitution.
>
> I represent a constituency who love and cherish this Union as much as any men in it, and who will sacrifice all that honest freemen, having a proper respect for themselves and their rights, can sacrifice for its maintenance. Beyond this I trust they will not be asked or expected to go.[43]

On the narrow issue of the admission of California as a state, Harris opposed it on the grounds that the area was simply too big, and that Congress had no way of knowing who among its burgeoning and shifting population had framed its constitution. But, Harris concluded, if California's statehood were combined with other matters raised by the proposed compromise measures, he would be willing to vote for her admission.[44]

41. *Cong. Globe*, 31st Cong., 1st Sess., 1850, Appx. 443–45. The privileges and immunities clause (U.S. Constitution, Art. IV, Section 2, Clause 1) states: "The Citizens of each State shall be entitled to all Privileges and Immunities of Citizens in the several States."

42. Atkins, "Politicians, Parties and Slavery," 28.

43. *Cong. Globe*, 31st Cong., 1st Sess., 1850, Appx. 446.

44. Ibid.

Harris's views were consistent with those of other Democrats on the Tennessee delegation. Andrew Johnson, representing a district in East Tennessee, echoed Harris's metaphor of an altar, and urged that, in the spirit of the Constitution to which all claimed allegiance, "we ought to all come forward and cooperate in erecting an altar to our common country, upon which each one of us . . . may sacrifice something to preserve the harmony that has heretofore existed between the extremes of the Union."[45] Andrew Ewing, representing the district which included Nashville, stated just a few days after Harris's speech that he was for the admission of California "if we can satisfactorily adjust the other questions connected with it, and thus let her enter our Union as a harbinger of peace and unity." In the end, the Tennessee delegation eventually supported most of the compromise resolutions.[46]

Back in the 9th District, the *Jeffersonian*'s Whig counterpart, the *Chronicle*, accused Harris of throwing firebrands and acting in bad faith in his speech, and saying that the congressman opposed California's admission unless as a slave state. Once the published speech made it to Clarksville, the *Jeffersonian* published a piece quoting the last few paragraphs of the speech, extolling Harris for his "good sense and patriotism." Harris sought to "make the admission of California the condition of the settlement of the slavery question," and, in the view of the *Jeffersonian*, was "using his best efforts to bring about an honorable and equitable compromise."[47]

Clay's proposal was a single legislative package, which, after being buffeted by amendments, was defeated at the end of July. The exhausted Clay left the compromise proposal in the hands of Senator Stephen A. Douglas of Illinois. Douglas's efforts were aided by the unexpected death of President Taylor that summer. Taylor's successor, Millard Fillmore, was more sympathetic to the South. Douglas eventually broke the logjam by breaking the "omnibus" bill into its several parts, and finding majorities for each component. Thus, Congressman Isham G. Harris could vote against the admission of California and the abolition of the slave trade in the District of Columbia, and vote for the rest, because the total compromise was not presented to him. Harris reasoned "that the measures of which the compromise bill was composed, some of them materially changed, were presented to

45. Ibid., 559.
46. Ibid., 451; Corlew, *Tennessee: A Short History,* 272.
47. "Gen. Harris and the Chronicle," *Clarksville Jeffersonian,* April 30, 1850.

him as independent measures, and that he voted for each upon its own merits, as his judgment approved or disapproved them."[48]

From the start of his political career, Harris made no secret of his political views. He did not doubt the constitutional right of property in man, and viewed the Wilmot Proviso and the men who supported it as the true enemies of the Union and the Constitution. Harris's campaign for reelection in 1851 was in essence a referendum on this political viewpoint. Harris's Whig opponent was Jacob G. Hornberger, a thirty-one-year-old Clarksville lawyer whose previous public service was as a public school commissioner. A "good speaker" who showed "some ingenuity in handling his points," the "gentlemanly" but youthful Hornberger likely undertook the impossible task of unseating Harris in order to make himself better known in legal and political circles.[49]

The three points on which Hornberger challenged Harris was the latter's positions on one of the various rivers and harbors internal improvements measures of the day, the Tariff of 1846, and the issues raised by the compromise of 1850. The rivers and harbors debate was typical of the age, and hinged upon the issue of whether Congress had the constitutional power to fund internal improvements. Citing President Polk's veto message of a similar message, Harris's view was that Congress should follow past precedent and authorize the states to levy duties based on the tonnage of vessels to fund improvements. The point of the debate over the tariff was to what extent the *ad valorum* principle should be used in levying tariffs. Rather than specific duties on specific goods, Harris advocated a tax on premised the value of goods, of whatever nature.[50]

On the issue of the compromise, Hornberger announced that he would have supported the Wilmot Proviso in 1846, and attacked Harris's votes against California statehood and the abolition of the slave trade in the District of Columbia as a rejection of the compromise as a whole. Harris effectively parried the charge by noting that only three Whigs had voted for every one of the compromise mea-

48. McPherson, *Battle Cry of Freedom*, 74–77; "The Congressional Canvass," *Clarksville Jeffersonian*, June 28, 1851.

49. "The Congressional Canvass," *Clarksville Jeffersonian*, June 28, 1851; "Harris and Hornberger at Paris," *Clarksville Jeffersonian*, July 30, 1851; 1850 and 1860 Federal Census, Montgomery County, Tennessee; Ursula Smith Beach, *Along the Warito or A History of Montgomery County, Tennessee* (Nashville: McQuiddy Press, 1964), 138, 160–61.

50. "The Congressional Canvass," *Clarksville Jeffersonian*, June 28, 1851; "Harris and Hornberger at Paris," *Clarksville Jeffersonian*, July 30, 1851; Yontan Eyal, "Trade and Improvements: Young America and the Transformation of the Democratic Party," *Civil War History* 51 (September 2005): 245, 257–63; "Very Summary," *Clarksville Jeffersonian*, July 19, 1851.

sures, and that his vote was exactly the same as that of Congressman Henry Foote of Mississippi, whom Hornberger considered to be a sound Union man. Consistent with the practice of the day in Tennessee, when each party claimed the other was a danger to the Union, on various occasions, Hornberger equated the Tennessee Democracy with "agitators, nullifiers, dis-unionists and fire-eaters," the nullifiers of South Carolina, and John C. Calhoun. Harris replied: "What have I to do with S. Carolina and her fire-eaters? There are extreme men South and extreme men at the North. Have I countenanced them? Have I shown them favor or friendship and helped them carry out their disunion designs?" In the end, it was clear that the otherwise personable Hornberger was simply overmatched. The *Jeffersonian* warned that Harris's friends might feel sympathy for his opponent. The paper's editor personally wished Hornberger all the good in the world, hoping that the next time he appeared it would be in a "better cause," and "against a less powerful and popular opponent than Isham G. Harris."[51]

Another of Harris's duties was to press the case for Governor Trousdale, whom the Whigs portrayed as a dangerous disunionist. Indeed, Trousdale was on record as willing to defend Southern rights "to the last extremity," and indicated only grudging acceptance of the compromise. His opponent, Judge William Campbell, deemed the compromise a "work of wisdom," which seems to have resounded well among his fellow Tennesseans, who, in general, favored the compromise. In the background was the abortive Nashville Convention of 1850, a gathering of delegates from the Southern states that was meant to solidify a united front on the issue of slavery. Tennesseans saw firsthand the radicalizing effect the fire-eating extremists of South Carolina had upon the Democratic delegates from Tennessee, and, indeed, the convention brought to light a factional dispute between hard-line and more moderate Tennessee Democrats. The split of the Democrats into "compromise" and "Southern rights" factions led to the sweeping Whig victory in 1851. Harris was able to hold his seat with a comfortable majority, but his "stirring appeals" on Trousdale's behalf were to less avail, as the Whigs again took control of the statehouse.[52]

51. "The Congressional Canvass" and "The Wilmot Proviso," *Clarksville Jeffersonian,* June 28, 1851; "Harris and Hornberger at Paris," *Clarkesville Jeffersonian,* July 30, 1851; Atkins, "Politicians, Parties and Slavery," 28; "Our Candidates," *Clarksville Jeffersonian,* August 2, 1851.

52. "The Congressional Canvass"; Atkins, "Politicians, Parties and Slavery," 29; Corlew, *Tennessee: A Short History,* 273; Thelma Jennings, "Tennessee and the Nashville Conventions of 1850," *Tennessee Historical Quarterly* 30(Spring 1971): 70, 79–80; St. George L. Sioussat, "Tennessee, the Compromise of 1850, and the Nashville Convention," *Tennessee Historical Magazine* 4 (December 1918):

Harris's views on the Nashville Convention are unknown. Publicly, he was pro-compromise, notwithstanding his fervent support of Trousdale. His votes in general sustained the compromise of 1850 with the exception of the California and District of Columbia measures. On the stump Harris repudiated "S. Carolina and her fire-eaters." As any successful politician, Harris had a sense for the sentiment of the voters, and must have known that the prevailing sentiment in his district, as elsewhere in the state, was for sectional compromise. Harris made it known that while he voted against the admission of California, if the measure would resolve the sectional unrest and restore the peace and harmony of the country, he would be for it. In his view, the goal of his party was to "remove the dangerous question [of slavery] from the arena of national politics." Harris's reelection was deemed, at least by his political allies, a vindication of his stand on the compromise.[53]

Early in the new session, Harris first came into conflict with another Tennessee congressman, fellow Democrat Andrew Johnson. On February 21, 1851, late in the second session of the 31st Congress, Johnson introduced a resolution calling for a constitutional amendment to change the method of electing the president and vice president by dividing the states into electoral districts. The resolution also called for direct election of senators and election of the judges of the Federal judiciary for twelve-year terms. There was no further significant action on the resolution in the 31st Congress. Johnson introduced a nearly identical resolution on February 2, 1852, and it was referred to the Committee on the Judiciary, of which Harris was a member.[54]

Johnson's proposal was coldly met in the committee, and Harris was asked to write the report. Years later, Harris recalled, "I did so and made a report that squelched the proposition. We sat down on it unceremoniously." The committee's report, and Harris's reply, was the subject of some words between the two, and

215, 243–47; Atkins, *Parties, Politics, and the Sectional Conflict in Tennessee,* 172–77; "Committee of Arrangements," *Clarksville Jeffersonian,* August 13, 1851; "How Was it Done?" *Clarkesville Jeffersonian,* August 28, 1851.

53. Sioussat, "Tennessee, the Compromise of 1850, and the Nashville Convention," 236–40; "Harris and Hornberger at Paris," *Clarksville Jeffersonian,* July 30, 1851; "Gen. Harris," *Clarksville Jeffersonian,* July 19, 1851; "The Congressional Canvass," *Clarksville Jeffersonian,* June 28, 1851; "Committee of Arrangements," *Clarksville Jeffersonian,* August 13, 1851.

54. *Cong. Globe,* 31st Cong., 2nd Sess., 1853, 627; U.S. *House Journal,* 31st Cong., 2nd Sess., 322; 1 *PAJ* 604–7; *Cong. Globe,* 32nd Cong., 1st Sess., 1852, 443; U.S. *House Journal,* 32nd Cong., 1st Sess., 306.

Harris was convinced that Johnson disliked him from that point, as Harris did not believe Johnson "ever forgave any man who he once disliked." Johnson's pet project during that time was a Homestead Bill, which Johnson believed was necessary to counteract efforts by the states, corporations, and capitalists in general to "parsel [sic] the entire public domain among themselves." Harris also voted against this measure, and was in fact the only Tennessee congressman to do so, which cannot have improved his standing with Johnson. Harris actually proposed an alternate measure that provided a complicated sliding scale for claimants to pay for the acreage they desired.[55]

Johnson believed Harris's stance on the Homestead Bill a political aberration within the Democratic Party.[56] Harris's position on the proposal, however, was consistent with his strong sectional stance. A number of Southerners feared the measure would encourage the incursion of foreign immigrants, most of whom would arrive with antislavery prejudices, thereby increasing the political imbalance already seen in the North's growing population advantage. A Democratic politician in Middle Tennessee later noted that Johnson's Homestead Bill was "not popular in the South." Harris's position on other measures during the 32nd Congress continued to reflect his pro-Southern viewpoints. Early in the first session, an odd dispute arose over a resolution welcoming the Hungarian patriot Louis Kossuth. Some Southerners in the House feared that Kossuth would be used by Free Soilers to advance their political agenda, and fell back on George Washington's admonition against foreign entanglements as their justification for a watered-down welcome. While he was as ready as anyone to "extend to Kossuth a personal compliment," Harris protested he was unwilling to abandon "the principle of non-intervention." He therefore moved an amendment that advised Kossuth: "Friendship with all nations—entangling alliances with none." The amendment and several like it failed, and the resolution eventually passed.[57]

On account of sickness, Harris missed a debate on April 5, 1852, on two resolu-

55. Jonathan Brownlow to O. P. Temple, January 1, 1896, O. P. Temple Papers, University of Tennessee Special Collections; A. Johnson to H. Greely, December 15, 1851, 1 PAJ 631–33; U.S. House Journal, 32nd Cong., 1st Sess., 705–6; Cong. Globe, 32nd Cong., 1st Sess., 1852, 707. Harris's conversation with Brownlow indicates the clash over the election resolution occurred in 1851, but the record shows it was not referred to the judiciary committee until 1852.

56. A. Johnson to William Lowry, December 14, 1856, 2 PAJ 460–62.

57. Cong. Globe, 32nd Cong., 1st Sess., 1852, Appx. 512; Herschel Gower and Jack Allen, eds., Pen and Sword: The Life and Journals of Randal W. McGavock (Nashville: Tennessee Historical Commission, 1959), 581; Cong. Globe, 32nd Cong., 1st Sess., 1851–52, 175, 187, 200. The Memphis Daily Appeal

tions offered by members from Georgia that, at least facially, pledged support for the compromise measures passed by the previous Congress. While the measures passed, they were criticized during the debate as being cynically worded so that one, regardless of his position on slavery, could claim support for the measures on the one hand, and then go home to his district and deny them on the other. Harris published a card in the *Congressional Globe* stating that he would have voted for both measures, believing that they "reflected the will" of most, if not all, of his constituency. A piece in the *Jeffersonian* confirmed that Democratic support for the pro-compromise measure was stronger than that of the Whigs, who had only been recently attacking Trousdale for an anti-compromise position.[58]

Harris's other guiding principle during his second term in Congress was strict examination of Federal expenditures. As has been seen, his alternative homestead proposal provided that there would be payment for the parcels subject to a homestead claim. As a member of the Judiciary Committee, he opposed a measure that proposed publishing the laws of the United States in the two papers having the largest weekly circulation in each congressional district, at the cost of an additional $80,000 over the system whereby they were published in the two largest newspapers of each state, sensibly noting that the public benefit of the measure was slight. A concern for the public purse also motivated a change of course on a bill providing for the assignability (transferability) of land warrants issued as bounties for service to the government. On January 24, 1852, Harris began spearheading an effort to pass a bill from the Senate on the subject, supposing "that some legislation on the subject is absolutely necessary." But less than two weeks later, Harris changed his tune, objecting to provisions of the bill that seemed to leave the government open to excessive claims from the agents appointed to register and receive the warrants. When challenged, he explained that he had introduced the measure in order to get it before the House, with the expectation that any defects would be exposed in the course of the debate. Upon scrutiny, Harris explained, he determined to correct the error.[59]

Even when expenditures were appropriate, Harris reviewed them carefully. In a debate over the disappearance of certain funds due the Seneca Indians by treaty,

---

noted some weeks later that the principle of non-intervention was also Andrew Jackson's. "Jackson and Intervention," *Memphis Daily Appeal*, February 12, 1852.

58. *Cong. Globe*, 32nd Cong., 1st Sess., 1852, 976–83; "Friends of the Compromise," *Clarksville Jeffersonian*, April 24.

59. *Cong. Globe*, 32nd Cong., 1st Sess., 1852, 379, 421, 451, 458–59, 463–68.

Harris questioned whether the fraud was due to an agent of the Federal government, in which case the Indians should be indemnified, or by an agent of the Indians, for which the government should not be liable. As chairman of the Committee on Invalid Pensions, Harris sought clarification as to its duties relating to the claims relating to the navy. Harris presented what the committee thought were appropriate claims, and was careful in cases that might produce large arrears, noting: "the principle upon which we proceed is, that [Congress's] neglect shall not prejudice his rights, while his own neglect shall prejudice that right." And, consistent with his position in the campaign against Hornberger, Harris continued to oppose tonnage duties unless the power was delegated to the states.[60]

At home, the Whig victory in 1851 began to bear bitter fruit for Harris and the Democracy of Tennessee. Led by Representative Gustavus Adolphus Henry of Montgomery County, the Whig-dominated General Assembly reapportioned Tennessee in a "remarkable and barefaced" gerrymander, one so epochal that a Democratic editor wrote: "In the history of gerrymanders, this will stand unparalleled in its unfairness." The "Henrymander," as the move became to be known, was contrived to give the Whigs eight of the ten congressional districts. Andrew Johnson and Harris were among the targeted Democratic congressmen. Henry County remained in a revamped 9th District, which now had a Whig majority of almost five hundred votes from the previous election. Harris's political ally, James Trimble Dunlap, his successor as state senator, made an effort to restore the 9th District to a "slight Democratic majority," but was defeated. The bill, passed on February 20, 1852, changed the political landscape dramatically, doing "yeoman's service" for the Whigs and inflicting "heavy damage" on the Democrats.[61]

The Democrats recognized that their split on the issue of slavery was the source of their problem. In March 1852, at the end of the disastrous legislative session, the Democratic members of the General Assembly published an address to the party faithful exhorting unity and organization, noting that the split on slavery was really a "shade of difference . . . in the degree of indignation felt at Northern aggression than in any proposed remedy or final action on the subject."

60. Ibid., 47, 235–39, 435–36, 2014.

61. Lewright B. Sikes, "Gustavus Adolphus Henry: Champion of Lost Causes," *Tennessee Historical Quarterly* 50 (Fall 1991): 173, 180; Atkins, *Parties, Politics, and the Sectional Conflict in Tennessee,* 181–82; "The Last and Worst Gerrymander," *Nashville Daily American,* January 22, 1852; "The Congressional Apportionment Bill," *Memphis Daily Appeal,* January 31, 1852; "Afternoon Session—District Congressional Bill," *Memphis Daily Appeal,* February 15, 1852; Chapter 196, *Acts of the State of Tennessee, 1851–52;* "The Whig Gerrymander," *Clarksville Jeffersonian,* February 25, 1852.

In spite of its recognition of the problem, the state party could not unite on a candidate for president, eventually sending a delegation to the national convention split between Lewis Cass and James Buchanan. While Democrat Franklin Pierce won the nomination and eventually the election, the Whigs carried Tennessee yet again, convincing enough of the electorate that the Democrats were a party of disunion.[62]

It was this atmosphere of party division and defeat that Green Harris contemplated in early 1853, with his congressional district now with a Whig majority. While Harris's proponents expressed no doubt that he would retain his seat notwithstanding the Henrymander, they began to lay the groundwork, with his acquiescence, if not his approval, to put his name forward as a candidate for governor in 1853. In January, the loyal *Clarksville Jeffersonian* ran a series of articles extolling Harris as a candidate, noting his past political success, his prowess as a speaker, and his effectiveness as a congressman, but also hastening to note that Harris in far off Washington had no foreknowledge of the paper's suggestion of his name for the office. Others in Harris's old congressional district took up his cause, as the Democratic conventions in both Henry and Dickson counties made it known that while they would loyally support the state party's candidate; Harris was their first choice for the nomination.[63]

Unfortunately, Harris was not the first choice of most of the rest of the state. While Harris's public position supported the compromise, he was clearly part of the Southern rights wing of the party, perceived as the cause of the party's loss in the previous two elections. On April 26, 1853, the night before the start of the convention, many delegates met in caucus, and it was agreed that a straw poll would be taken, and if a candidate received the votes of two-thirds of the counties, the caucus would recommend that person to the convention. The split between Unionist and Southern Rights candidates remained evident in the first poll; Andrew Johnson got thirty-two of fifty-four votes, while Harris and Judge W. C.

---

62. "An Address of the Members of the Legislature to the Members of the Democratic Party of Tennessee," *Clarksville Jeffersonian*, March 9, 1852; Atkins, *Parties, Politics, and the Sectional Conflict in Tennessee*, 183–85.

63. "The Last Gerrymander," *Clarksville Jeffersonian*, January 24, 1852; "The Next Candidate for Governor," *Clarksville Jeffersonian*, January 5, 1853; "The Eagle wishes to know . . .," *Clarksville Jeffersonian*, January 15, 1853; "The Eagle is condemned . . .," *Clarkesville Jeffersonian*, January 22, 1853; "Democratic Meeting in Henry," *Memphis Daily Appeal*, March 16, 1853; "Democratic Meeting," *Nashville Daily American*, April 13, 1853.

Dunlap of Memphis each got nine votes. By the time of the third poll, Harris was out of the running, and Johnson prevailed against former governor Trousdale, behind whom the Southern Rights candidates combined. Then, in a final dramatic anti-Johnson move, Nashville's Andrew Ewing was put forth as a candidate, but Ewing rose and asked that he be allowed to postpone an answer until the next day.[64]

After preliminary matters were disposed of the next day, Ewing declined the nomination, on the grounds that he had previously promised to support Johnson, Johnson's being the only name before the convention; Harris's name was then placed in nomination, but Harris's political ally, John DeWitt Clinton Atkins of Henry County, asked for it to be withdrawn. Harris had clearly taken the temperature of the meeting and did not want a formal vote ending in defeat. After other names were unsuccessfully floated, Johnson was made the unanimous selection of the convention. Ironically, the Henrymander proved to serve as a catalyst for the defeat of its author, as Johnson outpolled Gustavus A. Henry in the gubernatorial election in August.[65]

While they might not have supported him for governor, the Democrats in Harris's new district still deemed him the party's proper candidate for Congress. Harris had published a card before his term ended on March 4, 1853, stating that he would not be a candidate for a third term, having "resolved to quit politics and devote my life to the practice of law." What the effect of that resolution in light of a nomination for governor would have been is not known. That May, a number of possible candidates vied for the congressional nomination in the convention for the revamped 9th District. After two days of balloting, no agreement could be reached. Harris's name was then placed before the convention despite his published intention not to run, and on the first ballot he was nominated. Notwithstanding this compliment, Harris quickly declined. Tired of life as a congressman, he intended to resume his law practice.[66]

64. Atkins, *Parties, Politics, and the Sectional Conflict in Tennessee*, 185; "The State Convention—Preliminary Meeting," *Nashville Daily American*, April 28, 1853.

65. "The State Convention," *Nashville Daily American*, April 28, 1853; "The State Convention," *Clarksville Jeffersonian*, May 4, 1853; Robert H. White, *Messages of the Governors of Tennessee* (Nashville: Tennessee Historical Commission, 1959), 4:512–19.

66. "Democratic Meeting," *Nashville Daily American*, April 15, 1853; "Good Nominations," *Nashville Daily American*, May 14, 1853; Harris to Quintard, December 29, 1894, Quintard Papers; "Grim Death Claims a Great Statesman."

Harris later wrote: "The fact that I was so nominated after my card declining to be a candidate decided me to . . . move out of that Congressional District." His brother, William R. Harris, moved his practice from Paris to Memphis in 1851, and was appointed in June to the unexpired term of Judge William B. Turley of the Chancery Court. Elected to a full term in November 1851, William was fully established in the Memphis bar by 1853. It was only logical that his brother Green, having decided to escape his former life in politics, should move to Memphis in the winter of 1853–54.[67]

By any standard, Green Harris at age thirty-six was a successful man. He had proven himself in business, in the practice of law, and in politics. Furthermore, with Trousdale's eclipse, he was established as the future leader of the Southern Rights wing of the state Democratic Party, although he was careful not to be linked with the "fire-eaters" who advocated disunion. Unfortunately for Harris, the electorate was in the mood for compromise, meaning that Harris and those of his views on sectional issues were a distinct minority. Tired of Congress and doubtless leery of his prospects in his Henrymandered district, he faced the possibility that the Tennessee Democracy would be dominated by his newly made enemy, Andrew Johnson, for some years to come. As he had two decades before, he followed his older brother to greener pastures. The question would be whether he would be satisfied, after being in the center of his political universe for so long, with a quiet law practice on the Mississippi.

67. "Judicial," *Memphis Daily Appeal*, June 13, 1851; "Election of Judge," *Memphis Daily Appeal*, November 22, 1851; Harris to Quintard, December 29, 1894, Quintard Papers.

2 "MY BUSINESS WILL BE TO ADVOCATE THE PRINCIPLES AND PLATFORM OF DEMOCRACY" 1854–1860

When Green Harris took up his law practice in Memphis in 1854, the city had grown substantially from the small, rough river town of just a few years before. The census of 1840 showed a total free population of 1,799, with 221 slaves. By 1850, the population had grown to 8,841, and by 1854, thanks in part to expansion of the corporate boundaries, to 12,687. It teemed with commerce and the business class that went with it and a number of Irish immigrants in the 1850s soon provided a white underclass more numerous than the African American slaves. Further, as it always had, the river brought native whites who frequented a number of lower-class establishments where law and order was at best tenuous. Yet, muddy roads were planked, schools opened, and, a marvel for the time and place, five-story commercial buildings were erected.[1]

All of the business activity and growing population made Memphis a fertile area for a number of business and professional endeavors. The front page of the *Memphis Appeal* in mid-1854 published the names of cotton factors and commission merchants, doctors, confectionaries, hotels, steamboats, and, of course, lawyers. Among those of the bar publishing their cards was the firm of "W. R. & I. G. Harris," noting that their office was that previously occupied by another person and "nearly opposite [the] Odd Fellow's Hall."[2]

The Harris law practice prospered, and Green continued to build his reputation as a lawyer. In August 1855, the sheriff of Shelby County sought an opinion from prominent members of the bar construing the provisions of a statute relating

1. J. P. Young, *Standard History of Memphis, Tennessee* (Knoxville: H. W. Crew, 1912), 80–81, 92, 94; Gerald M. Capers Jr., *The Biography of a River Town, Memphis: Its Heroic Age* (Chapel Hill: University of North Carolina Press, 1939), 107–8, 111, 132.

2. *Memphis Daily Appeal*, July 6, July 26, September 26, December 17, 1854.

to voter eligibility. Harris, a member of the local bar for less than two years, joined seven other attorneys in rendering advice. William appears to have split his time between the practice and a local judicial position he first occupied in 1851. A vacancy occurred on the Tennessee Supreme Court, and perhaps in recognition of William's legal ability, or perhaps as an olive branch to warm what were probably cool relations with Green, Governor Andrew Johnson appointed William to the post on August 22, 1855. Considered by his fellow lawyers as "able, astute and discriminating," William was elected to a full eight-year term that December. Even after his brother went on the bench, Green continued, at least for a period, to advertise the firm with William's name joined with his.[3]

Although Green Harris moved to Memphis in part to escape politics, he continued to keep a high political profile. An overzealous fellow Democrat wrote the *Appeal* in February 1855 touting Harris's qualifications for an open state Senate seat. Having resumed his practice, and having recently been a possible candidate for governor, it was not likely a former congressman would accept a state Senate seat. Harris wrote the paper a few days later expressing his appreciation: "I cannot, under any circumstances, consent to become a candidate for the Senate." Harris kept his name at the forefront of the party, however, as he spoke on at least one occasion at a Democratic meeting.[4]

Harris's desire to grow his law practice inevitably came into conflict with his party loyalty. In early January 1856, the Tennessee Democratic state convention met in Nashville to prepare for the national election to be held that year. Before the convention, Harris was told that he would be selected as an elector-at-large, and he replied that he would not accept the post. Nominated, Harris immediately wrote a letter declining the post. But he was convinced by friends not to do so, notwithstanding the fact that he "then had a good law-practice, was making money & wished to keep out of politics." Accordingly, along with William H.

3. "Grim Death Claims a Great Statesman"; letter from Farrington et al., *Memphis Daily Appeal*, August 1, 1855; "Tribute of Respect to the Memory of the Hon. William R. Harris, Late One of the Judges of the Supreme Court of Tennessee," 37 Tenn. (5 Sneed) 731, 734; Caldwell, *Sketches of the Bench and Bar of Tennessee*, 159–60; "Hon. W. R. Harris—Supreme Judge," *Memphis Daily Appeal*, September 26, 1855; "The Election Today," *Memphis Daily Appeal*, December 1, 1855; "The Vote for the Judge of the Supreme Court," *Memphis Daily Appeal*, December 19, 1854; W. R. and I. G. Harris advertisement, *Memphis Daily Appeal*, December 1, 1855.

4. "Memphis," *Memphis Daily Appeal*, February 22, 1855; Harris letter, *Memphis Daily Appeal*, March 1, 1855; "The Democratic Meeting at Collierville," *Memphis Daily Appeal*, October 26, 1855.

Polk of Maury County, the former president's brother, Harris undertook the duty, which called for him to campaign statewide for the Democratic ticket.[5]

Governor Andrew Johnson remained the state's most prominent Democrat, but whatever *rapprochement* was achieved between Johnson and Harris by the appointment of William to the supreme court soon dissipated. Late in life, Harris recalled that Johnson made a speech in Nashville during this interval that the governor thought worthy of publication in pamphlet form "as the keynote of the campaign." While in Nashville on business, Harris went to Johnson's office at the Capitol at the governor's request. Johnson read his speech to Harris, and disclosed his plan to publish it. Harris said that it had better not be published, because the spokesmen for Millard Fillmore, the Know-Nothing candidate for president, would "be certain to read from it on the stump." When Johnson expressed a lack of concern, Harris said, "Then . . . I will denounce it on every occasion where it is quoted." An angry Johnson asked why, and Harris replied, "Because . . . I will not, by God, stultify myself by endorsing a lot of d——d Andy Johnsonisms as Democracy." Harris pointed out that no Democratic convention anywhere had adopted Johnson's "d——d hobbies," such as the direct election of U.S. senators, as part of their platform. Harris closed by saying, "My business . . . will be to advocate the principles and platform of Democracy and not *Andy Johnson's hobbies*." Harris bowed out of the room, and from that point on, the two were enemies, an enmity that lasted another nineteen years. The pamphlet, however, went unpublished.[6]

Harris had good reason to think that Johnson's peculiar ideas might be used against the Democracy. As the national Whig Party fractured in the early 1850s over sectional issues, a new party, the American Party, more commonly known as the Know-Nothings (from their secret antecedents and the stock answer "I don't know"), arose. For a short period in the mid-1850s, the Know-Nothings, which in Tennessee were basically former Whigs, formed the opposition to the Democracy. The main credo of the party, at least on the national front, was to take a "native American" stance that was basically anti-Catholic and anti-immigrant. In Johnson's last gubernatorial campaign, his opponent charged him with "radical" ideas,

5. "Democratic State Convention," *Memphis Daily Appeal*, January 13, 1856; Jonathan Brownlow to O. P. Temple, January 1, 1896, O. P. Temple Papers, University of Tennessee (quote); "Grim Death Claims a Great Statesman."

6. Brownlow to Temple, January 1, 1896, O. P. Temple Papers, University of Tennessee.

the very "d——d Andy Johnsonisms" Harris feared would be used against him in the campaign season of 1856.[7]

That summer, Harris and former Governor Neill S. Brown toured the state, Brown advocating the Fillmore candidacy on the Know-Nothing ticket, and Harris the Democratic candidate, James Buchanan. Brown, known for his debating skills, was a formidable opponent. Democratic correspondents reported from across the state that Harris clearly prevailed against Brown, challenging him to name a single time while Fillmore was in Congress that he had voted in favor of the "peculiar institution." Harris made the point that the Democracy was the only true national party, while Brown, who spoke platitudes about the Union, had no ideas on how to preserve it. The Know-Nothings countered during the course of the election that they were the true party of Union and that the Democrats harbored disunionists. In the course of the campaign, Harris showed up well. Little known outside of West Tennessee, Harris made a name for himself in other quarters of the state with his skillful and forceful debating. One glowing report came in from Fayetteville, in Middle Tennessee, extolling Harris's performance, and concluding that "Harris is greater than Andy Johnson." Forty years later, Harris recalled that he "never in his life made a canvass which was so satisfactory to himself and to his friends." The Whigs thought Brown got the better of the debate, the Democrats (save Andrew Johnson, Harris was told) thought Harris prevailed.[8]

In any event, Harris's candidate won. While the Know-Nothings tried to fill the vacuum left by the dissolution of the Whig Party, a faction called the "Old Line Whigs," fearful of what they deemed encroachments on Southern rights, refused to join with the Know-Nothings. The Democratic presidential candidate carried Tennessee for the first time in twenty-four years. Harris returned to Memphis in triumph, and celebrated at a "grand illumination" on November 11. Although the Democratic ticket had barely carried Shelby County itself, it seemed

7. Atkins, *Parties, Politics and the Sectional Conflict*, 194, 196–98, 201; Corlew, *Tennessee: A Short History*, 279; Paul H. Bergeron, Stephen V. Ash, and Jeanette Keith, *Tennesseans and Their History* (Knoxville: University of Tennessee Press, 1999), 106–7.

8. "Grim Death Claims a Great Statesman"; "A Challenge Not Accepted," *Memphis Daily Appeal*, August 2, 1856; "Harris and Brown," *Memphis Daily Appeal*, August 5, 1856; "Messrs. I. G. Harris and D. M. Currin" and "Additional Appointments of Gov. N. S. Brown and Gen. I. G. Harris," *Memphis Daily Appeal*, August 19, 1856; "Denying the Record," *Memphis Daily Appeal*, August 23, 1856; "The Speaking Yesterday," *Memphis Daily Appeal*, September 24, 1856; "T" letter, *Memphis Daily Appeal*, October 2, 1856; Atkins, *Parties, Politics and the Sectional Conflict*, 208; Brownlow to Temple, Temple Papers, University of Tennessee; Gower and Allen, eds., *Pen and Sword*, 378.

as if "the whole population" was out to hear Harris and other luminaries extol the party's victory. Harris was now well known as a loyal Democrat statewide, and had improved his political prospects quite considerably.[9]

Johnson determined to forgo a third term as governor to make a run for the U.S. Senate. But he withheld the announcement until January 1, 1857. Then, the *Nashville Union & American* announced that Johnson "neither expects nor desires the nomination." The state Democratic convention was originally scheduled for early January 1856, but Johnson had the meeting delayed to develop "public sentiment" in his favor for his run for senator. Therefore, the main party organ, the *Nashville Daily Union & American,* advocated a delay, claiming that there was not enough time for the various counties to elect delegates and have them travel during the bad weather months.[10]

Even before Johnson formally declined the possibility of a third nomination, Harris's name was before the public as a possible successor. Letters from various individuals appeared in the *Memphis Daily Appeal* proposing Harris carry the Democracy's standard in the coming election. One correspondent noted that West Tennessee had never provided a Democratic candidate for governor, and put forward Harris, "a man who is neither an old fogy nor a beardless youth, but full of the vigor of intellectual manhood, as was evinced by his able canvass during the last great campaign." The *Appeal* dutifully published letters and editorials from East and West Tennessee advocating Harris's candidacy, and, significantly, county conventions in a number of Middle Tennessee counties passed resolutions of preference for Harris. On December 27, 1856, the *Appeal,* again noting that West Tennessee had never had a candidate, endorsed Harris's candidacy, not because he was a West Tennessean, but "for the reason he is worthy, competent, patriotic and able, and that his services entitle him to this position."[11]

Other names that were mentioned for the nomination were Andrew Ewing,

9. Atkins, *Parties, Politics and the Sectional Conflict,* 203–4, 210–11; Corlew, *Tennessee: A Short History,* 281; Capers, *The Biography of a River Town,* 114; "That Demonstration," *Memphis Daily Appeal,* November 12, 1856.

10. "Democratic Convention," *Nashville Daily Union & American,* November 29, 1856; "State Convention Postponed," *Nashville Daily Union & American,* December 5, 1856; "Our State Convention," *Memphis Daily Appeal,* December 5, 1856; "The Gubernatorial Question," *Memphis Daily Appeal,* December 27, 1856; "Gov. Johnson—The Next Canvass," *Nashville Daily Union & American,* January 1, 1857; A. Johnson to William Lowry, December 14, 1856, 2 *PAJ* 460–61.

11. "Gubernatorial," *Memphis Daily Appeal,* December 4, 1856; letters from "Silas" and "Fayette," *Memphis Daily Appeal,* December 6, 1856; "The Next Governor—Gen. I. G. Harris," *Memphis Daily*

a Nashville lawyer and former congressman, and William H. Polk, Harris's fellow elector at large in the recent presidential canvass. Johnson correctly deemed Harris the favorite, but obtusely sought an approach to Harris through intermediaries "to set him right on the Homestead policy," the point of difference between the two in 1851. There is no evidence that the issue was ever broached with Harris. Polk soon made it clear that he was not a candidate. The Democrats of Davidson and Williamson counties advocated Ewing's candidacy, and opposition newspapers sought to infer that Harris did not want the nomination, thus clearing the way for Ewing. Undoubtedly with a great deal of truth, these papers also charged that Governor Johnson preferred Ewing to Harris. But the *Appeal* soon published an authorized statement that Harris would accept the nomination if tendered. Harris made too strong a favorable impression with party members across the state during the presidential canvass the previous year. Meanwhile, Ewing's candidacy made no headway. A brief effort testing Ewing's strength in a caucus the night before the meeting failed. On April 15, 1857, the Democrats unanimously picked Green Harris as the party's gubernatorial candidate.[12]

As was usual for the times, the *Appeal* noted that Harris had not sought the nomination, but accepted on the importunities of his friends and the call of duty. An official three-man committee notified Harris of his nomination, oddly con-

---

Appeal, December 19, 1856; "The Gubernatorial Question," *Memphis Daily Appeal*, December 27, 1856; "Democratic Meetings," *Memphis Daily Appeal*, December 14, 1856; "Democratic State Convention," *Nashville Daily Union & American*, December 9, 1856; "The Next Governor," *Memphis Daily Appeal*, December 27, 1856.

12. A. Johnson to William M. Lowry, December 14, 1856, 2 *PAJ* 461; "Hon. Isham G. Harris," *Memphis Daily Appeal*, January 29, 1857; "Democratic Meeting in Coffee," *Nashville Daily Union & American*, January 30, 1857; "Gen. Isham G. Harris," *Memphis Daily Appeal*, January 31, 1857; "Gen. Harris," *Memphis Daily Appeal*, February 14, 1857; "Hon. W. H. Polk," *Memphis Daily Appeal*, February 19, 1857; "Democratic Meeting in Madison," *Memphis Daily Appeal*, April 11, 1857; "Democratic Candidate for Governor," *Nashville Daily Union & American*, February 10, 1857; "Gen. Harris," *Nashville Daily Union & American*, February 19, 1857; "Democratic Meeting in Franklin," *Nashville Daily Union & American*, March 6, 1857; "Humphreys County Democratic Meeting," *Nashville Daily Union & American*, March 8, 1857; "We Understand that Mr. Andy Johnson," *Nashville Daily Union & American*, March 9, 1857; "Meeting of the Davidson Democracy," *Nashville Daily Union & American*, March 11, 1857; "Williamson County," *Nashville Daily Union & American*, March 13, 1857; "Democratic Meetings," *Nashville Daily Union & American*, March 15, 1857; "The Fourth District," *Nashville Daily Union & American*, March 27, 1857; "Hon. Isham G. Harris" and "Proceedings of the Democratic State Convention," *Nashville Daily Union & American*, April 16, 1857; Gower and Allen, eds., *Pen and Sword*, 408.

taining two future political rivals, William H. Polk and David M. Key. Even before the American Party had its candidate, its party organs attacked Harris on the basis that his votes on the compromise of 1850 and statements criticizing the Missouri Compromise of 1820 were both inconsistent internally and with his position on the Kansas–Nebraska Act, which allowed the residents of those two territories to decide if they wanted slavery. Eventually, the Americans nominated Robert Hopkins Hatton, a thirty-one-year-old lawyer who was serving his first and only term in Tennessee House of Representatives. The *Appeal* noted that Hatton was a "very respectable gentleman" who, it hoped, would be "satisfied with the honor of being named as a candidate for Governor, without indulging any extravagant expectations of ever occupying the Executive Chair."[13]

With Harris now a public figure of the first order, the Democratic Party organs did their part to increase his visibility, with stories relating to his visits to Nashville and his assistance to an orphan needing free legal assistance appearing in the papers.[14] A biographical sketch of Harris's life appeared in *Union & American*, emphasizing the economic disadvantage of his early life having been overcome by his ingenuity and hard work and noting his success at the bar and the eminence of his two brothers. Democratic voters were assured he had the right views, as "in politics, he is and ever has been a consistent Democrat of the Jefferson, Jackson and Polk school." Harris's personal attributes of "wisdom," "earnestness," and "unusual industry" were noted, and his comparative youth for the various political posts he had held to that point.[15]

As was the custom of the day, the two candidates' camps agreed on a series of "appointments" across the state, starting at Camden, in Benton County, West Tennessee, with the intention to move south to Memphis, across the southern portion of the state to Chattanooga, up into East Tennessee, and then back across

13. "Gen. Isham G. Harris, Democratic Nominee for Governor of Tennessee," *Memphis Daily Appeal,* April 17, 1857; "Proceedings of the Democratic State Convention," *Memphis Daily Appeal,* April 19, 1857; "Acceptance of Gen. Harris," *Memphis Daily Appeal,* May 1, 1857; "Gen. Harris' Record," *Memphis Daily Appeal,* April 19, 1857; "An Inconsistency that is Consistent," *Memphis Daily Appeal,* April 29, 1857; Robert M. McBride and Dan M. Robison, *Biographical Directory of the Tennessee General Assembly* (Nashville: Tennessee State Library and Archives and Tennessee Historical Commission, 1979–91), 1:344–45; "Know-Nothing Candidate for Governor," *Memphis Daily Appeal,* May 5, 1857.

14. "Hon. Isham G. Harris," *Nashville Daily Union & American,* May 10, 1857; "Gen. I. G. Harris," *Memphis Daily Appeal,* May 17, 1857.

15. "Gen. Isham G. Harris," *Nashville Daily Union & American,* May 27, 1857.

the northern portion of the state into Middle Tennessee. The first crowd was not large, owing to the sparseness of the population and the general lack of knowledge as to the appointment schedule. Unfortunately for Harris, he was somewhat ill that day, but according to a Democratic correspondent of the *Union & American*, he nonetheless bested Hatton on all subjects of debate.[16]

While there were charges of political inconsistency and countercharges, and various arguments relating to desirable public policy advanced by either side, no major issues were discussed. Hatton pushed a scheme whereby the Federal government could find a way to transfer the millions of acres of public land, or their value, to the states. With the new revenue, the states could eliminate their debt, build schools, or make internal improvements. Harris observed the Know-Nothings' Whig forebears, Daniel Webster and Henry Clay, rejected that scheme, and even John Bell, Tennessee's great surviving Whig, did not advocate the actual distribution of the lands. Harris argued that distributing the land would end up creating a deficiency in the Federal treasury. Seeking to tap the slaveholders' fear that immigrant voters would prohibit slavery, Hatton proposed that aliens should not be allowed to vote in territorial elections until they had been in the United States for twenty-one years. Harris replied that the issue should be left up to the territorial legislatures themselves, and that, as a result of the recent *Dred Scott* decision, alien voters could not bar slavery from the territories in any event. Indeed, it was the Know-Nothings, in their resistance to the repeal of the Missouri Compromise (in the Kansas–Nebraska Act), who sought to continue limits on slavery.[17]

The campaign was remarkable for an incident that occurred at Fayetteville, in Middle Tennessee, on June 13. Hatton was again pushing his alien suffrage argument and pronounced that the doctrine of allowing un-naturalized foreigners the right to vote was "infamous." According to witnesses favorable to Harris, the Democrat asked Hatton if he intended to apply the term *infamous* to him. Hatton replied, "Do you expect to intimidate me by coming forward and asking this question?" Harris protested that he didn't want to intimidate any gentleman, but again inquired whether the term *infamous* applied to him. Turning to the crowd, Hat-

16. "The Gubernatorial Canvass—Appointments for Speaking," *Memphis Daily Appeal*, May 22, 1857; "Opening of the Canvass," *Nashville Daily Union & American*, May 28, 1857; White, *Messages of the Governors of Tennessee*, 5:18. As newspaper accounts were highly politicized, it is difficult today to discern in any instance who "won" a debate.

17. Paul H. Bergeron, *Antebellum Politics in Tennessee* (Lexington: University Press of Kentucky, 1982), 129; "Discussion Between Messrs. Harris and Hatton," *Memphis Daily Appeal*, June 2, 1857.

ton replied, "Fellow citizens, I repeat that the policy is infamous, rank and smells to heaven, and those who advocate it are ——." At this point Harris struck him.[18] Harris's blow knocked Hatton off the platform, and his rough and tumble frontier political training took over, and he jumped off after his rival. After a short scuffle, "the parties were separated without injury." Hatton later told his wife that he only got hit once, on the shoulder, and was not even bruised.[19]

Harris appears to have perceived a need to quickly resolve the situation. Through intermediaries, the parties agreed to issue a joint statement assuring the public "that each acted upon a misconception of the language and intention of the other, and that therefore both have occasion to regret the unpleasant altercation that took place." This indeed seems to have been the case, and no further difficulties of a similar nature occurred during the campaign, which ended sooner than expected by mutual agreement because of the exhaustion wrought by their difficult schedule.[20]

Hatton confidently told his wife that Harris had hurt himself with his conduct at Fayetteville, and had heard "the Democrats are disappointed with Harris." Andrew Johnson also doubted Harris's approach to the campaign, and predicted Harris would not show well unless the Democratic legislative and congressional candidates brought out the vote. On August 6, Harris prevailed by over 11,000 votes, carrying all three grand divisions of the state, although the turnout for the election was less than the previous gubernatorial and presidential votes. The Know-Nothings as a party were effectively dead in Tennessee, shown not only by the result of the gubernatorial election, but the Democrats' large majority in the General Assembly. Seven of the ten congressional seats went Democratic as well. Although his inauguration was set for November 3, Harris arrived in Nashville on October 8, the very day of Andrew Johnson's election as U.S. senator.[21]

The sweeping nature of the Democratic victory of 1857 can be attributed to

18. "A Statement to the Public," *Nashville Daily Union & American*, June 19, 1857.

19. "Difficulty at Fayetteville Between the Candidates for Governor," *Nashville Daily Union & American*, June 16, 1857 (scuffle); James Vaulx Drake, *Life of General Robert Hatton* (Nashville: Marshall & Bruce, 1867), 122.

20. Drake, *Life of General Robert Hatton*, 122, 146–47; "A Statement to the Public," *Nashville Daily Union & American*, June 19, 1857 (joint statement); White, *Messages of the Governors of Tennessee*, 5:21.

21. Drake, *Life of General Robert Hatton*, 122, 123–24; White, *Messages of the Governors of Tennessee*, 5:22–23; Bergeron, *Antebellum Politics in Tennessee*, 129–30; "The Vote for Governor," *Nashville Daily Union & American*, August 21, 1857; Atkins, *Parties, Politics and Sectional Conflict in Tennes-*

several factors. First, Harris was simply a more formidable candidate than Hatton, whose youth and relative lack of political experience contrasted with Harris's vast experience. Hatton's affiliation with the politically bankrupt American Party was a liability for his candidacy as well. And, while there is not sufficient evidence to make a conclusive determination, Andrew Johnson's personal attention to the legislative races to ensure his election to the U.S. Senate can only have helped with the larger margins, although it should be recorded that based on available data, Harris carried the same number of counties in 1859 that he did in 1857, which suggests that Johnson's influence was not as great as might be supposed.[22]

As Harris was preparing to take office in October 1857, the financial upheaval known as the Panic of 1857 began to have some effect in Tennessee, although the crisis was somewhat muted there in comparison to states outside the South. The nation's financial system was based on "hard" money, that is, gold and silver specie, but banks would often issue notes in a variety of denominations for ease of commerce. The notes would be redeemable in specie by the banks that issued them. As the crisis deepened, banks began to suspend specie payments, often because they did not have the ready supply of hard money to redeem their notes. A week or so before Harris first arrived in Nashville, there was a run on the Bank of Nashville. The state's main financial institutions—the Bank of Tennessee, a state instrumentality, the Union Bank, and the Planters' Bank—made it known that they would never suspend specie payments.[23]

On November 3, Harris was formally inaugurated, in a ceremony that included prayers, patriotic music, a valedictory speech by Andrew Johnson, and an inaugural address by the new governor. While Harris touched on the banking and currency crisis and other local issues, much of his address was a discussion of where Tennessee fit into the Federal system. Harris spoke of "strict construc-

---

see, 212; Gower and Allen, eds., *Pen and Sword*, 435. Hatton would go on to be elected to Congress in 1859 as an Opposition candidate. He was elected colonel of the 7th Tennessee Regiment in 1861, and would die a brigadier general fighting for the Confederacy on May 31, 1862, at the Battle of Fair Oaks. Ezra Warner, *Generals in Gray: Lives of the Confederate Commanders* (Baton Rouge: Louisiana State University Press, 1959), 128.

22. Hopkins and Lyon, *Tennessee Votes, 1799–1976*, 40–41.

23. White, *Messages of the Governors of Tennessee*, 5:42–44, 51–52; Robert Love Partin, "The Administration of Isham G. Harris" (M.A. thesis, Peabody College, 1928), 19–21; "The Bank Excitement" and "Suspension of the Bank of Nashville," *Nashville Daily Gazette*, September 29, 1857.

tion" of the Constitution in the context of the "maintenance of all the reserved rights of the states." The new governor made a pointed reference to slavery, arguing that if Tennessee's institutions and rights were to be maintained, it was the duty of all the states, especially slave states, "to adhere with firmness and pertinacity to a strict construction of the Constitution, upon which rests the principle of 'non-interference by Congress with domestic slavery either in the States or Territories.'"[24]

While the sectional crisis lurked on the horizon, the state's banking crisis was of more immediate concern. To this point, the 1850s had been a prosperous decade for Tennessee banks. Entrepreneurs organized eighteen new banks during that interval, and capital, deposits, circulations, and loans all grew at a healthy rate. Established in 1838, the state-owned Bank of Tennessee was an occasional subject of political agitation since that time. Most of the governors since James K. Polk in the early 1840s had recommended liquidation, but it survived nonetheless. Harris, too, favored the gradual liquidation of the Bank of Tennessee. Until (if ever) liquidated, though, the bank played a significant role in the conduct of financial matters in the state. Notwithstanding the brave words and good intentions at the end of September, by mid-October the Bank of Tennessee suspended its payments in specie because other banks with which it had relationships had done so, and it did not seem prudent to expose the bank to a run on its hard money reserves. The resulting shortage of money affected the state's merchants and smaller banks, fortunately with little long-term effect.[25]

Harris renominated old Jacksonian Cave Johnson of Clarksville to the board of directors of the Bank of Tennessee the very day he took office. But thereafter, Harris spent some weeks studying the financial crisis, and his first formal message to the General Assembly on December 16, 1857, dealt almost exclusively with the "present panic and monetary derangement."[26] Concluding that an inflation of paper notes against specie was the problem, Harris proposed legislation requir-

24. White, *Messages of the Governors of Tennessee*, 5:25–34 (quoted material on 30).

25. Larry Schweikart, "Tennessee Banks in the Antebellum Period, Part II," *Tennessee Historical Quarterly* 45 (1986): 199, 206; C. L. Grant, "The Public Career of Cave Johnson," *Tennessee Historical Quarterly* 10 (1951): 195, 219; White, *Messages of the Governors of Tennessee*, 5:49; Partin, "The Administration of Isham G. Harris," 20; Gower and Allen, eds., *Pen and Sword*, 440.

26. *White*, Messages of the Governors of Tennessee, 5:34, 42–45; Grant, "The Public Career of Cave Johnson," 218–19.

ing that banks resume specie payments as soon as possible, that bank notes of denominations of $20 or less be phased out, that notes from banks outside the state of these lesser denominations be banned, that no bank in the state issue a note not payable in specie upon demand at the counter where issued, that no bank be allowed a ratio of 2:1 of circulating notes relative to specie or 3:1 of liabilities to note holders or depositors to specie in the vault, and that bank officers be required to file a sworn statement of condition with the state and publish the same in a Nashville newspaper. In Harris's view, the state had no business in the banking business, and he recommended the gradual liquidation of the Bank of Tennessee. Anticipating a problem that would strike the state twenty years later, Harris also recommended a constitutional amendment establishing a debt limit, and that "the faith and credit of the State be no further pledged in aid of internal improvement or otherwise," as the debt at that time was approaching $20 million.[27]

While the legislature did not wait for the governor's message to start on numerous banking bills of its own, Harris's message, with many proposals similar to those made by his predecessor, effectively "killed" the plethora of bills then pending, and a local political observer thought the message would induce the legislators to resume debate after Christmas. Even though the Democrats controlled the General Assembly, when the debate resumed, there was little consensus and much bickering. The extent of disagreement was highlighted when a senator and a representative engaged in a brawl in the Capitol itself. Eventually, on January 28, 1858, the General Assembly passed a measure that largely adopted Harris's recommendations, with the significant exception of that relating to the liquidation of the Bank of Tennessee.[28]

The political influence of the bank was unmistakable, and the Democratic Party split on the issue. Bank proponents advocated legislation that would increase the capital of the bank. One scheme to do so was to sell state bonds, a move that Harris pointed out lacked fiscal logic. Another scheme provided for the sale of the state's stock in the different turnpike companies in Tennessee. Again, on February 15, 1858, Democrats came to blows, as pro-bank Senator Joseph Knox Walker accused Senator Washington Curran Whitthorne of being drunk when the measure was being discussed, which Whitthorne denounced as a "G——d d——n lie." Walker struck Whitthorne in the face with a book, and a scuffle began that was broken up almost immediately. The vote proceeded, and Whitthorne

27. White, *Messages of the Governors of Tennessee*, 5:42–51.
28. Ibid., 5:51–53; Gower and Allen, eds., *Pen and Sword*, 447.

and other pro-Harris senators, such as his brother-in-law William E. Travis and speaker of the Senate John C. Burch, were defeated.[29]

Whitthorne would prove to be one of Harris's most faithful allies. Born in 1825, Whitthorne had a university education and studied law in the office of James K. Polk in Columbia. When Polk was inaugurated president in 1845, his young pro-tégé was appointed to clerkships in various government offices in Washington. On January 1, 1848, Whitthorne went to Mexico City carrying dispatches for the American minister there. Returning to Columbia in July 1848, he married a young relation of Polk's, and the couple had ten children, although four were tragically lost in an epidemic in the space of ten days. Entering politics, Whitthorne lost a race for a seat in the state House of Representatives in 1853. He was elected to the state Senate in 1855, and enjoyed the friendship of both Harris and Andrew Johnson.[30]

A diversion of editorial opinion at the main Democratic organ in Nashville, the *Daily Union & American*, further compounded the split in the party. This aggravated the situation further, to the extent that, in early March, one party loyalist felt that it would "run into the next canvass and cause our defeat." A bill to increase the Bank of Tennessee's capital was thought to be almost a foregone conclusion, but just at the right time, Harris sent a message relative to the Bank of Tennessee demonstrating that the bank historically did not produce the return on the capital it already had and that it would cost in interest to borrow in order to increase the capital. The divided editorial staff of the *Union & American* thought Harris provided "weighty arguments" against increasing the state debt to raise capital for the bank. A third and final reading on the bill in the House occurred on March 16, but the bill failed on the final reading by a "very decided" margin. Harris celebrated his victory at an oyster supper with some friends the following evening.[31]

The banking act passed on January 28 was amended on March 18 to throw

29. A. McCall to IGH, November 25, 1857, Harris Papers, TSLA; White, *Messages of the Governors of Tennessee*, 5:64–65; "Fight in the Tennessee Legislature," *Nashville Daily Gazette*, February 17, 1858; McBride and Robison, *Biographical Directory of the Tennessee General Assembly*, 1:101, 733–34, 754.

30. McKellar, *Tennessee Senators*, 417–20.

31. Gower and Allen, eds., *Pen and Sword*, 459; "The State Bank Bill," *Nashville Daily Gazette*, February 26, 1858; "The Tennessee Democracy on Banks and Banking," *Nashville Patriot*, March 16, 1858; "Hards and Softs," *Nashville Daily Union & American*, March 19, 1858; White, *Messages of the Governors of Tennessee*, 5:63–67; "The Governor's Message," *Nashville Daily Union & American*, March 4, 1858;

a sop to the disappointed proponents of the Bank of Tennessee, relaxing by six months the requirement of retiring small bills, authorizing the establishment of branches at Memphis and Knoxville, and making other favorable provisions. Many recognized that the irritating issue of the continued survival of the Bank of Tennessee remained unresolved. The opposition press mocked the Democrats for the split and the editors of the *Union & American* for their inconsistency. But Harris and his friends quickly smoothed over the rift, characterizing it as a "local issue" that distracted the party and the people from the more important sectional issue. Harris induced Whitthorne to write an anonymous editorial in the *Union & American* leaving the door open to attack the bank in the future, but reminding readers that the issue of Kansas's admission to the Union as a slave state was "more involved than all the Banks in Tennessee or the United States."[32]

The General Assembly adjourned on March 22, 1858. In addition to its efforts to address the financial crisis and the ongoing issue of the Bank of Tennessee, it followed the suggestion of former Governor Johnson and revised the Tennessee legal code, which was not again totally revised until 1932. And, reversing a previous trend, the legislature backed one of Harris's campaign promises and refused to borrow any further funds to aid railroads and other public improvements. This restraint was felt to have saved the state over $5.4 million, and improved its credit standing in the nation's financial markets.[33]

With the General Assembly dispersed back to their homes, Harris planned for the next year's political campaign and for further efforts to regulate the banks. He could claim success in his first year as governor, both in addressing the banking crisis and in helping to prevent yet another split in the Tennessee Democratic

---

"The Bank Bill" and "Tennessee Legislature," *Nashville Patriot,* March 17, 1858; "Bank Bill Defeated," *Memphis Daily Appeal,* March 17, 1858; Gower and Allen, eds., *Pen and Sword,* 459.

32. W. E. Travis to IGH, March 30, 1858, Harris Papers, TSLA; "The New Bank Bill," *Nashville Patriot,* March 20, 1858; "The Tennessee Democracy on Banks and Banking," *Nashville Patriot,* March 16, 1858; "State Bank at Memphis," *Memphis Daily Appeal,* March 19, 1858; "What is the Bank Creed of the Democracy," *Nashville Patriot,* March 23, 1858; "The Union and American," *Nashville Patriot,* March 26, 1858; "Bank Bill Defeated," *Memphis Daily Appeal,* March 17, 1858; "The Bank Bill," *Nashville Daily Union & American,* March 17, 1858; Whitthorne to IGH, March 27, 1858, and Whitthorne to IGH, April 4, 1858, Harris Papers, TSLA.

33. "The Legislature," *Nashville Daily Union & American,* March 28, 1858; White, *Messages of the Governors of Tennessee,* 5:83; "State Credit," *Memphis Daily Appeal,* March 31, 1858; "Retrenchment by the Democratic Party," *Memphis Daily Appeal,* April 3, 1858.

Party. If the survival of the Bank of Tennessee is counted as a defeat, Harris can be credited with demonstrating that its power was not overwhelming, and with further showing that it was not a good investment for the state.

The constitution of 1834 provided that the governor was to serve for two years, and could only serve for six years out of any period of eight. While his duties were to wield the "Supreme Executive power of the State," the office of the governor was actually quite limited, which gave Harris plenty of time to play cards with friends once the legislative session ended. While he could "recommend" measures to the General Assembly, he had no veto power over any measure it adopted, nor was he required to approve a law before it became effective. He was commander of the state's armed forces, which had little meaning in peacetime, offered rewards for the capture of fugitives (such as that issued for a former Tennessee secretary of state that summer), issued grants and commissions (usually empowering persons outside the state to notarize deeds for lands inside the state), and had the power to pardon and grant reprieves. The governor had the power to temporarily appoint persons to fill vacant offices when the legislature was not in session, and on occasion would be granted the power to appoint boards or commissioners granted by legislation. Even Andrew Johnson petitioned Harris to appoint the senator's friends to various posts, a prerogative Harris doubtless enjoyed. Under the constitution of 1834, the General Assembly would convene the first Monday in October after a general election and stay in session for about six months. Unless called into a special session for a specific item of business designated by the governor, they would not meet again until after the next general election, two years later. While the power of the office was limited, Harris had the influence that being the leader of the majority party in the legislature bestowed. The governor's largely successful maneuvering relating to the bank legislation reflected his skill in wielding that influence.[34]

The year 1858 proved to be personally volatile for the governor and his family. The Mississippi River steamer *Pennsylvania* was making the run from New Orleans to St. Louis at 6:00 a.m. on the morning of June 13, 1858, when, while south of Memphis, four of the vessel's eight boilers exploded, destroying the front third

34. White, *Messages of the Governors of Tennessee*, 5:86; "Gov. Harris offers a reward," *Nashville Daily Gazette*, June 13, 1858; F. W. Dunnington to IGH, June 7, 1858, Harris Papers, TSLA; Tenn. Const., Articles II and III (1834); see also Watters, "Isham Green Harris," 52–53; A. G. Watkins to IGH, February 22, 1858, A. Johnson and J. Jones to IGH, February 24, 1858, and A. Johnson to IGH, April 8, 1858, all in Harris Papers, TSLA.

of the boat. A great cloud of scalding steam enveloped the scene, severely injuring a number of the passengers, who not only were externally burned but also suffered lung injuries. Eventually, the survivors were brought to Memphis for treatment, many of whom, including Henry Clemens, the brother of Samuel Clemens, the future Mark Twain, expired. Unfortunately, the most prominent Tennessean on the *Pennsylvania* was Justice William R. Harris. Green was in Memphis when his brother arrived, and was constantly at his bedside. "Dangerously scalded," Justice Harris did not survive, passing on June 19. With the legislature adjourned, Governor Harris had the sad duty of appointing a successor to his brother, the highly recommended Archibald Wright of Memphis. William's death was not the only family news that year. Green and Martha saw the birth their son, another Isham G. Harris, in September 1858. Sadly, the family lost eight-year-old George Ludson Harris the day after Christmas that year.[35]

Unlike 1857, there was no question that Harris was to be the Democratic candidate for governor in 1859, a fact confirmed at the state convention in March. The bank issue continued to fester through the end of 1858, guaranteeing that it would be a concern in the 1859 campaign. Prominent Democrats and party newspapers spoke of reform that would effectively end the system as it then existed, but party leaders quietly tried to find a middle ground that would preclude the intra-party squabbling of the previous legislative term. Harris, who favored a more gradual demise for the bank, quietly cast about for a more pliable president for the Bank of Tennessee. The venerable Cave Johnson signified that summer that he might be willing to resign the presidency of the bank, which Harris's new friend Randal McGavock saw would "meet the approbation of all good democrats." Johnson did not resign, but would not be nominated for another term. The party platform on the bank issue eventually advocated reform based on hard currency, but acknowl-

35. Mark Twain, *Life on the Mississippi* (New York: Harper Brothers, 1905), 170–76; "Terrible Explosion on the Pennsylvania," *Memphis Daily Appeal,* June 15, 1858; "Death of Hon. Wm. R. Harris," *Memphis Daily Appeal,* June 20, 1858; "Supreme Judge—Hon. Archibald Wright," *Memphis Daily Appeal,* July 3, 1858; E. W. M. King to IGH, June 25, 1858, S. Milligan to IGH, June 26, 1858, J. B. Thornton to IGH, June 28, 1858, and undated petition from J. Wickersham et al. to IGH, all in Harris Papers, TSLA; U.S. Department of the Interior, Twelfth Census of the United States, 1900, Callahan County Texas (for Isham G. Harris the younger); George L. Harris marker, Elmwood Cemetery, Memphis.

edged "we are compelled to legislate under the circumstances by which we are surrounded."[36]

Harris alternated his time in this pre-election interval between Nashville, the state capital, where he lived in a little brick house on the side of Capitol Hill, and Memphis, where he maintained his residence. He owned a house in Memphis at 123 Exchange Street and a farm in the 12th District of Shelby County. Census records for 1860 indicate that Harris's farm had 280 improved acres and 170 unimproved acres. The farm land was valued at $5,600 and machinery and implements at another $400. Twenty slaves worked the farm, with a few mules and oxen. Of the slaves, there were 4 adult females, including 2 women over age 40. They were joined by 5 adult males, none over age 30, and 11 children, ranging from age 6 months to 16 years. As the average value of slaves in Tennessee in 1859 reached $854.65, the bondsmen themselves were a substantial asset. The farm produced 31 bales of cotton, which was remarkable for the amount of acreage and labor, and the 50 hogs present were probably raised for sale. The farm appears to have been contiguous to a slightly smaller farm owned by Martha's brother, James L. Travis, who lived there along with an overseer, the overseer's small family, and Travis's 14 slaves. It is likely that Travis and the overseer managed both farms in Harris's absence. While his modest salary as governor was likely not enough to support his lifestyle, his previous success as a lawyer, farming activities, legal work on the side, and likely other investments enabled Harris and his large family to live comfortably.[37]

36. "State Politics," *Nashville Union & American,* December 25, 1858; Bergeron, *Antebellum Politics in Tennessee,* 130; "Democratic State Convention," *Nashville Daily Gazette,* March 18, 1859; White, *Messages of the Governors of Tennessee,* 5:90; Gower and Allen, eds., *Pen and Sword,* 472, 481; F. W. Dunnington to IGH, June 7, 1858, Harris Papers, TSLA; "The Banks and the People," *Memphis Daily Appeal,* July 11, 1858; "The Democratic Party and the Bank Question," *Memphis Daily Avalanche,* July 15, 1858; Whitthorne to IGH, March 27, 1858, Whitthorne to IGH, April 4, 1858, and F. Dunnington to IGH, December 27, 1858, all in Harris Papers, TSLA; IGH to A. Johnson, September 7, 1858, and "The Tennessee Democracy on Banks and Currency," 3 *PAJ* 194–95; Grant, "The Public Career of Cave Johnson," 220; Philip M. Hamer, ed., *Tennessee: A History, 1673–1932* (New York: American Historical Society, 1933), 1:513.

37. Gower and Allen, eds., *Pen and Sword,* 506, 558; "Governor Harris," *Memphis Daily Appeal,* April 3, 1859; B. F. Lamb to IGH, January 30, 1858, Harris Papers, TSLA; Watters, "Isham Green Harris," 57–58; Eighth Census, 1860, Shelby County, Tennessee; Eighth Census, 1860, Productions of Agriculture, Shelby County, Tennessee; Eighth Census, 1860, Slaves, Tennessee; Donald L. Winters,

With no formal Whig or Know-Nothing party apparatus in place, the Democracy's opposition was aptly termed the "Opposition Party," contemptuously,
but somewhat accurately, described by a Democratic organ as "Old Whigs, apos-
tate Democrats, disguised Know-Nothings, fire-eaters and freesoilers." Building
a "party" network with remarkable speed, the Opposition adopted a platform that
condemned further agitation on slavery, and favored a tariff, the disposition of the
public lands, a probationary period for the naturalization of foreigners, "a sound
and well-regulated banking system," and prompt payment and non-extension of
the public debt. For governor, the Opposition nominated East Tennessean John
Netherland, a longtime Whig stalwart.[38]

The two sides agreed on the traditional tour of statewide speaking engagements, which stretched from May 1 at the Capitol in Nashville to August 2, 1859,
at Loudon in East Tennessee. As was usually the case, the evaluation of the prowess and effectiveness of the candidates' speeches depended on the hearer's political
perspective. From the view of the Opposition-aligned *Nashville Patriot*, the opening speeches resulted in Netherland having the "manifest advantage," although
the paper conceded Harris delivered a "well digested and delivered speech." Harris's friend, Randal McGavock, thought the governor's speech at the Capitol was
"able and dignified," while Netherland's was "filled with anecdotes and humorous
sayings, but not very sound." McGavock observed that his fellow Democrats "were
much gratified with Harris, and the Opposition pretended to be pleased with
Netherland."[39]

Unlike the canvass with Hatton, the bank controversy created a legitimate issue of local interest across the state. Netherland and his party opposed the Democratic position that the legislature should be allowed to modify or revoke bank
charters, pointing out that the banks paid money into the state's education fund.
Harris touted the success of his legislative program relating to the banks and the

Tennessee Farming, Tennessee Farmers: Antebellum Agriculture in the Upper South (Knoxville: University of Tennessee Press, 1975), 57–59; Mooney, "Some Institutional and Statistical Aspects of Slavery
in Tennessee," 199; Jones, *Major Edward Travis*, 37; "When Memphis was the Capital of Tennessee,"
Memphis Commercial Appeal, December 11, 1932.

38. White, *Messages of the Governors of Tennessee*, 5:91–92; "John Netherland," *Nashville Patriot*,
March 31, 1859; Bergeron, *Antebellum Politics in Tennessee*, 131.

39. Bergeron, *Antebellum Politics in Tennessee*, 131–33; White, *Messages of the Governors of Tennessee*, 5:93–97; "The Opening of the Canvass," *Nashville Patriot*, May 3, 1858; Gower and Allen, eds.,
Pen and Sword, 518.

state credit, and argued that no new charter should be granted or renewed without specified restrictions to guard against further abuse. Netherland agreed that there should be "restrictions," but the Democratic press charged that the Opposition never spelled out what those were to be. Harris and the Democrats also raised the sectional issue, charging that the Know-Nothings and the "Black Republicans" were in an unholy alliance to unseat the Democratic Party, the one true national party that stood in protection of "property rights" (i.e., in slaves). Netherland and the Opposition countered by charging that these claims were agitating this sensitive issue for political purposes, noting that the Opposition's position was not simply abolitionist.[40]

Harris was confident of reelection from the start, and even expected a larger majority than he had attained against Hatton. Indeed, the best argument in favor of his reelection was that he had done well in his first term. As noted by the Memphis Democratic papers, the *Avalanche* and the *Appeal*, the Opposition could not point to anything in Harris's first term to serve as a basis for arguing against a second. The *Avalanche* succinctly argued: "Is there any reason for a change? Has Gov. Harris done anything for which he ought to be turned out of office?" The *Appeal* sneered: "they have nothing, absolutely nothing, to harp upon." Just in case, though, Harris took time to write Andrew Johnson to request that he speak in a number of counties, observing that "we are stronger than at any previous period in our history, but over Confidence and inaction may produce a result which will cause us to regret our lethergy [sic]."[41]

When the election was held on August 4, Harris won by a margin of just over 8,000 votes, 3,000 less than in 1857. Reflecting greater voter interest in the issues of the day, there were almost 13,500 more voters than the previous election, and the majority of those were Netherland voters. The Democrats once again controlled the legislature, but, with no other explanation than the Henrymander, the Opposition elected seven of the ten congressional seats. While the Democrats still controlled the machinery of the state government, the thin margin between them and their opposition, Whig or otherwise, remained close to its historical trend.

40. Bergeron, *Antebellum Politics in Tennessee*, 132–33; "The Discussion Yesterday," *Memphis Daily Appeal*, May 21, 1859; "Won't Answer," *Memphis Daily Avalanche*, May 26, 1859; "The Gubernatorial Canvass," *Memphis Daily Appeal*, May 31, 1859.

41. Gower and Allen, eds., *Pen and Sword*, 523; "Gov. Harris has been," *Memphis Daily Avalanche*, May 21, 1859; "They Can Find Nothing Against Him," *Memphis Daily Appeal*, June 22, 1859; IGH to A. Johnson, July 7, 1859, 3 *PAJ* 285.

Both parties could celebrate the results, the Democrats their continued control, the Opposition the lesser margin of their opponent's victory, the congressional result, and the anticipation of victory in the next electoral cycle. Harris, McGavock, Dunnington, and other Democrats went out from Nashville to the Opposition Jubilee held August 30, to hear Netherland and other Opposition leaders speak. McGavock presciently observed: "Jno Bell is their man for the next Presidency, but they will be disappointed—the Black Republicans will want a man of their own . . . This is the first jubilee over a defeat I ever heard of."[42]

Just before the legislature opened in early October, the Democrats scheduled a jubilee themselves, which was inauspiciously rained out, requiring a shift of the speechmaking to the third story of the Davidson County courthouse. Having pressed the banking issue during the canvass, Harris lost no time proposing extensive restrictions on banks. McGavock deemed Harris's position "extremely hard" and noted that some Democrats were opposed to the governor's stance. In his legislative message dated October 4, 1859, Harris first noted that corporations, such as banks, were authorized by the state constitution when "deem[ed] expedient for the public good." It followed that the people, through the legislature, could also amend or repeal corporate charters when deemed expedient for the public good as well. Other proposals placed limitations on the amount and size of bank notes, provided for individual liability of bank stockholders, and imposed various means of state regulation.[43]

In addition, nineteen bills relating to banking were introduced in the legislature. The members' deliberations reduced that number to nine. Eventually, Chapter 27 of the Acts of Tennessee, 1859, passed on February 6, 1860. While some of Harris's proposals were adopted, others were improved upon and still others made less harsh. In the end, the advent of open sectional conflict in 1861 prevented a subsequent evaluation of the long-term effectiveness of this reform.[44]

Almost unbelievably, the Bank of Tennessee managed to survive yet again.

42. Bergeron, *Antebellum Politics in Tennessee*, 133–34, 164–65; White, *Messages of the Governors of Tennessee*, 5:97–98, 134; Atkins, *Parties, Politics and Sectional Conflict in Tennessee*, 216; "The Opposition of Tennessee," *Memphis Weekly Bulletin*, September 9, 1859; Gower and Allen, eds., *Pen and Sword*, 533.

43. Gower and Allen, eds., *Pen and Sword*, 538–39; White, *Messages of the Governors of Tennessee*, 5:97–99, 116–19, 137–38.

44. White, *Messages of the Governors of Tennessee*, 5:139–40; Partin, "The Administration of Isham G. Harris," 38–40; *Acts of State of Tennessee*, 1859, chapter 27.

Harris again strongly recommended its dissolution, and a bill for that purpose was introduced in the Senate by a staunch member of the Opposition, Dr. John W. Richardson. With apparent bipartisan support, the measure passed on the first two readings in the Senate, but was defeated by a 2–1 margin on the third on March 14, 1860, only one Democratic senator voting for dissolution. McGavock's observation relative to the harshness of Harris's position on the bank proved true, and it lessened Harris's effectiveness as a party leader. Near the start of the legislative session the previous October, Harris nominated an entirely new board for the bank, which was thought to be not as good as the previous board headed by Cave Johnson, who himself thought the new men were "principally . . . *the enemies* of the Bank without the *least experience* in banking." Cave Johnson, writing to Andrew Johnson, complained: "I have never known a high officer so utterly mistaken as to the true means of preserving the unity of his party in which he was more interested than any other person in the State, as our Governor." After a game of euchre with Harris and newspapermen E. G. Eastman and Henry Watterson, Randal McGavock wrote in his diary that Harris had "taken upon himself a great responsibility" in opposing the bank.[45]

Apart from banking, Harris had also recommended in his message to the General Assembly that it should consider leasing out the labor of the convicts in the state penitentiary. While a measure to do so passed the Senate on two readings, it failed on a third, and a similar bill in the House died. Harris took steps to complete the ongoing task of more accurately marking the state lines with Kentucky and Virginia, and actually took out a personal loan to make sure the work continued. The state reimbursed Harris in accordance with a special act, and legislation passed to pay the balance of the expenses of these two commissions and to fix the lines thus established. Salutary measures increasing the size of the state library and preserving Andrew Jackson's home, the Hermitage, also passed.[46]

Harris's power to influence events as governor stemmed more from his leadership of the ruling Democratic Party than from the constitutional authority of his office. He was effective in instances in which the party faithful were kept in line, such as the defeat of the proposal to raise the state debt limit. But the split of the Democratic Party on the issue of the Bank of Tennessee made it impossible for Harris to destroy that institution. It would not be the last time in Harris's ca-

45. White, *Messages of the Governors of Tennessee*, 5:140–50; Gower and Allen, eds., *Pen and Sword*, 542; C. Johnson to Andrew Johnson, January 8, 1860, 3 *PAJ* 369–71.

46. White, *Messages of the Governors of Tennessee*, 5:120–22, 125–27, 130–32, 153–62.

reer that divisions within the Democratic Party hindered its ability to govern. In the end, the bank was a purely local issue, which never obscured for Harris the greater issues posed by the growing sectional crisis. In his two election campaigns in 1857 and 1859, Harris pressed his opponents on their parties' position on Southern "property rights" and continually advocated the Democratic Party's protection of the same. That he never lost sight of the larger issues facing the state and the country is reflected not only in his campaign messages, but also in the letter ghostwritten by Whitthorne—the issues raised by slavery were much more important than those posed by any bank.

Only weeks after the 33rd General Assembly opened in early October 1859, John Brown's seizure of the Federal arsenal at Harpers Ferry, Virginia, brought the issue back before the public eye in a striking fashion. After some maneuvering, on December 2, 1859, the very day Brown's body started moldering in the grave, the legislature passed a resolution blaming the incident on the agitation brought about by the "treasonable 'irrepressible conflict' doctrine put forth by the great head of the Black Republican party" (i.e., Senator William H. Seward of New York).[47]

The legislatures of two other states, South Carolina and Mississippi, reacted by passing resolutions calling for a convention of the slaveholding states of the Union. When received by Harris in mid-February 1860, the governor transmitted these resolutions on to the General Assembly with a message dated February 28, with a recommendation that Tennessee not participate, in hopes "that wise, temperate, and firm councils may avert the impending evils." Eventually, the legislature passed a resolution that effectively concurred with the governor, expressing that the General Assembly deemed it "inexpedient" to appoint delegates to the proposed conference. While the General Assembly was moderate in its response to South Carolina and Mississippi, it was immoderate in another slavery-related issue. Each House passed a harsh bill to expel free African Americans from the state. But the two versions differed in detail to the extent that the General Assembly as a whole passed no law at all.[48]

The last great national institution outside of the Federal government itself was the Democratic Party. The national Democracy was starting to crack, as Southern party conventions the winter of 1860 instructed their delegates to walk out of the national convention if a plank of the party's platform supporting slavery in the na-

47. Ibid., 5:163–67.
48. Ibid., 5:169–208.

tional territories was not adopted. Juxtaposed against this was Senator Stephen A. Douglas's doctrine of popular sovereignty, leaving it to the residents of the affected territory to be the ultimate authority of whether slavery should be allowed. The Tennessee Democratic Party was also divided, although along more mundane political alliances and jealousies than great constitutional principles. The state Democratic convention met on January 18, and eventually endorsed a compromise platform that endorsed the U.S. Supreme Court's *Dred Scott* decision, which had the effect of making slavery legal in the territories, qualified by the position that the states had the right to determine whether or not to have slavery as a domestic institution.[49]

Harris's rivalry with Johnson continued to fester, as both were advocated in the Democratic press as possibilities for the 1860 presidential ticket. The *Memphis Avalanche* and the *Nashville Union & American* mentioned Harris as a possible part of a ticket with pro-Southern Northern Democrat Joseph Lane of Oregon or Daniel S. Dickenson of New York, a prospect that apparently gave Harris great delight. Prior to the state party convention, Cave Johnson wrote Andrew Johnson that a "*formidable* portion of our party . . . seem inclined to take up Genl. Lane and our Gov. in view [sic] under the hope that success may be achieved by humbuggery & the personal popularity of both of them; and thus enable them to continue the patronage they now enjoy." But at the convention, W. C. Whitthorne reported to Senator Johnson, "Gov. Harris acted like a man, repudiated the idea that he was to be brought into conflict with you." The state convention named Senator Johnson as its candidate for president, but a resolution complimentary to Harris was also passed, and the *Union & American* played off of that to suggest that Harris might be a Southern vice presidential candidate to balance the ticket with a Northern presidential nominee.[50]

Union feeling continued to run strong in Tennessee, even as the prospects for the unity of the national Democratic Party seemed to dim. In late 1859, Nashville hosted a celebration of the completion of the Louisville & Nashville Rail-

49. McPherson, *Battle Cry of Freedom*, 195, 214; Gower and Allen, eds., *Pen and Sword*, 553; Mary E. R. Campbell, *The Attitude of Tennesseans Toward the Union* (New York: Vantage, 1961), 109–10.

50. Watters, "Isham Green Harris," 69–70; Campbell, *The Attitude of Tennesseans Toward the Union*, 105, 111–12; C. Johnson to A. Johnson, January 8, 1860, 3 *PAJ* 369–71; Whitthorne to A. Johnson, January 19, 1860, 3 *PAJ* 388; W. H. Maxwell to A. Johnson, February 2, 1860, 3 *PAJ* 410–12; F. Dunnington to A. Johnson, February 13, 1860, 3 *PAJ* 425–26; Gower and Allen, eds., *Pen and Sword*, 553; Atkins, *Parties, Politics and Sectional Conflict in Tennessee*, 221.

road, which included dignitaries from Louisville. Seeking to address the most pressing issue of the day, the mayor and council of Louisville issued an invitation to Governor Harris and the legislature to attend a celebration there, citing the two states' love for each other and "common love for the Union." Harris replied, clarifying that the "bond of union" should be "maintained in all its parts, and each and all its quantities, in letter and spirit, as the only means of security equality to the states, justice to the citizens, and impetus to the Union forever." Anticipating, no doubt, that the celebration, held at the end of the January 1860, might blur the distinctions that he had articulated between unconditional Unionism and his view of the rights conferred by the Constitution, Harris personally declined the invitation, claiming he was "indisposed." Lizinka Brown, an eligible Middle Tennessee widow who was politically and socially connected, wryly wrote Senator Johnson that the governor was not "physically [indisposed]" but "morally and politically."[51]

In April, the Tennessee delegation went to Charleston pledged to vote for Andrew Johnson as the nominee for president. Johnson himself calculated that Stephen A. Douglas's nomination was a sure thing. Writing his son Robert, the senator observed that if Tennessee (i.e., Johnson) could secure the vice presidency, the presidency would be available four years later. With some prescience, Johnson further wrote, "I do not See how Douglas' nomination is to be Successfully resisted without great injury to the party and perhaps its overthrow." Whitthorne, who was functioning as sort of an emissary between Senator Johnson and Governor Harris, assured Johnson before the convention started that "I do not believe Gov. Harris or his friends will at all attempt anything that is not exactly right."[52]

Douglas's nomination was unpalatable to the fire-eaters of the lower South. The ultra-slavery position was impossible for Northern Democrats to advocate to their constituents. As a Cincinnati newspaper reporter observed: "The South has driven the Northern Democracy to the wall, and now insists upon the protection of slavery in the Territories. In other words, insists upon the political execution of every Northern Democrat, and the total destruction of the Democratic party."

51. Madison Bratton, "The Unionist Junket of the Legislatures of Tennessee and Kentucky in January, 1860," *East Tennessee Historical Society Publications* 7 (1935): 64–80; "Kentucky and Tennessee," *Daily* (Washington, D.C.) *National Intelligencer,* January 23, 1860; L. C. Brown to A. Johnson, February 2, 1860, 3 *PAJ* 407–8; see also R. Johnson to A. Johnson, February 5, 1860, 3 *PAJ* 415.

52. A. Johnson to R. Johnson, April 22, 1860, 3 *PAJ* 573; W. C. Whitthorne to A. Johnson, April 11, 1860, 3 *PAJ* 523–24.

Eventually, the delegations from the lower South (and slave-holding Delaware) left the convention. Sam Milligan, Andrew Ewing, Whitthorne, and a few others, armed with authority from Johnson, Senator A. O. P. Nicholson, and two of the three Democratic congressmen, managed to keep the Tennessee delegation from joining the fire-eaters. McGavock, who was present as an alternate, observed it "was a solemn sight to see these States leave the Convention . . . the scene . . . was distressing to an old democrat, who believes the salvation of the country depends on the perpetuity of the party."[53]

The convention could not agree on a nominee, and adjourned to meet in Baltimore on June 18. Johnson's prospects for the presidency remained murky, although his adherents held out hope that he might be nominated in Baltimore. At Charleston, after a number of ballots, Johnson's support began to break down as some of the Tennessee delegation advocated voting for the strongest Southern candidate, James Guthrie of Kentucky. Calculating that a split in the delegation would be most injurious to Johnson, Johnson's managers agreed; Ewing announced that Tennessee withdrew his name, and the delegation voted largely for Guthrie. While it is likely Harris worked to subvert Johnson's candidacy, the only direct evidence is Sam Milligan's observation to Johnson that he could see Harris's "hand wielded against you; and that accounts for so much hesitation in our delegation."[54]

Johnson and Harris had much in common. They both had humble beginnings and had worked their way to political ascendancy. Both were powerful stump speakers, both had loyal followings, and both were dedicated to the proposition that the Democratic Party should rule in Tennessee and the nation as a whole. They both were personally ambitious, a similarity that naturally brought them into conflict regardless of their political philosophy. But, even as Democrats, their political views differed. Johnson had ideas outside the Democratic mainstream, such as the Homestead Bill that first brought the two into conflict that Harris damned as "Andy Johnsonisms." Further, Johnson believed in the constitutional

53. Murat Halstead, *Caucuses of 1860. A History of the National Political Conventions of the Current Presidential Campaign: Being a Complete Record of the Business of all the Conventions: with Sketches of Distinguished Men in Attendance Upon Them, and Descriptions of the Most Characteristic Scenes and Memorable Events* (Columbus: Follett, Foster and Company, 1860), 42 (newspaper reporter's quote); Campbell, *The Attitude of Tennesseans Toward the Union*, 117–18; Whitthorne to A. Johnson, and A. Johnson to Whitthorne, both April 29, 1860, 3 *PAJ* 579; S. Milligan to A. Johnson, May 7, 1860, 3 *PAJ* 586; R. Johnson to A. Johnson, May 8, 1860, 3 *PAJ* 588–89; Gower and Allen, eds., *Pen and Sword*, 567.

54. Campbell, *The Attitude of Tennesseans Toward the Union*, 117–18; Halstead, *Caucuses of 1860*, 90; S. Milligan to A. Johnson, May 7, 1860, 3 *PAJ* 586.

rights that protected the institution of slavery, but not at the risk of dissolving the Union. Harris was a much more typical Southern Democrat. And he had made it clear, from the very start of his political career when he made the Wilmot Proviso a point of attack against his political opponents, that the protection of constitutional property rights was his fundamental principle. Harris's speech in April 1850 on the compromise of 1850 and his inaugural address as governor in 1857 demonstrate that he never wavered from this principle, even if to the point of destroying the Union in order to preserve his view of the Constitution.[55]

The rivalry between Harris and Johnson was understood among their friends, but was not publicized by either side. While Johnson was a Unionist and favored popular sovereignty, he cared little for Douglas. His goal, as was that of Harris, was to make sure that the regular Democratic organization in Tennessee stayed unified in the face of the Opposition, which was uniting behind John Bell as a presidential candidate on the ticket of the new Constitutional Union Party. While the Republican candidate, Abraham Lincoln, was realistically thought to be the favorite in the election of 1860, Lincoln would not be on the ballot in Tennessee. As always, the contest in Tennessee would be between the Democrats and the anti-Jacksonian/Whig/Opposition party.[56]

At Baltimore, the issue was between seating Douglas delegates from the states who left the Charleston convention, and the fire-eating, anti-Douglas men who had walked out in April. A compromise effort failed, but the all-or-nothing attitude of the "ultras" sealed the doom of the convention and the unity of the national Democratic Party. This time, when the delegates from the Southern states left, delegations from the upper South, including Tennessee, went with them. Nineteen of Tennessee's twenty-four delegates left, repaired to Richmond with the other bolters, and nominated Vice President John C. Breckinridge for president and Joseph Lane of Oregon for vice president. Three of Tennessee's remaining five at Baltimore joined with the majority to nominate Douglas.[57]

Johnson freed the Tennessee delegation from its commitment to support him

55. LeRoy P. Graf, "Andrew Johnson and the Coming of the War," *Tennessee Historical Quarterly* 19 (September 1960): 208–18; *Cong. Globe*, 31st Cong., 1st Sess., 1850, Appx. 443–46; White, *Messages of the Governors of Tennessee*, 5:30–31.

56. T. Newman to A. Johnson, May 15, 1860, 3 *PAJ* 600–601; Graf, "Andrew Johnson and the Coming of the War," 212–14; Campbell, *The Attitude of Tennesseans Toward the Union*, 119–21; Temple, *East Tennessee and the Civil War*, 126–29; Bergeron, *Antebellum Politics in Tennessee*, 147; see also Whitthorne to A. Johnson, July 24, 1860, 3 *PAJ* 649–51.

57. McPherson, *Battle Cry of Freedom*, 215–16; Campbell, *The Attitude of Tennesseans Toward the Union*, 121–23.

at the convention, expressing the hope that the delegation could join with others to find a consensus candidate. Harris went to Washington and then on to Baltimore with the Tennessee delegation. The governor's political opponents charged he had much to do with the Tennessee delegation's decision to leave the convention, which was highly likely. On June 30, 1860, the state party machinery met in Nashville to ratify the bolters' nomination of Breckinridge. Chairing the meeting, Harris expressed the conviction that the Tennessee delegation had done all it could to conciliate matters, "consistent with the maintenance of the Constitution of the United States, and the protection of the rights of the citizens."[58] Harris also deemed it so important to defeat Lincoln that even though he preferred Breckinridge, if it appeared that a vote for Douglas would ensure that defeat, he would "advise the Democratic electors chose by the people of Tennessee to vote for Judge Douglas." In Whitthorne's view, Harris crossed the line with that proposition, and actually damaged his ability to campaign for the Breckinridge ticket. Whitthorne deemed Douglas to have little support in Tennessee, although such was not the case in Harris's base in West Tennessee, where Douglas eventually outpolled Breckinridge in seven counties. A Douglas proponent advanced the same "fusion" proposition later in the campaign. While the bulk of the Douglas organization was unenthusiastic, the Breckinridge wing signaled it would accept the proposition, no doubt giving Harris a measure of satisfaction.[59]

Whitthorne was wrong. Harris campaigned quite effectively for the Breckinridge ticket. Johnson took the field late in the campaign, and but rejected a suggestion that he appear with Senator Nicholson, Andrew Ewing, and Harris in West Tennessee, where Douglas had his greatest strength in the state. Johnson was gloomy, and had little enthusiasm for Douglas and not much more for Breckinridge. Johnson was glad to hear that Harris was displeased with the size of the crowds, bitterly writing his son that "he is a small man at most and the more he is brought in Contact with the people the more apparent it will be." Harris no doubt had similar thoughts about the senator, and each would have greater occasion to hate the other after the election.[60]

58. Campbell, *The Attitude of Tennesseans Toward the Union*, 121–26 (Harris quote on 124); Marguerite Bartlett Hamer, "The Presidential Campaign of 1860 in Tennessee," *East Tennessee Historical Society Publications* 3 (January 1931): 9, 13.

59. Whitthorne to Johnson, July 24, 1860, 3 *PAJ* 649–51 (Harris quote in note 6); Bergeron, *Antebellum Politics in Tennessee*, 164; Campbell, *The Attitude of Tennesseans Toward the Union*, 130; Gower and Allen, eds., *Pen and Sword*, 579–80.

60. Campbell, *The Attitude of Tennesseans Toward the Union*, 124–25; A. Johnson to Nicholson, Au-

Regardless of the great issues of union, slavery, and constitutional rights espoused by the parties, Tennessee voting patterns held true to the same percentages they had during the 1850s. The Opposition vote was effectively the same percentage (47 percent) as it had been in the Fillmore–Buchanan election of 1856 and Harris's contest with Netherland the previous year. While Bell won Tennessee, the combined Democratic vote in the state equaled that of the previous contests. As expected, the Black Republican candidate, Abraham Lincoln, was elected to the presidency.[61]

Less than two weeks after Lincoln's election, the South Carolina legislature set the date for an election to choose delegates to a convention, which, on December 20, 1860, passed an ordinance of secession. By February 1, 1861, Mississippi, Florida, Alabama, Georgia, Louisiana, and Texas all followed South Carolina. Action was not as precipitous in Tennessee. Indeed, newspapers across the state in the weeks after Lincoln's election counseled restraint. But the pro-secession faction was on the move. In several corners of the state, local meetings were called to express views on the national emergency and to ask Harris to call the legislature into special session for consideration of the political situation. While these local meetings appeared to be nonpartisan in nature, they had a decided secessionist flavor to them. In Knoxville, attorney Oliver P. Temple and other Unionists discerned that a seemingly harmless meeting of this nature had as its goal stoking up secession sentiments. Temple's group succeeded in gaining an adjournment until Union sympathizers from the surrounding countryside could be mustered to provide the votes to defeat a resolution calling for the legislature to meet and to pass a resolution condemning secession. Temple was convinced that this meeting was significant in rallying East Tennesseans in their resistance to the secessionist cause.[62]

Temple acknowledged that the action of the Knoxville meeting did nothing

gust 23, 1860, 3 *PAJ* 659–60; Hamer, "The Presidential Campaign of 1860 in Tennessee," 15–16. There is some indication that Johnson and his adherents thought Harris was seeking to replace Johnson in the U.S. Senate, which makes little sense since Johnson had more than half of his term left. See W. H. Carroll to A. Johnson, January 2, 1861, 4 *PAJ* 117.

61. Bergeron, *Antebellum Politics in Tennessee*, 164–66; Campbell, *The Attitude of Tennesseans Toward the Union*, 134–36.

62. McPherson, *Battle Cry of Freedom*, 234–35; Campbell, *The Attitude of Tennesseans Toward the Union*, 136–44; J. Williams to IGH, December 8, 1860, Harris Papers, TSLA; Temple, *East Tennessee and the Civil War*, 147–66.

to prevent the legislature from meeting, which Harris, bowing to the will of the people, announced on December 8 that he would call for January 7, 1861, not only to consider the national political crisis, but also to deal with the ever-present banking issue. It is impossible to pinpoint exactly when Harris decided that disunion was appropriate, as he had always had strong pro-slavery views, but there seems to be no doubt that by the time he called the legislature into session, he was bent on secession, although subtlety was necessary, as most Tennesseans resented South Carolina's repudiation of the Union. Tennessee legal scholar Joshua W. Caldwell, a political contemporary of Harris in later years, wrote that Harris was "not a disunionist for the sake of disunion, but believed that the constitutional rights of the Southern States were being infringed so as to justify, indeed to require, secession." Harris's future enemy, Temple, cared little for the governor's reasons, but respected his ability. Temple saw Harris as "a man of remarkable energy and determination; ambitious, able and daring. In him the Southern leaders had an ally as bold as [William L.] Yancy or [Robert] Toombs, less brilliant, but with more prudence and discretion."[63]

As he prepared his message to the special session, Harris received a letter from his elder brother George Washington Harris, who, writing "Bro. Green" on December 18, 1860, advised, "Let the terms of our continued Union be so clearly stipulated as that there can be no misinterpretation of them." Harris also received letters of support and encouragement from a friend in Centerville believing that old political differences would be settled "on the common ground against coercion." But Sam Tate, president of the Memphis & Charleston Railroad, perhaps expressed best what Harris himself was likely feeling, when he wrote that he deemed the old government "gone," and that "it only remains for us to stand up and meet the Crisis like Men, do nothing except upon open, bold and dignified principles, & form the best government we can for the protection of our lives, Liberty & property & take the consequences."[64]

63. Temple, *East Tennessee and the Civil War*, 160, 167; Campbell, *The Attitude of Tennesseans Toward the Union*, 145, 153; H. Cox to A. Johnson, December 21, 1860, 4 *PAJ* 64; Joshua W. Caldwell, *Studies in the Constitutional History of Tennessee*, 2nd ed. (Cincinnati: Robert W. Clarke & Co., 1907), 267–68.

64. G. W. Harris to IGH, December 18, 1860, J. Williams to IGH, December 8, 1860, and S. Tate to IGH, December 10, 1860, all in Harris Papers, TSLA.

3 "FOR THE DEFENSE OF OUR RIGHTS AND THOSE OF OUR SOUTHERN BROTHERS"

1861–1862

With South Carolina out of the Union, and other Deep South states preparing to follow, the Tennessee General Assembly met in special session on January 7, 1861. Hot-blooded secessionists vowed in newspapers that the state would "not bow to the yoke of despotism," while moderate Unionists rejoined that "the course of the great and conservative State of Tennessee will never be determined or controlled by men whose passions thus take captive their reason and sense."[1] When the legislators began their work, they were met with a message from the governor. If there was any possible doubt as to Harris's views on the subject of secession up until this point, they were made clear to the members as well as the people as a whole. Harris later wrote that "any history of the secession of Tennessee that leaves out my message to the legislature in January 1861 would be very incomplete. That message distinctly and clearly presented the ground upon which I as Governor recommended separation or secession."[2]

Harris's message began with the premise, most recently set forth in the *Dred Scott* decision, that the Federal Constitution recognized the right of property in slaves, and like other property, property in slaves was entitled to the protection of the law throughout the Union. From that point, Harris embarked upon a slanted view of every "concession" on the slavery issue for the sake of peace since 1820 and Northern states' refusal to enforce laws relating to fugitive slaves, including an incident where the governor of Ohio failed to honor a request to issue a warrant for a man accused of stealing a slave from Tennessee. Harris charged that the anti-

1. "Shall Tennessee Submit?" *Nashville Daily Gazette*, January 9, 1861; "The Madness of the Hour," *Nashville Republican Banner,* January 9, 1861.

2. IGH to Marcus J. Wright, April 19, 1890, Marcus J. Wright Papers, Southern Historical Collection, UNC. For a view that Harris actually acted moderately at this time, see Horn, "Isham G. Harris in the Pre-War Years," 202–3.

slavery party in the North "has assailed our rights, as guaranteed by the plainest provisions of the Constitution, from the floor of each house of Congress, the pulpit, the hustings, the school room, their State Legislatures, and through the public press, dividing and disrupting churches, political parties, and civil governments."

Denouncing the "wrongs" that had gone on for "more than a quarter of a century," some of Tennessee's sister Southern states had determined to sever the ties of union. Harris argued that in the early years of the Republic when the South controlled the Federal government, "she . . . never attempted to encroach upon a single constitutional right of the North." He believed the time had come for the issue to be settled once and for all. Harris recommended that the issue of calling a state convention be submitted to the people, and that delegates be selected in case the convention was approved. The referendum would place the "whole matter in the hands of the people, for them, in their sovereignty, to determine how far their rights have been violated, the character of redress or guaranty they will demand, or the action they will take for their present and future security."

Harris went on to propose constitutional amendments that, given the resistance of the Northern part of the Democracy in the conventions of 1860, he must have known would never be accepted by the North. These included a line across the continent to the Pacific, south of which would forever be slave territory; a double recovery from states that failed to return fugitive slaves; protection for slave owners in transit through free territory; a prohibition on Congress abolishing slavery in the District of Columbia or on any Federal post in slave territory; and amendment of the previous four provisions contingent on the consent of all the slave states. Failing those or similar amendments that would "promise an equal amount and certainty of security, there is no hope of peace or security in the government."

Harris concluded the message with the reminder that the state's militia force was disorganized, and that the public arms available to the state required attention. Harris then turned to the financial crisis brought on by crop failure in the state the previous two years, and recommended that the legislature consider the measures it deemed appropriate to deal with the situation. He also noted that he intentionally avoided bringing up other issues of a general nature because of "the necessity of prompt and immediate action upon the absorbing questions connected with the political crisis of the day."[3]

3. White, *Messages of the Governors of Tennessee*, 5:255–69.

Historians who have recently studied the secessionist ideology that was developed in the final decades before the crisis of the secession winter of 1860–61 have noted the presence of a number of elements that were articulated to justify the doctrine. When examined in detail, Harris's message can be seen to contain many, if not all, of these elements. One element was the perceived threat of equality of the races and race mixing. In his speech, Harris accused Lincoln of asserting "the equality of the *black* with the *white* race."[4] The secessionists defensively condemned the increasingly militant antislavery and Free Soil rhetoric in the North. Harris observed abolitionists in the North spoke of the "irrepressible conflict" and, as noted above, spoke of the assault on slavery from every aspect of Northern society.[5] Secessionists feared that Northern antislavery agitators would incite a slave insurrection, which Harris alluded to by complaining of the adulation received by John Brown and others. The governor also darkly quoted a purported abolitionist motto: "Alarm to the sheep, fire to the dwellings, poison to the food and water of the slaveholders."[6] Secessionists vehemently condemned the resistance of Northerners to the right of slaveholders to take their property to the territories, recognized by the Supreme Court in the *Dred Scott* decision, upset not only by the failure to recognize their property rights as citizens, but also by the danger of free states upsetting the delicate balance of power between slave and free states. Harris spoke of that balance of power, and denounced the North's effort "to appropriate to itself, and to exclude the slaveholder from the territory acquired by the common blood and treasure of all the States."[7]

The secessionists recognized that the South's economic system was closely bound to slavery, and indeed concocted a political/economic theory that argued that the existence of slavery and a nonwhite working underclass was actually a

4. Charles P. Dew, *Apostles of Disunion: Southern Secession Commissioners and the Causes of the Civil War* (Charlottesville: University Press of Virginia, 2001), 29, 46, 48, 54; Eric H. Walther, *The Fire-Eaters* (Baton Rouge: Louisiana State University Press, 1972), 273; Steven A. Channing, *Crisis of Fear: Secession in South Carolina* (New York: Norton, 1970), 65–67; White, *Messages of the Governors of Tennessee*, 5:260.

5. Lacy K. Ford, *Origins of Southern Radicalism: The South Carolina Upcountry, 1800–1860* (New York: Oxford University Press, 1988), 349; Walther, *The Fire-Eaters*, 99; White, *Messages of the Governors of Tennessee*, 5:257, 260.

6. Channing, *Crisis of Fear*, 61–62; Dew, *Apostles of Disunion*, 33–34, 40, 66–67; Walther, *The Fire-Eaters*, 185.

7. Ford, *Origins of Southern Radicalism*, 349–50; Walther, *The Fire-Eaters*, 61–62, 143; White, *Messages of the Governors of Tennessee*, 5:256, 257.

better guaranty of republican liberty than enjoyed by the property-less "wage slaves" of the North. While Harris did not speak in such abstract terms, he recognized that slavery was "interwoven . . . with our wealth, prosperity and domestic happiness."[8] To the secessionist, preservation of Southern honor was at stake; to submit to the North's aggressive abolitionism would result in humiliation and subjugation. Secession, therefore, was the only way to ensure the defense of the South's true republican values. Harris spoke of "justice and honor," and of the need to ensure the guarantees he sought within the Union, or "in a homogenous Confederacy of Southern States."[9] These were all arguments that white Tennesseans recognized, and in most cases agreed with. Events would prove if they were sufficient in the minds of the electorate to actually justify secession.[10]

Harris's message was approved as that of a "patriot and statesman" by the pro-secession *Memphis Daily Appeal*. Harris's critics instantly recognized the message for what it was: an effort to impress "upon the people of Tennessee that the whole North is banded together in a war upon the Constitutional rights of the South." Given the revolutionary spirit of the times and the generally pro-Southern leanings of the legislature, it seemed to some that Tennessee was certain to secede. A secessionist newspaper posed the rhetorical question "shall Tennessee become one of the free and independent states of the Southern Confederacy, or the subjugated, voiceless province of the Northern Empire?" Even conservative voices spoke in terms of "Constitutional rights in the Union, or independence out of it."[11]

Considering the tenor of the times, what emerged from the special session on January 19 was a remarkably conservative measure. There would indeed be a question submitted to the voters of the state for "Convention" or "No Convention" on February 9. There would also be a slate of delegates elected at the same time

8. Channing, *Crisis of Fear*, 62–64; Ford, *Origins of Southern Radicalism*, 352–65; Walther, *The Fire-Eaters*, 33, 201–2; White, *Messages of the Governors of Tennessee*, 5:261.

9. Ford, *Origins of Southern Radicalism*, 372; Channing, *Crisis of Fear*, 142; Dew, *Apostles of Disunion*, 32, 58, 67; Walther, *The Fire-Eaters*, 6; White, *Messages of the Governors of Tennessee*, 5:261, 264.

10. Atkins, *Parties, Politics and the Sectional Conflict in Tennessee*, 228–29; Daniel W. Crofts, *Reluctant Confederates: Upper South Unionists in the Secession Crisis* (Chapel Hill: University of North Carolina Press, 1989), 94–100.

11. "Gov. Harris' Message," *Memphis Daily Appeal*, January 10, 1861; "Gov. Harris' Message," *Nashville Republican Banner*, January 15, 1861; Campbell, *The Attitude of Tennesseans Toward the Union*, 159; OR 52(2):4; OR (Series 4) 4(1):56; "The Questions for Tennesseans to Answer," *Nashville Daily Gazette*, January 16, 1861; "Last Appeal for the Union and the Constitutional Rights of the South," *Nashville Republican Banner*, January 12, 1861.

should the voters approve a convention, to save the state a second vote. But, conservatives added an amendment that provided that no measure passed by the convention that had "for its object a change of the position or relation of this State to the National Union or her sister Southern States" would be binding until ratified by a majority of the qualified voters of the state measured by the number of voters who voted in the election of 1859. Not only were there significant legal hurdles for an eventual secession vote, but the issue of a convention essentially became a referendum on immediate secession, which few in Tennessee desired at that time. An Opposition member of the legislature wrote Andy Johnson bragging that the "Union men whipt the Seceders out of their boots, and completely unhorsed his Excellency" (i.e., Harris).[12]

With the tone set by Harris's "hot blast" of a message, the rhetoric on both sides in the days leading up to the convention election was of the fieriest sort. The Unionist *Nashville Republican Banner* warned the public of "the vilest, most damnable, deep-laid, and treacherous conspiracy that was every concerted in the busy brain of the most designing knave." The secessionist *Nashville Daily Gazette* told its readers, "If you think you have rights and are the superiors of the 'black man,' then vote for men who will not sell you out, body and soul, to the Yankee Republicans—for men who would rather see Tennessee independent and out of the Union, then in the Union subjugated." Party lines, somewhat disrupted by the election of 1860, were crossed to a much greater extent as Unionist Democrats joined those of the Opposition to urge the election of Unionist delegates.[13]

Harris and his allies had badly miscalculated. The secessionists' efforts to defeat the provision calling for a popular vote ratifying the results of the convention, if called, the talk of the need to remilitarize the state, and the seeming rush toward dissolution caused uneasiness in the electorate. On February 9, "No Convention" won by almost 12,000 votes, carrying both Middle and East Tennessee. More strikingly, the total vote for Union delegates swamped that of the secessionists by more than 64,000 votes. Significantly, nearly half of the Democratic vot-

12. White, *Messages of the Governors of Tennessee*, 5:271–72; Campbell, *The Attitude of Tennesseans Toward the Union*, 159–60; "Convention of the People of Tennessee—Passage of the Convention Bill," *Nashville Republican Banner*, January 20, 1861; Crofts, *Reluctant Confederates*, 144–47; John W. Richardson to A. Johnson, February 8, 1861, 4 *PAJ* 266.

13. Temple, *East Tennessee and the Civil War*, 170; "Let every true, honest citizen," *Nashville Republican Banner*, January 22, 1861; "The Tennessee Convention," *Nashville Daily Gazette*, February 2, 1861; Campbell, *The Attitude of Tennesseans Toward the Union*, 173–74.

ers of 1860 refused to support a convention. Tennessee had emphatically repudiated secession—for the time being. While its Memphis competitor the *Avalanche*
lamented the betrayal of "the rights, interests and honor of a once noble State,"
the secessionist *Appeal* ominously warned "the election [of February 9] is but the
first act in the great drama which is yet to be played." And while the capital's
strongest Unionist paper, the *Republican Banner,* enjoyed the victory over the secessionists, it warned the North that a good faith effort should be made to settle
the crisis. While the election returns showed Tennessee was "overwhelmingly
for the Union," the *Banner* spoke for a number who were for the Union but who
were anti-coercion, warning that "her gallant people will submit to no rule in the
Union which is unjust or oppressive."[14]

Notwithstanding the lingering uncertainty, Harris's enemies gloated over his
defeat. The Unionist victory was credited to the influence of Andrew Johnson,
who remained virulently opposed to secession. One of Johnson's friends gleefully
wrote that the governor was "Check mated," and another crowed that "Gov. Harris is buried so deep that no political resurrection horn can ever toot him up." But
there was no admission of defeat from Green Harris, whose attitude was much
like that of his hometown *Appeal.* Soon after the election, he received the envoy
of the Georgia secession convention, Hiram P. Bell, who reported back to Georgia
that Harris "deplored" the result of the election, applauded Georgia's secession,
and "expressed the opinion that the withdrawal of Tennessee from the Government of the United States and its union with the Confederate States of America
was only a question of time." Doubtless reflecting his brother-in-law's view, W. E.
Travis wrote the *Avalanche* from Paris, advocating that the friends of secession
should be patient and await Northern efforts to coerce the South, in which event
Tennesseans would be ready to join the South. An Opposition paper reported that
Harris stated "he would sink the whole fifteen Southern States in the vortex of
destruction before he would accept the Crittenden proposal as a settlement of the
difficulty between the North and the South." The governor deemed it "the duty

14. Atkins, *Parties, Politics and Sectional Politics in Tennessee,* 239–41; Campbell, *The Attitude
of Tennesseans Toward the Union,* 175–77; White, *Messages of the Governors of Tennessee,* 5: 271–72;
Charles F. Bryan Jr., "The Civil War in East Tennessee: A Social, Political and Economic Study" (Ph.D.
dissertation, University of Tennessee, 1978), 37; Crofts, *Reluctant Confederates,* 104–6, 192; "The Result of Saturday's Election," *Memphis Daily Avalanche,* February 11, 1861; "The Election Yesterday—
The General Result," *Memphis Daily Appeal,* February 10, 1861; "What Was Decided Yesterday," *Nashville Republican Banner,* February 10, 1861.

and the right of South Carolina to take Fort Sumter; even if total destruction became necessary."[15]

Lincoln was inaugurated on March 4, 1861. The *Avalanche* advocated that Harris call another special session. In reply, the *Banner* mocked that it doubted that
the governor "*ever* wants to see the Legislature again." Although pro-secessionist
papers interpreted Lincoln's inaugural address as a "declaration of war," Unionists thought the speech "conservative and mild." Harris appears to have spent
much time in Memphis, while, in Middle Tennessee, secessionist agitation abated.
With Harris and the secessionists in eclipse, and leading Unionist Democrats and
Whigs cooperating in the wake of their victory in February, the Lincoln administration had the opportunity to strengthen Tennessee conservatives by the ju-
dicious dispensation of patronage. Bell personally went to Washington to confer with Lincoln. But he and other members of the Opposition were bypassed as
patronage dispensers in Tennessee in favor of Andrew Johnson, likely because
Lincoln and the Republicans had little knowledge of the political complexion in
Tennessee. Although Unionist, Johnson remained a Democrat. Patronage appointments strengthened his personal political position in the state, rather than the
larger Union cause. Members of the Opposition began to lose enthusiasm for the
Republican administration.[16]

The crisis did not alter the constitutional fact that 1861 was an election year.
The ultra-secessionist *Avalanche* pronounced the Democratic Party dead, killed

15. J. B. White to A. Johnson, February 22, 1861, 4 *PAJ* 329; Charles O. Faxon to A. Johnson, February 11, 1861, 4 *PAJ*, 274; R. M. Edwards to A. Johnson, February 11, 1861, 4 *PAJ*, 272–73; OR (Series 4) 4(1):180; "Letter from W. E. Travis, Esq.," *Memphis Avalanche*, February 20, 1861; "Our Governor to Sink us in the Vortex of Destruction," *Nashville Republican Banner*, February 19, 1861. The
Crittenden proposals were constitutional guarantees to slavery similar in many respects to those advanced by Harris in his January 8 message. Fort Sumter in Charleston Harbor was one of the two
remaining Federal installations in the territory of the new Confederacy. McPherson, *Battle Cry of
Freedom*, 252–53, 263–65.

16. "An Extra Session of the Legislature," *Memphis Daily Avalanche*, March 6, 1861; "Convening the Legislature," *Nashville Republican Banner*, March 12, 1861; J. Milton Henry, "The Revolution in Tennessee, February, 1861 to June, 1861," *Tennessee Historical Quarterly* 18 (June 1959): 99,
103–4, 110–15; Crofts, *Reluctant Confederates*, 266, 327–28; James L. Baumgardner, "Abraham Lincoln, Andrew Johnson, and the Federal Patronage: An Attempt to Save Tennessee for the Union?"
East Tennessee Historical Society Papers 45 (1973): 51, 57–60; Joseph H. Parks, *John Bell of Tennessee*
(Baton Rouge: Louisiana State University Press, 1950) 395–96; Campbell, *The Attitude of Tennesseans
Toward the Union*, 184–85; J. Fowlkes to A. Johnson, March 13, 1861, 4 *PAJ* 388; "Postmaster at Nash-
ville," *Nashville Republican Banner*, March 26, 1861.

on account of its resistance to abolitionism, and proposed a new States' Rights Party in its place. Newspaperman and former legislator John C. Burch contemplated raising the standard of rebellion in Nashville, exciting one admirer to advocate him as a possible candidate for governor for the Southern Rights Party. On the Unionist side, possible candidates were former Governor William B. Campbell, William H. Polk, the former president's brother, and colorful Knoxville newspaperman (and former circuit-riding preacher) William G. "Parson" Brownlow. Harris was constitutionally eligible for one more term as governor, but no man had held the office for more than two terms for over twenty-five years. While there was some talk of Harris replacing Johnson as senator, Johnson's term did not expire until 1863, and, if Harris achieved his goals, there would be no U.S. senator seat from Tennessee to fill.[17]

While there were efforts to schedule the usual nominating conventions in early May, events in South Carolina and Washington, D.C., in mid-April soon made the normal political process dramatically shrink in importance. In early April, a small garrison of U.S. troops still held Fort Sumter in South Carolina's Charleston Harbor. In response to their deteriorating supply situation, President Lincoln informed Governor Pickens of the Palmetto State that a peaceful resupply effort would be made. This forced the fledgling Confederate government's hand, and on April 12, Rebel forces at Charleston began a thirty-three-hour bombardment of the fort, which eventually forced the garrison's surrender. On April 15, Lincoln called on the various states for 75,000 men to suppress the "insurrection."[18]

The outbreak of open hostilities completely changed the situation. Northern states enthusiastically responded to Lincoln's call for troops. The upper South slave states of Arkansas, North Carolina, and Virginia moved rapidly to join the Confederacy. In East Tennessee, the secessionist wave broke on the sea wall of a largely undiminished core of Union support. But in Middle and West Tennessee, much of the remaining Unionist sentiment melted away under fiery secessionist rhetoric. While the principal Unionist newspaper in Middle Tennessee, the *Republican Banner*, counseled caution, it published a memorial from leading Unionists who called on the state to assume a state of armed neutrality. The *Memphis Daily Appeal* published a memorial from the citizens of Memphis to Harris the

17. "Old Party Issues Must Be Ignored," *Memphis Daily Avalanche*, March 14, 1861; "Hon. Jno. C. Burch" and "The Gubernatorial Election," *Nashville Daily Gazette*, April 3, 1861; OR 52(3):36; Campbell, *The Attitude of Tennesseans Toward the Union*, 185–88; Watters, "Isham Green Harris," 88–89.

18. McPherson, *Battle Cry of Freedom*, 271–75.

very day Fort Sumter changed hands, calling for a special session of the legislature for the purpose of joining the Confederacy.[19]

The crisis, and the opportunity it created, brought Harris swiftly back to Nashville from Memphis. On April 17, he met the Federal government's call for two regiments of militia with a defiant reply: "Tennessee will not furnish a single man for purposes of coercion but 50,000 if necessary for the defense of our rights and those of our southern brothers." That night, he appeared before a crowd at the Capitol to thunderous applause, and referring to his reply to the Federal authorities, "rather than sign such an order he would cut his right arm from his body—rather than utter it he would tear his tongue from the root." Harris offered to go to war as a common soldier, stating "if to say this was treason, then before God he was a traitor." On April 18, the governor issued a call for the legislature to meet a week later on April 25. On April 20, Harris dispatched Whitthorne to the seat of the Confederate government in Montgomery, Alabama, to confer with Jefferson Davis and Confederate Secretary of War Leroy P. Walker. Whitthorne was "fully advised" and was to "make known . . . the state of parties in our State, as well as our prospects, hopes, and apprehensions. Large accessions every day to the secession cause, and we confidently hope to stand with you under the Confederate flag very soon."[20]

Harris's messages to the Federal government signaled that while still nominally a member of the Union, Tennessee had assumed belligerent status on the side of the Confederacy in the strange new war. On April 19, Confederate Secretary of War Walker wrote asking for permission to erect a battery at Memphis, to which Harris assented, as he had already anticipated the necessity of fortifying the Mississippi. Tennessee had no real military structure during this interval, yet Harris for some weeks appears to have employed Tennessee's most famous Mexican War veteran Gideon J. Pillow in an anticipatory role as a military

19. Ibid., 274–84; Temple, *East Tennessee and the Civil War*, 179–188; Atkins, *Parties, Politics and Sectional Politics in Tennessee*, 244–46; Campbell, *The Attitude of Tennesseans Toward the Union*, 190–94; Charles L. Lufkin, "Secession and Coercion in Tennessee, the Spring of 1861," *Tennessee Historical Quarterly* 50 (Summer 1991): 98, 100–104; "Stand Firm," *Nashville Republican Banner*, April 18, 1861; "Self Defense" and "To the People of Tennessee," *Nashville Republican Banner*, April 19, 1861; "Memorial," *Memphis Daily Appeal*, April 14, 1861; "The Convocation of the Legislature," *Memphis Daily Appeal*, April 18, 1861.

20. "Governor Harris," *Memphis Daily Avalanche*, April 19, 1861; White, *Messages of the Governors of Tennessee*, 5:272–73; OR (Series 3) 1:81, 91–92; Harris to Cameron, April 17, 1861, Harris Papers, TSLA; OR 52(2):57; "Great Rectification at the Capitol," *Nashville Union & American*, April 18, 1861.

advisor. In the space of a single day, April 20, Pillow energetically appealed to the Confederate government for an officer with expertise in defensive works, dispatched John C. Burch to confer with the governor of Missouri about the Federal arsenal at St. Louis, and published an appeal in the Memphis paper of that name for fifty thousand volunteers. Within a few days, at Harris's request, Pillow traveled to Louisville to confer with Governor Beriah Magoffin of Kentucky relative to the defense of the Mississippi and returned to Memphis to begin erecting works for that same purpose. In the weeks that followed, Pillow would assert himself in the gray area between political and military matters, advising Harris on the need to fully mobilize the state and protesting that Harris should not have let a particular steamer pass through the blockade of the Mississippi at Memphis. While respectful in his replies to his general, Harris left no doubt he was in charge.[21]

Even without a state military organization, there were already three regiments in some state of readiness, organized by Peter Turney, William B. Bate, and George Maney. Like others, Turney and Bate had little enthusiasm for Pillow, and in the days after Fort Sumter, actually dealt with the Confederate government directly, perhaps because Harris had no official authority yet to offer Tennessee troops to the Confederacy. Other ardent secessionists, such as Harris's friends, Sam Tate of Memphis and John H. Crozier of Knoxville, apparently were on authorized state business when dealing with Confederate authorities. A call for three regiments for the defense of Virginia on April 22 highlighted Harris's ambiguous authority. Harris acknowledged he had no authority to send them, and there was concern that Tennessee might need its soldiers for its own defense. Therefore, Bate requested, likely at Harris's instance, that Tennessee be accorded the right to recall the units if necessary. Bate advised the Rebel government that he thought Harris would again run for governor, "and we want him right beyond cavil before the masses." The Confederate government agreed.[22]

The legislature assembled once more in special session on April 25, and was

21. OR 52(2):56–59, 63; Nathaniel Cheairs Hughes Jr. and Roy P. Stonesifer Jr., The Life and Wars of Gideon J. Pillow (Chapel Hill: University of North Carolina Press, 1993), 157; "Call for Tennessee Volunteers," Memphis Daily Appeal, April 20, 1861; Pillow to IGH, May 22, 1861, IGH to Pillow, May 24, 1861, Pillow to IGH, May 25, 1861, and IGH to Pillow, May 28, 1861, all in Harris Papers, TSLA.

22. Robert H. White, Development of the Tennessee State Educational Organization (Kingsport: Southern Press, 1929), 280; OR 52(2):59–60, 64, 67–70, 75, 79, 81, 90–91; OR (Series 4) 1:233; Hughes and Stonesifer, The Life and Wars of Gideon J. Pillow, 157–58; "The Meeting at the Capitol Last Night," Nashville Daily Gazette, April 23, 1861.

met by a message from the governor. Harris reminded the General Assembly of his January bill of complaint against the North and denounced Lincoln's call for troops. Harris recommended that the lawmakers declare Tennessee independent of the Federal Union, and that they should consider alignment with the Southern Confederacy as a matter of common defense. Harris further recommended a quick vote of the electorate to ratify the declaration and to affirm Tennessee joining the Confederacy. The governor then called for "such legislation as will put the State upon war footing immediately." All of this should be done quickly, as the members' "presence may soon be needed in the field, and if not, will be required at home for counsel among your constituents."[23]

Both houses went into secret session, and even Harris's message was withheld from the public for almost a week. During that time, Jefferson Davis's envoy, Henry Hilliard, arrived in Nashville. In an interview with the governor, Hilliard was told that Harris's recommendation that the declaration of independence be separated from the measure allying Tennessee with the Confederacy was to make sure Tennessee left the Union as soon as possible. While Harris was confident that Tennessee would eventually join the Confederate States, there was some sentiment in the state to form a "middle confederacy" of the Border States. Harris would not allow such a halfway measure. Obviously wanting to keep as much control over the process as possible, and likely recalling that the vote in February elected a majority of Unionist delegates, Harris told Hilliard he wanted the issues to go to the people as a direct vote, not wanting a convention "between himself and the people." Hilliard addressed a public joint session of the General Assembly on April 30, arguing "in favor of the immediate secession of Tennessee from the Union and the speedy accession of the State to our Confederacy." Hilliard's speech was met with great enthusiasm, and he and Harris later rode about the city giving brief speeches. Hilliard later recalled that "it was a brilliant scene."[24]

At this juncture, the result was a foregone conclusion. On May 1, the General Assembly authorized Harris to appoint commissioners to conclude a military league with the Confederacy. These commissioners drew up an agreement with Hilliard, which was submitted for approval on May 7. More significantly, the General Assembly passed an act to submit two questions to a vote of the people on

23. White, *Messages of the Governors of Tennessee*, 5:279–87.

24. Ibid., 5:287–88; "Gov. Harris' Message," *Memphis Daily Avalanche*, May 1, 1861; OR 52(2):75–78, 82–83; "Speech of Mr. Hilliard," *Nashville Daily Gazette*, May 1, 1861; Henry Washington Hilliard, *Politics and Pen Pictures at Home and Abroad* (New York: G. P. Putnam's Sons, 1892), 326–30.

June 8. The first question sought the approval of a "Declaration of Independence and Ordinance dissolving the Federal Relations between the State of Tennessee and the United States of America," and the second adopted or rejected the provisional constitution of the Confederate States. It was at this point the legislature's actions were revealed to the public. The *Nashville Union & American* assured its readers that the actions "but reflect the overwhelming voice of the people of Tennessee." Harris's plan, as described to Hilliard, had come to pass.[25]

Among the seceding states, Tennessee was unique in its "Declaration of Independence" and its bypassing of a convention on the question of secession. The proposed Declaration of Independence "waiv[ed] any expression of opinion as to the abstract doctrine of secession," and relied upon the sovereign right of the people to "alter, reform or abolish" their form of government. The right of revolution invoked by Harris's legislation appeared in the state constitution of 1834 in Article I, Section I.[26] But the preamble of the state constitution made reference to Tennessee's admission to and relation to the Union, and the document contained no less than nine references to the United States, including requirements that the governor and members of the General Assembly be citizens of the United States and that each officer of the state take an oath to support the Constitution of the United States.[27] A change in the state's relation to the Union was therefore constitutional in nature. In February, Harris and his political allies chose to submit the issue of secession to a convention, an accepted means of exercising the "sovereign power of the people." In May, the legislature framed a question to be submitted to a direct vote, as Harris argued "since it is only the voice of the people that is to be heard, there is no reason why they may not as readily and effectively express themselves upon an ordinance framed and submitted to them by the Legislature, as if submitted to them by a Convention." Yet, the General Assembly's only power to amend the constitution lay in Article XI, Section 3, whereby the group elected in 1859 would propose changes that would have to be passed by a two-thirds ma-

25. OR 52(2):84; OR (Series 4) 1:289–91, 296–98; White, *Messages of the Governors of Tennessee,* 5:289–94; "The Action of the Legislature," *Nashville Union & American,* May 8, 1861.

26. Tennessee Constitution of 1834, Art. I, Sec. 1 provided: "That all power is inherent in the people, and all free governments are founded on their authority, and instituted for their peace, safety and happiness; for the advancement of those ends, they have, at all times, an unalienable and indefeasible right to alter, reform or abolish the government in such manner as they may think proper."

27. Tennessee Constitution of 1834, Art. I, Sec. 25, 31; Art. II, Sec. 9, 10, 26; Art. III, Sec. 3, 5, 13; Art. IV, Sec. 1; Art. VI, Sec. 7; Art. X, Sec. 1.

jority by the members to be elected in August 1861, after which the issue would require a vote of the people.[28]

The vote held on June 8 ratified the Declaration of Independence and the state's joining the Confederacy by a majority of approximately 55,000 votes, although East Tennessee rejected the two questions by a two to one majority.[29] While there is an argument that the vote on June 8 ratified the action of the legislature, as seen above, a question from the legislature constitutionally required the approval of two separate General Assemblies before the vote. As Unionist East Tennessee lawyer Oliver P. Temple pointed out, during the interval between the passage of the act calling for the election on May 7, and the purported ratification on June 8, Harris, the legislature, and the state government allied itself to the Confederacy, politically and militarily. In Temple's view, the ratifying election could not cure an unconstitutional act, nor could it justify the state's open hostility to the United States in the interim period.[30]

Harris and his fellow secessionists were bent on revolution, and it could be fairly argued that they trampled on the Tennessee Constitution to accomplish that result.[31] Harris's central role in taking Tennessee out of the Union in the spring of 1861 cannot be underestimated, and is best summarized by Temple:

> It is sometimes said that great as was the influence of Governor Harris in causing the secession of Tennessee, he could not have accomplished this act alone; that it was the great events of 1861 that caused the withdrawal of the state, and that if he had opposed secession to his uttermost, the state still would have seceded. It is probably true that he alone could not have carried the state out of the Union. But that he exercised in this direction a more potent influence than any other man admits of little doubt. His position as governor, to say nothing of his ability, daring and exceeding aggressiveness, gave him immense power. With him alone was lodged the

28. Tennessee Constitution of 1834, Art. XI, Sec. 3; White, *Messages of the Governors of Tennessee*, 5:285, 288.

29. White, *Messages of the Governors of Tennessee*, 5:302–4; OR (Series 4) 1:901.

30. Temple presents a scathing critique of the secessionists' course of action and legal position. Temple, *East Tennessee and the Civil War*, 205–15.

31. Ultimately, a failed revolution is a rebellion. This was confirmed by a "schedule" to the state constitution adopted in 1865 that held that the actions taken by the state government after May 6, 1861, were "unconstitutional, null and void from the beginning."

right and the discretion of convening the legislature, which right he exercised twice, by means of which the state was finally withdrawn from the Union.[32]

In leaving the Union, and in entering a military alliance with the Confederacy, Tennessee joined the Confederacy's war with the United States, requiring military preparedness. On May 6, the legislature passed a measure to raise a provisional army of 55,000 volunteers to defend the state.[33] The army would be funded by the sale of $5 million in war bonds, as the state had no resources to meet the extraordinary demand of raising and equipping an army. Initially, Harris had little luck in selling the bonds. While the officers of the Bank of Tennessee were inclined to help, they advised Harris that without the assistance of the state's largest private banks, the Union and Planters banks, the funds could not be raised. Harris had several interviews with the officers of these two institutions, and soon saw they were reluctant to help. Viewing the situation as a military necessity, Harris once again went to the reluctant officers and "made those Gentlemen clearly understand that if they did not co-operate with the Bank of Tennessee in meeting these financial necessities, that I would do so, or take the assets of the Banks out of their hands and place them in the hands of a receiver who was friendly to the Confederate cause." The next morning, each begrudgingly informed the governor that the private banks would accept the bonds. In the end, the banks together purchased more than $1 million of the bonds. But, since that amount was not all that was needed, the legislature had to authorize Harris to convert 60 percent of the remaining amount as legal tender treasury notes.[34]

With this money, Harris funded a remarkable effort to equip the military force authorized in early May. Even before the authorization passed, Harris organized a "preliminary and informal" military and financial board, which purchased "large

32. Temple, *East Tennessee and the Civil War*, 217 (see also 218–19). This passage was inferentially discussed with Harris in late 1895 by John Brownlow, the son of "Parson" Brownlow, who assured Harris that Temple would "tell you took Tennessee out of the Union but will do justice to your character as a man." J. Brownlow to Temple, January 1, 1896, O. P. Temple Papers, University of Tennessee.

33. White, *Messages of the Governors of Tennessee*, 5:294.

34. White, *Development of the Tennessee State Educational Organization*, 277–81 (the referenced pages are the transcript of a deposition given by Harris in 1872); "A Legal Relic of the War," *New York Times*, April 26, 1876; White, *Messages of the Governors of Tennessee*, 5:311; IGH to Pillow, June 21, 1861, Harris Papers, TSLA.

supplies" of food, clothing, and war materiels. This quick movement "enabled the State to secure a large amount of articles of indispensable necessity that in a short time afterward could not be purchased at any price; and much of what was still attainable and important to the service soon rose to enormous rates." Private citizens also aided in an unofficial manner, and "rendered efficient and valuable services as auxiliaries in the great work of preparation." Once a formal board was authorized, Harris appointed influential citizens such as prominent Whig editor Felix K. Zollicoffer (whom Harris soon appointed a general), former rival Gustavus Henry (soon to be elected Confederate senator), William G. Harding of the famed Belle Meade Plantation, and Clarksville attorney James E. Bailey. While hampered by shortages, the blockade, and the cessation of communications with the North, the board procured supplies, organized the manufacture of arms and ammunition, procured property for the camps of instruction, and paid the troops. These efforts benefited the Confederacy as a whole, as Jefferson Davis later wrote that they provided the new government "much relief" during its initial period of shortages.[35]

The initial focus of Tennessee's defensive measures was in the far western reaches of the state, along the Mississippi River. As discussed above, Pillow's early efforts were geared toward the river defenses there, and efforts were made to focus the Confederate government on the area. There were a number of reports of large concentrations of Federals at various points in the North preparing to descend the river, which certainly increased tensions in that part of the state. But, contrary to the assertions of Thomas L. Connelly, the eminent historian of the Army of Tennessee, Harris did not "neglect" the important potential invasion routes of the Tennessee and Cumberland rivers. Even before secession, he assigned Adna Anderson, "one of the ablest and most widely known engineers in the South," to "locate and construct defensive works on the Cumberland and Tennessee rivers." Soon thereafter, surveyor and topographer Wilber F. Foster was detached from the 1st Tennessee Regiment to assist Anderson. The party set out for the area between the two rivers on May 10, and they marked the position of a "water battery" at what would later be called Fort Donelson on the Cumberland River; a force of workmen was assigned to start work on the position. A proposed position was selected for a work on the Tennessee, but as no workmen were avail-

35. OR 52(2):158–59; Dillard Jacobs, "Outfitting the Provisional Army of Tennessee: A Report on New Source Materials," *Tennessee Historical Quarterly* 40 (Fall 1981): 257–71; Jefferson Davis, *The Rise and Fall of the Confederate Government* (New York: D. Appleton & Co., 1881), 1:408.

able for that project, nothing further was done by the Anderson/Foster party. Harris later dispatched military officers Daniel S. Donelson and Bushrod Johnson to make their own review. Johnson strongly recommended a position at Kirkman's Landing, but the need to stay out of Kentucky limited the Tennessee's military options.[36]

Kentucky's political position at this time was a blessing and a curse. Like Harris, pro-secessionist Governor Beriah Magoffin refused to provide troops in response to Lincoln's call after Fort Sumter. But the Kentucky legislature eventually passed a resolution calling for the state's strict neutrality in the sectional struggle. Simon Bolivar Buckner, the pro-Southern commander of the Kentucky State Guard, assured Federal commander Major General George B. McClellan that he would resist any effort by Tennessee troops to cross into the state, and left McClellan to tell Harris the same thing. Buckner told Harris that McClellan would not occupy Kentucky with Federal troops, either, ensuring that the Commonwealth would not be an avenue of invasion. Accordingly, Harris made sure to caution Pillow to keep his troops out of Kentucky. Harris also stayed in touch with Magoffin, seeking assurance that no invasion force was assembling in the Commonwealth. As long as Kentucky remained demilitarized, Tennessee was safe from its immediate North, although a significant portion of the state troops was massed in camps of instruction near the Kentucky border. This advantage was offset by the determination that the best defensive positions to guard the state from a water-borne invasion along the Mississippi, Tennessee, and Cumberland rivers were actually in Kentucky.[37]

36. "Our River Defenses," *Memphis Daily Appeal*, April 27, 1861; OR 52(2):72–73, 80, 89–91, 93–94, 100; Horn, *The Army of Tennessee*, 48; Thomas L. Connelly, *Army of the Heartland: The Army of Tennessee 1861–62* (Baton Rouge: Louisiana State University Press, 1967), 20–21, 27, 39; E. C. Bearss, "The Construction of Fort Henry and Fort Donelson," *West Tennessee Historical Society Papers* 21 (1967): 24–26; Bromfield Ridley, *Battles and Sketches of the Army of Tennessee* (1906; reprint, Dayton: Morningside, 1995), 64–65; B. R. Johnson to IGH, June 11, 1861, and IGH to B. R. Johnson, June 14, 1861, both in Harris Papers, TSLA; Benjamin Franklin Cooling, *Forts Henry and Donelson: The Key to the Confederate Heartland* (Knoxville: University of Tennessee Press, 1987), 14; William Preston Johnston, *The Life of Gen. Albert Sidney Johnston* (New York: D. Appleton & Co., 1879), 407; B. Magoffin to IGH, August 12, 1861, Beriah Magoffin Papers, LC. Historian Larry Daniel has written an effective rebuttal of Connelly's various criticisms of Harris in the early days of the war. Larry J. Daniel, "In Defense of Governor Isham G. Harris," *North & South* 7 (May 2004): 74–79.

37. Nathaniel S. Shaler, *Kentucky: A Pioneer Commonwealth* (Boston: Houghton, Mifflin & Co., 1885), 241–48; OR 2:674, 4:122; OR 52(2):378; Harris to Pillow, June 1, 1861, and Harris to Pillow,

While the focus of the state military authorities against outside invasion was to the north and west, internal problems remained in East Tennessee, although there were hopeful reports that sympathy with the secessionist cause was growing. If so, it was not growing fast enough. Even as most of the state saw secession as the inevitable result of the Lincoln administration's "coercion," East Tennessee's most strident newspaper editor, William G. "Parson" Brownlow, condemned Harris and the General Assembly for their secret proceedings, restrictive war measures, and massive expenditures on the Provisional Army. While the state mobilized for war, prominent citizens in East Tennessee, including Brownlow, Temple, and others, called for a convention of conservatives to assemble in Knoxville on May 30. Mass meetings in that section of the state selected delegates, and rallied the population to the Union cause. The convention heard speeches from Andrew Johnson, Congressman Thomas A. R. Nelson, and former Congressman Thomas D. Arnold. The meeting adjourned to meet again in Greeneville on June 17, after the election on June 8.[38]

East Tennessee's divergence from the rest of the state in the crisis of 1861 had a number of possible causes. Historically, Tennessee's unique geography dictated the state's segmentation into three regions, or "grand divisions." Indeed, since the constitution of 1834, the "grand divisions" have been a legal as well as a geographic distinction. The most populated area of East Tennessee was mainly the valley watered by the southward-flowing Tennessee River and its tributaries. The valley was somewhat isolated by the Unaka Mountains to the east and the Cumberland Plateau to the west, which was compounded by the difficulty of navigating the Tennessee River as it passed out of East Tennessee into Alabama. Middle Tennessee is essentially bounded by the Cumberland Plateau on the east and the Tennessee River on the west, there flowing north, and consists of a central basin ideal

June 12, 1861, both in Harris Papers, TSLA; Connelly, *Army of the Heartland*, 40–41; Daniel, "In Defense of Governor Isham G. Harris," 76; Johnston, *The Life of Gen. Albert Sidney Johnston*, 407; Bearss, "The Construction of Fort Henry and Fort Donelson," 27; Hughes and Stonesifer, *The Life and Wars of Gideon J. Pillow*, 168–69.

38. "The Spirit in East Tennessee," *Nashville Union & American*, May 18, 1861; "Has it Come to This?" *Knoxville Whig*, May 4, 1861; "Governor's Message," *Knoxville Whig*, May 11, 1861; "Diabolical Legislation," *Knoxville Whig*, May 18, 1861; Temple, *East Tennessee and the Civil War*, 340–43; Charles F. Bryan Jr., "A Gathering of Tories: The East Tennessee Convention of 1861," *Tennessee Historical Quarterly* 39 (February 1980): 27, 30–31, 36–38; Bryan, "The Civil War in East Tennessee," 40–52.

for agricultural pursuits, surrounded by hills of the Highland Rim. West Tennessee is bounded by the Tennessee on the east and the Mississippi River on the west. Acquired by the Chickasaw Purchase of 1818, it was the last of the three to be settled.[39]

Because theirs was the first region to be settled, East Tennesseans enjoyed early political control of the state, but by 1815, Middle Tennesseans took control of the government, and, on the basis of larger population, retained that control for much of the antebellum period. Resentments arose in the late 1830s when measures for internal improvements in East Tennessee were defeated by the Middle Tennesseans in the legislature, to the point that there was an initiative for separate statehood for East Tennessee in the early 1840s that acquired some early momentum but eventually failed. The lack of hard-surfaced roads and the unreliability of river transportation meant that until the advent of railroads into the region in the 1850s, East Tennessee's commerce with the outside world was largely by wagon train or by driving livestock to market outside the state. Isolation from potential markets had a substantial adverse impact on the region's wealth.[40]

While, as noted above, East Tennessee was the center of early antislavery agitation in the state, the height of that movement had passed by 1830, and even at its heyday only involved a minority within the region. By 1860, most East Tennesseans neither had sympathy for the slaves nor desired their freedom. Practically, however, slavery was not as central a component of the economic system of East Tennessee as it was in the rest of the state. East Tennessee's soil and shorter growing season did not foster the cotton production seen in West or Middle Tennessee, thus obviating the need during the greater part of the antebellum period for the large slave population required to cultivate that labor-intensive crop. Accordingly, by 1860, East Tennessee contained only about 10 percent of the state's slave population. Not surprisingly, the greatest concentration of slaves in the state was in the more conducive regions in the central basin of Middle Tennessee and in the bottomlands of West Tennessee. Fewer slaves meant fewer slaveholders. That and the lack of wealth generated by the cash crops grown and harvested by slaves ac-

39. Tennessee Constitution of 1834, Art. VI, Sec. 1; Bergeron, Ash, and Keith, *Tennesseans and Their History*, 2–4; Bryan, "The Civil War in East Tennessee," 8.

40. Noel C. Fisher, *War at Every Door: Partisan Politics and Guerilla Violence in East Tennessee, 1860–1869* (Chapel Hill: University of North Carolina Press, 1997), 10, 15–16, 17; Bryan, "The Civil War in East Tennessee," 12–13, McKenzie, *One South or Many*, 55, 192.

centuated the differences that already existed between East Tennessee and most of the rest of the state.[41]

In the decade before the war, however, some of the differences related to slavery began to abate. For most of the antebellum period, East Tennessee looked to the North for its commercial contacts. With the advent of railroads in the 1850s, however, the region finally had a relatively easy connection with the markets of the southern Atlantic seaboard. The demand for the region's wheat crop enabled its farmers to finally have a cash crop to rival cotton and tobacco farther to the west, and actually fostered a growth in the slave population. Towns grew and sprouted up along the railroad line and contacts with and visitors from the lower South increased substantially. Concomitantly, the business and professional classes that prospered from those contacts had an interest in their continuation. The areas that the railroad did not touch did not experience this wave of prosperity or the contacts with the lower South.[42]

It is difficult to draw sweeping generalizations as to how these various factors made East Tennessee a bastion of Unionist sentiment and accordingly an unending source of trouble for the secessionists. As historian Noel Fisher has noted, "a large number of factors, including party affiliation, slaveholding, residence, political and personal conflicts in the antebellum period, and business contacts, influenced individual choices for or against the Confederacy."[43] Certainly, the economic and social investment in slavery was not as significant in East Tennessee, where only about 10 percent of the slaveholders of the state lived. Indeed, that number must have fostered a suspicion that many East Tennesseans were encouraged to feel by Andrew Johnson and his allies: that secession was a device by elitist slaveholders to create a government where the non-slaveholding common man would be unable to affect the interests of the slaveholders at the ballot box.[44]

With the remainder of the state carrying the issue in favor of secession, East Tennessee secessionists hoped that their Unionist compatriots would patriotically

41. Fisher, *War at Every Door*, 15–21; Patton, "Progress of Emancipation in Tennessee," 89–95; Winters, *Tennessee Farming, Tennessee Farmers*, 119, 135–37; Bryan, "The Civil War in East Tennessee," 13–16, 19–22.

42. W. Todd Groce, *Mountain Rebels: East Tennessee Confederates and the Civil War, 1860–1870* (Knoxville: University of Tennessee Press, 1999), 9–20, 29–45; Bryan, "The Civil War in East Tennessee," 23–24.

43. Fisher, *War at Every Door*, 173.

44. Atkins, *Parties, Politics and the Sectional Conflict in Tennessee*, 250–52; Bryan, "The Civil War in East Tennessee," 12; Crofts, *Reluctant Confederates*, 158.

accept the result and join the rest of the state in the Confederacy. But the East Tennessee convention resumed in Greeneville, although with a smaller number of Unionists. While debate raged on over exactly what stand to take relative to the action of the state government, eventually resolutions were passed that maintained that the action of the legislature was unconstitutional, and that delegates be sent to Nashville to petition the legislature to allow East Tennessee to itself secede from the state and remain in the Union. The legislature made a show of considering the request, but eventually laid it over to the body to take office in October 1861. But that new legislature never took up the issue. The section, largely unhappy, remained with the state within the Confederacy.[45]

Andrew Johnson did not appear at Greeneville. Sensing danger, he left his home in Greeneville soon after the June election and traveled to the North through the Cumberland Gap. There indeed appears to have been an effort to set Johnson up on a charge of treason, as a forged letter purportedly from Johnson to a friend in the North asking for money for arms was "intercepted" and sent to Harris. The *Richmond Enquirer* called for Johnson's arrest for treason. Johnson, perhaps anticipating a quick end to the war and the restoration of his political fortunes as a leader of the Tennessee Democracy, saw fit to write the *Nashville Union & American* to denounce the forgery, "perpetrated" to damage not only Johnson, but the Union Party of the state. In a speech at Lexington, Kentucky, Johnson charged that Tennessee secessionists were out to make the governor "King Harris." The senator denounced the secret actions of the legislature, claimed the vote on secession was coerced, and said before he would "submit to the Southern Confederacy & call Davis or Harris Master, he would yield to the Autocrat of Russia." As bitter and formidable an enemy as Johnson was, he was gone. Parson Brownlow and other Unionists remained, however, and Brownlow's columns were laced with the bitterest attacks against Confederate politicians, although he did not directly call for rebellion against the Confederate state government.[46]

Despite these verbal blasts, Harris resolved to treat East Tennessee with "for-

45. "The Election and Its Result," *Knoxville Daily Register,* June 11, 1861; Bryan, "A Gathering of Tories," 42–45, 47; White, *Messages of the Governors of Tennessee,* 5:311–15; "Division of the State," *Knoxville Whig,* July 13, 1861; Bryan, "The Civil War in East Tennessee," 62–63.

46. Temple, *East Tennessee and the Civil War,* 344; A. Johnson to A. Lawrence (forgery), June 6, 1861, 4 *PAJ* 484; A. Johnson to *Nashville Union & American,* June 30, 1861, 4 *PAJ* 527–28; "Speech at Lexington, Kentucky," 4 *PAJ* 437–38; E. Merton Coulter, *William G. Brownlow: Fighting Parson of the Southern Highlands* (1937; reprint, Knoxville: University of Tennessee Press, 1999), 160–62.

bearance and conciliation," in hopes that the people of the section would go along with the pro-secession result of the June 8 election. As a result, Harris was careful to keep Confederate troops in general and men recruited in West Tennessee away from East Tennessee. Even then, the governor suspected that many in East Tennessee "are bent on rebellion and desperate resistance to any attempt which may be made to put it down." Having trampled the state constitution in connection with Tennessee's departure from the Union, Harris recognized his authority in East Tennessee was limited to arrests that could be accomplished in his role as a military commander, presumably matters of open armed resistance. As governor, he had "no power over the punishment of crime, prosecution must come from a different quarter." Harris's policy of forbearance had two immediate consequences. First, it obviously left East Tennessee short of loyal troops to oppose invasion from a Federal force in Kentucky should the United States decide to violate the Commonwealth's "neutrality." Second, the governor was uncomfortable with Pillow instituting offensive moves into Missouri. While Harris favored an advance into Missouri as a means of bolstering Tennessee's defenses in the western part of the state, he delayed the movement until the policy of the Unionists in East Tennessee was "fully developed."[47]

The General Assembly reassembled on June 17 to act on the change of government ratified by the June 8 election. The Confederate flag flew over the Capitol. In the remaining two weeks of the special session, Harris proposed a number of small practical measures relating to Tennessee's new status as a Confederate state and the existence of hostilities with the North. The governor also submitted a list of nominations for a number of positions within the Provisional Army, including future generals John P. McCown, Alexander P. Stewart, William H. Jackson, and Bushrod R. Johnson.[48]

The uproar over secession and the entry into armed struggle did not alter the fact that an election was constitutionally required on the first Thursday in August 1861. Unionist sentiment at the first of that summer initially preferred, but

47. IGH to L. P. Walker, May 25, 1861, IGH to Pillow, June 20, 1861, IGH to Pillow, June 21, 1861, IGH to Pillow, June 30, 1861, IGH to Rowles et al., July 4, 1861, all in Harris Papers, TSLA; IGH to Thomas C. Lyon, August 19, 1861, under title "Gov. Harris and Tom Lyon," *Brownlow's Knoxville Whig and Rebel Ventilator,* January 9, 1864.

48. "Raising the Confederate Flag on the Capitol of Tennessee," *Nashville Union & American,* June 18, 1861; White, *Messages of the Governors of Tennessee,* 5:306–11, 317, 699; "Governor's Message," *Memphis Daily Appeal,* June 22, 1861.

did not nominate, former Governor William B. Campbell, while the secessionists suggested, but did not nominate, Harris. Late in June, the main Opposition newspaper in Nashville, the *Republican Banner*, proposed William H. Polk of Maury County, a brother of James K. Polk. Various reasons were given for proposing someone other than Harris, including a supposition that he would become a Confederate senator and the claim that Harris would be a divisive force in the effort to reconcile East Tennessee to secession, "as her people are *especially* embittered against him."[49]

Even without their candidate having announced his intention to run, Harris's supporters responded that the exigencies of the ongoing revolution and the new state of war required his experience and "comprehensive wisdom," and that he was "EMPHATICALLY THE REPRESENTATIVE MAN OF TENNESSEE." The argument was also advanced that Harris could not be replaced because of his work on the war effort. Indeed, argued the *Memphis Daily Appeal*, Lincoln, his cabinet, Andrew Johnson, and other Black Republican sympathizers would rejoice if Harris were not returned. Harris was also due the "opportunity of carrying forward to its consummation a policy of which he [was] the chief instigator." Finally, on July 17, the *Nashville Union & American* published a letter from Harris to Sterling Cockrill, a prominent secessionist, indicating that while he had originally intended not to run for reelection prior to the commencement of the war, he was willing to serve "this great cause" in any position. The governor's feelings of gratitude to his fellow-citizens and his sense of duty would "not allow me to decline a position accepted in time of peace, the duties of which have been rendered so highly responsible, important and arduous by a state of war."[50]

Although now a candidate, Harris declined to participate in the traditional campaign appearances across the state, as "the many responsible duties devolving upon the office, the proper discharge of which cannot be safely delayed, require my constant presence and attention at the Department." Combining the war effort with politics, Harris wrote to President Davis advocating that certain former Whigs, including Zollicoffer, be appointed to Confederate generalships. Polk picked up the support of the East Tennessee Unionists when their candidate

49. Campbell, *The Attitude of Tennesseans Toward the Union*, 210–11; White, *Messages of the Governors of Tennessee*, 5:319–22, 326 (quote).

50. "Our Next Governor," *Memphis Daily Appeal*, June 25, 1861; "Gov. Harris," *Memphis Daily Appeal*, July 7, 1861; "The Duty of the People of Tennessee," *Memphis Daily Appeal*, July 9, 1861; "Letter from Gov. Harris," *Nashville Union & American*, July 17, 1861.

proved to be ineligible for the office, Parson Brownlow's *Whig* noting that Polk would do the region justice, "the very thing that Harris and his party would never do." Also at issue in the election were the approval of the permanent Confederate Constitution and seats in the General Assembly, which would continue to have to pass on war measures. In the end, Harris was elected by a majority of over 31,000 votes, the constitution was ratified by a large margin, and a majority secessionist legislature was returned. The *Union & American* observed that Harris's majority was "sufficiently overwhelming to prove that, while he was faithfully attending to the Executive office, the people were taking care that his valuable services should be secured again to the State, as long as they may deem it important for him to serve them." Such was not the case in East Tennessee, where Polk won by a wide margin, which Parson Brownlow attributed to the fact that the people of that section "cherished towards Harris, hostility, deep and lasting, and not without cause." Nor was it necessarily the case in West Tennessee, where Harris's brother George W. D. Harris thought the campaign against his brother was particularly filled with falsehoods and misrepresentations.[51]

Harris's ultimate goal was to turn the state army over to the Confederacy. The problems created by the demand of the government at Montgomery that Tennessee place eight regiments into Confederate service confounded the governor in late May. The Rebel government only had enough muskets in the state to equip four of the regiments, and asked Harris to equip the others with "country rifles" and to make sure that the government muskets were distributed to Confederate troops. Harris initially thought that four of the regiments then in West Tennessee would be willing to enter the Confederate army, and made sure he mentioned that he supposed the government would attend to the subsistence, pay, and transportation of these troops. But while a number of the state troops were willing to go into the Confederate service, enough in each unit were not willing to do so, some indignant that they did not have the same weapons as the troops going to Virginia. In the days before the June 8 election Harris was unwilling to disorganize the Provisional Army by making drafts from its units to make up the new Confederate regiments. Seeing no point in keeping the Confederate government arms out of the hands of troops that could use them to defend the state, Harris requested that

51. "Letter from Gov. Harris"; White, *Messages of the Governors of Tennessee*, 5:329–32; IGH to J. Davis, July 13, 1861, Harris Papers, TSLA; J. Davis to IGH, July 17, 1861, 7 *PJD* 245–48; "The Election," *Nashville Union & American*, August 3, 1861; "The Election of Governor," *Knoxville Whig*, August 10, 1861; G. W. Harris to IGH, August 11, 1861, Harris Papers, TSLA.

the rule restricting the use of the muskets be relaxed, but never received a satisfactory answer.[52]

On June 24, Harris dispatched Landon C. Haynes with a letter to President Davis to send official notification of Tennessee's independence and to discuss transferring the Provisional Army of Tennessee to Confederate service, but got no response. On June 29, the legislature passed a joint resolution tendering the Provisional Army of Tennessee to the Confederate States. Again, Harris transmitted the tender to Davis, noting that "the provisional army of Tennessee is composed of twenty-two regiments of infantry, two regiments of cavalry, ten companies of artillery, engineer corps, ordnance bureau, &c." Finally, on July 5, the government responded, informing Harris that Confederate officers would receive muster rolls of the various units, and informing him that Major General Leonidas Polk, a former Tennessean and the Episcopal bishop of Louisiana, was now in command in that military department and would supervise the transfer. Ironically, Polk originally went to the Confederacy's new seat of government at Richmond because, in May, Harris had requested him to use his influence with old friend Davis to see to equipping the Tennessee troops and urge "prompt measures" to defend the Mississippi Valley.[53]

In the following weeks, Harris worked out the details of the Provisional Army's transfer to the Confederacy. One problem that the two governments encountered was that there were certain positions in the Tennessee army—"adjutant-general, quartermaster-general, surgeon-general, inspector-general, and commissary-general"—and their various assistants that were not recognized under Confederate law. The Richmond government promised to consider the displaced officers for similar posts, and requested that Harris give his recommendations. Another issue was the mountain of supplies accumulated for the provisioning of the Provisional Army and their transfer to the Confederacy, and the related issue of the Confederate government's reimbursing the state for the same. From his headquarters in Memphis, Polk weighed in on these and other issues, and joined sev-

52. L. Walker to IGH, May 20, 1861, IGH to Walker, May 25, 1861, IGH to Pillow, May 25, 1861, IGH to Pillow, May 28, 1861, IGH to Walker, May 28, 1861, IGH to Pillow, June 21, 1861, all in Harris Papers, TSLA; Connelly, *Army of the Heartland*, 29.

53. IGH to J. Davis, June 24, 1861, 7 *PJD* 210; OR Series 4, 1:411, 417; OR Series 1, 4:362–63; IGH to Pillow, June 30, 1861, Harris Papers, TSLA; William M. Polk, *Leonidas Polk, Bishop and General* (New York: Longmans, Green & Co., 1915), 1:353–55; Joseph H. Parks, *General Leonidas Polk, C.S.A.: The Fighting Bishop* (Baton Rouge: Louisiana State University Press, 1962), 166–67.

eral citizens in recommending the disappointed Gideon Pillow, now a Confederate brigadier, for major general.[54]

Rumors abounded. The press asserted that the process of assimilation was being delayed by Harris's insistence that his appointees be given preference in the Confederate service. Harris published a card denying this rumor and asserting that there was no strife or misunderstanding between the two governments. But Harris did say that he "shall continue to insist . . . upon having full justice done to the State in the general and staff appointments," although he had "not at any time doubted the disposition of the President to do ample justice to Tennessee and Tennesseans" in that regard. His political organ, the *Appeal*, asserted that the issues relating to the transfer of 25,000 men took time, and that Harris's efforts on behalf of his officers were to be expected. Consistently, on August 1, Harris sent the Confederate War Department a list of those appointed to positions in the Provisional Army, along with comments as to qualifications and who should not be reappointed. As he would later in the war, Harris sought to advance the interests of Tennesseans in the Confederate service. In his transmittal letter to the secretary of war, Harris informed the Confederate government he deemed it important that the Provisional Army be organized into units commanded by Tennesseans. But not all of Harris's appointments were honored, even at the highest rank, as two brigadier generals of the Provisional Army were not retained by the Confederate government.[55]

East Tennessee continued to simmer. Violence and intimidation on both sides persisted through the summer, and Harris's attitude toward the Unionists there began to harden. Polk and Harris recommended and the government appointed Brigadier General Felix K. Zollicoffer as the Confederate commander in East Tennessee. Zollicoffer was given a broad mandate to protect the vital railroad running through the region, guard against arms being smuggled to the disaffected Unionists, make efforts to reconcile the people of East Tennessee to the Confederacy, and, failing that, to prevent their organizing against the government. Zollicoffer warned the population that resistance to the Confederacy would not be tolerated, but then made assurances that if there were no resistance, they would not be disturbed by the government. While there were sporadic efforts to break up Unionist

54. OR 4:363–64, 371–76.

55. "Letter from Gov. Harris" and "Gov. Harris and the Transfer of the Provisional Army," *Memphis Daily Appeal*, July 24, 1861; IGH to Walker, August 1, 1861, with enclosure of officer list, Harris Papers, TSLA; OR 4:398.

organizations and some arrests, Zollicoffer pursued Harris's initial policy of avoiding a heavy hand in East Tennessee in the name of the Confederate government.[56]

In the first half of August, Harris made a trip to Richmond to confer with the government on East Tennessee and various other issues, but kept it secret. He arranged an appointment to confer with Zollicoffer, who was still technically under Harris's command, but asked him to *say nothing about it, as I have great horror of general or public attentions.* There is no record of Harris's discussions with the government, but it is likely that, in addition to the transfer of the army and the appointment of officers, the threat to Tennessee along the Kentucky state line was discussed. Before his trip, he addressed yet another letter to Governor Magoffin, protesting the organization and arming of Federal troops in the commonwealth. Harris thought Magoffin powerless to stop it in any event, and told Zollicoffer to take steps to "secure all the mountain passes so as effectively to prevent invasion as well as to arrest and crush out the first budding of organized rebellion." On August 16, Harris urged Secretary of War Walker to organize camps of instruction in East Tennessee, and urged the concentration of 12,000 to 14,000 men in that part of the state, noting that with more troops, he could enforce a more energetic policy. These steps were necessary, as "we can temporize with the rebellious spirit of that people no longer."[57]

The confused nature of the Confederate command structure in Tennessee no doubt taxed Harris in July and August. As noted above, Zollicoffer's East Tennessee command remained under Harris's supervision into August. And while Polk assumed command of his department in July, it only extended to the west bank of the Tennessee River. Effectively, the defense of Middle and East Tennessee remained in the hands of state authorities during that time. Harris wrote Zollicoffer on August 16 that he did "not think it at all probable that there will be any demonstration of a hostile character in Kentucky at any very early day if indeed there is at all." Taking no chances, though, the same day Harris complained to Secretary Walker that "having sent from Middle Tennessee 3 Regiments to East Tennessee, and 5 to West Virginia, and Genl. Polk and Genl. Pillow having moved some 6000 men from West Tennessee to Missouri, it leaves us very much exposed upon the

56. Fisher, *War at Every Door,* 41–50; Bryan, "The Civil War in East Tennessee," 71–72; S. R. Anderson to J. Davis, June 29, 1861, and J. W. Rogan to J. Davis, July 1, 1861, 7 *PJD* 218; OR 4:364–67, 374, 378.

57. IGH to Zollicoffer, August 4, 1861, IGH to Magoffin, August 4, 1861, Harris Papers, TSLA; OR 4:379.

Kentucky border, too much so if our Kentucky friends should attempt some hostile movement."[58]

The work on the forts blocking access to the state by means of the Tennessee and Cumberland rivers demonstrated Harris's dual expectation that there was no immediate threat from Kentucky and that the Confederate government would soon assume responsibility for the defense of the state. As noted above, Harris moved fairly quickly to dispatch officers to identify appropriate points for fortifications along each of the rivers. In mid-June, Colonel Augustus Heiman's 10th Tennessee Regiment began work on Fort Henry on the Tennessee, and a 32-pound smoothbore was mounted and test-fired by July 12. But at Fort Donelson on the Cumberland little work was done in July, although there were troops stationed in the vicinity of nearby Dover. The experience of Captain Jesse Taylor of the Provisional Army's artillery corps reflects the confusion created by the transfer of responsibility to the Confederate government. Around the first of September, Taylor was dispatched to Fort Henry because Harris feared there was no experienced artillerist at that post. Taylor thought the fort poorly positioned from a military standpoint, but when he reported it back to Harris and his staff, he was told that the position was chosen by competent military officers, which, given the limitations imposed by Kentucky neutrality that summer, was true. Taylor then scouted around and was amazed to discover from marks on the surrounding trees that the work was subject to flooding. Taylor's report to Nashville after this later discovery received the response that the defense of the area had been assumed by the Confederate authorities and to report the situation to them. While in the light of subsequent events this episode makes Harris and his advisors appear uninterested, the problem appears to have been caught in the transition from state to Confederate authority, a situation that naturally called for deference by state authorities.[59]

All during the summer of 1861, Harris had applied his considerable energy to the raising, equipping, and provisioning of an army and his political skill toward assimilating that army into that of the Confederate states, knitting old-line Whigs into the Confederate cause, and giving East Tennessee a chance to resign itself to

58. Connelly, *Army of the Heartland*, 43; IGH to Zollicoffer, IGH to Walker, August 16, 1861, Harris Papers, TSLA.

59. Bearss, "The Construction of Fort Henry and Fort Donelson," 28–30; Cooling, *Forts Henry and Donelson*, 14; Jesse Taylor, "The Defense of Fort Henry," in *Battles and Leaders of the Civil War*, ed. Robert U. Johnson and Clarence C. Buel (New York: The Century Co., 1881), 1:368–69.

its role as part of a Confederate state. Political calculation and military necessity had also driven the whole issue relating to Kentucky. Harris prodded Magoffin as to Kentucky's proclaimed neutrality and reminded him that Tennessee respected the same only so long as the Federal government did the same, while the state actually lacked sufficient armed troops to do much even if Kentucky became a Federal base. Because he could actually do little else, Harris played off of Kentucky's "neutrality" in order to buy time for the Confederate government to assume responsibility and arm the troops necessary to guard the state's northern border.[60]

Harris's political defense of that border came to naught in early September. Gideon J. Pillow, long a proponent of the move, urged Polk in late August to seize Columbus, Kentucky, noting its strategic position on the Mississippi, arguing "Kentucky neutrality is no longer regarded." Even as Pillow clumsily urged a Confederate advance into the Commonwealth, both President Davis and Governor Harris wrote Governor Magoffin to reassert the Confederate government's commitment to Kentucky's neutrality, and to express the hope that Kentucky would honor the concept in its relation with both warring powers. It was manifestly the intention of the Confederate government to continue Harris's policy toward Kentucky, although Harris recognized that affairs in Kentucky were so uncertain as to preclude an advance into Missouri. While Polk later claimed lack of specific information on the subject, it seems unlikely an officer commanding the department to which Kentucky neutrality was so important was ignorant of his government's policy.[61]

Demonstrating a propensity for self-willed action that would manifest itself again later in the war, Polk determined that regardless of the political consequences, military necessity demanded that he occupy Columbus on the Mississippi and Paducah at the mouth of the Tennessee before the Federals beat him to it. On the night of September 3, forces under Pillow moved into Kentucky and ad-

60. OR 4:531; IGH to Magoffin, August 30, 1861, Harris Papers, TSLA; see also Magoffin to IGH, August 12, 1861, Magoffin Papers, LC. In his dissertation on Harris, George Wayne Watters concludes that in the transition from state to Confederate direction of military affairs, each "assumed the other was taking proper actions." Watters, "Isham Green Harris," 99. Historian Larry Daniel has the more accurate view that Harris repeatedly sought direction from Richmond during this period. Daniel, "In Defense of Governor Isham G. Harris," 77.

61. OR 3:686–87; OR 4:180, 399; Davis to Magoffin, August 28, 1861, 7 *PJD* 310; IGH to Magoffin, August 30, 1861, Harris Papers, TSLA; Polk, *Leonidas Polk*, 2:18–19; Steven E. Woodworth, "'The Indeterminate Quantities': Jefferson Davis, Leonidas Polk, and the End of Kentucky Neutrality, September, 1861," *Civil War History* 38 (December 1992): 289–91.

vanced on Columbus. A horrified Harris notified Davis of the move, and appealed to him to withdraw the troops. He also quickly dispatched three commissioners to Frankfort to attempt to repair the situation, and sent a message to Magoffin that the move had been "without my knowledge or consent, and, I am satisfied, without the knowledge or consent of the President." Davis ordered Secretary of War Walker to direct Polk to withdraw, and to ask Harris to inform Magoffin of the order.[62]

Despite Harris's best efforts to restore a pillar of his strategy to defend Tennessee from the North, the damage was done. A little known Union brigadier, Ulysses S. Grant, moved quickly to seize Paducah, and Unionists in the Kentucky Senate passed a resolution against the Confederate incursion. After over ten days of indecision, Davis finally determined to accept Polk's claim of military necessity. But, on September 10, the president placed a layer of authority over Polk by naming General Albert Sidney Johnston as commander of Department No. 2, which encompassed the entire state of Tennessee as well as surrounding areas. Johnston went to Nashville to confer with Harris, and arrived in the capital to the great joy of its inhabitants. Once there, the new commander decided since the political question was effectively answered by the action of the Kentucky legislature, there was no going back, a conclusion with which Harris likely concurred, although his "dissatisfaction" no doubt lingered for some time. Acting on what was seen at Richmond and in Nashville as necessity, Johnston then ordered Confederate troops to advance to Bowling Green, Kentucky, even as Zollicoffer occupied the Cumberland Gap.[63]

While Tennessee's strategic situation became much more difficult with the need to defend the line established in Kentucky, Johnston's arrival and assumption of command relieved the governor of what remained of his military responsibilities, except those of tidying up the loose ends of the transfer of the Provisional Army to the Confederacy and the Confederate military's continued pleas, requests, and demands for support of all kinds. The state's Herculean effort to field, equip, supply, and pay an army from virtually nothing had been, given the circumstances, quite successful. But it had also been expensive, and even as the

62. OR 4:179–81, 189–90; IGH to Magoffin, September 4, 1861, Harris Papers, TSLA; IGH to Davis, September 4, 1861, endorsement of Davis to Walker, 7 PJD 325; Davis to Polk, September 5, 1861, 7 PJD 327.

63. OR 4:190–91, 192–94, 402–4; Johnston, *The Life of General Albert Sidney Johnston*, 292, 306–7; Woodworth, "'The Indeterminate Quantities,'" 292–97; Connelly, *Army of the Heartland*, 52–55, 64–65.

official date of transfer of July 31, 1861, came and went, ongoing expense and past debt began to catch up. During August and September, Harris and the Military and Financial Board fought on two fronts, the first to continue supply soldiers who were now the Confederate government's responsibility, and the second to get funds from the general government to reimburse the state and avoid a collapse of its credit.[64]

Amid editorial expressions of hope that it would not stay in session long, the new legislature convened in Nashville on October 7, 1861. Harris sent the assembly a message on all that had transpired since Lincoln's election, and the "disregard of the rights and privileges of the people" by the Republicans. Harris extolled the state's remarkable achievement relating to the creation of the Provisional Army, the patriotism of the men who rushed to the standard, and the competent job of organization performed by the officers. Harris also gave account of the expenditures of the Military and Financial Board, and the transfer of military supplies and procurement contracts to the Confederate government. The governor described the need to divide the state into Confederate congressional districts, and the need for financial conservatism in light of the war. If the state were at peace, the various issues relating to the state banks might need attention, but were not "deemed appropriate" at that time because of the war. Indeed, very little else but the war was deemed significant, and the domestic issues discussed by Harris related to the war, such as speculation and profiteering.[65]

One of the few significant actions of the regular session of the General Assembly in the fall of 1861 was an act passed to declare all white males between the ages of eighteen and forty-five as the state's Reserve Military Corps, while white males from forty-five to fifty-five were a Military Corps "for the defence of the State." This was an expansion of the authority of the Act of May 6, 1861, under which, on August 7, Harris had called for the organization of thirty thousand men as a Reserve Corps. Additionally, the General Assembly approved another issue of state bonds, created an Ordnance Bureau, and confirmed an additional list of officers. With the exception of arranging for Tennessee's representation in the Confederate Congress, the session accomplished very little, as even a measure to suppress the fraud and profiteering that Harris called to the legislature's attention was laid on the table. Suggested as a candidate for one of the Confederate

64. OR 4:401–2, 406, 410–11, 431, 436, 441, 446; OR 52(2):130, 140–41, 159–60.
65. "A Brief Session," *Nashville Union & American,* October 6, 1861; see also "The General Assembly—Short Session," *Memphis Daily Appeal,* November 8, 1861; White, *Messages of the Governors of Tennessee,* 5:332–50.

senator positions, Harris felt it his duty to remain in his newly reelected position as governor. No doubt on account of the press of war business, Harris's inauguration ceremony was a short affair, as was his inaugural address: "Gentlemen of the Convention: Having been elected to the office of Governor for another term, I am here to take the oath of office, which I am now ready to do."[66]

Even though the normal machinery of the state government effectively remained in stasis on account of the war, Harris continued his exertions to meet the military necessities of the Confederate forces protecting the state. Dismayed by the weakness of his new command, Johnston called on Harris for an additional thirty thousand volunteers on September 21. The Confederate government's inability to arm the men it had continued to be a problem, so Johnston requested that the volunteers that assembled be asked to bring their own weapons. Johnston expressed a preference for volunteers who would volunteer for the duration of the war, but his need was so great men who only enlisted for a twelve-month period would be accepted. According to the *Nashville Union & American*, Tennesseans for some reason had a "prejudice" against volunteering for more than twelve months. On September 26, Harris issued a call for an additional thirty thousand volunteers, saying that "volunteers for the war are greatly preferred, but will be accepted for the term of twelve months." Initial indications appeared to be that a sufficient number of volunteers would appear, but that proved not to be the case. In mid-October, the governor thought it necessary to address problems created by the call with the president. Harris predicted it would be difficult to raise the new force without some promise they would be appropriately armed. He also asked for the return of the Tennessee regiments then in Western Virginia, and predicted dire consequences should the Confederate line in Kentucky fail. Harris thought a winter campaign in Kentucky would put the Federals on the defensive and thereby protect Tennessee and inspire the new recruits.[67]

The state and Confederate government still struggled over the details relating to the organization of the Tennessee troops, as to both the new levies and those

66. White, *Messages of the Governors of Tennessee*, 5:351, 355–57, 701–2; Frank Moore, ed., *The Rebellion Record: A Diary of American Events* (New York: G. T. Putnam, 1863), 2:489; "Confederate States Senator," *Nashville Union & American*, October 16, 1861; "Tennessee Legislature," *Memphis Daily Appeal*, November 5, 1861.

67. OR 4:417–18, 442, 449–50; "Confederate Volunteers for the War," *Nashville Union & American*, September 21, 1861; "Proclamation," September 27, 1861; "Tennesseans to the Rescue" and "Response to the Governor's Proclamation," *Nashville Union & American*, September 29, 1861; "Three Cheers for Giles," *Nashville Daily Gazette*, October 12, 1861.

raised in the original Provisional Army. Considerable correspondence passed between Harris's state headquarters and the adjutant general's office in Richmond as to the proper numbering and designation of the regiments, and the "confusion . . . caused by having several regiments with the same designation." Harris detailed the new state adjutant general, W. C. Whitthorne, just back from service in Virginia, to report on the status of the Tennessee troops. After straightening matters out as best he could, Whitthorne concluded that the power to alleviate the confusion lay with the Confederate War Department.[68]

Harris continued to receive reports on the inadequacy of the garrisons and armaments of Fort Henry and Fort Donelson, the defense of the latter being critical to that of Nashville itself. It was a "matter of general remark" in the city that its defenses needed to be "*considerably* strengthened." Harris also made sure that Johnston was aware that a large portion of Tennessee's iron industry was in the area. In late October, Johnston assigned his chief engineer, Major J. F. Gilmer, "for the purpose of determining upon the most eligible sites for the erection of such works as will completely defend the city from all approaches of the enemy by means of the river." Johnston supposed that slave labor would be available to erect the fortifications, but the Confederate government was disappointed in its efforts to get laborers. Gilmer and Johnston sought Harris's aid in mobilizing sufficient labor, but at the end of December Harris was forced to admit: "I must say that the response to my appeal for laborers has not thus far been as flattering as I had wanted and expected." Harris hoped to mobilize as many as six hundred, but Gilmer thought a thousand were necessary, and even that many laborers would take two or three months to get the works constructed. Gilmer's predicted interval would prove to be insufficient. Not wanting to leave a stone unturned, in early December, Harris endorsed a letter from prominent citizens to Albert Sidney Johnston to encourage the construction of a gunboat on the Cumberland. But after analyzing the issue, Gilmer determined that time and available materials made the proposition unachievable, concluding "the best reliance for defense will be batteries ashore, in combination with such obstructions as may be devised in the channel under the guns of the works."[69]

On the eastern flank of Johnston's front, Zollicoffer occupied a thin front in

68. V. Groner to IGH, November 11, 1861, November 25, 1861, Harris Letterbook, Harris Papers, LC; OR 52(2):211–12; "General Order," *Nashville Union & American,* December 7, 1861; William S. Speer, *Sketches of Prominent Tennesseans* (Nashville: Albert B. Tavel, 1888), 48.

69. A. Heiman to IGH, October 18, 1861, Harris Papers, TSLA; "City Defenses," *Nashville Union & American,* September 18, 1861; "Defences on the Tennessee and Cumberland," *Nashville Union*

Kentucky with about 3,500 men, while the rest of his only partially armed and organized troops remained in East Tennessee to watch the Unionists and guard the railroad line. During the early fall, Zollicoffer conducted fairly successful raids against Union positions in his area, but was repulsed at Wildcat Mountain in October. Late that month, fearful of a Federal advance, he shifted his focus toward the Cumberland Plateau, in order to cover all possible Federal avenues of advance into East Tennessee. While Zollicoffer planned his defense from without, unrest continued within. The situation was exacerbated by a more heavy-handed policy from the Confederate government toward Unionist sympathizers, although even that policy was to a large degree ineffective. On the Federal side, a plan to come to the aid of the loyal East Tennesseans resulted in a plan to facilitate an anticipated Federal invasion by destroying a number of railroad bridges between Bridgeport, Alabama, just to the west of Chattanooga, and Bristol, on the Virginia state line. The Federal army did not advance into the state, but some of the bridges were burned, resulting in significant disruption of communication along the rail line. In response, the Confederate government dispatched heavy reinforcements to that part of the state, summarily executed four of the conspirators, and arrested and eventually banished Parson Brownlow to Federally controlled territory.[70]

Harris received a warning in late October from the president of the East Tennessee and Georgia Railroad that a "Lincoln force" was organizing in Zollicoffer's rear in East Tennessee, waiting only for a Federal advance to strike. Harris was further warned that the Unionists were in full contact with Federal forces in Kentucky, and that "there is no giving way in the hostile feeling in East Tennessee. This you may rely on and time will convince you." When the bridge burners struck, Johnston urged Harris "to use every exertion to ascertain the extent, power and organization of this insurrection if as I fear one exists, and most urgently I press your excellency to leave no means untried to put arms into the hands of your unarmed levies." Harris responded on November 12 with a message

& *American*, November 10, 1861; OR 4:476, 506–7, 557–58; OR 7:741, 748–49, 757, 794–95; OR 52(2):229; Gilmer to Whitthorne, January 4, 1862, Harris Letterbook, Harris Papers, LC.

70. James W. McKee Jr., "Felix K. Zollicoffer: Confederate Defender of East Tennessee, Part I," *East Tennessee Historical Society Publications* 43 (1971): 35, 48–58; OR 4:476–77; OR 7:740; Fisher, *War at Every Door*, 50–60; David Madden, "Unionist Resistance to Confederate Occupation," *East Tennessee Historical Society Publications* 52–53 (1980–81): 22–39; "Latest News From the South," *Philadelphia Inquirer*, November 21, 1861.

to President Davis informing him that he would be sending ten thousand men, all he could arm, to the region, and again requesting the return of the Tennessee troops in Virginia. In the end, meting out justice to the conspirators and the general security of the region became the responsibility of the Confederate War Department, which in mid-December appointed a new commander over Zollicoffer, Major General George B. Crittenden.[71]

On the Western end of the line, the Union's energetic Brigadier General Ulysses S. Grant dispatched a small force down the Mississippi from Cairo, Illinois, to raid Belmont, Missouri, across the great river from Polk's heavily fortified post at Columbus, Kentucky. Launching his attack on November 7, 1861, Grant achieved an initial success, but Confederate reinforcements and the skillful use of the larger-caliber guns in the Columbus works drove the Federals back in a near rout. Grant's aggressive move, however, made the Confederate military nervous, and a few days later, Polk, Pillow, and Johnston requested that Harris call out the state militia, fearing an invasion by one force down the Mississippi and another toward Nashville.[72]

The call for the militia came in the wake of weeks of difficulties attending Harris's September call for volunteers. At the root of the problem was the continual shortage of arms. Because of the shortage, it was the policy of the Confederate government not to arm troops that had volunteered for only twelve months in favor of men who had enlisted for three years or the duration of the war. On November 3, Johnston informed Harris of that policy, and also told him that unarmed troops enlisted for the shorter period would be disbanded. Harris protested, believing it would have a demoralizing effect, and stated he could arm the men, even if only with sporting guns, if given time. Johnston agreed to suspend his order for an interval, and informed the government of his action. The scare of mid-November induced the general government to lift Johnston's ban, although the ban on arming the short-term men with Confederate government weapons stayed in effect. For his part, Harris made a proclamation requiring the incoming volunteers to bring weapons with them. The governor also made appeals to the public for "every effective double barrel shot gun and sporting rifle which they have." In each instance, the government would pay the owner the value of the weapon. On November 20, the General Assembly passed a law that established

71. OR (Series II) 1:835–36, 838, 841, 848–56.

72. Nathaniel C. Hughes Jr., *The Battle of Belmont: Grant Strikes South* (Chapel Hill: University of North Carolina Press, 1991), 36–37, 78–177; OR 4:560–61, 564–65; OR 7:690, 703–4.

a state ordnance bureau to acquire and manufacture weapons, ammunition, and accoutrements. It also required militia men to bring weapons when called, empowered Harris and his agents to seize weapons, and fixed a method for providing compensation.[73]

Weapons were not the only problem, however. Some volunteers that fall decided they wanted to join regiments of the original Provisional Army, for whom a few months had expired from their original term of enlistment. Harris issued an order prohibiting this practice, providing that such volunteers would be placed into the new units. Another problem was that some companies formed in connection with the September call did not have the minimum number of men required by law, which Harris prohibited. Harris also called on the commanders of the various camps of instruction to provided detailed information relative to the new levies, and required that before new units were received at the camps, the Confederate supply officers would be able to supply the troops with the necessary camp equipage and subsistence.[74]

With these problems, it is not surprising that as of mid-November, the September call for thirty thousand troops resulted in a turnout of not more than ten thousand new recruits. Therefore, the militia call requested by Johnston, which was issued on November 19, 1861, was also for thirty thousand men. Officers of the militia divisions in Middle and West Tennessee were to have their men ready to march on November 25, "unless in the meantime a sufficient number of volunteers shall have tendered their services to fill this requisition." On November 25, Harris issued a follow-up order to clear up a misconception that volunteers would not be accepted from militia companies after that date, providing that if volunteers came from a particular unit, that unit would be credited with those men, as twelve-month men were "much preferred" to militia.[75]

The suggestion of coerced military service and the unfortunate use of the

73. Connelly, *Army of the Heartland*, 94–95; OR 4:505, 518, 553, 558, 565; "Proclamation by Isham G. Harris," *Nashville Union & American*, November 7, 1861; "Arms for our Volunteers," *Nashville Union & American*, November 12, 1861; "To the People of Tennessee," *Nashville Union & American*, November 14, 1864; "To the Owners of Guns," *Nashville Daily Gazette*, November 14, 1861; "To the People of Tennessee," *Memphis Daily Appeal*, November 15, 1861; *Public Acts of the State of Tennessee, 1861–1862*, chapter 55; "Tennessee Legislature," *Nashville Union & American*, November 21, 1861.

74. "Special Order No. 8," *Nashville Union & American*, October 15, 1861; "General Orders—No. 10," *Nashville Union & American*, October 29, 1861.

75. "Arms for our Volunteers," *Nashville Union & American*, November 12, 1861; "General Order No. 12," *Nashville Union & American*, November 20, 1861; "Call for the Militia—Governor Harris'

term *draft* by the *Union & American* resulted in some unrest. The *Nashville Daily Gazette* published a series of articles claiming that a draft impugned the honor of the state and suggested that such a means of raising troops was a device of tyranny. On December 1, 1861, the *Gazette* piously declared, "Draft the people of Tennessee, and the name of the present Executive of the State, *Isham G. Harris,* becomes forever infamous, and justly a by word and a reproach." The *Gazette* also published letters from anonymous citizens complaining that state workers and those with army contracts were being unfairly exempted from service, and that doctors were giving false certificates of exempting medical conditions.[76]

The apparent inconsistency of the government in seeking to disband unarmed volunteers for lack of arms and then the militia call "caused considerable feeling in certain quarters, and much exasperation." There were incidents of unrest in at least Nashville and just to the south in Williamson County, and it was reported in a Northern newspaper that Harris stayed in his hotel room "under strong guard, for fear of assassination by the incensed people." But in the end, by its own admission, the *Gazette* was almost alone in its criticism. The *Banner,* quick to note "we have never been an ardent advocate of Gov. Harris, or his measures," pointed out that the emergency declared by Albert Sidney Johnston must first be addressed, and there would be "time enough to settle our account with Gov. Harris, if we have any to settle." The *Union & American,* while confessing confusion as to the previous orders of the Confederate War Department to disband the twelve-month regiments, noted Harris was only responding to Johnston's call. It explained that while "an increase in the volunteer force was preferable," the emergency at hand called for a quicker means of raising troops, "hence the propriety of such an order as would meet the emergency, and at the same time furnish such of our citizens as preferred enlisting in the volunteer service an opportunity of doing so." The *Patriot* observed that the difference between the time the volunteers were disbanded and the time the militia was called was that in the latter instance, the state gov-

Proclamation," *Memphis Daily Appeal,* November 22, 1861; "General Order No. 13," *Nashville Union & American,* November 26, 1861.

76. "Volunteers," *Nashville Union & American,* November 23, 1861; "The Call for the Militia," *Nashville Union & American,* November 24, 1861; "Tennessee Patriotism," *Nashville Daily Gazette,* November 28, 1861; "Must the Odium Endure?" and "It was Unnecessary," *Nashville Daily Gazette,* December 1, 1861; "Read It," *Nashville Daily Gazette,* December 2, 1861; "The Difference," *Nashville Daily Gazette,* December 5, 1861; "Army Contracts," *Nashville Daily Gazette,* November 28, 1861; "Attention Militia," *Nashville Daily Gazette,* November 30, 1861.

ernment had the power to impress private firearms. Harris, stated the *Patriot*, was simply acting as the agent of the Confederate government in responding to Johnston's call. In the end, opined the *Memphis Daily Appeal*, the call was a failure, as the "manner of the detail was an insult, and therefore, regarded as a thing not of patriotism, but oppression."[77]

Demonstrating that the government at Richmond still did not appreciate the situation, in late December Polk asked for authority to arm twelve-month men, but Secretary of War Judah Benjamin dismissed the request, noting they were "immensely expensive and utterly useless." Unfortunately, almost all of Harris's volunteers were twelve-month men. Polk's command, for example, including the critical points at Forts Henry and Donelson, had eight regiments of twelve-month men. Benjamin went so far as to order the dissolution of one unarmed regiment, which Johnston was quick to address, as it ignored the practicalities of the situation in Tennessee. Benjamin relented, and asked Whitthorne to relay an apology to the governor for the government's reaction. Benjamin asked that Whitthorne "tell [Harris] that if he knew the incessant and ingenious attempts to force by indirection the acceptance of twelve months unarmed men against the steady refusal of the department, he would not be surprised at any effort to repress promptly such disingenuous practices."[78]

By raids, troop movements, and sham advances, Johnston kept the larger masses of the Federals from testing his thin line during the late fall and early winter of 1861. On the other hand, the Confederates were continually fearful of Federal advances, and Johnston was particularly concerned with an attack on his position at Bowling Green. Of course, Johnston's greatest problem was a lack of armed troops, and he complained to the War Department on Christmas Day that while the governors in his area had "seconded his appeals," the response was less

77. "Some time ago, Gov. Harris," *Nashville Patriot*, December 1, 1861; "The Militia," *Nashville Patriot*, December 3, 1861; "Old Williamson All Right," *Nashville Union & American*, December 10, 1861; Moore, ed., *The Rebellion Record*, 4:25; "The Nashville Daily Press," *Nashville Daily Gazette*, December 4, 1861, see also "A Mistaken Haste," *Nashville Daily Gazette*, December 5, 1861, reprint from the *Memphis Argus*; "The Call for the Militia," *Nashville Union & American*, December 4, 1861, reprint from the *Nashville Banner*; "Gov. Harris and the Militia," *Nashville Banner*, December 1, 1861; "The Militia—Its Organization," *Memphis Daily Appeal*, December 18, 1861.

78. OR 7:795, 798, 807, 822–28; Connelly, *Army of the Heartland*, 91, 94–95; M. H. Wright to W. C. Whitthorne, December 10, 1861, A. S. Johnston to IGH, December 10, 1861, A. S. Johnston to W. C. Whitthorne, January 13, 1862, and J. P. Benjamin to W. C. Whitthorne, January 16, 1862, all in Harris Letterbook, Harris Papers, LC.

than was desired. A letter the same day to Harris detailed Johnston's concerns relative to Federal intentions and implored that Harris "forward . . . every man at your disposition." Johnston also made sure to thank Harris for "the energetic and efficient co-operation which I have received from you and Tennessee since I assumed command."[79]

Harris replied on New Year's Eve, detailing the difficulties he faced in mobilizing men. He proudly noted that as of that date, Tennessee had mobilized or was mobilizing enough men to field sixty-six units of infantry, artillery, and cavalry. The governor wrote that Middle and West Tennessee had contributed the bulk of those men, which was an "immense tax" on the population of those sections. No doubt exasperated by the uproar of the previous weeks, Harris observed that the problem was not men, but weapons. The state's supply of arms was exhausted by the prior levies, and unlike certain of her sister states, Tennessee "had no United States arsenal or depository of arms within her limits from which her troops might have been supplied."[80]

The year 1861 demonstrated the depth of Harris's commitment to the secessionist cause, the energy and intellect that he applied to further that cause, and the extralegal (if not illegal) lengths he was willing to go to in order to make sure Tennessee was firmly aligned with the cause. From the beginning of the year, his principal goal was to guide Tennessee into the Confederate fold. With the exception of his miscalculation that led to the defeat in the February referendum, Harris was able to correctly gauge the political currents that resulted in the majority vote approving Tennessee's "independence" and alignment with the Confederacy in May and June. Indeed, Harris was able to ride the rising tide of secessionist sentiment to trample on the Tennessee Constitution and ignore the checks and balances on precipitous changes to that document contained therein. As Oliver P. Temple observed, Harris's "ability, daring and exceeding aggressiveness" gave the governor "immense power," which he used with great effectiveness for the secessionist cause.[81]

Once aligned with the Confederacy, Harris relentlessly mobilized the state

79. Connelly, *Army of the Heartland*, 75–77; OR 7:792–95.

80. OR 7:811–12. On January 28, 1862, Whitthorne reported that "volunteering has about ceased," especially in Middle Tennessee. W. C. Whitthorne to A. S. Johnston, January 28, 1862, Harris Letterbook, LC.

81. Temple, *East Tennessee and the Civil War*, 217.

for war, working to create a military organization for the defense of the state that could easily be integrated into the Confederate service. Historian Thomas Connelly has rightly recognized Harris for his role in creating the core of the Confederate Army of Tennessee, to the extent of stating that if any man could claim to be its "father," that man would be Harris. But Connelly criticized Harris for creating a number of problems for the Confederacy as it assumed the role of defending the state. Among the matters Connelly faults Harris for include "haste" in taking Tennessee out of the Union, the governor's purported overconfidence in his defense strategy, a failure to establish a proper working relationship with the Confederate government, and the inability to quell unrest in East Tennessee.[82]

On the whole, these criticisms are unfair. While Harris actually had much to do with hastening the state out of the Union, he was acting no more hastily than the authorities of the other states of the upper South. Indeed, if Harris had waited too long, the secessionist passion of the spring and early summer of 1861 may have cooled, and the opportunity for Tennessee to join the Confederacy lost. Likewise, Harris's defense strategy did not betray overconfidence so much as it recognized that the most immediate threat to the state as it armed itself for war came from the rivers that ran on a north-south axis, a recognition that ultimately proved true in 1862. While Harris had hope that Kentucky's "neutrality" would serve as a long-term protection to the state, it in fact served to protect that quarter until weeks after the Confederate government assumed responsibility for its defense, and the protection that Kentucky's "neutrality" afforded, uncertain though it may have been in the long run, was most certainly lost by men acting under the authority of the Confederate government.[83]

Connelly also faults Harris for failing to establish a proper working relationship with the authorities in Richmond. But the historical record is replete with evidence that Harris tirelessly sought to coordinate the state's military efforts with those of the Confederacy. The state's three most organized and trained regiments went to Virginia in the spring of 1861 at the request of the Rebel government and stayed there while the threat to Tennessee grew. After a prodigious undertaking to raise and equip a state army to turn over to the Confederacy, a process that severely strapped the financial resources of the state, Harris and his officials spared no effort to have the state army transferred to the new national authority. The

82. Connelly, *Army of the Heartland*, 25, 44–45.

83. Daniel, "In Defense of Governor Isham G. Harris," 74–79. Kermit L. Hall, "Tennessee," in *The Confederate Governors*, ed. W. Buck Yearns (Athens: University of Georgia Press, 1985), 194.

Confederate government time and time again made calls on Tennessee for more armed men, yet its own policy hindered Harris's efforts to satisfy those calls.[84]

It is also difficult to see what more effective measures Harris could have taken in East Tennessee. It should be recalled that he enjoyed significant support in that section of the state in the elections of 1857 and 1859, and it is likely he did not deem the people of the area a lost cause for the Confederacy. Although it seems strange in light of his complete disregard of the state constitution, Harris also felt legal constraints in dealing harshly with the people there, as there was no open rebellion until the bridge burners made their move in November 1861. From that point, East Tennessee became a military problem for the Confederate government.

While Harris's efforts were not perfect, when the balance is struck it appears that the raising, mobilization, and equipping of the Provisional Army of Tennessee gave the Confederacy a significant early advantage that the Confederate government was either unable or unwilling to build upon. While it is unclear how long Kentucky's "neutrality" would have lasted, it certainly would have been more difficult for the Federal government to disregard if Polk had stayed south of the state line in September 1861. Confederate military authorities had plenty of time from the late summer of 1861 to the winter of the next year to build adequate fortifications on the Tennessee and Cumberland rivers, but failed to do so. Keeping armed Tennesseans needed to defend Tennessee in Virginia and failing to arm men willing to serve in Tennessee was ultimately the fault of Jefferson Davis's government, not that of Green Harris.

The lull the Confederates enjoyed along the line defending Tennessee from the north lasted until January 19, 1862. Finding Zollicoffer in an advanced position on the north side of the Cumberland River in southeastern Kentucky, the new Confederate commander in that region, Major General George B. Crittenden, ordered an attack on Federal forces at Logan's Crossroads, near a stream known as Fishing Creek. The ensuing battle, known by the name of either geographic feature, or by that of Mill Springs, was a Confederate disaster, resulting in a rout of Crittenden's small division and the death of Zollicoffer. The eastern flank of Johnston's line had, for all practical purposes, ceased to exist, as Crittenden's diminish-

---

84. Connelly gives Harris and his officials due credit for the raising and organization of the Provisional Army, as well as its fine logistical support. Connelly, *Army of the Heartland*, 45.

ing force retreated back across the state line to Livingston, and then Gainesboro, on the Cumberland River. Johnston informed Harris of the defeat on January 22, after reading an account in a Louisville newspaper. Reports then began to stream in to Harris from Knoxville as to the details and extent of the disaster.[85]

Gloom pervaded in Nashville as Zollicoffer's remains lay in state in the House of Representatives chamber in the Capitol at Nashville. There, a large number of persons paid respect to the fallen hero, who lay with his sword across his "faultlessly arranged" uniform. On February 2, Zollicoffer's war-horse accompanied the funeral procession to Nashville's Old City Cemetery, where Bishop James H. Otey conducted Episcopal burial services. The same day, Union troops embarked on their transports at Cairo, Illinois, and began their trip south up the Tennessee River to Fort Henry. The long-feared Northern invasion of Tennessee was at hand.[86]

85. James W. McKee Jr., "Felix K. Zollicoffer: Confederate Defender of East Tennessee, Part II," *East Tennessee Historical Society Publications* 44 (1972): 17, 27–40; Connelly, *Army of the Heartland,* 97–99; OR 7:103–4; "Battle on Fishing Creek!" and "Death of Gen. Zollicoffer," *Knoxville Daily Register,* January 24, 1862; A. S. Johnston to IGH, January 22, 1862, and G. Monseratt to IGH, January 23, January 24 (2), January 25 (2), 1862, all in Harris Papers, TSLA.

86. Ridley, *Battles and Sketches of the Army of Tennessee,* 41; Raymond E. Myers, *The Zollie Tree* (Louisville: The Filson Club Press, 1964), 128–29; OR 7:126, 579–80.

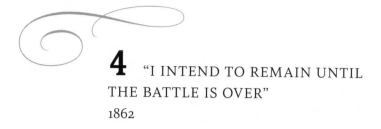

4 "I INTEND TO REMAIN UNTIL THE BATTLE IS OVER"
1862

Accompanied by a strong force of gunboats, Federal Brigadier General Ulysses S. Grant sailed two divisions of his command up the Tennessee. A winter of confused and often lackadaisical effort on the part of the Confederate military relating to the defenses on the Tennessee resulted in the fall of Fort Henry on February 6, 1862, after a relatively short engagement with the Union gunboats. Captured with the token garrison left to surrender the fort, the unfortunate Captain Jesse Taylor saw his warning of the previous year vindicated. A Federal boat literally sailed into the fort from the overflowing river to accept its surrender. With Fort Henry reduced, marauding Federal gunboats sailed upriver as far as Florence, Alabama, severing the railroad between Nashville and West Tennessee and doing a great deal of other damage to materiel and morale.[1]

Faced with the reality of the loss of Fort Henry, on February 7, Harris communicated the situation as he knew it to Secretary of War Benjamin, and called for reinforcements to defend Tennessee "from Cumberland Gap to Columbus." That same day, however, the Confederate high command in the West met at Bowling Green. The military chiefs decided that Federal control of the Tennessee River, coupled with the belief that Fort Donelson was "not long tenable," required the withdrawal of Polk's force at Columbus back into Tennessee and the force at Bowling Green south of the Cumberland. The generals also recognized the possibility of further retreat, south out of Tennessee altogether.[2]

It is unclear exactly when Harris was informed of these conclusions, but it

---

1. Stephen D. Engle, *Struggle for the Heartland: The Campaigns from Fort Henry to Corinth* (Lincoln: University of Nebraska Press, 2001), 45–59; Edwin C. Bearss, "The Fall of Fort Henry," *West Tennessee Historical Society Papers* 17 (1963): 85–107; Taylor, "The Defense of Fort Henry," 371; OR 7:122–24, 153–57.

2. OR 7:860–62.

was probably no later than the following day, as he advised Johnston to remove the army's meat stores at Nashville farther south. But it was not the governor's intention to relinquish Nashville without a fight. On February 10, as Grant waited for the muddy roads from Fort Henry to Fort Donelson to dry, Harris petitioned the government at Richmond for ten thousand small arms, confidently claiming that he could put a force that large into the field "instantly." Secretary Benjamin replied the next day, noting that arms and reinforcements were on their way, urging Harris to "do your best and we will spare no effort."[3]

Having no control over events at Fort Donelson, Harris's best would not be enough. While the Bowling Green force toiled its way toward Nashville, Harris's ally Gideon J. Pillow and Brigadier General John B. Floyd reinforced the fort, in hopes of holding it long enough for the Bowling Green column to get safely south of the Cumberland. Pillow concluded, or at least gave Johnston the impression, that the fort could be held. Pillow's staff officer John C. Burch wrote Harris with details of the surrender of Fort Henry, emphasizing that Donelson "*will not be surrendered.*" The repulse of an attack by the dreaded Federal gunboats on February 13 and again on the 14th appeared to confirm Pillow's evaluation, but diverted attention somewhat from the arrival of the bulk of Grant's army. During the course of the fighting, Pillow dispatched several optimistic messages to Harris, the last on February 13 reporting that the garrison had "injured the gun boat materially" and "repulsed the enemy everywhere." Finally concluding late on February 14 that the true threat to the Rebel position was Grant's land force, Floyd ordered an attack for the morning of the 15th, which opened a route of escape. Indecision on the part of Floyd and Pillow frittered away this opportunity, and early on February 16, the decision was made to surrender the fort.[4]

In Nashville, the populace was disturbed by the news of the evacuation of Bowling Green. This unease was compounded by the sight of unusual movements in the Commissary and Ordnance departments, "it being argued that if the authorities thought it prudent to remove the public stores, they could not regard Nashville as entirely safe." Nonetheless, the reports from Donelson were all of Confederate success, especially against the fearsome gunboats. Dispatches during the day on Saturday, February 15, all reflected impending Rebel victory, and

3. Connelly, *Army of the Heartland,* 135; Cooling, *Forts Henry and Donelson,* 116–21; OR 7:869, 872.

4. Cooling, *Forts Henry and Donelson,* 138–39; Connelly, *Army of the Heartland,* 117–25; Burch to IGH, February 9, 1862, and Pillow to IGH February 11, 12, and 13, 1862, Harris Papers, TSLA.

the majority of the populace expected to awaken the next day with news of further success.[5]

By this point in time, Albert Sidney Johnston was in the Nashville suburb of Edgefield, just north of the city across the Cumberland River. That day, Harris sent a message to Johnston, urging reinforcement of the troops at the fort and offering the full support of the state authorities. Having received the effectively the same glowing intelligence as the general populace concerning the events of February 15, Johnston went to bed believing that Floyd and Pillow won a great victory that day. That false impression was shattered shortly after 5:00 a.m. the morning of February 16, when news of the fort's surrender awakened Johnston. Understanding that Nashville was defenseless, Johnston issued orders for the troops from Bowling Green, under Major General William Joseph Hardee, to move southeast to Murfreesboro.[6]

The governor was likely advised of the disaster near the same time as word reached Johnston. Harris rode across to Edgefield to consult with the army commander. As Harris later reported to the General Assembly, "I called upon General Johnston to tender to him all of the resources of the State which could be made available, with my full co-operation in any and all measures of defense of our State and Capitol." Harris purportedly told Johnston that if he would defend Nashville, he would mobilize "ten or twenty thousand additional troops from Tennessee within a few days." Johnston replied that unarmed, untrained, and undisciplined troops were useless. "Your first duty, Governor, is to the public trusts in your charge." Johnston advised Harris to remove the state's archives and records, and gave orders to facilitate their transportation. "The Legislature," Johnston said, "can also adjourn to some other place. You can do no further good here now, and I think you should take the public archives under your especial charge."[7]

Harris quickly concluded that without Johnston's aid, "it would have been

5. J. Miller McKee, "The Evacuation of Nashville. The Panic that Succeeded the Fall of Fort Donelson—Incidents Connected with the Surrender of the City," in *The Annals of the Army of Tennessee and Early Western History*, ed. Edwin L. Drake (Nashville: A. D. Haynes, 1878), 219–24.

6. OR 7:883; Connelly, *Army of the Heartland*, 127, 132–33.

7. White, *Messages of the Governors of Tennessee*, 5:365–66; "Gov. Harris and the Evacuation of Nashville," *Chattanooga Daily Rebel*, September 13, 1862; "Gov. Harris and the Defense of Chattanooga," *Chattanooga Daily Rebel*, September 16, 1862; Johnston, *The Life of Gen. Albert Sidney Johnston*, 499.

worse than folly" to attempt the capital's defense, although an order went out to
the local militia commander to "call out the entire force" under his command and
hold it subject to Johnston's orders. The governor acted rapidly to move the state
government out of the doomed city. At the Capitol, anxious members of the General Assembly convened in an emergency session and appointed a committee to
communicate with the governor. They reported that Harris intended to convene
the legislature in Memphis on February 20, and a vote was taken to meet upon
that call. Harris then issued a proclamation for the members of the General Assembly to assemble at Memphis on that date, "for the dispatch and transaction of
such business as may be submitted to them."[8]

The rapid fall of the city later gave birth to an unfavorable rumor concerning
the governor. In the weeks and months following the evacuation, published reports appeared stating that, upon receiving the news of the fall of Fort Donelson, Harris galloped through the streets of Nashville "proclaiming to every body
the news that Donelson had fallen; that the enemy were coming and might be expected hourly, and that all who wished to leave had better do so at once." These reports were eventually branded as a "malicious fabrication without the semblance
of truth" in two articles published the following September in the *Chattanooga
Daily Rebel*, which relied on "gentlemen of high character and intelligence who
were in Nashville" to tell the true story "in justice to Gov. Harris." The *Rebel* assured its readers of Johnston's "unbounded confidence" in Harris, and that the
governor, "though willing to make a stand and fight for Nashville, yielded to the
judgment of General Johnston and acted upon his advice" to evacuate.[9]

Regardless of their source, the rumors of the disaster on the Cumberland soon
reached the bewildered populace of Nashville, and a number of "anxious inquir-
ers" appeared at Harris's office, seeking definitive word on the extent of the crisis.
Harris, doubtless fully employed with the job of moving the state government
and its records to Memphis, declined to issue a proclamation. A special train was
procured to convey the state archives out of the city, and that afternoon Harris,
his department heads, and a number of the legislators boarded the train, which
headed southward. Later that evening, the train stopped in Columbia, about forty
miles south of Nashville, where Harris and Adjutant General Whitthorne ad-

8. White, *Messages of the Governors of Tennessee*, 5:364, 367; OR 7:887.

9. "The Nashville Panic," *Knoxville Daily Register*, March 16, 1862; "Gov. Harris and the Evacuation of Nashville," *Chattanooga Daily Rebel*, September 13, 1862; "Gov. Harris and the Defense of
Chattanooga," *Chattanooga Daily Rebel*, September 16, 1862.

dressed a large crowd. Whitthorne, a resident of Columbia, darkly advised his fellow citizens to "flee and follow them and burn every building and every blade of grass and to leave a devastated waste before the invading foe."[10]

Arriving in Memphis, Harris dispatched a message on February 18 to President Davis advising him of the fall of Fort Donelson and the imminent loss of Nashville. Asking for the government's plans, Harris stated that he would "rally all the Tennesseans possible and go with them myself to our army." The same day, he issued a proclamation to the people of Tennessee, announcing the removal of the government to Memphis and calling for volunteers to repel the Yankee invasion. Seeing his duty in terms of his role as commander in chief of the state's forces, Harris stated he would be leaving "the officers of the State to the immediate discharge of their duties," while he would "repair to the field . . . [of] battle where the fortunes of all are to be lost or won."[11]

On February 20, both Johnston and Beauregard sent messages to Harris asking that he go to Jackson to confer with Beauregard. When he received Beauregard's message, Harris declined, as he was preparing to return to Nashville within an hour or two. Beauregard answered, suggesting Harris take a special train to Jackson for the meeting, and then take another to Corinth, Mississippi, to intercept the Nashville train he planned to take. Harris accordingly met with Beauregard for an hour, during which the general communicated his decision to evacuate Polk's troublesome fortress at Columbus, Kentucky. Beauregard asked Harris to convey his desire that Johnston concentrate his forces at Corinth. Harris then traveled to Corinth, and then on to Nashville, staying in the crumbling capital until at least the morning of February 22. He then followed the army to Murfreesboro, where he delivered Beauregard's message to Johnston.[12]

At Murfreesboro, Harris began a practice that he continued through the war: rallying the Tennessee troops. Joining the army at Murfreesboro was the 20th Tennessee Infantry, veterans of the Confederate disaster at Mill Springs just over

10. McKee, "The Evacuation of Nashville," 226; Jill K. Garrett and Marise P. Lightfoot, eds., "Excerpts from the Diary of James W. Matthews," in *The Civil War in Maury County, Tennessee* (Columbia, Tenn.: Privately published, 1966), 126; William J. Andrews, "In the Days of the Past," in *Maury County, Tennessee Historical Sketches* (Columbia, Tenn.: Privately published, 1967), 40.

11. ORN, Series I, 22:824; *Memphis Daily Appeal*, February 20, 1862.

12. Johnston, *Life of Gen. Albert Sidney Johnston,* 506; OR 7:895–96; Alfred Roman, *The Military Operations of General Beauregard,1861–1865* (New York: Harper & Brooks, 1883), 1:506; James A. Hoobler, ed., "The Civil War Diary of Louisa Brown Pearl," *Tennessee Historical Quarterly* 38 (Fall 1979): 308, 318.

three weeks before. Harris and Whitthorne made speeches "to encourage [the men] in the sadness they felt in leaving their homes, friends and State, to the mercies of an advancing foe." While the speeches were no doubt appreciated, the historian of the regiment recalled that they were "unnecessary," for when the orders came to march, "we fell into line like soldiers and patriots and left all behind, many of us to return no more."[13]

At the end of February, Johnston, at Beauregard's urging, decided to unite Hardee's former Bowling Green force with Polk's Columbus men and reinforcements from the Deep South at the important rail junction of Corinth, Mississippi. While Harris noted after the war that he was with Johnston during most of the time from the retreat from Nashville to the concentration at Corinth, indications are that Harris went some distance from the army during the month of March 1862. While he was certainly in Memphis for part of that time, early in the month Harris availed himself of an opportunity to remove "a portion of my negroes and plantation stock" to the relative safety of a farm he rented in Clarksville, Texas. Presumably he kept Johnston and Beauregard advised of his whereabouts, because on March 7, the governor sent a message from Clarksville to Major General Earl Van Dorn, Johnston's deputy in the Trans-Mississippi, to the effect that Beauregard had telegraphed Harris to ask Van Dorn to move his troops to join the Creole on the Mississippi. On that date, Van Dorn was far west of the Mississippi, fighting the Battle of Pea Ridge in northwest Arkansas, and would not join Beauregard until April.[14]

By March 24, the governor was back in Memphis, writing Jefferson Davis to

13. W. J. McMurry, *History of the Twentieth Tennessee Regiment Volunteer Infantry, C.S.A.* (Nashville: The Publication Committee, 1904), 203.

14. Connelly, *Army of the Heartland*, 138–39; Harris to C. T. Quintard, December 29, 1894, Quintard Papers; Johnston, *Life of Gen. Albert Sidney Johnston*, 731; White, *Messages of the Governors of Tennessee*, 5:369; Edward M. Coffman, "Memoirs of Hylan B. Lyon, Brigadier General, C. S. A.," *Tennessee Historical Quarterly* 18 (March 1959): 52; U.S. State Department, *Papers Relating to Foreign Affairs Accompanying the Annual Message of the President to the First Session, Thirty-Ninth Congress, 1865,* Part III (Washington, D.C.: Government Printing Office, 1866), 528; OR 8:771; Arthur B. Carter, *The Tarnished Cavalier: Major General Earl Van Dorn, C. S. A.* (Knoxville: University of Tennessee Press, 1999), 53–63, 69–71. The conclusion the farm was rented stems from the fact that the records of Red River County, Texas, do not reflect that Harris owned a farm there. But, there is an account that the governor of Missouri rented a farm in that area for his slaves in 1862, indicating either that the account is wrong as to which governor, or that more than one governor thought it was a good idea. Author's telephone conversation with Red River County Clerk's office, May 30, 2006; Pat B. Clark, *The History of Clarksville and Old Red River County* (Dallas: Mathis, Van Nort & Co., 1936), 181.

advise him of the General Assembly's act of March 18, 1862, authorizing the mobilization of the "whole military strength of the state" and the transfer of any part of the state force to the Confederate army for a period of twelve months. Repeating his appeal to Secretary Seddon the month before, Harris pleaded for ten thousand small arms he understood had been landed at Charleston, as he had "exhausted the guns of my state."[15]

The act to which Harris referred was an amendment of the militia law originally passed in October 1861, and was introduced on February 13, while events were taking their course at Fort Donelson. In his legislative message of February 20, Harris recommended passage of the measure, noting that the amendment "will not only enable the Executive to fill promptly all requisition made by the Confederate Government upon Tennessee for her just proportion of troops but also give full power to discipline for efficient service in the field the whole Military Strength of the State." The act's comprehensive nature gave reason for some pause, although the difficulty of assembling a quorum of the General Assembly in Memphis delayed its passage as much as the reservations of skeptics in that body. Several amendments were introduced, and the bill bounced back and forth from one house of the legislature to another. The editors of the *Knoxville Register* doubtless reflected some of the skepticism of the act's opponents, sensibly noting that without the necessary arms and equipment, Harris's *levee en masse* might do more harm than good, taking men from their farms during spring planting. "Place this vast, heterogeneous, undisciplined, unarmed, unfed and unmilitary mass of men in the field and it will melt away like snow in the spring." The *Register* called for a "less suicidal and more efficient means" to aid the cause. Notwithstanding reservations of this nature, the General Assembly passed the law one day before it adjourned, as it turned out, for good, at least as a Confederate entity. Like the October version of the law, the entire white male population of the state between the ages of eighteen and forty-five was subject to military service, but in this instance could be called up by the state in anticipation of transfer to the Confederate army. The troops so raised were to be commanded by the governor so long as they remained in state service, but any requisition upon the state by the Confederate government would be filled.[16]

Turning from the military to the financial on March 28, Harris wrote

15. Harris to Davis, March 24, 1862, Harris Papers, TSLA. See *Public Acts of Tennessee, 1861–62*, chapter 26.

16. White, *Messages of the Governors of Tennessee*, 5:351, 368–70; "The Call for the Militia," *Knoxville Daily Register*, February 28, 1862.

Christopher G. Memminger, the Confederate secretary of the treasury, relative to Tennessee's contribution to the government's war tax. Harris reported that the only means of raising the funds assessed was to issue state bonds, but that the state was "paralyzed" with the "presence of an invading army," which would delay the governor's making the necessary negotiations. "Therefore the only possible assurance that I can give you at this time is that all that is possible for me to do in the matter shall be promptly done."[17]

Harris was in Memphis until at least April 1, when he wired Johnston at Corinth that he would see the general the next day. Johnston named the force at Corinth the Army of the Mississippi, effectively designating the component parts from Columbus, Bowling Green, and the Gulf Coast as corps under their familiar commanders. Approximately twenty-three miles away, back across the Tennessee state line at Pittsburg Landing, Ulysses S. Grant massed approximately 30,000 troops, with another 20,000 or so nearby, in preparation for a move against the Memphis & Charleston Railroad. Both sides expected about 25,000 men of Major General Don Carlos Buell's Army of the Ohio to join Grant from Middle Tennessee in a few days, so the Confederates determined to strike the Federals at Pittsburgh Landing before that junction occurred.[18]

Moving out on the morning of April 3, the Rebels intended to attack the morning of April 5. Unfortunately, the raw troops' lack of discipline and the narrow roads, made more difficult by a rainstorm on the night of April 4, caused a day's delay of the attack to the morning of April 6. Upon his return to the army, Harris assumed the role of a volunteer aide to Johnston, but availed himself of the opportunity to address Colonel William B. Bate's 2nd Tennessee on April 3 on the coming battle. While Harris rode along the Rebel lines with Johnston around mid-day of April 5, a scout informed the general that there were a good many more Federals at Pittsburg Landing than were expected. After what appeared to the governor to be a moment of profound thought, Johnston turned to Harris and fiercely said: "I would fight them if there is a million of them! I have as many men as can be well handled on this field, and I can handle as many men as they can." That night, Harris took supper with an old friend, Colonel Christopher H. ("Kit") Williams of Memphis and four other members of the 27th Tennessee Infantry. In the distance, the bands of the unsuspecting Federals in the camps near Pittsburg Landing were

17. Harris to Memminger, March 28, 1862, Harris Papers, TSLA.

18. IGH to A. S. Johnston, April 1, 1862, Fort Donelson/Lloyd Tilghman Files, Eleanor S. Brockenbrough Library, Museum of the Confederacy; Wiley Sword, *Shiloh: Bloody April* (1974; reprint, Dayton, Ohio: Morningside, 1988) 35–44, 92–97; OR 10(2):49–52, 370–71; OR 10(1):385, 567.

heard playing national airs. The next day, Williams and all but one of Harris's dinner companions were killed or wounded.[19]

Harris was doubtless up before dawn on the "remarkably bright and beautiful" morning of April 6. Gathered at headquarters with Johnston were corps commanders Major General Braxton Bragg, Major General William J. Hardee, Beauregard, and others. Hearing the opening guns about a half mile away in the forest, Johnston rode forward just before dawn on his fine thoroughbred, Fire Eater, leaving Beauregard in charge at army headquarters. In his capacity as a volunteer aide, Harris appears to have accompanied Johnston throughout the morning, as the army commander rode about urging his troops forward.[20]

In the early afternoon, the Rebels encountered what Harris termed an "obstinate stand" on the Confederate right, near the famous Peach Orchard. Elements of Major General John C. Breckinridge's Reserve Corps were directed to assault the area in an effort to turn the Federal left. At some point, Breckinridge rode up to Johnston and complained that a Tennessee regiment of Colonel Winfield S. Statham's brigade "won't fight." The regiment, the 45th Tennessee, was an inexperienced unit, raised in November 1861. Instead of advancing, the regiment remained sheltered behind the crest of a small hill, and only isolated groups would advance to a fence line and fire at the enemy instead of the entire unit. When he heard Breckinridge complain, Harris asked which command it was, and requested permission from Johnston to go to the regiment. Johnston agreed, and Harris aligned the men in an appropriate fashion. Johnston then ordered preparations for a charge, and Breckinridge expressed doubts that the unit would make the charge. Johnston said, "Then, I will help you." "We can get them to make the charge." Harris, having returned to report that the 45th was finally in line, was sent back to the Tennesseans to encourage them to charge.[21]

19. OR 10(1):385–6; Alexander P. Stewart, "The Army of Tennessee: A Sketch," in *Military Annals of Tennessee: Confederate*, ed. John Berrien Lindsley (1886; reprint, Wilmington, N.C.: Broadfoot, 1995), 1:72–73; IGH Compiled Service Record, M-331, NA; Jill K. Garrett, ed., *Confederate Diary of Robert D. Smith* (Columbia, Tenn.: Captain James Madison Sparkman Chapter, UDC, 1997), 10; OR 5:1079 (Bate's men ordered to Tennessee from Virginia); Johnston, *The Life of General Albert Sidney Johnston*, 569–70; John M. Taylor, "Twenty-Seventh Tennessee Infantry," in Lindsley, ed., *Military Annals*, 1:418–20.

20. OR 10(1):403; Sword, *Shiloh*, 147–48; Larry Daniel, *Shiloh: The Battle That Changed the Civil War* (New York: Simon & Schuster, 1997), 144–45; IGH to William Preston, April 6, 1862, Series 1, Box 13, Folder 140, SNMPA (this document is a typescript of a letter Harris wrote that evening in William Preston's pocket notebook, now in the National Archives).

21. OR 10(1):404; Johnston, *The Life of General Albert Sidney Johnston*, 610–11; Civil War Cen-

Harris observed that "Gen. Johnston rushed in front of the line of battle, rallied the troops, ordered and led the charge." Breckinridge and his staff led troops in the advance on another portion of the line. And, riding among the 45th Tennessee and dismounting, the governor pulled his pistol, harangued the men "in a few stirring, thrilling words," and then joined the assault, advancing "from a half to three fourths of a mile." According to an account in the *Memphis Daily Appeal*, it took three assaults for the 45th to prevail. Elsewhere on the line, Harris observed the 19th Tennessee deliver and receive a fire that he later said "was as heavy as any he had heard, and as heavy as any in the war." The Confederate assault as a whole was a success, turning the flank of Brigadier General Stephen A. Hurlbut's division.[22]

With the 45th advancing, Johnston moved forward with the rest of the line, and sat on Fire Eater alone about in the center of the Rebel line. Resuming his role as Johnston's aide, the governor rode up, "elated with his own success and with the vindication of his Tennesseans." In Harris's view, Johnston, too, was happy, as the commander's "face expressed a soldier's joy and a patriot's hope." Johnston remarked, "Governor, they came very near putting me *hors de combat* in that charge," showing Harris where a ball had ripped the sole off his boot. Harris asked if Johnston was wounded, and was told "no." The discussion was interrupted by the fire of a Federal battery, and Johnston dispatched Harris to order Statham to assault the battery.[23]

Harris delivered the order, and returned to Johnston, who was sitting alone under a large oak tree, and reported, "General, your order is delivered and is being executed." As Harris spoke, he saw Johnston reel in his saddle, and the governor steadied the general with his arm. Pulling close to Johnston, Harris looked him in the face and asked, "General, are you wounded?" Johnston replied in "a very deliberate and emphatic tone," "Yes, and I fear seriously." Harris and Johnston's

---

tennial Commission, *Tennesseans in the Civil War* (1964; reprint, Knoxville: University of Tennessee Press, 2000), 1:273–74.

22. IGH to Preston, April 6, 1862, Series 1, Box 13, Folder 140, SNMPA; Johnston, *The Life of General Albert Sidney Johnston*, 611, 613; "Gen. Albert Sidney Johnston," *Confederate Veteran* 3 (March 1895): 86; "Gov. Harris in the Field," *Memphis Daily Appeal*, April 9, 1862; W. J. Worsham, *The Old Nineteenth Tennessee Regiment, June, 1861–April, 1865* (Knoxville: Paragon Printing, 1902), 39; Sword, *Shiloh*, 260–70; Daniel, *Shiloh*, 218–25.

23. Johnston, *The Life of Gen. Albert Sidney Johnston*, 613–14.

quartermaster, Captain W. L. Wickham, held Johnston on either side and guided his horse from the crest of the hill to a ravine, where the army commander was lifted from his horse and laid on the ground. Harris dispatched Captain Wickham for the first surgeon he could find, and then to go on and locate Dr. D. W. Yandell, the army's medical director. Harris also sent a nearby soldier for any member of the general's staff that could be found. Harris searched for wounds, and found a wound in the right leg from which the general was "bleeding profusely."[24]

Johnston never spoke another word. Harris poured a small amount of brandy in his mouth, which the general swallowed, but he could not repeat the procedure. Just as Johnston was taking his last breath, his aide, Colonel William Preston arrived, and was present when the general expired. Harris and Preston agreed that Preston would convey Johnston's body to headquarters, and that Harris should report the death to Beauregard, who was now in command of the Army of the Mississippi. At about this time, Harris's nephew, Pink, the son of his brother James, rode up and said, "Uncle Isham, Father has just been killed." Major James Trousdale Harris of the 15th Arkansas was the second Harris on the field of Shiloh to lead troops with a drawn pistol that day, but unlike his brother, who escaped unscathed, the major was killed. To compound the family's loss, William R. Harris's son John Clinton Harris was also killed in the battle. Harris later said that he "learned just there that there was a wide difference between war on paper and war on the field."[25]

Since his own horse wandered off when Harris dismounted, the governor mounted Fire Eater, but found that he was wounded, so he rode him to a point where an orderly was keeping two fresh horses, and proceeded to report to Beauregard. Harris expected to find Beauregard, who had been in ill-health since Harris had seen him at Jackson in February, in his ambulance at headquarters in the rear. But Beauregard was off near Shiloh Church. At about 3:00 p.m., Harris located the general and advised him of Johnston's demise. After expressing regret, Beauregard stated, "Everything seems to be going on well on the right." Harris

24. IGH to Preston, April 6, 1862, Series 1, Box 13, Folder 140, SNMPA; D. W. Reed to Basil Duke, July 20, 1906, Series 1, Box 13, Folder 140, SNMPA; Johnston, *The Life of Gen. Albert Sidney Johnston*, 614.

25. Johnston, *The Life of Gen. Albert Sidney Johnston*, 614; OR 10(1):404, 581; William R. Harris family monument at Elmwood Cemetery, Memphis, viewed by author June 15, 2006; W. Thomas Cardin, "History of Pisgah," in *Flournoy Rivers' Manuscripts and History of Pisgah*, comp. Clara M. Parker and Edward Jackson White (Pulaski, Tenn.: n.p., n.d.), 20.

agreed, and Beauregard said "the battle may as well go on." Harris replied that "he certainly thought it ought." Harris then rode away, but soon returned and said to Beauregard, "I came here as a volunteer aide to General Johnston; as he has fallen I no longer have any duties to perform. I intend to remain until the battle is over, and would like to be useful, if there are duties you can assign me to." Harris's offer was "courteously accepted."[26]

By dark that night, both sides were exhausted. Convinced that Grant was whipped, Beauregard sent a telegram to Richmond that evening announcing both Johnston's death and a "complete victory." Likewise, Harris took time to send a similar dispatch to the Memphis Daily Appeal, in which the governor reported: "We have had a hard fought battle, and our victory is complete—Relative loss not known, but it is heavy on both sides." But even in victory, the Army of the Mississippi was wounded and disorganized, and the men suffered in a heavy rain during the night and under intermittent shelling by two Federal gunboats on the Tennessee River. The Rebels would discover the next morning that not only was Grant not completely whipped, but he had fresh troops on the field, including significant elements of Buell's Army of the Ohio.[27]

Beauregard was misled by a dispatch that placed Buell too far away to relieve Grant. Therefore, he was unpleasantly surprised by "a hot fire of musketry and artillery" at about 6:00 a.m. on the morning of April 7. The Confederates were slowly pressed back, out of the Federal camps that they had occupied the night before in apparent triumph. Harris again assumed his role of aide to Beauregard and morale-builder to the Tennesseans. On one occasion during the day, he conveyed an order from Beauregard to Colonel Robert F. Looney of the 38th Tennessee to make a charge on the Federals. At another point, Brigadier General S. A. M. Wood of Alabama, while waiting in reserve, noticed Beauregard and a gentleman who he later determined was Governor Harris among a couple of regiments to his right, and recorded that Harris "made them a speech."[28]

Beauregard initially hoped for reinforcement by fresh Confederate troops from

26. Johnston, The Life of Gen. Albert Sidney Johnston, 615–16; Roman, The Military Operations of General Beauregard, 1:297, 537; OR 10(1):387.

27. OR 10(1):384, 387; Knoxville Register, April 11, 1862; Sword, Shiloh, 364–82; Daniel, Shiloh, 262–66; T. Harry Williams, P. G. T. Beauregard: Napoleon in Gray (1955; reprint, Baton Rouge: Louisiana State University Press, 1995), 140–43.

28. OR 10(1):387, 594; Marcus J. Wright, "Thirty-Eighth Tennessee Infantry," in Lindsley, ed., Military Annals, 1:505.

Arkansas. But when he was told the troops were still miles away, it became apparent that the army was in danger of being overcome by exhaustion and overwhelmed by the fresh Federal troops. Harris pulled Colonel Thomas Jordan, Beauregard's chief of staff, aside, and asked if Jordan "did not regard the day as going against us irremediably, and whether there was not danger in tarrying so long in the field as to be unable to withdraw in good order." Jordan agreed, and moments later, spoke to that effect to Beauregard, who had doubtless already determined "to withdraw from so unequal a conflict." Orders were accordingly dispatched, and the Army of the Mississippi began to pull off the field, falling back to Corinth as successive lines of defense covered the retreat. Harris accompanied Beauregard and one of his aides back to Corinth, where they arrived late that night.[29]

The ferocity of the fight and the horrific casualties suffered profoundly affected both sides. But, for the Confederates, the failure at Shiloh cut short the anticipated counteroffensive to recover the losses of the previous winter. There would be no triumphant return for Harris to Nashville for the foreseeable future, and what was left of West Tennessee was now in danger of Union occupation. On a personal level, Johnston's death in the governor's arms, coupled with the news of his brother's death, were blows from which Harris apparently never recovered. It would be thirty-four years before the governor would return to that bitter field.[30]

The Confederate defeat at Shiloh frustrated the hope that the territory lost to the Federal breakthrough in the winter of 1862 would be restored to the Confederacy. To varying degrees, Federal control spread across West and Middle Tennessee, although Confederate cavalry units, guerrillas, and bushwackers continued to operate in those areas while the main field armies faced each other across the state line in Mississippi. Still convinced that the secessionists were a minority in Tennessee, Abraham Lincoln moved quickly to establish a government in Nashville that loyal Union men could rally to. While there were other potential candidates, in the end Lincoln chose the one man available to him who had unquestioned loyalty to the Union, the prestige of having formerly sat in the governor's chair, and the stubborn fortitude necessary to undertake the job. Late in the eve-

29. OR 10(1):388; O. Edward Cunningham, *Shiloh and the Western Campaign of 1862*, ed. Gary D. Joiner and Timothy B. Smith (New York: Savas Beatie, 2007), 364–65; Thomas Jordan, "Notes of a Confederate Staff Officer at Shiloh," *The Century Illustrated Monthly Magazine* 29 (November 1884–April 1885): 633–34; Roman, *The Military Operations of General Beauregard*, 1:533.

30. Engle, *Struggle for the Heartland*, 161–65; Reed to Duke, July 20, 1906, SNMPA.

ning of March 12, 1862, Andrew Johnson returned to Nashville as the new Federal military governor of Tennessee. Clothed with wide powers, Johnson was tasked to restore a state government loyal to the United States.[31]

Johnson moved quickly against prominent secessionists within his reach, and obtained indictments for treason against Harris, S. R. Anderson, and Pillow on June 2. But because he believed that the people of Tennessee had been swayed from their true Union path by a virulent minority of Rebels, he pursued a mild policy against the rebellious populace of Middle and West Tennessee, ironically similar to that pursued by Harris in East Tennessee in the summer of 1861. As Harris before him, Johnson eventually found that the greater portion of the population was indeed in sympathy with the enemy, if not actively supporting him, and, like Harris, began to take more active measures against the resistance to his government that in the end did little to change the hearts of the majority.[32]

Two groups in Middle and West Tennessee benefited from the Federal occupation, although not without some difficulty. Unionists recovered a tenuous influence over the government, as it was the policy of the Lincoln government to reestablish a loyal government in Tennessee as quickly as possible. Seeds of future discord were sown when leading Middle and West Tennessee Unionists, former Whigs, clashed with Johnson over the harsher policy he pursued as 1862 wore on. The other group that obviously benefited was the African American slaves of the invaded and occupied areas. With peacetime legal processes suspended, the old slave code eventually became unenforceable as local officers' powers were suspended by Federal military orders. As a result, the very structure of slavery began to rapidly decay, even though some Federal officers in the first months of the occupation actually returned escaped slaves to their owners. Nonetheless, a signifi-

31. Peter Maslowski, *Treason Must Be Made Odious: Military Occupation and Wartime Reconstruction in Nashville, Tennessee, 1862–1865* (Millwood, N.Y.: KTO Press, 1978), 22–26; Introduction, 5 *PAJ* xxxii–xxxvii; Nathan K. Moran, "'No Alternative Left': State and County Government in Northwest Tennessee During the Union Invasion, January–June, 1862," *West Tennessee Historical Society Papers* 46 (1992): 13, 26–33; Stephen V. Ash, "Sharks in an Angry Sea: Civilian Resistance and Guerrilla Warfare in Occupied Middle Tennessee, 1862–1865," *Tennessee Historical Quarterly* 45 (Fall 1986): 217, 218–21.

32. Maslowski, *Treason Must Be Made Odious*, 53–57, 74–80; Walter T. Durham, *Nashville, The Occupied City: The First Seventeen Months—February 16, 1862, to June 30, 1863* (Nashville: Tennessee Historical Society, 1985), 151; Ash, "Sharks in an Angry Sea," 218–20; Noel C. Fisher, "'Prepare Them for My Coming': General William T. Sherman, Total War, and Pacification in West Tennessee," *Tennessee Historical Quarterly* 51 (Summer 1992): 75, 76–77.

cant percentage of slaves within Union lines, perhaps as many as 20 percent, ran away from their owners. The Federal authorities would struggle with the exact legal status of these "contrabands" for months to come.[33]

For almost a month after the Battle of Shiloh, the two armies lay in their respective cantonments at Pittsburg Landing and Corinth. In that interval, the Confederate defenses on the Mississippi suffered another loss as the fortress and garrison at Island No. 10 in extreme northwest Tennessee surrendered the night of April 7–8, 1862. This effectively put Memphis close to the front lines, as its defense was now based on the battered Army of the Mississippi at Corinth and Fort Pillow, sited on bluffs above the Mississippi about thirty-five airline miles upriver from Memphis.[34]

Harris was back in Memphis by April 12, issuing an order for a state official to track down what happened to arms supplied by the state when the Confederate government provided new weapons for a body of Tennessee troops. The *Memphis Daily Appeal* for April 18 expressed gratitude to the governor for a synopsis of the Conscription Act passed by the Confederate Congress two days previously. Among its provisions was the drafting of soldiers already in the army for another two years of service, although the men were given the consolation of electing their officers in the new organization. Harris returned to the army and spoke on the subject to a very large audience of volunteer soldiers at Colonel Robert M. Russell's headquarters the evening of April 30 for about an hour, followed by another speaker. One observer noted, "I think the speeches both had a good effect for the southern Cause." This may have been one of several speeches Harris gave on the subject, as on May 2, Major General Hardee requested Harris to address his troops at the governor's "earliest convenience."[35]

On May 3, 1862, the Federal force at Pittsburg Landing, now effectively an army group under the direction of the overall Union commander in the West, Major General Henry Wager Halleck, moved out from Pittsburg Landing in a slow

33. Maslowski, *Treason Must Be Made Odious*, 19–20, 80–82, 98–100; John Cimprich, *Slavery's End in Tennessee, 1861–1865* (Tuscaloosa: University of Alabama Press, 1985), 31–45; Nathan K. Moran, "Military Government and Divided Loyalties: The Union Occupation of Northwest Tennessee, June 1862–August 1862," *West Tennessee Historical Society Papers* 48 (1994): 91, 93–97.

34. OR 8:89; 10(1):776–77.

35. Executive Order, April 12, 1862, Harris Papers, TSLA; Memphis *Daily Appeal*, April 18, 1862; Ann York Franklin, comp., *The Civil War Diaries of Capt. Alfred Tyler Fielder, 12th Tennessee Regiment Infantry, Company B, 1861–1865* (n.p., 1996), 48; Roy to IGH, May 2, 1862, Harris Papers, TSLA.

advance toward Beauregard's works around Corinth. Halleck would not fully close up on those works until the last week of the month. While Beauregard watched for opportunities to take offensive action, he and his corps commanders all concluded that in light of the poor state of the Rebel army and the overwhelming numbers of Yankees, prudence dictated a retreat. Therefore, on the night of May 29, the Army of the Mississippi began a retreat south to Tupelo, Mississippi. With Corinth abandoned, the line protecting Memphis became unraveled. Fort Pillow was abandoned on June 4, and Memphis fell to a Federal gunboat flotilla on June 6.[36]

As late as June 1, Harris was expressing to newspapermen confidence in Confederate success at Corinth, even as the Army of the Mississippi moved south. But, with his connections within the army's high command, it is likely the governor knew that the position could not be held, nor, therefore, could Memphis. Whatever machinery of the state government that remained in Memphis was transferred to Chattanooga late in May, and Harris with it. The *Knoxville Register* reported that the governor, Whitthorne, and other state officials were in Chattanooga on May 31, and that Harris "paid a flying visit" to Knoxville on June 1 and returned to Chattanooga the following day. The paper noted Harris "seemed in excellent health."[37]

Although Chattanooga was about 220 miles from the main armies at Corinth, Federals in Middle Tennessee threatened the town. At intervals in May, Union and Confederate cavalry alternatively raided and clashed in northern Alabama and Middle Tennessee. In late May and early June, a Rebel force under Colonel John Adams camped in Sweeden's Cove, just on the east side of the Cumberland Plateau about thirty-five miles west of Chattanooga, preparing to cross into Middle Tennessee. The morning of June 4, Federals under Brigadier General James S. Negley made a forced march into Sweeden's Cove, catching Adams by surprise and routing his command, causing it to flee in "the wildest disorder." Adams's men streamed back to Chattanooga in confusion, leaving the way open for Negley to make a rapid descent upon the town.[38]

Fortunately for the Confederates, who had less than two thousand men to defend the town, Negley's orders were to only make a reconnaissance in force. Finding the Rebels holding the town strongly entrenched to dispute a crossing, Negley's men contented themselves with shelling the town the afternoon and evening of June 7 and for about three hours the morning of June 8. The effectiveness of the

36. Engle, *Struggle for the Heartland*, 174–84; OR 10(1):775–77, 898–903, 908.
37. *Knoxville Daily Register*, June 3, 1862.
38. Connelly, *Army of the Heartland*, 189; OR 10(1): 894–96, 904–5.

bombardment differed depending on the color of one's uniform, but it is likely the Federals' view of the damage wrought was deceived by the confusion, smoke, and excitement.[39]

The Federal raid certainly caused some excitement among the state's bankers. On June 7, Harris received a terse telegram from Granville C. Torbett, president of the Bank of Tennessee, then at Marietta, Georgia, asking that the governor "see that the assets of the Union Bank at Chattanooga are sent south." Much closer to the action was Dr. James G. M. Ramsey, president of the Knoxville branch of the Bank of Tennessee and Confederate States "Depository" for Tennessee. Traveling to Knoxville through Chattanooga, Ramsey heard the sound of cannon fire coming from the town. Concerned with the safety of his treasury assets in East Tennessee, Ramsey went into town with a doctor friend from Cleveland and found the governor near Chattanooga's principal hotel, the Crutchfield House. Harris asked: "What has brought you *old* men to this post of danger?" Ramsey replied that knowing that Harris would "*seek* the post of danger, and as he was not invulnerable, we desired to be on hand and render our professional assistance to him and his comrades if wounded." The governor told them that the cannon fire had come from across the river, and "that there was little injury suffered, and that the enemy had retired with some loss." Fragments of the shells were lying about on the streets, and Ramsey took some as souvenirs.[40]

Even as Negley retired from his raid on Chattanooga, Henry Halleck ordered Major General Don Carlos Buell to advance with his Army of the Ohio into Middle Tennessee, repairing the Memphis & Charleston as he proceeded eastward. While Federal elements remained as close as Battle Creek, about twenty-five miles to the west of Chattanooga, through June and most of July the bulk of Buell's mobile force of about 25,000 was strung out across north Alabama repairing the railroad, building bridges, guarding lines of communication, and fighting off Confederate cavalry raids. Notwithstanding these delays, by July 28, Buell had the road repaired from Nashville to Stevenson, Alabama, where the Nashville & Chattanooga intersected with the Memphis & Charleston.[41]

39. OR 10(1):905, 919–22.

40. Torbett to IGH, June 7, 1862, Harris Papers, TSLA; J. G. M. Ramsey, *Dr. J. G. M. Ramsey: Autobiography and Letters,* ed. William B. Hesseltine (1954; reprint, Knoxville: University of Tennessee Press, 2002), 103–4; see also "From Chattanooga," *Knoxville Daily Register,* June 12, 1862.

41. Don Carlos Buell, "East Tennessee and the Campaign of Perryville," in Robert Underwood Johnson and Clarence Clough Buel, *Battles and Leaders of the Civil War* (reprint, New York: Thomas Youseloff, 1956), 3:35–38.

During this interval, Harris energetically assisted the Confederate war effort in a number of ways. From Chattanooga on June 16, he telegraphed Rebel commanders in Knoxville with intelligence of a Federal move on Kingston in East Tennessee. On July 11, Harris issued General Order No. 7, for the establishment of an encampment of state troops organized in accordance with the militia laws passed in 1861 and 1862, appointing their officers and allocating funds for that purpose. The order also empowered the adjutant general to remove the encampment "to such point as the public service may require," tacitly recognizing the danger from Buell's approaching force.[42]

Later in July, Harris returned to the Army of the Mississippi, now at Tupelo. On Sunday, July 20, along with Leonidas Polk he watched a "grand review of Cheatham's division." An observer noted that the "troops presented an imposing sight as the several brigades passed in review with banners floating to the breeze and bayonets gleaming brightly in the morning sunbeams." As many of Cheatham's regiments were troops originally raised by Harris in 1861, the governor must have felt a special pride in the martial display.[43]

Notwithstanding this display, Harris was at Tupelo on serious business. While, at the end of June, Bragg detached a division under Major General John P. McCown for the defense of Chattanooga, there was still some doubt as to how the main body of the Rebel forces in the West would be utilized. Although Bragg recognized that the loss of Chattanooga would be a "disaster," as late as July 4, he was deciding between a move around the flank of the Federal position at Corinth or crossing the Tennessee and an advance on Nashville. Harris conferred with Bragg probably on or before July 20, by which time the commander determined on the advance across the river into Middle Tennessee. To his delight, Harris learned of Bragg's expectation to return the governor to the capital by the end of August.[44]

Harris did not let Bragg's assurances of the recovery of Middle Tennessee distract him, however, from the immediate problem of the defense of Chattanooga. He convinced Bragg to send two of Cheatham's brigades (those of brigadier generals Dabney Maury and Daniel Donelson) to Chattanooga. These additional five thousand troops, added to what Kirby Smith already had in East Tennessee, would enable the Confederates to "successfully prevent Buell from crossing the river, and

42. OR 16(2):687; "General Orders No. 7," *Chattanooga Daily Rebel,* August 9, 1862.

43. "Diary of Rev. J. G. Law," *Southern Historical Society Papers* 12 (May 1884): 215.

44. OR 16(2):710; Grady McWhiney, *Braxton Bragg and Confederate Defeat in the West* (1969; reprint, Tuscaloosa: University of Alabama Press, 1991), 1:266–67; OR 16(2):710.

indeed defend our line of railroad from [Chattanooga] to the Virginia line." Although it is doubtful that there was ever any contemplation of abandoning Chattanooga, Harris got credit in the press for "using all his influence" to prevent such, and for taking "necessary steps to have the place properly defended, because he well knew that the loss of Chattanooga was irreparable."[45]

The governor also sought to reinforce East Tennessee from other quarters. On July 12, he wrote Confederate Secretary of War George W. Randolph to propose sending the three remaining Tennessee regiments in Virginia to Kirby Smith's command. Harris suggested that their thin ranks could be better recruited in Tennessee. The government's response to the suggestion came from President Davis himself, who wrote on July 29 declining to send the regiments away from the "glory" of defending Richmond, but agreed they should be recruited and hoped that Harris would aid in that effort, and perhaps in raising a fourth regiment so that they all might be brigaded together. Harris replied on August 8 that the expected advance into Middle Tennessee would yield "a large number of volunteers, yet not a sufficient number to fill all of our now skeleton regiments," which would necessitate ordering "the conscripts of the State into service." Harris hoped to have Whitthorne appointed to command the Tennesseans in Virginia, while it seems Davis and Randolph were much more interested in having Tennessee send conscripts rather than a new officer.[46]

Bragg rapidly changed his mind as to the practicality of the plan he outlined to Harris. Even as the governor was writing confidentially to Andrew Ewing in Middle Tennessee about the coming offensive, 34,000 Rebel troops were en route to Chattanooga from Tupelo. Bragg made the decision to move to Chattanooga as early as July 21, telegraphing President Davis of the move, and explaining in a telegram the following day that "obstacles in front coupled with danger to Chattanooga induce a change of base." Bragg expected to take the offensive from Chattanooga, and Rebel cavalry was "paving the way for me in Middle Tennessee and Kentucky."[47]

45. OR 16(2):710; "Gov. Harris and the Defense of Chattanooga," *Chattanooga Daily Rebel*, September 16, 1863. It is possible Harris briefly visited Richmond during this time period, as there is an indication that he conferred personally with Jefferson Davis at some point before August 7, 1862. OR 17(2):669–70; see also Moran, "Isham Harris and Confederate State Government in Tennessee" (Ph.D. dissertation, University of Memphis, 1999), 131.

46. OR 52(2): 333, 339.

47. OR 52(2): 330–31.

Harris would have agreed with Bragg's evaluation of the effectiveness of Rebel cavalry, especially that of Forrest, as he characterized Forrest's activities in Middle Tennessee that summer as "brilliant," vengefully observing that the raider had "proved himself a scourge to the vandal cut-throats." Harris served as a conduit to Forrest from Bragg's headquarters, and in return received communications from Forrest as to conditions in Middle Tennessee.[48]

Although Harris must have been surprised by Bragg's sudden change of plan, the anticipated result, the liberation of Middle Tennessee, remained the same. Bragg and Kirby Smith conferred on July 31, and agreed that while Bragg awaited the arrival of his wagons and artillery, which, unlike his infantry, moved by road from Tupelo, Kirby Smith would move against the Federal position at Cumberland Gap, and then join Bragg for a move into Middle Tennessee, with the aim of cutting Buell off. Kirby Smith then embarked on a march that took him, contrary to his agreement with Bragg, far past Cumberland Gap. Reinforced by detachments from Bragg's army, Kirby Smith's men reached Lexington, Kentucky, on September 1. Kirby Smith's march north had ceased to be a complement to Bragg's move into Middle Tennessee against Buell, and became instead an independent effort to occupy the Bluegrass area around Lexington.[49]

Harris's friend, Colonel Randal McGavock, recently exchanged after his capture at Fort Donelson, encountered the governor and his staff in Chattanooga on August 14. McGavock noted that Harris was trying to raise a state force and had named Brigadier General Samuel Read Anderson as its commander. Either Anderson, who was assisting in the state service after resigning his Confederate commission on account of ill health, or the prospect of raising additional troops, inspired little confidence in McGavock, who wrote: "I hope he will succeed but I have my doubts."[50]

Meanwhile, Bragg was left with little choice but to stay in supporting distance of Kirby Smith. The Army of the Mississippi marched out of Chattanooga on August 28, and moved across Walden's Ridge into the Sequatchie Valley, heading north. Confederate chaplain Dr. Charles Todd Quintard, looking for his brigade's line of march, encountered Harris with Bragg and Simon Bolivar Buckner on

48. OR 16(2):710; Forrest to IGH, August 12, 1862, Harris Papers, LC (reporting no Federals at Lebanon).

49. OR 16(2):741; Connelly, *Army of the Heartland*, 209–20.

50. Gower and Allen, eds., *Pen and Sword*, 662; Warner, *Generals in Gray*, 10. Anderson held the state rank of major general.

Walden's Ridge that day, and Quintard recalled that the governor "put us right as to our way." The army rested around Sparta on the Cumberland Plateau for a few days the first week of September. There, Harris made his final pitch for a move directly on Nashville, but was rebuffed by Bragg. The march would continue north, not west.[51]

While Harris accompanied Bragg and his men into Kentucky, he did not abandon his hope that Nashville could be recaptured. Leaving Bragg the evening of September 17, after the surrender of the Federal garrison at Munfordville, Harris traveled back into Middle Tennessee to Lebanon, about thirty miles east of Nashville. There, on September 20, he wrote to Major General Sterling Price, in command of the Rebel forces in north Mississippi, advising him of Bragg's victory, anticipated movements, and the weakness of the Federal position in Tennessee with Buell in Kentucky. Harris wrote that the Federal garrison at Nashville was five thousand to eight thousand troops, which he had "no means of dislodging until you can reach there." Harris inquired as to Price's position, "the route by which you will approach Nashville, the probable time it will take you to reach that city, and the probable force you will be able to reach the city with." Harris pledged full cooperation with Price's anticipated movement.[52]

Unfortunately, on September 20, Price was moving away from Nashville, extricating his army from a potential trap at Iuka, Mississippi, after a hard fight there the day before with the Union forces of Major General William Starke Rosecrans. Responding to Harris on September 28, Price kept the hope of an advance toward Nashville alive, telling Harris that his army had joined that of Major General Earl Van Dorn that day, and promising that they would "at once proceed northward." The combined force attacked Rosecrans again, this time at Corinth on October 3 and 4, and was once again repulsed. Harris would get no help from Mississippi.[53]

Even as Confederate forces moved north, Harris worked to augment their ranks. On September 6, Harris issued General Order No. 9, requiring the judges and chairmen of the various county courts to appoint persons to enroll conscripts

51. Charles Todd Quintard, *Doctor Quintard, Chaplain C. S. A. and Second Bishop of Tennessee*, ed. Sam Davis Elliott (Baton Rouge: Louisiana State University Press, 2003), 50–51; McWhiney, *Braxton Bragg and Confederate Defeat*, 282–83; OR 16(1):261.

52. OR 16(2):858.

53. Peter Cozzens, *The Darkest Days of the War: The Battles of Iuka and Corinth* (Chapel Hill: University of North Carolina Press, 1997), 118–25, 159–279; OR 17(2):715.

under the Confederate conscription law of April 16, 1862. Failure to comply would result in a fine and imprisonment. The editors of the *Chattanooga Daily Rebel* succinctly stated the governor's policy: "There is no escape. The law is to be enforced." The new department commander, Major General Samuel Jones, sought a personal interview with Harris relative to the execution of the conscription law, and sought suggestions "as to the best mode of executing the law for the best interest of the country." Harris likely met with Jones on this subject during a visit to Knoxville on October 2. It was rumored that Harris was opposed to receiving any more volunteers, "and in place thereof, is in favor of a rigid and remorseless enforcement of the conscription." Newspapers in East Tennessee protested this policy, deeming it more likely to create "more harm than good." Harris was urged to "take a wise, liberal and comprehensive view of the condition of things around him."[54]

East Tennessee continued to be a problem for the Confederacy. While Unionist townsmen maintained a "prudent silence" and facial neutrality toward the war, outside Confederate-garrisoned areas, military-aged men flowed out of the region into Kentucky, where they would be armed and organized for Union service. Confederate conscription officers accordingly had difficulty finding qualified men for Rebel service, and they often had to recruit twice as many men to offset the possibility of desertion. Not unlike their secessionist counterparts in Middle and West Tennessee, Unionist partisans roamed the region, terrorizing, intimidating, and killing secessionists. At one point in April 1862, there were armed anti-Confederate bands in twenty-five of the region's thirty-one counties. Individual Confederate troops were ambushed, and columns subjected to sniper attacks. Confederate strength was sapped by the need to guard railroad lines and bridges, and Unionists of all ages and sexes provided the Federal army intelligence on Confederate troop movements. As a result, Confederate troops increased the severity of their suppression efforts.[55]

In Middle and West Tennessee, the Confederate resurgence of the late sum-

54. "General Orders No. 9," *Chattanooga Daily Rebel*, September 12, 1862; OR 16(2):862; *Knoxville Daily Register*, October 2, 1862; "Gov. Harris," *Knoxville Register*, October 5, 1862 (reprint from *Athens Post*).

55. Robert Tracy McKenzie, "Prudent Silence and Strict Neutrality: The Parameters of Unionism in Parson Brownlow's Knoxville, 1860–1863," in *Enemies of the Country: New Perspectives on Unionists in the Civil War South* (Athens: University of Georgia Press, 2001), 83, 90; Fisher, *War at Every Door*, 66–78; Bryan, "The Civil War in East Tennessee," 111–13.

mer and fall of 1862 emboldened secessionist resistance efforts. Even in the bleakest days of the winter and early spring of 1862, much of the populace had a belief in victory that propped up Confederate morale during that difficult time. During the summer, transient but spectacular captures of Federal garrisons at Murfreesboro and Clarksville and news of successful raids elsewhere reinforced the belief of many Tennesseans, also held by Green Harris, that the Confederacy would regain the lost portions of the state. The Confederate advance into Kentucky and the Federal army's withdrawal from Middle Tennessee in pursuit only reinforced such feelings. As events would transpire, the aroused feelings of the populace fed the hope that Nashville would be recovered.[56]

Hopeful reports filled East Tennessee newspapers, as it was reported from Nashville that Andrew Johnson was drunk and the city was to be evacuated. The *Daily Rebel* reported that the railroad from Chattanooga to Nashville was open for ever greater stretches, it being anticipated on September 21 that the rail link to the capital could be established within ten days "if the military authorities protect the road . . . and the Yankees will have entirely left Nashville by that time." By the end of September, the hopeful and energetic governor had established his headquarters at Murfreesboro, from where on October 1, the railroad was open back to Chattanooga. On October 7, the line was reported open to Lavergne, just seventeen miles from Nashville. It was also reported that judicial elections held under Federal auspices in Middle Tennessee would be "held null and void" and that Harris would order new elections.[57]

Harris made one last attempt to obtain aid from regular Confederate forces. Major General John C. Breckinridge's division, which had been campaigning in the lower Mississippi Valley, was moving to join Bragg in Kentucky, as it was thought that this prominent Kentuckian would rally the men of the Bluegrass State to the Rebel cause. On September 29, Harris telegraphed Secretary Randolph from Chattanooga, advising him of conditions in Nashville, the governor

56. Steven V. Ash, *When the Yankees Came: Conflict and Chaos in the Occupied South, 1861–1865* (Chapel Hill: University of North Carolina Press, 1995), 38–39, 50; Benjamin Franklin Cooling, *Fort Donelson's Legacy: War and Society in Kentucky and Tennessee, 1862–1863* (Knoxville: University of Tennessee Press, 1997), 85–98, 128.

57. *Knoxville Daily Register*, August 31, 1862; "Judicial Elections in Middle Tennessee," *Chattanooga Daily Rebel*, September 20, 1862; "From Nashville" and "The Train on the Nashville Railroad," *Chattanooga Daily Rebel*, September 21, 1862; "Letter from the Rangers," *Houston Tri Weekly Telegraph*, October 27, 1862; "Ho, for Murfreesboro!" *Chattanooga Daily Rebel*, October 1, 1862; *Chattanooga Daily Rebel*, October 7, 1862.

having been in the vicinity the day before. Harris reported that he had "the city surrounded by a cloud of cavalry," but had no artillery or infantry. Harris asked that the former vice president of the United States and his troops be ordered to divert to Nashville instead. Randolph replied the next day, declining to give Breckinridge orders different from any he might have received from Bragg.[58]

Harris's "cloud of cavalry" were local "companies and battalions" organized by the citizens of the counties surrounding Nashville to counteract foraging expeditions from the garrison of Nashville, which increased as the railroad connections to the North were interdicted as the men guarding the lines followed Buell into Kentucky or were drawn into the fortified lines at the capital. Overall, the Federals went fifty days without any supplies other than what could be drawn from the surrounding countryside, but in the end only suffered "inconvenience." Toward the end of September, Harris ordered S. R. Anderson to "take charge of all [the state] cavalry organizations and direct their movements so as to most effectively repress [the] predatory forays" of the Federals."[59]

While the Federal departmental commander, Major General Don Carlos Buell, felt that in the emergency Nashville could be abandoned, he recognized that Harris's force was not sufficiently organized to threaten even the weakened Federal garrison. Buell's attitude irritated Andrew Johnson, who was grimly determined to hold on to the capital. The Federal commander at Nashville was Brigadier General James S. Negley, who just a few months before had scattered Rebel cavalry in Sweeden's Cove. Seeing that Anderson was concentrating his largely irregular force at Lavergne, and hearing that they had an "avowed intention of assaulting Nashville," Negley determined to "check this project with a sudden blow," and organized a strike force of 2,600 men to assault the Rebels. Many of the Rebel Tennesseans were without arms, and most were certainly without proper cavalry weapons, such as sabers and pistols. In addition to his irregular state forces, Anderson had the four hundred men of the 32nd Alabama Infantry and a small force of regular cavalry, which General Jones authorized Harris to order to Murfreesboro to cooperate with the state troops in the area, as well as a single battery of artillery. Jones warned that they should be "constantly on the alert to prevent being surprised themselves."[60]

58. Connelly, *Army of the Heartland*, 208; OR 16(2):888, 891.

59. "Correspondent of the Daily Rebel," *Chattanooga Daily Rebel*, October 12, 1862; OR 16(1):258, 261.

60. Cooling, *Fort Donelson's Legacy*, 126–28; OR 16(1):258, 1020; 16(2):890, 916; "Correspondent of the Daily Rebel."

Negley marched out of Nashville the evening of October 6, forming a two-prong attack, one force advancing down the Murfreesboro road with a force of 400 cavalry and 400 infantry, and another force of 1,600 infantry making a flanking march to the south of Lavergne. Early on the morning of October 7, the Rebels formed their lines in anticipation of the movements of the apparent main force, Anderson dismounting some of his irregular cavalry as infantry to support the regulars and deploying one piece of artillery. The gun was put out of action early in the fight, as a lucky Federal shot exploded its ammunition chest. Suddenly, Negley's flanking column arrived, confirming General Jones's warning and creating a "disgraceful surprise." The Rebels held out under this attack from two quarters for about a half-hour, and while the account in the *Rebel* indicated that while part of the Rebel command fell back in "admirable order," other parts panicked. Negley was likely more accurate when he reported a flight "in the wildest disorder" and that the Confederate "defeat was complete."[61]

News of the disaster made its way to Murfreesboro, where Forrest and one of his veteran battalions had recently arrived, in order to lend his unique talents to the efforts to pressure the Federals in Nashville. The cavalryman rushed out to Lavergne, but found that Negley, with his mission accomplished, had returned to the environs of Nashville. While Forrest pushed his small relieving force to within six miles of the city, the battle was effectively over. Anderson's career, at least as a field officer, was also over, as Forrest took over the task of training and organizing the irregulars into his type of partisan cavalry. Harris's efforts to raise troops was somewhat repudiated in this process, as it was reported his "clouds of cavalry" were raised by offering enlistees the opportunity to choose the organizations in which they were to serve. Bragg objected, and ordered that the troops be placed in organizations that already existed and the state force entities be disregarded.[62]

Bragg's Kentucky campaign reached its apogee as a result of the fighting the next day, October 8, between the Army of the Ohio and the Army of the Mississippi at Perryville, Kentucky, and the troops of both armies thereafter began a slow movement back to Tennessee. In the interval, the governor was able to extend a courtesy to Andrew Johnson and his family, as Johnson's wife, seeking to join the Federal military governor in Nashville, was detained by Forrest. Har-

61. OR 16(1):258, 1020–21; "Correspondent of the Daily Rebel"; OR 16(1):261.

62. Robert Selph Henry, *"First With the Most" Forrest* (1944; reprint, Wilmington, N.C.: Broadfoot Publishing, 1987), 102–5.

ris and Andrew Ewing secured permission from Richmond for her party to proceed. In late October, Harris finally got his wish for regular Confederate troops as
Breckinridge arrived in Murfreesboro with his division from Knoxville. There was
a meeting in Murfreesboro between Harris, Breckinridge, Forrest, Confederate
Congressman Henry Stuart Foote, and Ewing, in which Harris used "very strong
persuasions" to use the collection of forces at Murfreesboro to assault Nashville.
The Federal defenses at the capital were accordingly tested to no avail on November 4. Federal reinforcements arrived soon afterward. What chance there was to
seize Nashville while the main Federal army was in Kentucky was gone.[63]

Harris's efforts to direct the military strategy of the Confederacy did not dimin-
ish his responsibilities as governor to the rump of the state that remained under
Confederate control. On October 7, a piece in the *Knoxville Register* complained
that Harris had failed to provide for the distribution of salt, an absolute necessity for the preservation of meat in those days. The paper noted that he alone, "of
all the Governors of the Southern States, has adopted no measures by which the
people of Tennessee may 'save their bacon.'" Conceding that its comments were
"salty," the paper made it clear that its editor thought Harris should stick to his civilian job. The *Register* said the governor should leave military affairs to the Confederate government and devote himself to civil matters, observing, "he should,
if possible, see that the poor, many of whom are beggared by a fierce revolution,
are not reduced to absolute starvation. His well known energy can obviate this
anticipated evil."[64]

But there seems to have been little Harris could have done. The state's contrac-
tor was reported to be "straining every nerve to furnish Tennessee with salt," but
there was only so much available. The plan was to have by December four hundred to five hundred bushels of salt a day "for the use of the people of the state, to
be equally distributed among the counties within our lines according to population." The measure was applauded as one that would combat extortion relative to
the distribution of this vital commodity. The results were uneven, as salt prices

63. Ibid., 105–6; OR 16(1):256–64; John Savage, *The Life and Public Services of Andrew Johnson,
Seventeenth President of the United States, Including his State Papers, Speeches and Addresses* (New York:
Derby & Miller, 1866), 275; Charles Johnson to Andrew Johnson, October 12, 1862, n3, 6 *PAJ* 23; "Gov.
Johnson's Family at Nashville," *Daily* (Washington) *National Intelligencer*, October 29, 1862. Harris's
papers at TSLA contain a typescript of a Philadelphia "Press" account dated November 6, 1862, rela-
tive to the November 4 "demonstrations" against Nashville.

64. *Knoxville Daily Register*, October 7, 1862.

fluctuated wildly from $10 a bushel wholesale to $102 a sack sold by speculators on the street in Chattanooga. Lack of transportation and damage to the railroad from Virginia inflicted by Federal raiders compounded problems, and at least one proposal appeared in a Middle Tennessee newspaper suggesting means of extracting salt from the soil on the floor of smokehouses.[65]

Another issue relating to feeding the people of Tennessee arose that fall when Harris issued an order that prohibited the sending of provisions out of the state. The *Fayetteville Observer* caustically noted that if Harris would prevent corn from being made into whiskey, "he would do much more good, and prevent any scarcity of corn meal and flour." This criticism obviously made its way to the governor, as the very edition of the *Observer* that complained of Harris's order reported the "good news" that whiskey-making had indeed been ordered stopped.[66]

Food was indeed a problem. As the armies glowered at each other from their respective positions in Nashville and Murfreesboro, conditions in Middle Tennessee continued to deteriorate for the populace there. In the space of time since the Confederate evacuation in February, the region suffered from the destruction wrought by retreating Rebels seeking to deny industry, infrastructure, and supplies to the enemy. Although the Federal army committed most of the depredations, both armies foraged heavily in the rich farm areas of the section, taking food, money, and valuables, burning fence rails, and seizing livestock. No doubt compounding the decline was the lack of labor due to the erosion of slavery and many of the young men serving in the army. Not all destruction was for military necessity; there were many cases of spiteful acts. When, for example, the Federals recaptured Clarksville in October 1862, they pillaged the town with a vengeance.[67]

The Federal policy of "collective punishment" in areas of partisan activity also contributed to the impoverishment of the citizens. In mid-1862, Military Governor Johnson issued an order that directed imprisonment and financial compensation from secessionists in an area where guerrillas mistreated Unionist citi-

65. "Salt-Salt-Salt," *Athens Post*, October 10, 1862; "His Excellency," *Chattanooga Daily Rebel*, December 9, 1862; "Salt for the People," *Chattanooga Daily Rebel*, December 16, 1862; "Salt for Franklin County," *Winchester Daily Bulletin*, November 25, 1862; "Rather Salty," *Winchester Daily Bulletin*, December 12, 1862; "Salt, Salt!" *Athens Post*, December 10, 1862; "To the Public," *Winchester Daily Bulletin*, January 17, 1863; "To the Readers of the Fayetteville Observer," *Fayetteville Observer*, October 16, 1862.

66. "He Forbids It" and "Good News—The Latest," *Fayetteville Observer*, November 6, 1862.

67. Ash, *Middle Tennessee Society Transformed*, 84–92; Cooling, *Fort Donelson's Legacy*, 106–7, 172.

zens. In West Tennessee, which swarmed with Confederate partisans, Federal commander Major General William T. Sherman employed the concept in a much harsher fashion. In retaliation for partisan attacks in October 1862, Sherman sent a regiment to destroy all the "houses, farms and cornfields" in the area where the attacks occurred. The previous month, an attack on a Federal steamer in the Mississippi near the town of Randolph in Tipton County resulted in the burning of every structure there but one. Later, a similar attack along the Cumberland River near Palmyra resulted in the town's shelling by Federal gunboats.[68]

The *Knoxville Register* took Harris to task again in November, noting that his presence in East Tennessee would remedy defects in the enforcement of the Confederate Conscription Act in the recalcitrant counties of the region. In Carter County, a faithful enrolling officer was removed for failing to obey the instructions of the chairman of the county court, who wanted to exempt some of his "special friends." The newspaper argued that Harris, using his militia powers as governor, could muster the militia in those areas and order them to Knoxville, where the conscripts could be designated. The previous month, a rumor started that the Confederate government planned to suspend enforcement of the Conscription Act in Tennessee, causing Harris to telegraph Davis for confirmation, admonishing "if so, it is most unfortunate as it should be enforced with vigilance." There was no relaxation of conscription, Davis's reply explaining that the War Department was only receiving five regiments enrolled before October 1 under a special law. Indeed, Davis beseeched Harris for replacements for existing regiments, to the extent that Harris explored ways to raise regiments in areas behind Union lines in Tennessee.[69]

Notwithstanding his civilian duties in East Tennessee, Harris remained either at his headquarters at Murfreesboro or at Tullahoma, where Bragg first assembled the main body of his army after its transfer from East Tennessee, preparatory to moving on to Murfreesboro. Given Harris's devotion to the recovery of the occupied portions of the state, he was doubtless pleased when, on November 20, Bragg renamed his force the Army of Tennessee. Bragg told Harris he was confident he

68. Mazlowski, *Treason Must Be Made Odious*, 66–67; Cooling, *Fort Donelson's Legacy*, 165; Ash, "Sharks in an Angry Sea," 227; Fisher, "Prepare Them for My Coming," 77–80.

69. "Where is Governor Harris," *Knoxville Register*, November 13, 1862; "Conscription," *Knoxville Daily Register*, October 21, 1862; "The New Regiments—Conscription," *Knoxville Daily Register*, November 25, 1862; IGH to Jefferson Davis, October 24, 1862, 8 *PJD* 464; OR Series 4, vol. 2, 148; Fisher, *War at Every Door*, 110–12 (Fisher succinctly discusses the pros and cons of strict enforcement of conscription at this point of time in East Tennessee); OR 52(2):391.

could defeat the Federals if they came out of Nashville and if not, by cutting lines of communication, could keep the Yankees hemmed in close to the capital. Harris was therefore "tolerably confident" of the prospect of the Confederacy holding Middle Tennessee.[70]

One of Harris's roles was to exert his political influence on the part of Tennesseans in the Confederate army. During this interval, Harris worked hard to have his friend, Colonel Marcus J. Wright, appointed to a field command as a brigadier general, writing a "strong" letter on Wright's behalf for Cheatham to sign, and another for himself. Wright was stationed in McMinnville as commander of the post and the nearby camp of instruction for conscripts. The governor also induced Bragg and Leonidas Polk to request Wright's appointment. Harris promised Wright that the War Department "shall have no peace" until the appointment was made, and even stated that if he had to go to Richmond to secure Wright's appointment, he would do so, confidently stating that the word *fail* was "not in my vocabulary." Harris took advantage of a letter to President Davis on November 30 reporting on the status of recruitment in Tennessee to urge Wright's appointment. Davis visited the Army of Tennessee at Murfreesboro in mid-December, lifting spirits with a grand review of the army and casting gloom with his detachment of the army's largest division to Mississippi. Harris likely was able to press for Wright's promotion personally with the president during this visit, as he was finally able to telegraph Wright from Murfreesboro on December 14 announcing his appointment.[71]

Bragg soon had occasion to miss the transferred division. On December 26, Rosecrans marched out of his camps near Nashville toward Bragg's position at Murfreesboro. By the evening of December 30, the contending armies were deployed to the west of the town, each anticipating launching an attack the next morning. Bragg's attack early on the morning of December 31 was successful to the point that it is easy to speculate that the missing division might have tipped

70. "From the Chattanooga Rebel—The Situation," *Montgomery* (Alabama) *Advertiser,* November 25, 1862; OR 16(2):411; IGH to M. J. Wright, November 23, 1862, Wright Papers.

71. IGH to Wright, November 23, 1862, Wright Papers; IGH to Davis, November 30, 1862, 8 *PJD* 524; IGH to Wright, November 30, 1862, Southern Historical Collection, UNC; Thomas L. Connelly, *Autumn of Glory* (Baton Rouge: Louisiana State University Press, 1971), 40–41; A. M. Manigault, *A Carolinian Goes to War,* ed. R. Lockwood Tower (Columbia: University of South Carolina Press, 1983), 53; "President Davis at Murfreesboro," *Chattanooga Daily Rebel,* December 17, 1862; Marcus J. Wright, *Diary of Brigadier-General Marcus J. Wright, C. S. A., April 12, 1861–February 26, 1863* (n.p., 193?), 8.

the balance decisively in Bragg's favor. As it was, there was an obstinate day-long fight that, in the end, resulted in the bloody exhaustion of both forces.[72]

As he had Johnston and Beauregard at Shiloh, Harris served as an aide for Bragg during the fight. And, as after the close of the fighting at Shiloh, Harris made sure the newspapermen, and thereby his constituents, knew that he was on the field in person. On December 30, he telegraphed the *Daily Rebel* of preliminary artillery fights and infantry skirmishing, noting, "a fierce battle is expected to-morrow." On the evening of December 31, he telegraphed the paper with news of the battle, reporting that the battle had lasted from about 5:30 a.m. to 5:00 p.m., and that the Rebel "left wing drove the enemy's right back upon Stones River." Harris went on to state that four batteries and four thousand prisoners were captured. Accounting for casualties, Harris noted: "Loss heavy on both sides. Relative loss not known." A shorter message to the *Rebel* also dated December 31 reported on prisoners and captured artillery, and proudly closed: "Men never fought better than our men have today."[73]

New Year's Day 1863 found the armies still facing each other on the battlefield. Harris reported in a telegram to the *Rebel* that there was some skirmishing, and that he perceived the Federals were retreating, but such was not the case. In strengthening his lines, Rosecrans ordered the occupation of high ground on the east bank of Stones River, ground that Bragg feared would enable the Federals to bombard Polk's position on the Confederate right. Accordingly, Bragg ordered an attack on the new Federal position on January 2, 1863, which Rosecrans's men bloodily repulsed. Fearing that his bloodied army would have to face a reinforced Federal army, Bragg decided to withdraw, and the army retreated fifteen to twenty miles south, behind the Highland Rim.[74]

Thus ended 1862, a year in which Harris's role as the head of the civilian government of Confederate Tennessee changed significantly. While Harris and the state government struggled to function within the rump remaining under Confederate

72. Herman Hattaway and Archer Jones, *How the North Won: A Military History of the Civil War* (Urbana: University of Illinois Press, 1983, 1991), 317–22.

73. "To the Rebel," *Chattanooga Daily Rebel*, January 1, 1863; "The Great Battle," *Chattanooga Daily Rebel*, January 2, 1863.

74. "Special Report to the Daily Rebel," *Chattanooga Daily Rebel*, January 3, 1863; Peter Cozzens, *No Better Place to Die: The Battle of Stones River* (Urbana: University of Illinois Press, 1990), 174–98; OR 20(1):670; Connelly, *Autumn of Glory*, 66–69.

control, the overwhelming need to mobilize what remained to the Southern cause in an effort to regain what was lost in Middle and West Tennessee necessarily lowered the priority of purely civilian matters. While Harris was criticized by newspaper editors in East Tennessee for shirking his civilian duties in order to focus on the military, the realities of 1862 cannot be ignored. Since early February, the state was on the front line of the war and had seen two great battles and innumerable smaller skirmishes. The recapture of Nashville, which seemed so tantalizingly close in the fall of 1862, would have gone a long way toward restoring Confederate military fortunes and proving to the civilian population of Tennessee that Harris's administration was still the legitimate state government. As the battlefield was in Tennessee, and the largest contingent of troops in the Army of Tennessee was Tennesseans, Harris's presence with the army and his continued efforts to strengthen it are difficult to criticize.

At Murfreesboro, as at Shiloh, Harris proved himself useful to the army commander in the midst of battle. A correspondent of the *Daily Rebel* admiringly reported that "our distinguished Executive, Governor Harris, has been on the field with General Bragg every day since the battles began, displaying that devotion to our cause which is the ruling sentiment with him."[75] In recognizing Harris's contribution on the field of battle, Braxton Bragg provided Harris with the ultimate response to those who chided him for not attending to his civilian duties:

His Excellency Isham G. Harris, Governor of Tennessee, and the Hon. Andrew Ewing, member of military court, volunteered their services and rendered me efficient aid, especially with the Tennessee troops, largely in the ascendant in this army. It is but due to a zealous and efficient laborer in our cause that I here bear testimony to the cordial support given me at all times since meeting him a year ago in West Tennessee by His Excellency Governor Harris. From the field of Shiloh, where he received in his arms the dying form of the lamented Johnston, to the last struggle at Murfreesborough, he has been one of us, and has shared all our privations and dangers, while giving us his personal and political influence with all the power he possessed at the head of the State government.[76]

75. "A Letter from the Battle Field," *Chattanooga Daily Rebel*, January 8, 1863.
76. OR 20(1):671.

5 "IN THIS STRUGGLE FOR NATIONAL INDEPENDENCE"
1863

As the Army of Tennessee settled behind the Highland Rim, Isham G. Harris was called on once again to operate in his element, politics. Yet the exigencies of the war made the execution of the familiar unfamiliar. First, the retreat from Murfreesboro brought to the surface differences that existed between Braxton Bragg and his principal officers, differences that required Harris to exercise his influence in the high command of the army in an effort to smooth matters over. Second, Harris's third term as governor was in its final months. A means was required to hold elections, both to comply with the state constitution and to demonstrate the Confederate state government of Tennessee was still a viable entity with over half the state at least nominally occupied by the Federals. As events would transpire, both efforts were only partially successful.

In the days following the army's retreat from Murfreesboro, Bragg was uncertain as to where to stop the army's withdrawal, and considered pulling back to the line of the Elk River. Perhaps scouting out that position, Bragg appeared in Winchester on January 5, and made a speech promising that Tennessee would not be "left to the mercy of the Abolitionists." Bragg stayed in Winchester until January 10, by which time he decided to halt the retreat in the Duck River Valley, behind the Highland Rim in Coffee and Bedford counties, and departed for Tullahoma, where Harris and his staff were located.[1]

During this interval, Bragg became aware of criticism arising from his retreat from Murfreesboro, after announcing a glorious victory after the fighting on December 31, and the initial confusion relative to the extent of the army's withdrawal. Incredibly, he polled his staff as to the advisability of his remaining in command

1. "General Bragg," *Winchester Daily Bulletin*, January 6, 1863; "General Bragg and staff," *Winchester Daily Bulletin*, January 11, 1863; Connelly, *Autumn of Glory*, 69; "The Situation," *Chattanooga Daily Rebel*, January 11, 1863.

and, to his astonishment, they returned an opinion that he should ask to be re-lieved. Against the advice of his staff, he then wrote his corps and division com-manders asking them to recall that they, too, had deemed a retreat from Murfrees-boro advisable, and vaguely posed the question whether he had lost the confidence of his officers. The responses he got were unexpectedly adverse. Perplexed as to why Bragg would invite the public judgment of his subordinate officers, Jefferson Davis ordered his theater commander, Joseph E. Johnston, to the scene to assess the situation and "decide what the best interests of the service require."[2]

During this interval, Harris was at or near army headquarters at Tullahoma, and undertook to write Davis on January 17. In a letter endorsed by Bragg, the governor praised the actions of the Army of Tennessee at Murfreesboro, but ex-pressed his fear that Bragg would be forced to retreat farther. Bluntly asking if the government were ready to lose Tennessee, Harris asked for reinforcements from Virginia and Mississippi and reported on efforts to enforce conscription.[3]

When Johnston arrived in Tullahoma at the end of January, he consulted with Bragg, Polk, Hardee, and Harris. Johnston found that the two lieutenant generals lacked confidence in Bragg, but that it stemmed from the previous fall's opera-tions in Kentucky, not the recent fight at Murfreesboro. Johnston noted that Har-ris, too, thought that the problem arose in Kentucky, but that the lack of confi-dence was "declining." Harris also told Johnston that the removal of Bragg would be a greater "evil" than the lack of confidence expressed by his officers. This epi-sode demonstrated the influence Harris had within the army's officer corps. John-ston noted that "the general officers converse" with Harris "more freely probably than with their military superiors." Indeed, a correspondent for the *Rebel* later wrote that Harris was not only "respected by the Generals," but that he was "gen-erally popular in the army" as well. Recognizing Harris's influence in the officer corps, Chaplain Charles Todd Quintard asked his assistance in seeking a pardon for two Tennesseans sentenced to death for desertion.[4]

The ranking Tennessean with the army was Benjamin Franklin Cheatham, who had, at least during the initial part of the fighting at Murfreesboro, performed rather poorly, possibly because of excessive fortification with alcohol. Bragg be-

2. Connelly, *Autumn of Glory*, 74–76, McWhiney, *Braxton Bragg and Confederate Defeat*, 374–79; OR 23(2): 613–14.

3. IGH to Davis, January 17, 1863, 9 *PJD* 33.

4. OR 23(2):624; "By Grapevine or Otherwise," *Chattanooga Daily Rebel*, March 18, 1863; Elliott, ed., *Doctor Quintard*, 73. One deserter was shot, the other spared. Ibid., 75.

lieved such was the case, and undoubtedly grimly let his disapproval be known. For his part, Cheatham told Harris that he never would go into battle under Bragg again, but Harris expressed to Johnston confidence "that he can control that officer and bring him to his senses." While Cheatham remained with the army, John P. McCown, another Tennessee general, was removed. Suspended from his division command on technical grounds, McCown's actual failing was incompetence, fully demonstrated at Murfreesboro. Cheatham mattered to the Tennessee troops, McCown did not. Perhaps frustrated by Harris's preference for his old friend Cheatham, McCown complained that the Confederacy was a "*damned stinking cotton oligarchy*" created "for the benefit of Isham G. Harris and Jeff Davis and their damned corrupt cliques."[5]

On February 12, Johnston reported that the Army of Tennessee was "well clothed, healthy and in good spirits," and that such was, in his view, "positive evidence of General Bragg's capacity to command." Acknowledging that the army's two corps commanders, Polk and Hardee, preferred Johnston himself to assume command, Johnston thought his doing so would be "inconsistent" with his "personal honor" and recommended that Bragg be retained. The situation dragged on until March, when Davis simply ordered Johnston to assume command, but Johnston incredibly demurred, deeming it inappropriate to relieve Bragg while his wife suffered from a deathly illness. By the time of her recovery, Johnston was himself incapacitated with a flare-up of the wound he had received at Seven Pines in May 1862. Bragg remained in command of the Army of Tennessee for the coming campaign.[6]

In 1862, Harris's eldest son, Eugene Travis Harris, served as a volunteer aide on Cheatham's staff. On September 22 of that year, the members of Tennessee's congressional delegation united to recommend Eugene's appointment as a cadet. He was described as "a young man of good mind, intelligence and moral character." On January 20, 1863, Tennessee's newest brigadier, Marcus J. Wright, requested that Eugene be appointed to his staff as aide-de-camp, tacitly acknowledging the governor's friendship and his role in Wright's promotion. Eugene's

5. Christopher Losson, *Tennessee's Forgotten Warriors: Frank Cheatham and His Tennessee Division* (Knoxville: University of Tennessee Press, 1989), 90–97; OR 23(2):624; Connelly, *Autumn of Glory*, 80–81; Steven E. Woodworth, *Jefferson Davis and His Generals: The Failure of Confederate Command in the West* (Lawrence: University Press of Kansas, 1990), 196–97; McWhiney, *Braxton Bragg and Confederate Defeat*, 375.

6. OR 23(2):632–33; McWhiney, *Braxton Bragg and Confederate Defeat*, 380–88.

appointment as an aide-de-camp with the rank of 1st lieutenant eventually came through, to rank from January 20, 1863.[7]

Wright was originally assigned to command the famous Kentucky Orphan Brigade, whose commander had been killed at Murfreesboro. In late January, however, politics intervened as Davis had Kentuckian Brigadier General Benjamin Hardin Helm appointed to command the Orphans. Accordingly, Wright was given command of the brigade of Tennesseans formerly commanded by Brigadier General Daniel S. Donelson. Then, in March, Richmond directed that Wright be given command of the brigade of Arkansas troops formerly commanded by Patrick Cleburne, then under the command of Brigadier General Lucius E. Polk. Both Bragg and Johnston disapproved of the change, and Harris telegraphed Tennessee Congressmen John V. Wright and J. D. C. Atkins, tersely stating "get order countermanded. It is important." Wright stayed with his Tennessee brigade, and Polk remained in command of the Arkansas men.[8]

It was likely no secret that Harris had worked hard for Wright's promotion. Doubtless, this led to the conclusion by Colonel John Houston Savage of the 16th Tennessee of that brigade that Harris opposed his promotion to the position. With the exception of military service in both the Seminole and Mexican wars, Savage's early career was fairly similar to that of Harris. Born in 1815, he studied for the bar and eventually entered Congress in 1849, the same year as Harris. Savage later wrote that he held a grudge against Harris and Andrew Johnson for their supposed contribution to his reelection defeat in the 1850s. Like, Harris, Savage was known in Congress as a states' rights advocate, and after Tennessee seceded, he was elected the colonel of the 16th and led the regiment in heavy fighting at Perryville and Murfreesboro. Hearing that Savage blamed him for opposing his promotion, Harris told Wright that Savage was "very much mistaken" as the governor "never even placed a pebble in his path." Resigning in a huff from the army, Savage would prove to be a bitter and lifelong, if not a very effective, enemy.[9]

The first of the year brought into focus changes that affected Union-occupied Tennessee and Andrew Johnson's efforts to organize a Union party around which to

7. Eugene T. Harris Compiled Service Record, M-331, NA.

8. Wright, *Diary of Brig. Gen. Marcus J. Wright*, 8; OR 20(2):497; OR 23(2):620–21, 688, 726; "An Interesting Batch of Telegrams," *Confederate Veteran* 2 (April 1894): 110.

9. IGH to Wright, February 12, 1863, Wright Papers; John H. Savage, *The Life of John H. Savage: Citizen, Soldier, Lawyer, Congressman, Before the War Begun and Prosecuted by the Abolitionists of the*

build a new and loyal civilian government in Nashville. On January 1, 1863, the Emancipation Proclamation went into effect, freeing the slaves in areas still in rebellion against the U.S. government. Although Tennessee was specifically exempted from the effect of the proclamation, it spotlighted one of several significant differences among the Unionists. The difference first appeared in the late summer of 1862, when Johnson began to take harsher measures against the secessionists in the population after his initial leniency proved ineffective. Conservative elements in the Unionist ranks, led primarily by prominent prewar Whigs, continued to advocate lighter measures, in hopes that the Union could be restored with as little damage to the prewar state of things as possible. Later in the year, West Tennessee's most prominent Unionist, Emerson Etheridge, rejected a federal judgeship as a means of illustrating his strong opposition to emancipation. The Radicals, as the faction desiring harsher measures came to be known, advocated limitation of the franchise to those who could show unconditional support for the Union throughout the crisis, economic punishment for the disloyal, and immigration from the North and Europe. A conservative in many ways himself, Andrew Johnson himself initially opposed emancipation, but pressure from Lincoln and the practicalities of the military governor's position required his acquiescence in and eventual advocacy of emancipation. The significant differences between the two factions of the Unionist "party" would carry into the postwar period.[10]

What was left of the institution of slavery continued to deteriorate, even if the Emancipation Proclamation did not apply to the state. Contrabands, as the practically but not legally freed slaves were called, were concentrated in camps or in the Federally garrisoned towns. In the crisis of the late summer of 1862, contrabands were impressed into service by the Federal army to build fortifications around Nashville. Because they were unpaid, often mistreated, and poorly provided with food, shelter, and clothing, the morale of the former slaves suffered during this interval. Nonetheless, they recognized that their condition had essentially changed, and notwithstanding the neglect of the Federal authorities, their enthusiasm for the Union cause remained. As 1863 wore on, it was but a short step to move from

---

Northern States to Reduce the Descendants of the Rebels of 1776, who Defeated the Armies of the King of . England and gained Independence for the United States, Down to the Level of the Negro Race (Nashville: John H. Savage, 1903), 66–67, 73–77, 144–46.

10. Maslowski, Treason Must Be Made Odious, 80–84, 147; Cimprich, Slavery's End in Tennessee, 98–117; Introduction, 6 PAJ xlvii–xlviii.

employing the contrabands on fortifications to begin arming them to fight for the Union.[11]

Harris's role at army headquarters required that he stay at Tullahoma, occupying "a little white cottage on the out skirts of town." This regimen agreed with the governor, as it was noted in the winter of 1863 during a visit to Winchester that he "look[ed] remarkably well, and [was] in fine spirits." In March, there was a grand review of Hardee's Corps, and the martial scene was described in the *Winchester Daily Bulletin*. The governor was noted to be among the luminaries present at the stirring event: "His Excellency, Gov. Isham G. Harris, was in attendance, his countenance exemplifying that degree of earnestness so characteristic of the patriot."[12]

Harris's sojourn with the army, however, did not insulate him from the politics of state government. On January 23, a letter appeared in the *Rebel* calling for "Gubernatorial action in an early convening of the Legislature of Tennessee." The correspondent noted that it seemed "highly important in view of the present revolutionary condition of things, and the circumstances attendant upon the fact that half of our territory is in the hands of our enemies and the term of office of the Governor and the members of the Legislature is approaching an end." The next day, in Richmond, Tennessee's congressional delegation "united in the recommendation to Governor Harris to convene the legislature of that state."[13]

The newspapers in the part of the state still under Confederate control agreed. The *Rebel*, for example, saw "no reason why the General Assembly of the State could not be convened now as well as when our State capital was in our possession. There is much business of vital interest to the commonwealth to be transacted and a great deal of good might be accomplished." Harris's viewpoint is not directly recorded, but it can be concluded that he was not in favor of the idea. In mid-February, he was visited by Confederate Congressmen William G. Swann and Joseph Heiskell in order to discuss the possibility of calling the legislature. It was

11. Cimprich, *Slavery's End in Tennessee*, 17, 46–59, 65, 100–101; Maslowski, *Treason Must Be Made Odious*, 100–103.

12. By Grapevine or Otherwise"; "Review of Gen. Hardee's Troops at Tullahoma," *Winchester Daily Bulletin*, March 21, 1863.

13. "Gov. Isham G. Harris," *Winchester Daily Bulletin*, January 24, 1863; "The State Legislature," *Chattanooga Daily Rebel*, January 23, 1863; "Tennessee Legislature," *Winchester Daily Bulletin*, January 29, 1863.

determined that the extra session was "impracticable," as a quorum of members were not inside Confederate lines.[14]

Still, some were of the opinion that Harris should be doing something. In late February or early March, the *Athens Post* accused the governor of "masterly inactivity." Changing its position somewhat, the loyal *Daily Rebel* responded by pointing out the obvious fact that the most realistic potential for something being done was with the army, not the governor. "In any event, what can we, the people, or he, the Governor, do?" The *Rebel* observed that the legislature could not meet without a quorum, and a constitutional convention would lack validity with no participation from Middle and West Tennessee. These "facts of law" were effectively "an answer to every enquiry and a defense of Governor Harris." Returning to the subject three days later, the *Rebel* mocked that if the governor's critics "will undertake to legislate the army of General Rosecrans out of the state by an act of the General Assembly, and can satisfy anybody that such a scheme is practicable, the Governor, we are sure, will lose not a day till the labor is accomplished."[15]

In March, the *Winchester Daily Bulletin* reported that it had been "settled" that there would be no election for governor should the Federals continue to hold Middle and West Tennessee when the time came for the elections in August.[16] The governor, who had been publicly silent to this point, responded, writing the *Bulletin* from Tullahoma on April 3, declaring "that it is settled by the Constitution of Tennessee that there shall be an election for Governor, Senators, and Representatives, on the first Thursday in August, and there is no power in or out the State which can change or annul this constitutional requirement." Therefore, Harris continued, the election would be held, and when the time was right, the state government would "take all necessary preparatory steps" for the election. Requesting that all political differences be put aside, Harris wrote: "we should select a good and true man for each position, in whose support all true patriots cordially unite." Harris's proposition made sense to the *Athens Post*, the publisher of the "masterly inactivity" comment. It "cordially endorse[d] the suggestion," and expressed the

14. Moran, "Isham G. Harris and Confederate Government," 157–58; "A recent telegraphic dispatch," *Chattanooga Daily Rebel*, January 30, 1863; "Our Congressmen and the State Government," *Knoxville Daily Register*, February 20, 1863.

15. "Let us turn for a moment," *Chattanooga Daily Rebel*, March 3, 1863; "We recur to our state affairs," *Chattanooga Daily Rebel*, March 6, 1863.

16. "It has Been Settled," *Winchester Daily Bulletin*, March 21, 1863.

"hope that there is patriotism enough and a spirit of self-sacrifice sufficient to adopt it and carry it into effect."[17]

Making an effort to restore political normalcy that spring, Harris attended to the various duties that his dual position as governor and aide and confidant to the high command of the Army of Tennessee entailed. An early concern was the sickness and death in February 1863 of William F. McGregor, the state treasurer. As the state constitution gave Harris the power to temporarily fill the vacancy until the next session of the legislature, the governor appointed Joel Allen Battle, a former brigadier general of the state militia, who served as the colonel of the 20th Tennessee Infantry early in the war, until incapacitated by a falling tree limb at Shiloh and captured. Not exchanged until September 1862, Battle lost his command of the regiment during the army reorganization that May.[18]

Battle soon needed Harris's assistance. Having already had two sons killed at Shiloh, Battle learned in early May 1863 that one of his daughters, Fannie, had been arrested with a friend and confined at Camp Chase, Ohio. According to one account, the ladies were arrested for "passing the Federal lines without authority" and were "to be imprisoned for the war." Battle beseeched Harris to intervene with Johnston or Bragg to see if they could do anything to secure the young women's release. Harris sprang into action, first discussing the matter with Bragg, and then addressing Secretary of War James A. Seddon, requesting assistance. Seddon referred the matter to the Confederacy's agent for prisoner exchange, Robert Ould, who was able to secure the ladies' release on May 13, 1863.[19]

While Harris remained near army headquarters at Tullahoma, what was left of the machinery of the state government, which included State Treasurer Battle, John Edward R. Ray, the secretary of state, and likely James Trimble Dunlap, the state comptroller, was headquartered at Winchester, farther behind the lines. An example of what must been several communications from the governor to these officers survives in a letter dated April 9, 1863. There, Harris instructs Ray to issue a pardon to a "convict" on the condition that the man "enlists in the Confed-

---

17. "From Gov. Harris," *Athens Post,* April 17, 1863; "Gov. Harris," *Athens Post,* April 17, 1863.

18. IGH to J. E. R. Ray, February 19, 1863, Harris Papers, TSLA; "Wm. F. McGregor," *Chattanooga Daily Rebel,* March 1, 1863; McBride and Robison, *Biographical Directory of the Tennessee General Assembly,* 1:35–36; Lindsley, ed., *Military Annals,* 382–83.

19. OR Series II, 5:943–44; "Col. Joel E. Battle," *Winchester Daily Bulletin,* March 20, 1863; "W. S. Rosecrans—The Dog," *Montgomery Advertiser,* April 26, 1863.

erate army." The letter then requests information relative to the bond issues made to prosecute the war, so that the governor could give the Bank of Tennessee "a statement of what is due the Bank from these two sources." Harris also points to a legal opinion from Judge Archibald Wright of the state supreme court that Ray and Dunlap could not collect certain fees under existing law.[20]

Having proposed a means to have an election of "good and true" men, Harris spent some time traveling in the rump of the state still under Confederate control with Washington Barrow, who had been imprisoned by Andrew Johnson for a short period the previous year as a "political offender." Harris and Barrow visited Athens on April 25, 1863, and the *Athens Post* noted the "general expression" Barrow should run for governor. Although the *Post* was critical of Harris in the past, the same article stated: "The present Executive, who has so ably discharged the duties of the office in the trying times which have been upon us for the past two years, is ineligible under the Constitution for a re-election, having served three terms." A visit to Knoxville occurred a day or two before, and Barrow's potential candidacy was mentioned there, too.[21]

In addition to the election due in August for members of the General Assembly and the office of governor, the Confederate Congress faced the issue of passing legislation to accommodate the changed conditions in Tennessee relative to election of representatives to Congress. Like the method suggested for state offices by Harris, the act provided for election by a general ticket. Although there initially was a veto on Confederate constitutional grounds by President Davis, a second version of the bill that addressed some of Davis's concerns was passed, and the election was set for August 1863.[22]

On May 23, 1863, a call for a state convention was published in the *Chattanooga Daily Rebel,* signed by several hundred individuals, mostly from the army. At the head of the list of signatories appeared Harris, General Cheatham, and Senator Gustavus A. Henry. The document fixed the meeting for June 17, 1863, at

20. Moran, "Isham G. Harris and Confederate Government," 148–50; McBride and Robison, *Biographical Directory of the Tennessee General Assembly,* 1:217, 609, 821; IGH to J. E. R. Ray, April 9, 1863, Harris Papers, TSLA.

21. "Gen. Barrow," *Athens Post,* May 1, 1863; McBride and Robison, *Biographical Directory of the Tennessee General Assembly,* 1:30; "Distinguished Visitors," *Knoxville Register,* April 24, 1863; "Our Next Governor," *Knoxville Daily Register,* May 5, 1863.

22. Moran, "Isham G. Harris and Confederate Government," 169–76; "Congressional Elections in Tennessee," *Knoxville Daily Register,* May 5, 1863.

Winchester, and urged: "*We must* exhibit to the enemy our unalterable firmness of purpose and determination to preserve and perpetuate our free institutions."[23]

In spite of the serious purpose, there were comic overtones. The *Knoxville Register* and *Athens Post* both suggested Chattanooga was a more "accessible place" for the meeting, setting off a bitter response from the *Winchester Daily Bulletin*, which had previously mocked Chattanooga's smell, arguing Winchester's perceived advantages over Chattanooga: "Everything is cleaner, everything is cheaper, everything is better and more plentiful, the mind can work more freely, and Winchester is just as accessible as that hole called Chattanooga." Another article in the *Knoxville Register* reported that it "was wickedly said," that, after the return of peace, "there were at least one thousand men among the volunteer soldiers of Tennessee who expected to succeed Governor Harris because of their various achievements on ensanguined battle fields." No one dreamed, however, that these candidates "displaying their wounds" would make themselves available before peace was achieved.[24]

As called for, the delegates convened at 9:00 in the morning on June 17, 1863, in the Presbyterian church in Winchester.[25] In the end, it was not Barrow, but the distinguished Judge Robert Looney Caruthers who was nominated for governor. Candidates were also secured for the state's Confederate congressional seats. After Caruthers's nomination, Colonel A. W. Campbell moved a vote of thanks for Harris, endorsing the governor's "wise and patriotic administration" and rendering "heartfelt thanks for his untiring devotion to the interests and honor of the State, and the fidelity with which he has discharged the important trust the people have confided in him."[26] Harris responded to this resolution and the "loud calls of the Convention" with "a brief and forcible address," which one observer termed "powerful."[27]

23. "To the People of Tennessee," *Chattanooga Daily Rebel*, May 23, 1863; "To the People of Tennessee," *Fayetteville Observer*, June 4, 1863; "State Convention," *Winchester Daily Bulletin*, June 2, 1863.

24. "Chattanooga is a 'sweet scented place,'" *Winchester Daily Bulletin*, February 2, 1863; "State Convention," *Winchester Daily Bulletin*, June 2, 1863; "The campaign for office," *Montgomery Advertiser*, May 22, 1863.

25. "We are requested to state," *Winchester Daily Bulletin*, June 17, 1863; "The Convention," *Winchester Daily Bulletin*, June 19, 1863; "State Convention," *Fayetteville Observer*, June 25, 1863. For a thorough discussion of the proceedings, see Moran, "Isham G. Harris and Confederate Government," 189–97.

26. "State Convention of Tennessee," *Chattanooga Daily Rebel*, June 21, 1863.

27. Ibid.; "The Convention," *Winchester Daily Bulletin*, June 19, 1863.

Unfortunately for Harris and the other Confederate Tennesseans, events at the front just a week later cast serious doubt on the prospects for a successful election. On June 24, 1863, Rosecrans finally moved against Bragg's line of defense, seizing Hoover's Gap on the far right of the Confederate line and pouring troops through to threaten Bragg's line of supply back to Chattanooga. Bragg abandoned his lines at Tullahoma the night of June 30, and retreated to the line of the Elk River. During these movements, Chaplain Quintard encountered Harris, who "looked very bright and cheerful" and said, "To-morrow morning you will be roused up by the thunder of our artillery." No doubt to Harris's consternation, the next morning the army retreated through Winchester to Cowan, at the western foot of the Cumberland Plateau. By the evening of July 2, the army was in motion across the plateau toward Chattanooga, from whence it had started eleven months before. Once again, the little town on the banks of the Tennessee was the de facto capital of Confederate Tennessee.[28]

The loss of Middle Tennessee to the numerically superior Federals once again underscored the need for more troops. On June 6, the Confederate government called for six thousand men from state of Tennessee for local defense and special service for six months from August 1, 1863. Harris issued a stirring proclamation on June 22, appealing for volunteers for this service, stating that as much as the state had "already done in this struggle for national independence, I am proud to know that she is able and willing to do more, and that she will persevere to the end of the struggle, however long or bloody it might be." Even with the enthusiastic approval of the *Knoxville Register* and *Chattanooga Daily Rebel*, the appeal was not very successful among the people of East Tennessee, "half of whom," Harris ruefully wrote to Seddon on July 24, "sympathize with our enemy." This fact was publicly acknowledged in the *Rebel*, where it was stated on July 26 that "the full measure of six thousand men are not expected from the limited portion of the State now in our possession." A letter from Whitthorne was published near the end of the month emphasizing that the troops were not meant to be sent outside Tennessee, but "only to meet the enemy when he actually comes to pillage and destroy his own and the premises of his neighbor, and upon sudden invasions."

28. Steven E. Woodworth, *Six Armies in Tennessee: The Chickamauga and Chattanooga Campaigns* (Lincoln: University of Nebraska Press, 1998), 19–46; Elliott, ed., *Doctor Quintard*, 76; "Letter from Chattanooga," *Knoxville Daily Register*, July 7, 1863.

The call, which promised some success before the retreat across the Cumberland Plateau, ended up raising less than two thousand men.[29]

What little success the Confederates had in recruiting the ranks of the Army of Tennessee to that point in 1863 could be credited to Harris's friend, Gideon J. Pillow. For the first three months of the year, Pillow found his true calling at the head of the Volunteer and Conscript Bureau of the Army of Tennessee, using small forces of cavalry to obtain men for the army. Unfortunately, the Confederate War Department eventually stopped Pillow's activities, determining that he interfered too much with the regular process of conscription.[30]

The emergency conditions of the summer of 1863 gave Pillow an opening to resurrect his powerful position. In mid-July, Joseph E. Johnston asked for authority to enforce the conscript law in Tennessee, Alabama, and Mississippi. Johnston was given the authority, and immediately placed Pillow back in charge. Emboldened, Pillow wrote to Confederate Adjutant General Samuel Cooper on August 7, urging that his former methods be expanded to the rest of the Confederacy, or at least into Georgia. Pillow got the qualified endorsement of Georgia Governor Joseph E. Brown and the enthusiastic endorsement of Bragg, Johnston, and Harris. From bitter experience, Harris wrote that the conscript law's system was "defective." Recruiting the armies "require[ed] systematic effort and force" and Pillow, in Harris's view, had the necessary experience to do so in a most efficient manner. In replying to Johnston, Seddon noted that Pillow's previous actions were often extralegal, which caused a number of "remonstrances, indignant and bitter." Pillow retained the authority given him by Johnston, and did good work in the late summer and fall of 1863, but never got the expanded authority he had requested.[31]

Harris sought to link Pillow's recruiting efforts with the conduct of the elec-

29. OR Series 4, vol. 2, 666–69; "The State Military Corps—Letter from the Adjutant General," *Chattanooga Daily Rebel,* July 29, 1863; "Requisition on Tennessee for Six Months Troops," *Knoxville Daily Register,* June 26, 1863; "The Call of Governor Harris," *Chattanooga Daily Rebel,* June 28, 1863; "The Governor of Tennessee," *Chattanooga Daily Rebel,* July 26, 1863, see also "General Order, July 22, 1863," *Chattanooga Daily Rebel,* July 23, 1863, clarifying the terms of the call to an age group of men not subject to conscription.

30. Connelly, *Autumn of Glory,* 109–10; Hughes and Stonesifer, *The Life and Wars of Gideon J. Pillow,* 260–65.

31. OR Series 4, vol. 2, 748–53; Hughes and Stonesifer, *The Life and Wars of Gideon J. Pillow,* 267–73.

tion on August 6. Harris secured Bragg's cooperation in sending Confederate cavalry into West Tennessee in order to facilitate the election in that area. It seemed to the governor that at the same time, Pillow could recruit the temporarily reoccupied area. Harris sent Pillow a dispatch on July 29 from Chattanooga notifying the general of the enterprise and suggesting that Pillow deputize Harris's election superintendents, Colonel Alexander William Campbell and a Captain Clark with full recruiting powers. Unfortunately, Campbell was captured at Lexington in West Tennessee. Alerted, the Federals took steps to disrupt efforts to recruit and hold elections as far north as Paris, Tennessee.[32]

Harris apparently remained in Chattanooga through the election.[33] On election day, the *Rebel* urged: "Everybody vote." Federal efforts in West Tennessee appear to have substantially disrupted what chance there was to hold the election there, but some counties in Middle Tennessee were able to vote. The election went on as it normally would have in East Tennessee, and the Tennesseans in the army were able to vote as well. Because of events in late August and early September, the results of the election for the Tennessee legislature were never reported.[34]

Hopeful in his anticipation that he might be relieved of his office, Harris planned to formalize his service in the army. Long before the election, it was suggested that, at least in one regard, Harris was the equal or superior of any other officer in the Army of Tennessee. In March, a reporter heard that "a distinguished officer in command of department . . . expressed the opinion that the dispatches, letters, etc. transmitted by Governor Harris to Richmond, evince a clearer military sagacity than those of any one connected with the army of the West." The department commander, Bragg, still maintained a healthy respect for Harris on August 7, the day after the election, writing President Davis that he should consider a military appointment for Harris, and stating, "if I had a vacant Brigade I should gladly recommend him for it." Seddon thought political rather than military reasons compelled the appointment, and Davis determined to ask Bragg's advice on the timing of an appointment and the nature of Harris's potential position.[35]

32. OR 24(3):560, 562; Warner, *Generals in Gray,* 42.

33. The correspondence at OR Series 4, 2:752 indicates the governor was in Chattanooga on August 8.

34. "The Election," *Chattanooga Daily Rebel,* August 6, 1863; Moran, "Isham Harris and the Confederate State Government in Tennessee," 201–8.

35. "By Grapevine or Otherwise," *Chattanooga Daily Rebel,* March 18, 1863; Bragg to Davis, August 7, 1863, 9 *PJD* 322.

Harris's unique relationship to the Confederate army's high command in the West once more became evident in August. On August 12, Harris wrote Davis from Columbus, Mississippi, seeking the president's assurance that Lieutenant General John C. Pemberton would not be put back in command of the army there, which he had surrendered to Major General Ulysses S. Grant the month before. This effectively echoed a letter from Hardee on the same subject dated August 6. Hardee was sent to Mississippi in mid-July to help Johnston repair the disarray created by the Federal invasion subsequent to the fall of Vicksburg. Davis replied to Harris on August 17 with the assurance the governor sought, noting that Hardee was then in command of the troops there, and he ranked Pemberton. Harris appears to have been so concerned by the threat that Pemberton would resume command of the Vicksburg troops that he made a flying visit to Richmond at that time. In any event, a formal order was issued on August 19, parceling out the Vicksburg parolees by state, and appointing Hardee commander of those from Louisiana and Mississippi.[36]

Events in Tennessee soon brought Harris back to Chattanooga. On August 21, Rosecrans began a series of moves calculated to confuse and deceive Bragg relative to the route of the Federals' advance on Chattanooga. The most spectacular was a Federal column's appearance on Stringer's Ridge, on the north bank of the Tennessee opposite the town, just as a portion of the populace was in church to observe a day of fasting, humiliation, and prayer proclaimed by Jefferson Davis. By the time Harris returned to Chattanooga on August 24, many of the "public institutions" had already fled, leaving little more than the *Daily Rebel* and its staff and the Confederate military. Among the "institutions" removed, or soon to be removed, were the post office, the telegraph office, and the records of the state of Tennessee.[37]

Harris dispatched a terse plea to President Davis on August 30 for arms for

36. IGH to Davis, August 12, 1863, 9 *PJD* 341, also in Jefferson Davis Papers, Louisiana Historical Association Collection, Tulane (confirms Harris at Columbus); Nathaniel Cheairs Hughes Jr., *General William J. Hardee: Old Reliable* (Baton Rouge: Louisiana State University Press, 1965) 157–59; OR 52(2):514–17. Relative to Harris's visit to Richmond, see "Governor Harris," *Chattanooga Daily Rebel,* August 25, 1863, which reports a return to Chattanooga from Richmond, and IGH to Mrs. General Ewell, March 7, 1863, George Washington Campbell Papers, LC, noting Harris visiting Richmond "repeatedly" in the previous eight months.

37. Woodworth, *Six Armies in Tennessee,* 54–56; Elliott, ed., *Dr. Quintard,* 77; "Governor Harris" and "The Rebel," *Chattanooga Daily Rebel,* August 25, 1863; "Removed," *Montgomery Weekly Advertiser,* August 26, 1863.

exchanged prisoners and recruits, which ended: "if you can re-enforce this line it is of the highest importance." Davis replied on September 1 that arms were on the way, and that he hoped that militia and local defense troops from Tennessee, Georgia, and Alabama would provide "accessions to the army." While reinforcements were indeed on their way from Mississippi and Virginia, they would not arrive in time to save Chattanooga from Rosecrans's advance, or for that matter, Knoxville from that of Union Major General Ambrose Burnside, both of which were evacuated in the first nine days of September.[38]

Buckner's withdrawal ended, for all practical purposes, the largely unsuccessful Confederate effort to pacify East Tennessee. Like the Federals in Middle and West Tennessee, the Confederate government had underestimated the depth of the opposition in East Tennessee, which itself contributed to a dangerous inconsistency in policy toward the recalcitrant Unionists. At times, while the government at Richmond tried leniency, local secessionists used the legal process and other means to oppress Unionists. The Confederate draft would at times be suspended, then reinstated. The Unionist majority in the region did little or nothing to support the Confederate government, and often actively supported the partisans that roamed the area. Parties on both sides used the disorder to settle personal or political differences in a violent fashion, and as time wore on, frustrated Confederate soldiers acted as badly in East Tennessee as the Federals in Middle and West Tennessee, which exacerbated already hard feelings. Finally, as in the other two grand divisions of the state, the disorder, retaliation, and unrest caused by the military occupation of an area with an unfriendly population resulted in the destruction of property and much human suffering.[39]

The loss of the bulk of East Tennessee must have finally brought home to Harris the futility of the summer's effort to seat a new legislature and thereby obtain release from office. Under Article III, Section 4 of the Tennessee Constitution of 1834, Harris remained governor until his successor "shall be elected and qualified." According to Article III, Section 2, qualification occurred when the returns from the election were opened up and published "in the presence of a majority of the members of each House." Of course, the "military necessities" of the late summer of 1863 made it "impossible to convene the legislature."[40] Harris later wrote

38. OR 52(2):519, 520; Woodworth, *Six Armies in Tennessee*, 62–66.

39. Bryan, "The Civil War in East Tennessee," 115–17; Fisher, *War at Every Door*, 119–21.

40. Tennessee Constitution of 1834, Art. III; "The Three Governors of Tennessee," *Knoxville Daily Register*, September 19, 1863.

that he made an earnest effort to elect Judge Caruthers, and after the election, the governor declared, he "made every effort possible to get the Legislature together to have him *qualified*. But it was impossible. Therefore I remained Governor under the Constitution until a successor was *elected and qualified*."[41]

The Confederacy got a brief surge of hope that a portion of Tennessee might be recovered that September. Rosecrans's advance southwest of Chattanooga dangerously separated his army, during an interval in which Bragg was being reinforced from other quarters of the Confederacy. Harris was privy to the movements of the two armies to the extent understood by Bragg and his staff, and approved of Bragg's evacuation of Chattanooga and withdrawal into northwest Georgia in order to "move with his whole force to meet the enemy in the field to take his chances to regain Chattanooga & Tennessee by not only whipping him, but crushing him." During this interval, on September 10, 1863, Harris gave a speech to Tennessee troops of Cheatham's Division of the plan to "fall on and destroy two of [Rosecrans's] corps before the other corps could come up." In the course of the speech, Harris told the Tennesseans that "he wished to make one more Fourth of July speech after the war was over, to tell how well the Tennessee troops had fought."[42]

Bragg indeed made efforts to fall upon the separated segments of the Army of the Cumberland, which were ultimately frustrated by the failure of his subordinates. Harris wrote of the chance missed on September 11, 1863, at McLemore's Cove, west of Lafayette, Georgia, where Major General Thomas C. Hindman, in command of three Rebel divisions, failed to attack a large element of the Federal XIV Corps. Bragg, Harris and others "stood on Pidgeon [sic] Mountain from daylight until 9 o'clock at night anxiously expecting and listening for Hindman's guns, but not a gun was fired." The Federals escaped, and, Harris sadly wrote, "the golden moment was allowed to pass."[43]

Bragg marched to cut Rosecrans's army off from Chattanooga. Approaching from the southeast, the Army of Tennessee crossed Chickamauga Creek in an effort to interdict the Chattanooga–Lafayette road. The armies met "in two days of

41. IGH to D. B. Cooper, December 15, 1888, Duncan Brown Cooper Papers, TSLA.

42. Woodworth, *Six Armies in Tennessee*, 68–77; IGH to Mrs. General Ewell, George Washington Campbell Papers; IGH to D. B. Cooper, December 15, 1888, Cooper Papers; OR 30(3):581.

43. Woodworth, *Six Armies in Tennessee*; IGH to Mrs. General Ewell, March 7, 1864, George Washington Campbell Papers.

hard fighting" that resulted in Rosecrans's tactical defeat, but the Federals' retreat into Chattanooga meant that the strategic goal of Bragg's attack was not achieved. A "keen-eyed" Harris was seen riding along the battle line by a young Georgia soldier, showing as much interest as any of the generals. Another observer saw that the governor was "there encouraging by act, deed and word, the men of his state." In addition to his service on Bragg's staff, Harris continued his practice of making quasi-official battle reports to Tennessee newspapers, on September 20 telegraphing to the *Memphis Daily Appeal,* then based in Atlanta, that the Army of Tennessee had been successful in driving the enemy from his positions in the first day's fighting, but "the engagement [was] not yet decisive." Harris reported heavy casualties on both sides, including prominent officers who were killed and wounded. Harris concluded: "Troops never fought better than ours. They are in high spirits, and ready to meet the enemy again to-morrow."[44]

Harris thought that the Federals were "whipped, badly whipped" on September 20, "and if he had been vigorously pursued from the field he would have been crushed." But uncertainty at army headquarters the night of September 20 as to whether the Federals remained on the field prevailed, although at least Leonidas Polk and his subordinate, St. John Richardson Liddell, told Bragg that the Army of the Cumberland had retreated. As Harris wrote some months later, "when the firing ceased instead of following up a victory which had cost us so much & by which we had fairly won all the territory to the Mississippi river, we quietly bivouacked on the field." Harris later told Secretary of War Seddon that "Bragg did not know that a victory had been won, and when told that Rosecrans would escape during the night, would not hear of it, but insisted that a severe battle would have to be fought the next day." That next day, September 21, Harris once more telegraphed the *Appeal,* reporting a "complete" victory, and that the army was "in fine spirits, ready and eager for a vigorous pursuit."[45]

While the Army of the Cumberland was in substantial disarray, the Army of

44. Woodworth, *Six Armies in Tennessee;* IGH to Mrs. General Ewell, March 7, 1864, Campbell Papers; "The Twentieth Georgia Regiment at the Battle of Chickamauga," *Southern Historical Society Papers* 16 (1888): 384, 386; Robert G. Stone letter, September 29, 1863, Stone Family Papers, University of Georgia; "The Battle of Chickamauga," *Macon Weekly Telegraph,* September 30, 1863; OR 30(3):791.

45. Connelly, *Army of the Heartland,* 228–29; St. John Richardson Liddell, *Liddell's Record,* ed. Nathaniel Cheairs Hughes Jr. (Baton Rouge: Louisiana State University Press, 1997), 146–47; IGH to Mrs. General Ewell, March 7, 1864, Campbell Papers; Robert Garlick Hill Kean, *Inside the Confed-*

Tennessee was not in much better shape. In the end, Bragg settled on investing Chattanooga by occupying Missionary Ridge, Chattanooga Valley, and Lookout Mountain. While the Confederates waited for the bluecoats to starve, surrender, or leave, the conflict between Bragg and his officers that necessitated Harris's involvement earlier in the year once more burst into flames, this time with little hope of reconciliation. Harris, seizing an opportunity in the afterglow of Chickamauga, wrote Davis recommending Forrest for promotion on September 24. But, on September 28, Bragg ordered Forrest to turn his command over to Wheeler, which eventually resulted in Forrest's departure from the army. On September 28, Bragg removed Polk and Hindman for their failures during the past weeks, and in turn on October 5 suffered "much distress, & mortification" when a petition gotten up by twelve corps, division, and brigade commanders addressed to the president respectfully suggested that Bragg should be removed from his command.[46]

Present with the army at this juncture was an aide of President Davis, Colonel James Chestnut. Lieutenant General James Longstreet, Robert E. Lee's primary lieutenant and the commander of the troops brought from Virginia to reinforce Bragg, spoke with Chestnut and told him of the dissenters' "distressed condition." Chestnut telegraphed the president that a personal visit to the Army of Tennessee was "urgently demanded." Therefore, Davis traveled to army headquarters on Missionary Ridge. On the morning of October 10, the president was saluted by the commanders of the corps and divisions in full dress, and reviewed the army with bands playing and martial pomp and ceremony. This stirring scene did not mask the problems between Bragg and many of his officers, and Davis eventually concluded that the Army of Tennessee lacked "that harmony among the highest officers which is essential to success." Harris felt that Bragg was "a much abler and better man than the world was willing to believe," but that he "had, to a great extent lost the confidence of the officers and men of the army," which proved to be "an element of weakness." Davis eventually sustained his commander, which failed to resolve anything. Hardee returned to the army, replaced in Mississippi

---

erate Government: The Diary of Robert Garlick Hill Kean, Head of the Bureau of War, ed. Edward Younger (New York: Oxford University Press, 1957), 425; OR 30(3):791.

46. Larry J. Daniel, Days of Glory: The Army of the Cumberland, 1861–1865 (Baton Rouge: Louisiana State University Press, 2004), 336–39; Connelly, Autumn of Glory, 231–41; IGH to Jefferson Davis, September 24, 1863, 9 PJD 403; OR 52(2):529; W. W. Mackall to wife, October 5, 1863; William W. Mackall Papers, Southern Historical Collection, UNC.

by Polk. Then, while reinforcements swelled the Federal forces at Chattanooga, Longstreet was dispatched in early November to attack the Federals at Knoxville along with 17,000 men and as many of the dissenting officers as Bragg could send with them. The troops remaining with the army were then reorganized, in order to place the remaining dissenters with officers loyal to Bragg.[47]

Given Harris's previous important role in the politics of the Army of Tennessee's high command, it is difficult to imagine that Davis did not consult the governor for his views during his visit to Chattanooga. While Harris was sympathetic to Bragg, the reorganization of the army, especially in its effects on Tennessee officers and troops, must have given the governor some pause. Harris had yet another meeting with Davis and with Confederate Vice President Alexander Stephens in Atlanta on October 30, possibly to discuss the reorganization. Regardless, the disruption of the reorganization, in combination with the loss of Longstreet's troops and the growing strength of the Federal army facing Bragg, did not make the task of the soldiers of the Army of Tennessee holding on to this one last corner of Tennessee any easier.[48]

The end came on November 25. In the preceding two days, the Federals seized Orchard Knob, providing an advanced position toward Missionary Ridge, and Lookout Mountain, driving the Army of Tennessee back to Missionary Ridge itself. Grant assigned the main effort against the ridge to his trusted lieutenant, William T. Sherman, who with the major part of the Federal Army of the Tennessee, reinforced by other elements, was to attack the northern end of Missionary Ridge. Another Federal column was to move across Chattanooga Valley and attack up the ridge north from Rossville, Georgia, just across the state line. Sherman's attack stalled, and the Rossville column was delayed by a destroyed bridge. Grant ordered a diversionary attack by four divisions of the Army of the Cumberland against the center of Missionary Ridge. The Rebel line was stretched thin, especially on the left.[49]

Bragg's headquarters on Missionary Ridge was roughly in the area where the

47. OR 30(4):728; 52(2):538; "Our Army Correspondence," *Memphis* (Atlanta) *Appeal*, October 15, 1863; OR 31(3):609, 618, 685–86; IGH to Mrs. General Ewell, March 7, 1864, Campbell Papers; Connelly, *Autumn of Glory*, 245–46, 250–54, Woodworth, *Six Armies in Tennessee*, 176–79.

48. Editorial note, 10 *PJD* 48.

49. Woodworth, *Six Armies in Tennessee*, 180–200; *Supplement to the Official Records of the Union and Confederate Armies* (Wilmington, N.C.: Broadfoot Publishing Co., 1994–2004), 6:106–7.

right of Alexander P. Stewart's division joined the left of the division commanded by William B. Bate. Earlier on November 25, Stewart received orders to move his rightmost formation, the Louisiana brigade commanded by Colonel Randall Gibson, to the left of army headquarters. When the Army of the Cumberland advanced after 3:30 that afternoon, Bragg discovered a gap in his line and dispatched Governor Harris to find troops to fill the gap. Harris went to Gibson "in great haste and told [him] that the space in front of Army Headquarters had not been occupied and that the General commanding directed it to be covered immediately." Gibson moved north to the defense of headquarters, but neither he, nor Bragg, nor Harris advised Stewart of the move, which opened a gap between Gibson and the next regiment down the line, that of Otho French Strahl. The Federals eventually penetrated that gap, as well as one that opened to the right of headquarters, and the Rebel line on the ridge collapsed in the waning afternoon light.[50]

Whatever his faults, Braxton Bragg was no coward, and he did his best to rally his disintegrating line, riding under fire among his men, waving his cap, and "beseeching them to hold their ground." One newspaper writer reported that "Gen. Bragg and Gov. Harris, seeing the lines upon the left centre begin to waver, dashed forward right into their midst and begged the men to hold the position at all hazards. They seemed to be perfectly indifferent to death." Bragg's staff, of which Harris was a member, was lauded in his report for "their gallant and zealous efforts under fire to rally the broken troops and restore order, and for their laborious services in conducting successfully the many and arduous duties of the retreat."[51]

Once the army got away toward Dalton, Harris, Whitthorne, Senator Gustavus Henry, and certain ill and wounded officers, including Marcus J. Wright, went on to Atlanta, arriving on November 27. Wright and his brigade, including young Eugene Harris, fought in support of the Rebel forces on the northern end of Missionary Ridge, and therefore avoided the rout on the center and left. Unfortunately, Wright's brigade train was captured by a column of Federal cavalry, causing the loss of the personal baggage of Wright's officers and men and of Governor

50. OR 31(2):740; ORS 6:107–9, 113–17; "Battle of Chattanooga," *Southern Banner* (Athens, Ga.), December 16, 1863.

51. "Battle of Chattanooga"; "The Battle of Missionary Ridge," *Daily Columbus Enquirer*, December 4, 1863; OR 31(2):665–67.

Harris, who lost "his body servant, horse and the greater part of his wardrobe." Fortunately, while Eugene was slightly wounded and lost his horse, he escaped serious mishap.[52]

Harris's quick trip to Atlanta appears to have had, in part, the purpose of putting the best face on matters, letting it be known "that though our defeat may be regarded as something of a disaster, it is not one of such magnitude as first reports from the field were well calculated to make it." Harris minimized the killed and wounded, and "though somewhat mortified [was] not at all despondent in consequence of [the] reverse." The governor reported to another paper that "the army is settling down into an available position around Dalton, with its spirit unsubdued by the late reverse." The respect shown for Harris's views indicates that he came out of the campaign that fall with the esteem of his countrymen for his efforts on behalf of the Southern revolution. A month earlier, a correspondent of the displaced *Rebel* stated that Harris had suffered all of the army's "hardships, privations and dangers," ate of "the hard fare, and slept with [the army] on the ground," sharing "the privations of his country men" and fighting with the army "in all its battles." For that, the correspondent wrote, "history will do justice to Gov. Harris."[53]

From Atlanta, Harris went to Richmond. G. C. Torbett, president of the Bank of Tennessee, came to Harris with an order from the Confederate secretary of the treasury impressing the coin reserves of the bank, then in Georgia. Harris hastened to Virginia to meet with Secretary of the Treasury Christopher G. Memminger and President Davis. There, the governor explained that the bank's assets "were not the property of a private corporation, that they belonged to the whole people of Tennessee, and were a sacred trust in the hands of the officers of the bank, and protested against the impressments or seizure of the coin." The order was countermanded, and the coin stayed in possession of the bank's officers.[54]

While the governor was at the capital, the respective houses of the Confederate Congress extended to Harris "the privilege of the floor" of the Senate and, with Howell Cobb and Robert E. Lee, a seat within the bar of the House, "as a tes-

52. "Personal" and "In the late capture and destruction," *Memphis* (Atlanta) *Appeal*, November 28, 1863; OR 31(2):706–9; IGH to Mrs. General Ewell, March 7, 1864, Campbell Papers.

53. "Our Reverse," *Memphis* (Atlanta) *Appeal*, November 28, 1863; "The Front," *Daily Columbus Enquirer*, December 6, 1863; "Gov. Harris, of Tennessee," *Knoxville* (Atlanta) *Register*, October 14, 1863.

54. "Yesterday's Speaking," *Knoxville Daily Tribune*, October 19, 1876.

timonial of the great respect which this House entertains for them." With the issue of the bank resolved, Harris took the opportunity to urge the assignment of General Joseph E. Johnston, no favorite of President Davis, to the command of the Army of Tennessee. Harris later wrote that he spent three weeks urging Johnston's appointment, joining several influential politicians and generals who also backed the Virginian. While Johnston was no favorite of Davis, the president suppressed his objections, appointing Johnston on December 18, 1863.[55]

Harris returned to the army from Richmond in late December. Even with Johnston in command, there was one last episode of the division among the army's higher officers that marked Bragg's tenure. On the evening of January 2, 1864, Major General Patrick R. Cleburne, who, just five weeks before, had distinguished himself in the defense of Missionary Ridge and the subsequent retreat, presented a proposal to the higher officers of the Army of Tennessee that slaves be armed to offset the South's manpower disadvantage, and that those that so served be given their freedom at the war's conclusion. The proposal received only the open support of Cleburne's friend and former law partner, Major General Thomas C. Hindman, and was met by the violent objections of others. While Harris was not present during the presentation, upon reflection, he felt it his "duty to communicate the facts" to the president. Harris feared that the "knowledge of the fact that this policy is so advocated by officers so high in rank and who have been uniformly so efficient would produce the greatest possible discontent." Harris noted his highest regard for those officers who spoke in favor of the proposal, but expressed the hope that the matter might be "smothered so as to not gain publicity," which is what eventually occurred. The Confederacy was not quite ready for so revolutionary a measure.[56]

Thus, for the Army of Tennessee, 1863 ended in the manner it had started, with controversy among the members of its high command. Harris loyally tried to sustain Bragg during these struggles, while maintaining contacts with his opponents, such as Cheatham and Hardee. While the conflict in the army's high command was not the sole cause of the loss of Tennessee, it was a significant contributing factor. To Harris, the loss at Chattanooga would have never occurred but for

55. IGH to Mrs. General Ewell, March 7, 1864, Campbell Papers; S. Doc. No. 512, 58th Cong., 2nd Sess., *Journal of the Confederate Congress*, 3:476, 6:531; Woodworth, *Jefferson Davis and His Generals*, 256–59; OR 31(3):842.

56. "The Re-Enlistment Race," *Memphis* (Atlanta) *Appeal*, April 20, 1864; Woodworth, *Jefferson Davis and His Generals*, 262–63; IGH to Davis, January 16, 1864, 10 *PJD* 177–78; OR 52(2):595, 608.

the lack of execution by Bragg's lieutenants in McLemore's Cove. This view was shared by his fellow Tennessean, Major General A. P. Stewart, who wrote, "whatever apologies may have been offered for this failure, the *real* cause of it was the lack of confidence on the part of the superior officers of the Army of Tennessee in its commander."[57]

The Confederate military failure in Tennessee frustrated Harris's efforts to rebuild the state government and restore constitutional processes. While Harris and the political and military leaders of Tennessee strived mightily to create the semblance of a normal functioning state government in the spring and summer of 1863, in the end, the Federal advance wiped out what little had been gained. Harris personally hoped to pass the reins of his office to Judge Caruthers and join the army on a more formal basis, but in the end, his situation remained ambiguous. Nonetheless, he skillfully made it known that he had done all he could to restore the state government in unoccupied areas, and made sure that what remained of his constituents knew he was at the front with the Tennesseans serving the Confederacy.

57. IGH to Mrs. General Ewell, March 7, 1864, Campbell Papers; A. P. Stewart to Bragg, March 19, 1864, Palmer Collection of Bragg Papers, Western Reserve; A. P. Stewart, "The Army of Tennessee: A Sketch," in Lindsley, ed., *Military Annals*, 81.

6 "TENNESSEE, A GRAVE OR A FREE HOME"
1864–May 1865

After its loss at Chattanooga, the Army of Tennessee settled down for a winter during which Joseph E. Johnston and his officers would restore its strength and the confidence of its men. The new year of 1864 would see Harris continue his role as an advocate and morale-booster for the Tennessee troops in the army. And, with the Army of Tennessee no longer holding on even to the slightest sliver of the state, Harris would search for ways to stay in contact with his people and to continue his efforts to recruit Tennesseans for the Confederate war effort. With restless energy, he ranged across the western Confederacy, relentlessly pursing these two goals.[1]

Bragg's reorganization of the Army of Tennessee the previous fall hit Tennessee units the hardest. Cheatham's Division, formerly almost entirely composed of men from the Volunteer State, retained only Marcus J. Wright's brigade for the Battle of Chattanooga. This created a great deal of dissension among the Tennessee troops, of which Harris was doubtless painfully aware. Back at Dalton on January 9, 1864, Harris wrote Secretary of War Seddon requesting that Johnston have the authority to undo Bragg's changes. Carefully noting that the letter was written without Johnston's knowledge or consent, Harris expressed the opinion that the Tennesseans would do better under their old commanders. A few days later, Johnston made the same request, and eventually obtained the authority to reconstitute the division to its former character.[2]

Another Tennessean disaffected by Bragg was Nathan Bedford Forrest. After leaving the Army of Tennessee in late September 1863, Forrest assumed command of West Tennessee, and by December, was back in the state raising a new com-

1. Richard M. McMurry, *Atlanta 1864: Last Chance for the Confederacy* (Lincoln: University of Nebraska Press, 2000), 37–38.

2. OR 32(2):537–38; Losson, *Tennessee's Forgotten Warriors*, 118, 133–35.

mand. After several of his usual hairs-breadth escapes, Forrest was back in Mississippi by the first of 1864, and met at Meridian, Mississippi, on January 13, 1864, with Leonidas Polk, the department commander, and Major General Stephen D. Lee, its cavalry commander, to report on his recent efforts. Likely present at that meeting, and certainly present at Meridian three days later, was Isham G. Harris. Harris returned with Forrest to his headquarters in north Mississippi, first at Como, and then at Oxford. In keeping with his efforts to exert influence on behalf of Tennessee commanders and troops, the governor lost little time writing President Davis that Forrest's efforts at recruiting and organizing a command were suffering from competing demands from Mississippi state authorities and the Confederate War Department.[3]

Harris and Forrest were doubtless acquainted from their prewar days in Memphis. Forrest enlisted as a private soldier in June 1861, but several citizens of Memphis respected Forrest and petitioned Harris to offer him a command. Harris knew "Forrest well and had a high regard for the man." The governor telegraphed that Forrest should go to Memphis, and with Polk's help, "procured authority for him to raise a regiment of cavalry for the Confederate service." Forrest embarked on a career that, as early as 1864, made him a legend. The cavalryman and his governor had had a number of opportunities to spend time together during the war, and Harris likely wanted to confer with Forrest about conditions in West Tennessee and the prospects for recruiting there, although a friend noted that Harris was "pining for action" at this time. An officer's diary recorded that Harris spoke to his company on February 4 at Oxford, which was likely a common occurrence during that interval.[4]

While Harris was in Mississippi, a new Federal threat appeared. On February 2, William T. Sherman set two Federal army corps in motion from their camps east of Vicksburg on a march aimed at Polk's headquarters at Meridian, Mississippi. In North Mississippi Forrest's scouts, including former Atlanta newspaperman George W. Adair, read the signs of the impending advance, observing that

3. Brian Steel Wills, *A Battle From the Start: The Life of Nathan Bedford Forrest* (New York: Harper-Collins, 1992), 148–56; IGH to Jefferson Davis, January 16, 1864, 10 *PJD* 177–78; OR 32(2):601–2, 650.

4. Wills, *A Battle from the Start*, 45; James R. Chalmers, "Forrest and His Campaigns," *Southern Historical Society Papers* 7 (October 1879): 449, 455; John Allen Wyeth, *Life of Lieutenant-General Nathan Bedford Forrest* (New York: Harper and Brothers, 1899), 23–24; "Isham G. Harris as Warrior and Fugitive," *Atlanta Constitution,* August 1, 1897; William W. Chester, ed., "The Diary of Captain Elisha Tompkin Hollis, CSA," *West Tennessee Historical Society Papers* 39 (December 1985): 83, 91.

the Federals had evacuated Corinth and most of West Tennessee. Forrest prepared a detailed dispatch to Polk. Likely because Harris intended on returning to Dalton at that time in any event, the governor was dispatched with Adair to deliver the message. Leaving Oxford on February 9, they discovered that the Confederate rolling stock in the area had been moved to prevent its capture or destruction. Accordingly, they traveled from Okolona to Artesia, a distance of more than forty miles, by handcar, assisted by two Negro workmen. Adair later described the trip: "Jolting, jolting, bouncing we went all day and then all night, making such progress as we could." Oftentimes, he and Harris would have to help the workmen push the car up a difficult grade, but on the down grade they would "let her rip." Adair recalled, "I have frequently thought of that trip since, the governor of a great state with coat off and perspiration rolling down his face, pushing a dirty hand car."[5]

Harris and Adair reached Artesia and found that a train would be up the next day after some remnants of stores that were being removed by the Confederate government. They arrived outside of Meridian just as the Confederate troops evacuated the place, moving east into Alabama. While the loss of Meridian, a significant military logistical center, was a severe blow to the Confederacy, Harris was fortunate not to be killed or captured by the swarming Federals. Indeed, in a contemporary letter to a Georgia newspaper, Adair commented: "You will observe that the Governor and myself conducted our trip with signal good luck and at an opportune moment." Even though Polk was unable to resist Sherman's advance, much to Sherman's disgust Forrest successfully intercepted a Federal cavalry expedition from Tennessee intended to join with the main column at Meridian.[6]

After his experience in Mississippi, Harris returned to the encampment of the Army of Tennessee at Dalton, Georgia, for an interval, and was pleased to find that General Johnston had the full confidence of the officers and men of his army. Writing Lizenka Brown Ewell, he observed, "I have never seen the Army of Ten-

5. Buck T. Foster, *Sherman's Mississippi Campaign* (Tuscaloosa: University of Alabama Press, 2006), 21, 31–32, 43–44; OR 32(2):346–47; IGH to Jefferson Davis, January 16, 1864, 10 *PJD* 177–78; "Colonel Geo. W. Adair," *Atlanta Constitution,* October 2, 1892; "Isham G. Harris as Warrior and Fugitive," *Atlanta Constitution,* August 1, 1897; "Correspondence from General Forrest's Command," *Macon Daily Telegraph,* February 20, 1864.

6. "Isham G. Harris as Warrior and Fugitive," *Atlanta Constitution,* August 1, 1897; "Correspondence from General Forrest's Command," *Macon Daily Telegraph,* February 20, 1864; Foster, *Sherman's Mississippi Campaign,* 92–93; Wills, *A Battle from the Start,* 159–68.

nessee in better spirit than at this time." Notwithstanding the morale of the army, Harris deemed the situation facing Tennessee and the Confederacy as "rather a gloomy one." But, if the revolution were to fail, "the fault is our own." Harris expressed the view that the problem was that the Confederates had failed to properly mass their forces, mistakenly spreading them out by trying to hold too much territory. Harris thought the proper strategy was to combine the Army of Tennessee with Longstreet's small force in upper East Tennessee, Polk's Mississippi army, and Beauregard's forces in and around Charleston. "If it is done I have high hopes of a brilliant campaign, but if the old defensive policy is adhered to, I confess I have little hope for Tennessee or the Confederacy, I am resolved however, to bide the fortunes of the struggle and press forward to the end, be that end bright & successful or dark and bloody."[7]

Harris confided to Mrs. Ewell he was leaving Dalton that very night, March 7, 1864, for Mississippi "to join Forrest and make a raid into West Tennessee and visit my long neglected wife and boys, hope to return in about 6 weeks." Although Eugene was with General Wright, Martha and his other boys were back in Paris, where they had moved after the fall of Memphis in 1862. Fortunately, they were not annoyed by Federal authorities and were "comfortably situated." At that juncture, Harris had not seen them for two years. Harris hoped to bring his next oldest son, James, out of West Tennessee if he was "fortunate as to get home." Forrest's success in West Tennessee in December doubtless planted a seed that there was more to be accomplished there. With the Federal cavalry routed out of North Mississippi, the time seemed ripe to return to West Tennessee, then a no-man's land "infested" by "guerrillas, horse-thieves, and robbers." Particularly irksome to the cavalryman were the oppressive actions of Colonel Fielding Hurst, commanding a Tennessee Unionist cavalry regiment, among which was the imprisonment of Reverend George W. D. Harris, the governor's brother.[8]

Hurst's activities were a symptom of the affliction brought upon West Tennessee by the war. Before secession, he was a wealthy slaveholder owning a tract straddling the Tennessee River in Middle and West Tennessee. Hurst was also a

7. IGH to Mrs. General Ewell, March 7, 1864, Campbell Papers.
8. Ibid.; OR 32(1):611; OR 32(3):118. There is no reason to think Harris's long absence from his wife suggests that there was a feeling of estrangement between them. Martha preferred the company of her extended family during much of Harris's political life, and it must have seemed she would be safest in her own community, even behind Federal lines, rather than among strangers in the rear of the Confederate army.

vocal Unionist, and ended up in prison in Nashville until liberated when the city fell in 1862. Subsequently, Hurst was placed in command of the Federal 6th Tennessee Cavalry, which operated in West Tennessee from November 1862. Hurst and his men, often with the tacit if not explicit approval of his Federal superiors, practiced "hard war" upon the secessionists of the region. In February, several acts of murder and torture could be ascribed to Hurst's command. Hurst's imprisonment of Reverend Harris must have made Governor Harris very uneasy, although eventually the old preacher was released.[9]

When Forrest moved north from Columbus, Mississippi, on March 16, 1864, Harris was with him. At or near Purdy, Tennessee, not far from the Shiloh battlefield, Company G of the 7th Tennessee Cavalry split off from the main column, which was bound for Jackson and eventually Paducah, Kentucky. Under the command of Captain Felen F. Aden, the forty-man company escorted Governor Harris to Henry County. Just across the Henry County line, Aden's men encountered a force of Federals, and after a "sharp engagement," forced the Federals to retire. Since a reward had been offered for Harris's capture, Aden did not pursue the enemy with his small force, but was able to escort the governor on to Paris. In addition to presumably spending time with his family, Harris and the men with him were to bring back to Forrest every man between the ages of eighteen and forty-five.[10]

Forrest reported Harris at Paris as late as April 10, the same date that he announced to his superior, Major General Stephen D. Lee, his intention to move the next day with two of his brigades to Fort Pillow. At the time, the fort was garrisoned by white West Tennessee Union troops and by a contingent of United States Colored Troops, a mix of "renegades" and former slaves that invoked anger and disgust among Forrest's men. The Rebels arrived at the fort, on the Mississippi River, near dawn on April 12. During the course of the day, the gray cavalrymen first invested and then attacked the fort. An effort at surrender negotiations broke down, and Forrest eventually sent his men swarming over the ramparts of the fort. In the melee that followed, a number of Federal soldiers were killed,

9. Andrew Ward, *River Run Red: The Fort Pillow Massacre in the American Civil War* (New York: Viking, 2005), 9–10, 79–80, 102–4; Tennessee Civil War Centennial Commission, *Tennesseans in the Civil War* (Nashville: n.p. 1964), 1:333–35; Gary Blankinship, "Colonel Fielding Hurst and the Hurst Nation," *West Tennessee Historical Society Papers* 34 (1980): 71, 82–84.

10. OR 32(1):611; OR 32(3):779, 832; Lindsley, ed., *Military Annals*, 641; J. P. Young, *The Seventh Tennessee Cavalry: A History* (1890; reprint, Dayton: Morningside, 1976), 83.

some while trying to surrender. Although each side disputed the events of that day, Forrest's lieutenant Tyree Bell admitted there was "promiscuous shooting for some time."[11]

Fort Pillow was in some ways a microcosm of the internecine struggle within the larger sectional war. Occupying Fort Pillow were 266 men of the Federal 13th Tennessee Cavalry, white Unionist West Tennesseans who included a number of deserters from the Confederate army. Joining them were the 25 men of Company D, 2nd United States Colored Light Artillery, and 246 men of 4 companies of the 6th United States Colored Heavy Artillery. Each group was made up of men that were the natural enemies of Forrest and his hard-bitten secessionist troopers, many of whom were likely veterans of the partisan warfare in West Tennessee before joining Forrest's cavalry, and doubtless all of whom regarded the colored troops as inferiors, if not a little short of animals. Regardless of the intention of Forrest and his officers, there seems to be little doubt that many of the Federal survivors of the assault were massacred by the enraged Confederates.[12]

The Federal authorities accused the Rebels of murder, and the Northern press lost no time in labeling the affair a massacre. The Confederates, led by Forrest, disputed that claim. Harris wrote a letter to an Atlanta newspaper with an account of what transpired. During the final assault, Harris wrote, while "a few, black and white, threw down their arms and made signs of surrender—but at the same time the men on each side of them still retained their arms and kept up a constant fire and show of resistance. In the heat, din and confusion of a fire at such close quarters there was no chance for discrimination." Forrest became "sickened" with the slaughter, and ordered it stopped. In Harris's view, "[there was] not the semblance of a shadow of truth in the Federal exaggerations of wholesale slaughter." It is not certain whether Harris was actually at Fort Pillow. It will be recalled that the governor was reported at Paris, more than a hundred miles from Fort Pillow, on April 10. On the other hand, a ride of that distance was not impossible, and Har-

11. OR 32(3):779; Nathaniel Cheairs Hughes Jr., Connie Walton Moretti, and James Michael Browne, *Brigadier General Tyree H. Bell, C.S.A.: Forrest's Fighting Lieutenant* (Knoxville: University of Tennessee Press, 2004), 115–30; Wills, *A Battle from the Start*, 180–96.

12. Ward, *River Run Red*, 74–76, 128–29, 150, 152. Modern interpretation tends to label the affair as a massacre. Ibid., 227; John Cimprich, *Fort Pillow, A Civil War Massacre, and Public Memory* (Baton Rouge: Louisiana State University Press, 2005), 108–24. Cimprich states that Harris was at Fort Pillow, but appears to base his conclusion solely on the fact that Harris wrote a letter descriptive of the affair. Ibid., 103.

ris was reported to be with Forrest "during the greater part of his campaign" and visited all but three counties in West Tennessee during that time.[13]

A month in West Tennessee was enough, especially with the Army of Tennessee's spring campaign looming. Harris left Jackson for Polk's headquarters at Demopolis, Alabama, on April 20. A week's travel brought him to the bishop, who reported to President Davis on April 27 that Harris had related "a very favorable account of things" in West Tennessee and was "highly gratified with the state of feeling among the people." Rightly or not, given his previous experience, Harris was convinced by his trip to West Tennessee that, given time, he could raise as many as thirty thousand additional troops for the Confederacy, an opinion he communicated to Braxton Bragg, now President Davis's military advisor.[14]

Regardless of the accuracy of his estimate of the fertility of the West Tennessee recruiting ground, Harris left Tennessee for Dalton with Forrest's respect. An article appeared in an Atlanta newspaper a few weeks later lauding Harris as the "The Battle Governor of Tennessee." The article reported: "It is said that that brave man Forrest was asked by Tennesseans what sort of a soldier Isham G. Harris made? 'By G-d,' said the General, 'Harris is a fighting Governor. Whilst some Governors stay at home to quarrel with Jeff Davis, our Governor has been with me to fight Yankees!'" Harris was noted to have been on the fields of Shiloh, Murfreesboro, and Chickamauga, and with Forrest on his campaign. Such qualities, suggested the paper, merited Harris consideration for president of the Confederacy when Davis's term ended.[15]

Harris likely reached the Army of Tennessee around the first of May, and resumed his unique role as an advocate and encourager for the Tennessee troops of the army. For example, a Tennessee officer appealed to Harris as a witness that his regiment had been the first to offer to volunteer for the remainder of the war. An observer noted that Harris "never lost touch" with the Tennessee troops. Upon his arrival at Dalton, General Johnston asked the governor to "go around among the boys and 'stir 'em up a bit.'" Harris took newspaperman Henry Watterson with him on his tour, and they visited "every sector of the army." Watterson recalled: "Threading the woods of North Georgia on this round, if I heard it once I heard it

13. OR 32(1):617–18; OR 32(3):822, 832; "The Fort Pillow Affair—Refutation of Federal Slanderers," *Macon Daily Telegraph*, May 5, 1864; "The Fort Pillow Affair—Refutation of Federal Slander," *Montgomery Weekly Advertiser*, May 11, 1864.

14. OR 32(3):798, 832; Connelly, *Autumn of Glory*, 324.

15. "The 'Battle Governor of Tennessee,'" *Atlanta Southern Confederacy*, June 15, 1864.

fifty times shouted from a distant clearing: 'Here comes Gov-ner Harris, fellows; g'wine to be a fight.' His appearance at the front had always preceded and been long ago taken as a signal for battle." Indeed, that was the case as Sherman was preparing to advance on Atlanta. On May 6, Harris wrote Marcus Wright, then in command of the Post of Atlanta, that he expected fighting at any time, but that the army was in "splendid condition." Anticipating a "glorious victory," the governor promised to visit after "the storm blows over."[16]

True to Harris's prediction, the Federal advance began in earnest on May 6, and Harris was with the army as it began the long struggle for Atlanta. As the fighting began, the *Appeal* reported that Harris cheered the Tennessee troops by being there, "as he never fails to be, when a fight is on hand . . . Harris breathes the air of home to the troops. He appears among them constantly, delivers the most encouraging addresses, and is met with enthusiastic expressions of welcome." Unfortunately for the Confederates, the quick, glorious victory Harris anticipated became, in reality, a campaign of hard fighting and maneuver that forced the army first from its fortified camp at Dalton, then across the Oostenaula River. Harris was reported on May 15 to have accompanied a wounded nephew, Private Richmond P. Kirby of the 5th Tennessee, down on the train from the front to Wright's residence in Atlanta. By May 19, however, the governor was back at army headquarters, then near Cassville, bringing lunch for some of the staff.[17]

An anticipated great battle at Cassville did not occur. On May 23, Sherman threw his armies across the Etowah River, outflanking Johnston's heavily fortified position at Allatoona Pass on their western side, and marched for Dallas, intending to attack the Rebel base at Marietta from that direction. For the next six weeks, the armies would struggle in this region. While the Confederates were able to blunt the Federal advance with tactical successes at New Hope Church

16. Letter from Colonel S. S. Stanton, *Memphis* (Atlanta) *Appeal*, April 20, 1864; Henry Watterson, "*Marse Henry*": *An Autobiography* (New York: George H. Doran Co., 1919), 1:80–81; OR 32(3):581–82; IGH to Marcus J. Wright, May 6, 1864, Marcus Joseph Wright Papers.

17. OR 38(1):59; "General Johnston's Army," *Memphis* (Atlanta) *Appeal*, May 9, 1864; McMurry, *Atlanta 1864*, 62–74; "The Front," *Memphis* (Atlanta) *Appeal*, May 15, 1864; OR 38(3):984. The last citation is to the "journal" of Lieutenant T. B. Mackall, which has been shown to be unreliable on the dispute between Joseph E. Johnston and John B. Hood. See Richard M. McMurry, "The Mackall Journal and Its Antecedents," *Civil War History* 20 (December, 1974): 311, 328. However, it is considered useful on mundane details, such as Harris's lunch. Ibid., 328n33.

(May 25), Pickett's Mill (May 27), and Kennesaw Mountain (June 27), Sherman inexorably maneuvered the Army of Tennessee back toward Marietta and eventually, early in July, across the Chattahoochee, the last of the river barriers between the Union army and Atlanta. During that interval, the fighting and constant exposure to the elements ground down both sides with casualties, sickness, and exhaustion. With the larger army, this process naturally favored Sherman. The most notable Confederate loss occurred on June 14, when Harris's friend, Leonidas Polk, who in May had brought his corps-sized army from Mississippi to reinforce Johnston, was killed by a Federal shell at Pine Mountain. Confederate Tennesseans suffered another loss just a few days later with the death of former Congressman Andrew Ewing, who served as a colonel on military court duty. Harris chaired a committee of expatriate Tennesseans that passed a resolution honoring Ewing.[18]

While a newspaper report noted Harris, along with Judge Archibald Wright and Colonel Joel A. Battle, the state treasurer, was at the front on June 17, there were still attenuated aspects of state business that required the governor's attention. When David M. Currin, the congressman from the Confederate 11th Congressional District, died, Harris issued a proclamation on June 24 calling for an election to fill the vacancy. Of course, the only possible voters for the district, then in far-away West Tennessee, were soldiers and expatriate citizens. Reports also trickled in from the election held the previous year, as members of the legislature who could, notified the governor of their whereabouts. Harris provided counsel and information for his friend, Dr. J. G. M. Ramsey of Knoxville, whose son was wounded and captured at the Battle of Piedmont on June 5, 1864. Eventually, Harris's unceasing activity since before the fall of Missionary Ridge caught up to him. On July 16, Harris rode along the lines with war correspondent Felix Gregory de Fontaine, who, like Watterson had in May, observed that Harris's appearance brought a prediction from the soldiers that a fight was in the offing. The next day, as the Federals ground inexorably closer to Atlanta, Harris left the front,

---

18. OR 38(1):65; OR 38(3):616; Rachel Sherman Thorndike, ed., *The Sherman Letters: Correspondence Between General and Senator Sherman From 1837 to 1891* (New York: Charles Scribner's Sons, 1894), 234–35; Jacob D. Cox, *Atlanta* (New York: Charles Scribner's Sons, 1892), 64; McMurry, *Atlanta 1864*, 86–118; "The Fall of Lieutenant General Polk," *Atlanta Southern Confederacy*, June 16, 1864; "Death of Col. Andrew Ewing," *Atlanta Southern Confederacy*, June 19, 1864; "Death of Colonel Andrew Ewing, of Tennessee," *Chattanooga Daily Rebel*, June 18, 1864.

and went south of Atlanta to Griffin, Georgia, "to recruit his exhausted frame, worn out with the army in the front."[19]

Harris's physical exhaustion was matched by the exhaustion of President Davis's patience. By July 17, the date that Harris was reported at Griffin, Sherman had been across the Chattahoochee River about a week. Joe Johnston failed to stop the Federal tide, and furthermore could not explain to Davis how he expected to hold Atlanta. Davis therefore determined to replace Johnston, although he had few candidates to succeed the Virginian. Picking, most likely, the least qualified of the realistic options available to him, Davis relieved Johnston and elevated the army's youngest corps commander, John Bell Hood, to the post. When Harris returned to the army after his rest, Hood was in command.[20]

Understanding that his mandate was to drive Sherman away from Atlanta, Hood attacked the Federals on the north side of the city along Peachtree Creek on July 20, on the east side on July 22 in the Battle of Atlanta, and at Ezra Church on the west side on July 28. While the Army of Tennessee suffered casualties it could not sustain, its sudden aggressiveness made Sherman more cautious, and thus bought the beleaguered Rebels in the city some time. Harris, now serving Hood in much the same manner as he had the army's previous commanders, remained optimistic and believed the city would not fall. His optimism, however, did not blunt his sharp perception. A young friend of George Adair's reported a large Federal cavalry raid south of the city, which Hood initially disbelieved. Harris, however, remarked, "I am inclined to believe Adair's friend is right." Indeed, the raid occurred, although it was decisively defeated by Confederate forces, and its commander, Major General George Stoneman, was captured.[21]

The Confederacy's tenuous hold on Atlanta lasted through August. From the last little corner of Confederate Tennessee at Bristol, Dr. Ramsey telegraphed Har-

19. "From the Army of Tennessee," *Chattanooga Daily Rebel,* June 20, 1864; "A Proclamation," *Chattanooga Daily Rebel,* June 28, 1864; "Important to Tennesseans," *Memphis (Atlanta) Appeal,* June 25, 1864; W. W. Gray to IGH, August 19, 1864, Harris Papers, TSLA; F. H. Fulkerson to IGH, March 14, 1864, Harris Papers, TSLA; Hesseltine, ed., *Dr. J. G. M. Ramsey,* 192–96; "Governor Harris, of Tennessee," *Chattanooga Daily Rebel,* July 17, 1864; "Our Army Correspondence," *Daily* (Columbia) *South Carolinian,* July 21, 1864; "Gov. Harris of Tennessee," *Athens Southern Watchman,* July 20, 1864.

20. McMurry, *Atlanta 1864,* 117, 138–40.

21. Ibid., 141–59. "Isham G. Harris as Warrior and Fugitive," *Atlanta Constitution,* August 1, 1897. This account, which also appeared in *Confederate Veteran,* was disputed by E. T. Sykes, a member of General W. H. Jackson's staff. "Error in the Harris-Adair Art.," *Confederate Veteran* 5 (September 1897): 453.

ris that he should press for additional troops in that quarter and come there himself so that they might "make further efforts for the Southern Confederacy." Harris replied on August 21, stating he was "physically unable" to come to Bristol and that it was "impossible" to provide the troops requested. The same day Harris expressed his regrets to Dr. Ramsey, William T. Sherman made the decision to march the bulk of his army south of Atlanta to sever its last rail line to the rest of the Confederacy. While the Army of Tennessee bravely marched out to do battle at Jonesboro, Hood's battered force simply did not have the manpower to prevail. During the night of September 1–2, 1864, the Army of Tennessee evacuated Atlanta.[22]

Harris left the doomed city with his friend, George Adair, who was in charge of Hood's headquarters wagons. Accompanying them were newspapermen Harvey Watterson and John Happy, Harris's servant, Ran, and Adair's servant, Wash. With the possible exception of the two servants, all were despondent, as they "felt that the cause for which we had all sacrificed so much was doomed. Harris, proud, defiant man that he was, was the sickest man I have ever seen. He sat there gloomy and quiet, but without a thought of surrender." A humorous incident may have helped lift the gloom, as the party shared a campfire with chaplain Dr. Charles Todd Quintard. A major rode up to their fire and heard those present addressing Quintard as "doctor." The man was dying for a drink, and thought that Quintard might be a source of a medicinal dram, swearing: "You know how it is yourself, old fellow, and if you'll only help, why God d——." Adair provided him with a drink, but mentioned that Quintard was a chaplain. The refreshed officer quickly rode away.[23]

The next few days were spent in dealing with the details of the defeat. Marcus Wright and his staff, including Eugene, were at Macon, and Harris went there and observed that the army was in "good condition." On September 10, Major William Clare of Hood's staff was given the task of superintending the removal of civilians from Atlanta who did not want to remain in the Federally occupied city. Adair and Harris accompanied Clare and assisted in that task. Hood, in the meantime, did what he could to restore the army, and the commanding general told Davis that he expected to move his force over to the railroad to Montgomery, so he could operate on Sherman's communications. He also requested that Davis, or at least

22. IGH to Ramsey, with Ramsey endorsement, August 21, 1864, Ramsey Family Papers, University of Tennessee; McMurry, *Atlanta 1864*, 167, 170–75.

23. "Isham G. Harris as Warrior and Fugitive," *Atlanta Constitution*, August 1, 1897.

Bragg, visit the army. Expecting to "judge better the situation," and afterward determine the next best move, Davis personally set out for the army's new base at Palmetto, Georgia.[24]

Arriving at Palmetto on September 25, Davis conferred with Hood and his corps commanders, several "prominent Georgians," including Major General Howell Cobb, and doubtless Harris. Speeches were made to the troops, some of whom were unenthusiastic and cried out that Johnston be restored. After a day of inspections, the president was serenaded by the band of the 20th Louisiana Regiment, and he responded with a "short and spirited speech," followed by Hood, General Cobb, and Harris. In the days succeeding the fall of Atlanta, Hood sent messages to Richmond indicating he felt the officers and men of the Army of Tennessee had let the nation down. At Palmetto, Davis learned that Hood was thought lacking by all three of his corps commanders. Unable to restore Johnston, Davis created a theater command over Hood, commanded by Beauregard. Corps commander Lieutenant General William J. Hardee was relieved and sent to command on the Atlantic coast, and Frank Cheatham succeeded him by seniority of rank.[25]

While with Harris, Davis may have advised the governor of an opportunity to actually command troops. Although the bulk of the Tennessee troops were with the Army of Tennessee, two thin brigades fought near the Confederate capital at Richmond, Virginia. Archer's Brigade was the remnant of the Tennessee troops who bravely marched off to the Commonwealth in 1861, and its men fought as part of the Army of Northern Virginia on its many battlefields. Bushrod Johnson's brigade was originally a unit of the Army of Tennessee, but was detached with Longstreet to invest Knoxville in late 1863. Cut off by the loss of Chattanooga, Johnson's Brigade became a part of the troops defending the capital. In late August, a proposal was made to consolidate the two brigades. Lizenka Brown Ewell's husband, Lieutenant General Richard S. Ewell, suggested that Harris be appointed to command both brigades. Johnson believed that the governor would "add by his name and influence to the strength of [the] command." Harris's response to this proposal, assuming he was advised of it at all, was not recorded, although it is doubtful he would have desired a military command a year before. But commanding

24. OR 38(5): 1023–24, 1029; OR 39(2):828; Davis, The Rise and Fall of the Confederate Government, 564–65.

25. Davis, The Rise and Fall of the Confederate Government, 564–65; Connelly, Autumn of Glory, 470–73; OR 38(5):1021, 1023; OR 39(1):805, 842, 870; "General Hood's Army," Daily Columbus Enquirer, September 30, 1864; Hood, Advance and Retreat, 253.

troops in Virginia would deprive him of the opportunity to return to Tennessee with the Army of Tennessee.[26]

When Davis left the army, Harris traveled with him to Montgomery, Alabama, and was present at a speech given at the Alabama Capitol on September 29. With the prospect of a campaign that might reach into Tennessee before them, Harris purportedly told Davis that if Sherman could be defeated, Tennessee would furnish at least fifty thousand new men. Harris again appeared at Macon on October 2, and was at Talladega on October 8, en route with Beauregard to Hood's headquarters, then at Cave Spring, Georgia. While Harris was gone from the army, Hood crossed the Chattahoochee and was operating on Sherman's railroad line, overrunning small garrisons at Big Shanty and Acworth. Beauregard and Harris arrived at Hood's headquarters at Cave Spring, Georgia, near the Alabama line, on October 9. There, Beauregard met with Hood for the first time, and there was distressed by the Texan's lack of preparation in changing his base to Jacksonville, Alabama. While at that point Hood was likely already thinking about going cross-country toward the Tennessee River, he left Beauregard with the impression that he was going to stick close to Sherman.[27]

The army moved again to interdict the Western & Atlantic, this time at its old base at Dalton on October 13. The primary garrison there was the 44th United States Colored Infantry. About mid-day, Hood sent a flag of truce into town with Harris and another member of Hood's staff to demand the town's surrender. After ascertaining that the Confederate force was very large, the post commander asked to see the forces confronting him, but was refused. Harris and the officer told the commander "that two corps, Cheatham's (Hardee's old corps) and Stewart's, were in the immediate front of Dalton, and that another corps, S. D. Lee's, was in easy supporting distance, and that they were determined to take the place, cost what it might; that no quarter would be given, &c." The Federals surrendered. Unfortunately, the black soldiers were treated very badly by Confederate authorities.[28]

From Dalton, Hood moved toward LaFayette, where he briefly thought of en-

26. OR 42(2):1264–65, 1284–87, 1289; OR 42(3):1154. For the makeup of the two brigades at that time, see OR 42(2):1213, 1219.

27. "President Davis at the Capitol," *Macon Daily Telegraph*, October 2, 1864; "Speech at Greensboro," 11 *PJD* 91–92; "Gov. Harris," *Macon Daily Telegraph*, October 2, 1864; "The Montgomery Mail," *Daily Columbus Enquirer*, October 13, 1864; Connelly, *Autumn of Glory*, 480–82; Roman, *Military Operations of General Beauregard*, 2:281.

28. OR 39(1):717–21; "The Fortune of War," *Newark (Ohio) Daily Advocate*, May 29, 1899; Elliott, ed., *Doctor Quintard*, 175.

gaging Sherman, but his officers convinced him the army was not able to do so. Determining then to advance across the Tennessee, Hood moved the army westward to Gadsden, Alabama, where Beauregard caught up with him on October 21. Harris was not with the army, as apparently he was dispatched to Selma, Alabama, to confer with Lieutenant General Richard Taylor concerning the possible move into Middle Tennessee. On October 24, Taylor sent Forrest, then operating in West Tennessee, a message that detailed the steps Taylor had undertaken to facilitate Hood's move. Taylor noted that Harris was then at Selma, but proposed to join Forrest. Taylor stated he would "soon send Brigadier General Marcus J. Wright to Tennessee for the purpose of getting out the State reserves. He will be directed to be governed by your views and those of Governor Harris in the execution of his mission, and to report through you to me. General Hood's movement is intended to extend to the occupation of Middle Tennessee, and in that connection your proposed movement will be most advantageous to the final result of his campaign." Some inkling of these Rebel plans, likely inspired by the chaos of Forrest's operations in the state, occasioned a rumor among the Federals that Harris was going to convene a short session of the "Rebel legislature" at Jackson.[29]

Even as Hood moved westward, Sherman was arguing for permission to be allowed to move the bulk of his army to the Georgia seacoast at Savannah, which was eventually granted. By mid-November, the Army of Tennessee was at Florence, Alabama, preparing to cross the Tennessee and advance into the Volunteer State. Sherman, on the other hand, marched out of Atlanta on November 16, heading toward Savannah and the sea. On November 21, Hood's approximately thirty thousand-man army began its advance into Tennessee, its three corps marching north on roughly parallel routes. Facing them at Pulaski, Tennessee, were approximately 25,000 Federals, which, under the orders of Major General George H. Thomas in Nashville, quickly retreated to Columbia, north of Pulaski on the Duck River.[30]

At the Tennessee state line, a sign greeted the Tennesseans of Cheatham's Corps: "Tennessee, A grave or a free home." As Hood crossed the line, he received a formal welcome from Harris. Because he was Tennessee's leading Confederate citizen, Harris's presence with the army and his potential influence on the people

29. Connelly, *Autumn of Glory*, 483–84; OR 39(2):831, 845–46, 459. Beauregard seems to have lost track of Harris during this interval. OR 39(1):846; OR 52(2):763.

30. Anne J. Bailey, *The Chessboard of War: Sherman and Hood in the Autumn Campaigns of 1864* (Lincoln: University of Nebraska Press, 2000), 44–45, 48–55, 72, 77–78.

of Middle Tennessee was considered important. By November 25, Harris, riding with Forrest, encountered Quintard near one of the Polk estates in Maury County, just outside of Columbia. The next day, Harris was with Hood at the home of one of Leonidas Polk's brothers, Hamilton Place, and he spent much of the day greeting the various officers of the army. Unquestionably, this was a time of great elation for the governor. On November 28, a soldier wrote a letter that observed that Harris was with the army, "and it would do you good to see the placid, genial smile of his well known features, beaming all the brighter the farther we move into the heart of this once beautiful but much oppressed country." Not only did the soldier see the happiness of the governor, but the "glowing faces and brightened eyes" of the people of Middle Tennessee as they welcomed back "the veterans who have been so long exiled from their homes; so long looked for and so little expected."[31]

Already suffering from Union depredations for over two years, that "much oppressed country" suffered yet again. Retreating Federal troops destroyed bridges and burned homes. While there was rejoicing that the army was once more at home, wary merchants refused to sell goods for the almost worthless Confederate money. Indeed, while the countryside still seemed a "paradise" to some used to the bleak country in Northern Georgia and Alabama, the Rebel soldiers themselves stripped what little was left to some residents, taking food, burning fence rails, and seizing livestock. What little local government Andrew Johnson's military government was able to restore by that point in 1864 was disrupted by the Confederate invasion, as Unionist local officials and sympathizers fled the oncoming gray horde.[32]

Not wanting to face Hood with the Duck River at his back, the Federal commander, Major General John Schofield, withdrew from Columbia to the other side of the Duck. It was likely at this juncture that Harris sent a message south announcing that all of Tennessee south of the river was in Rebel hands, and reporting that the populace and the army were "in high spirits." On November 28,

31. Mrs. D. Giraud White, *A Southern Girl in '61: The War-Time Memories of a Confederate Senator's Daughter* (New York: Doubleday, Page & Co., 1905), 213–14; "The Tennessee Frost," *Daily Columbus Enquirer,* December 1, 1864; OR 52(2):771; Elliott, ed, *Doctor Quintard,* 182; "From Tennessee," *Macon Daily Telegraph,* December 16, 1864 (quotation).

32. Elliott, ed., *Doctor Quintard,* 182–86, 196; James Lee McDonough, *Nashville: The Western Confederacy's Last Gamble* (Knoxville: University of Tennessee Press, 2004), 46–47; see, generally, Ash, *Middle Tennessee Society Transformed,* 84–105.

Hood received a message from Beauregard urging speed, as Sherman was moving rapidly through Georgia. Hood intended to beat Schofield to Nashville "or make him go there at the double quick." He devised a plan to "go through the woods" by crossing the Duck River to the east of Columbia, and march rapidly to Spring Hill, about eight miles to the north on the main road from Columbia to Franklin.[33]

Hood arose at 3:00 a.m. on November 29 and had prayer with Doctor Quintard, telling the priest that "the enemy must give me fight, or I will be at Nashville before tomorrow night." Leaving Lee with two divisions to demonstrate against the Federal position at Columbia, Hood moved his remaining seven divisions to the east. The army's lead elements crossed the Duck before sunrise, and began a rapid march intended to "reach the enemy's rear and cut him off from Nashville." Hood rode at the head of his lead element, Cleburne's Division, followed by the other two divisions of Cheatham's Corps, with Stewart's Corps and Johnson's Division of Lee's Corps behind. At Spring Hill, the Federals had a large number of wagons, guarded by a few miscellaneous units and detachments. In late morning and early afternoon, bolstered by the timely arrival of Major General David S. Stanley and the two lead brigades of his Fourth Corps, this miscellaneous force succeeded in holding Forrest and his men out of the town.[34]

Harris rode with Hood and his staff, which reached the house of Absalom Thompson just south of the town in the mid-afternoon. At this juncture, the stories and recollections of the various witnesses begin to diverge.[35] Two statements relating to that fateful afternoon and evening have been attributed to Harris. The first in time was purportedly privately given to Campbell Brown, his friend Lizenka Brown Ewell's son, in 1868. The second was a letter written in May 1877 relating to a particular incident the evening of November 29. Both conflict in certain specifics with the published accounts of the various Confederate officers present. Harris's account as given to Campbell Brown states that Cheatham was ordered to form his two leading divisions and interdict the pike that ran

33. Bailey, The Chessboard of War, 80–82; OR 45(2):649; Elliott, ed., Doctor Quintard, 184–85.

34. Elliott, ed., Doctor Quintard, 185; Hood, Advance and Retreat, 284; OR 45(1):113–14, 652; Wiley Sword, The Confederacy's Last Hurrah: Spring Hill, Franklin and Nashville (Lawrence: University Press of Kansas, 1992), 117–20.

35. The following discussion is meant to place the account attributed to Harris by Campbell Brown in the context of other witnesses to the events of November 29, 1864, and is not intended as a comprehensive portrayal of the events at Spring Hill, which, at this point, have confounded historians for more than 145 years.

through Spring Hill from Columbia to Franklin—Schofield's line of retreat. Those at Hood's headquarters initially heard some skirmishing, but not the sound of a full-fledged attack. According to the Brown/Harris account, eventually Hood dispatched Harris to Cheatham to see what was transpiring. Harris could not find Cheatham, but found Major General John C. Brown, who showed Harris that the Federal line overlapped his on the right and suggested that another unit form on his right. Harris sent word to Hood that Stewart's Corps, then at Rutherford Creek, should be sent forward to that spot. Harris then found Cheatham, who had been occupied getting Major General William B. Bate's division in line. Cheatham and Harris rode back to find Hood, who told the corps commander to suspend his movement until Stewart could come up on his right.[36]

While Hood agreed that he sent Harris forward to determine the situation, he stated that Harris was his third messenger to Cheatham, rather than the first, as the Campbell Brown account suggests. Hood makes no mention of any order halting Cheatham while Stewart came up, and in fact wrote that he asked Cheatham why "in the name of God . . . have you not taken possession of that pike?" Further, neither Cheatham nor Brown mentions any contact with Harris that afternoon. On the other hand, Cheatham wrote that the "dramatic scene" of a confrontation between Hood and Cheatham "only occurred in the imagination of General Hood," and Brown recalled that it was decided to suspend his attack until Stewart came up.[37]

The Campbell Brown account states that it was then about 5 o'clock, and Hood related that he had ordered Stewart to move beyond Brown's right to the turnpike, and that he had furnished Stewart with a guide for that purpose. Nothing more occurred until about 8 o'clock, when Stewart and Forrest appeared at Hood's headquarters. Stewart said that he had met an officer who could put him across the pike, so he dismissed his guide. After dark, the officer halted them short of the pike, but Stewart was reluctant to push his men because they were tired from the long march, and he was ignorant of the ground and of the enemy's force in front. According to the Campbell Brown account, Harris related that Hood became irritated when Stewart showed great reluctance to put a brigade across the pike, and

36. Terry L. Jones, ed., *Campbell Brown's Civil War: With Ewell and the Army of Northern Virginia* (Baton Rouge: Louisiana State University Press, 2001), 164–66.

37. Hood, *Advance and Retreat*, 285–86; Benjamin F. Cheatham, "The Lost Opportunity at Spring Hill, Tenn.—General Cheatham's Reply to General Hood," *Southern Historical Society Papers* 9 (October, November, and December 1881): 524–26, 530, 538.

turned to Forrest and asked if he could do so, and Forrest said he could if he could get ammunition. Both then left, and the headquarters party went to bed. Harris expressed the belief that both Stewart and Forrest disobeyed orders by failing to block the pike.[38]

Forrest's report makes no mention of this incident. Stewart wrote that after Cheatham's last division (Brown's) crossed Rutherford Creek, he was ordered to deploy along the creek. When he finally was ordered to cross the creek, it was between sunset and dark. "Old Straight" rode forward to confer with Hood, who complained "bitterly" that his orders had not been obeyed. Stewart was given a guide and ordered to move one wing of his corps across the pike, while the other should extend into Cheatham's rear. Stewart and his men followed the guide through the dark, and eventually located Forrest's headquarters. While conferring with the cavalryman, another guide from Hood appeared with different instructions. Stewart then followed this new guide, until he located Brown and learned that his new instructions would mean his corps would form away from the pike. Feeling it was a mistake, Stewart ordered his exhausted men to bivouac, and arrived about 11:00 p.m. at Hood's headquarters, where Stewart explained the confusion. Hood "remarked, in substance, that it was not material; to let the men rest; and directed me to move before daylight in the morning, taking the advance toward Franklin." As can be seen, Stewart's account differs from that of Campbell Brown in several particulars, including the time of night, the lack of a confrontation with Hood, and the story of the guide. What can be gleaned from Hood's report and autobiography supports Stewart on each of these specific points. More significant, Hood provided Stewart a letter in April 1865 stating, "You did all that I could say or claim that I would have done under similar circumstances myself."[39]

38. Jones, ed., *Campbell Brown's Civil War*, 168–69.

39. OR 45(1): 653, 712–13, 754; Cheatham, "The Lost Opportunity at Spring Hill," 555; Hood, *Advance and Retreat*, 286. I engaged in this analysis in more detail in *Soldier of Tennessee: General Alexander P. Stewart and the Civil War in the West* (Baton Rouge: Louisiana State University Press, 1999), 232–34. There, I concluded that the preponderance of the evidence is in Stewart's favor, which remains my opinion. Assuming on the basis of this preponderance that the discrepancy is on the part of the Brown account, it is difficult to ascertain whether the fault is with Brown's recall of his conversation with Harris or with Harris's memory of events. In a recent book by historian James Lee McDonough, my conclusion in *Soldier of Tennessee* was questioned on the basis of a letter written by Stewart in 1895 quoted in J. P. Young, "Hood's Failure at Spring Hill," *Confederate Veteran* 16 (January 1908): 25, 39, that says that Stewart states he was ordered to place his right across the pike. McDonough, *Nashville: The Western Confederacy's Last Gamble*, 74. But Young's account was exten-

Harris related one final effort in his conversation with Brown, which was similar in substance to a letter the former governor wrote in 1877. According to Brown, Harris told him that about 3:00 a.m., an ordinary soldier came to head-quarters and asked to see Hood. The man had wandered into the Federal lines and found things in confusion there. Hood's adjutant general, Colonel Arthur Pendleton Mason, was ordered to have Cheatham "send at least a reg't out to fire into them & throw them into confusion." Hood and Harris then went back to sleep. The attack was not made, however, and the next morning Hood made harsh remarks about Cheatham. Mason called Harris aside and confessed that he fell asleep before getting the order out. Harris insisted that Mason relate the matter to Hood, in fairness to Cheatham, which Mason eventually did.[40]

In the night, Schofield marched his men through Spring Hill and on to Frank-lin. As Hood bitterly stated, "Thus was lost a great opportunity of striking the enemy for which we had labored so long—the greatest this campaign had offered, and one of the greatest during the war." After the Battle of Franklin, Hood made private comments to Harris and others that exonerated Cheatham for the failure at Spring Hill, and supposedly provided Cheatham a letter, which the Tennessean later lost. But when Harris was asked to comment on Hood's report in Richmond a few months later, he found that the report did not correct the adverse refer-ences to Cheatham. Harris insisted on having that "corrected," and "after a while got most of it struck out or changed." Nonetheless, Hood's report as published re-mained quite critical of Cheatham.[41]

After the war, the incident spawned a number of accounts from the Confed-erate participants that day and evening, but Harris's public pronouncements seem to have been limited to his letter to Porter, the sole purpose of which was to clear Cheatham. Save his conversation with Campbell Brown, whatever he may have said in private has not been recorded. In 1894, when Bishop Quintard was work-ing on his memoir of the war, he asked Harris to provide an account of Spring Hill. Harris "decline[d] to discuss it." Harris noted that in his official report Hood

---

sively analyzed in *Soldier of Tennessee*, and supports the conclusion that Hood gave Stewart later or-ders that inadvertently contradicted the original order for Stewart to put his right across the pike.

40. Jones, ed., *Campbell Brown's Civil War*, 168; IGH to James D. Porter, May 20, 1877, in Cheatham, "Lost Opportunity at Spring Hill," 532.

41. Jones, ed., *Campbell Brown's Civil War*, 169–70; Cheatham, "Lost Opportunity at Spring Hill," 532; OR 45(1):652–53.

censured both Cheatham and Stewart, yet gave each letters of exoneration. Harris wrote that he was there, and knew "much, if not all that occurred," but could not say any one officer was responsible. Harris deemed the matter an "old sore" that did not need to "bleed again."[42]

The next morning, November 30, 1864, the frustrated Army of Tennessee marched north to Franklin, with Hood intent on catching Schofield before he could complete his retreat to the defenses of Nashville. Schofield's army took position behind breastworks on the south side of the town, but their commander fully intended to abandon the town and continue his withdrawal to Nashville if left unmolested. But Hood had no such intention. Late that afternoon, the army's two lead corps, Cheatham's and Stewart's, attacked the Federals in their strong works on the southern fringe of the town. The result was a bloody repulse that cost the Army of Tennessee perhaps as many as seven thousand casualties. Subsequently, Harris penned one of his newspaper reports that detailed the attack on November 30 and Hood's intention to resume the attack early the next day, but for the Federal withdrawal. Harris reported the deaths of Major General Patrick R. Cleburne; brigadier generals Hiram B. Granbury, John C. Adams, and Otho F. Strahl; and States Rights Gist. Brigadier General John C. Carter was mortally wounded, and Tennesseans Major General John C. Brown and William A. Quarles were seriously wounded. Although he doubtless knew how badly the Army of Tennessee was injured, Harris accentuated the positive, and wrote that 1,300 prisoners and 6,000 stands of arms were captured. The governor also stated that the "Army is in fine health and excellent spirits, and confident of success."[43]

Hood doggedly pursued the Federals to their well-fortified lines around Nashville. Polk's son-in-law, Colonel W. D. Gale, wrote his wife on December 9 and described a scene where parts of the city were in the Rebel army's sight, "but between us and them there bristles on every hill a fort and . . . long lines of rifle pits connecting them, with the dark blue line of armed men that tells us too plainly that our way is not open." In the place of familiar stands of timber, there were "frowning forts and grim redoubts." Harris was at army headquarters, but likely ventured about seeking to raise morale. Quintard traveled to Franklin with the governor on December 7, and encountered him again with Secretary of State Ray

42. IGH to Quintard, December 29, 1894, Quintard Papers.
43. Bailey, *The Chessboard of War*, 95–111; Sword, *The Confederacy's Last Hurrah*, 185–244, 269; ORS 7:677–78; "The Fight at Franklin, Tenn.," *Daily Columbus Enquirer*, December 11, 1864.

on December 13 on the road to Franklin, where Harris gave Quintard "some letters and a copy of his excellent proclamation." Harris's proclamation called on Tennesseans to "arise" and went on to exhort: "We have driven the enemy in confusion to your capital, and now stand before the bristling fortifications which surround it. He can, must and will be driven from this last stronghold, and beyond the limits of our State. We are here for the purpose of redeeming and protecting Tennessee or finding graves upon her soil." On December 12, Harris found time for the one great social event of the army's stay near the capital, as Major William Clare, Hood's staff officer who had shepherded refugees with Harris outside Atlanta, married a local belle, which was followed by a grand celebration the home of John Overton, Traveler's Rest.[44]

Newspaper articles from Georgia reflect that Harris's account of the Battle of Franklin was not his only optimistic report. One message reported that Thomas was being pressed back on Nashville, the other that the skeletal Tennessee regiments would be "filled." Reality proved to be something quite different. Ground down in the Atlanta Campaign and gutted at Franklin, the Army of Tennessee could barely field 25,000 men, while Thomas had over 70,000 at his disposal. And exposed as the Confederate troops were during bitter winter weather between December 8 and 13, the number of effective troops was probably much less. The result was almost inevitable. Using overwhelming advantage in numbers and the mobility of Major General James H. Wilson's cavalry, Thomas struck the Confederate left flank on December 15, 1864, almost swamping A. P. Stewart's decimated corps. Incredibly, Hood and the army were able to retreat to a second line of defense to fight again on December 16, but another crushing attack on the Rebel left flank, this time held by Cheatham's men, dissolved a large portion of the army into a rout.[45]

Pursued by the vengeful Yankees, the army streamed south, across the Har-

44. W. D. Gale to wife, December 9, 1864, Gale–Polk Papers, Southern Historical Collection, UNC; Elliott, ed., *Doctor Quintard*, 192, 194–96; "The Rebellion," *New York Times*, December 25, 1864. While there is no specific record of Harris at the Clare wedding, he did sign the Traveler's Rest guest book, which also bears the signatures of Hood, Forrest, Stewart, Cheatham, Lee, Jackson, Loring, French, and Quintard. David Currey, Traveler's Rest curator, to author, July 6, 2005.

45. "Our Army in Tennessee," *Macon Daily Telegraph*, December 9, 1864; "There's Life in the Old Land Yet," *Macon Daily Telegraph*, December 31, 1864; OR 45(1):55, 679; Connelly, *Autumn of Glory*, 507–12; McDonough, *Nashville*, 155–264.

peth, through the blasted landscape at Franklin, and on to Columbia. There, on December 18, Quintard and Lieutenant Colonel J. P. Johnson sought to convince Hood that he should try to hold the line of the Duck River for the winter. Quintard recorded that early the next morning, Forrest arrived and forcefully argued the army should continue south across the Tennessee. Harris, "in whose judgment [Quintard had] great confidence, thinks it is the best we can do." The army accordingly moved from Columbia toward the Tennessee River at Bainbridge, Alabama. Quintard attached himself to Harris for the following day's trip, which ended at the home of Nathan Adams in Pulaski, as he knew the governor "would not be detained en route."[46]

On Christmas Day, as the remnants of the Army of Tennessee struggled southward, Harris wrote President Davis to report that Confederate forces had not been in Tennessee long enough to successfully recruit. Harris also told Davis that from his viewpoint, even though the campaign had ended disastrously, "I am not able to see anything that General Hood has done that he should not, or neglected anything that he should have done, which it was possible to do; indeed, the more that I have seen & known of him and his policy, the more I have been pleased with him, and regret to say that if *all* had performed their parts as well as he, the results would have been very different." The army completed its crossing early on December 28, and moved slowly to camps around Tupelo, Mississippi. Notwithstanding Harris's endorsement, Hood requested to be relieved of command. Beauregard was directed to place Lieutenant General Richard Taylor in command of the army, and to bring what troops that could be spared from the army to Georgia and South Carolina.[47]

By the first of February, it was determined that all three of the Army of Tennessee's corps, less a few detachments, should be dispatched to reinforce the troops opposing Sherman's march from Savannah into the Carolinas. Harris, too, left Tupelo, heading for Richmond. The governor was at Augusta, Georgia, on February 13, en route to Columbia, South Carolina, in an effort to confer with Beauregard. It is unlikely the two were able to meet in the South Carolina capital, as Sherman's army was on its outskirts on February 16. Harris was likely at Winns-

46. Sword, *The Confederacy's Last Hurrah,* 394–403; Elliott, ed., *Doctor Quintard,* 107n26, 200–201, 205.

47. IGH to J. Davis, December 25, 1864, 11 *PJD* 248–49; OR 45(1):674; OR 45(2):781, 784–85, 789, 805.

borough, South Carolina, on February 18, as Beauregard sent him a message there in care of South Carolina Governor Andrew G. Magrath. Harris skirted about the advancing Federals, and arrived in the capital before February 25, as he was granted the privilege of the floor of the Confederate Senate on that date.[48]

According to the account given Campbell Brown in 1868, one of Harris's purposes in going to Richmond was to lobby for the promotion of Cheatham to lieutenant general. Likely, Harris also followed up on his recommendation that Forrest be promoted to the same grade. But it appears those were secondary purposes. Harris not only felt it necessary to report on the true state of affairs in the West, including the greatly diminished strength of the Army of Tennessee, but also to determine for himself the prospects of the tottering Confederacy. The Campbell Brown account relates that when Harris got to Richmond's Spotswood Hotel, one of Hood's staff officers saw him in the lobby. Soon, the man appeared at Harris's door, bearing a request that he immediately come to Hood's room, as he was staying there as well. Harris initially demurred, as he was tired and wanted a bath. But the man insisted, and Harris went to the general's room, where he found Hood wanted him to listen to him read and then comment on his official report of his tenure as commander of the Army of Tennessee. Harris was shocked to see that Hood had not corrected his initial criticism of Cheatham's conduct at Spring Hill, and observed that Hood made gratuitous criticisms of Joseph E. Johnston, which the governor felt were inspired by Davis and Seddon. While Hood argued over the points relating to Johnston, he eventually concurred, but said it was too late to change. Harris was able to help the general correct aspects of the report, especially relating to Cheatham. Brown related that "during the whole of this remarkable interview, [Harris] was struck with the fact that Hood was a puppet in the hands of others who were sacrificing him to gain their own ends—and striking through him a blow at Gen'l Johnston."[49]

Hood's invasion delayed, but did not stop, the culmination of Andrew Johnson's military governorship, the reinstitution of a civilian government for Tennessee. In

48. Horn, *Army of Tennessee*, 422–23, 430; OR 45(2):800; OR 47(1):3; OR 47(2):1078, 1172, 1221; IGH to Duncan Brown Cooper, December 15, 1888, Cooper Papers; S. Doc. No. 512, 58th Cong., 2nd Sess., *Journal of the Confederate Congress*, 4:601.

49. Jones, ed., *Campbell Brown's Civil War*, 170–71; 11 *PJD* 374n6; IGH to Duncan Brown Cooper, December 15, 1888, Cooper Papers, 11 *PJD* 34n6.

November 1864, Lincoln was reelected as president with Johnson as his vice president, to take office in early March 1865. A Unionist "preliminary state convention" met in Nashville in January 1865 and quickly became a constitutional convention. Through his closest ally, Samuel Milligan, Johnson exercised great influence upon the gathering. The convention adopted proposed constitutional amendments abolishing slavery, repudiated the 1861 "declaration of independence," and nullified the actions of the Rebel state government after May 6, 1861. It called for an election ratifying these provisions, and, if ratified, for a vote for governor and for members of the legislature. The constitutional convention then became a political nominating convention and selected William G. Brownlow for governor. The election was a foregone conclusion. With the tacit agreement of Andrew Johnson, his old enemy, Parson Brownlow, succeeded him as governor of Tennessee.[50]

The new legislature met in April 1865, even as the Confederacy spiraled into its final days of ruin. It quickly ratified the Thirteenth Amendment to the U.S. Constitution, which also abolished slavery. Then, it began to consider issues of franchise, both for the African American population, whether formerly free or slave, and for the soon to be ex-Confederates. The issue of Negro suffrage was too controversial a subject to deal with at that time, so the Unionist legislature, with both Radical and Conservative elements, but a Radical majority, addressed the subject of the white franchise. The measure that was finally passed effectively disenfranchised all but a small Unionist minority. Tennessee was firmly under Radical control.[51]

By the time of Harris's arrival in Richmond, John C. Breckinridge was the secretary of war in the place of Seddon. During his short tenure to that point, Breckinridge had taken stock of the situation facing the Confederate army and government, and had concluded that collapse was imminent. In a letter dated March 9, 1865, Robert E. Lee stated that it was likely the Army of Northern Virginia would not be able to defend the lines about Richmond and Petersburg much longer, and that Federal superiority in numbers and resources made effective resistance by the forces in North Carolina and elsewhere unlikely. It was in this interval that Har-

50. White, *Messages of the Governors of Tennessee*, 5:394–400; Wilson D. Miscamble, "Andrew Johnson and the Election of William G. ("Parson") Brownlow as Governor of Tennessee," *Tennessee Historical Quarterly* 37 (Fall 1978): 308–20.

51. White, *Messages of the Governors of Tennessee*, 5:400, 426–38.

ris had a meeting with Davis, Breckinridge, and Lee. As he recalled some years later, "I realized the fact that the fall of the Confederacy was only a question of time, and a short time."[52]

As he prepared to leave Richmond, Harris was approached by Congressman J. D. C. Atkins. Atkins explained that his family was in Texas, and he needed funds to join them. Harris told Atkins that he was due his salary from the state, and would set aside $750 in gold for that purpose. The officers of the state and of the Bank of Tennessee were located at Greensboro, Georgia, to the west of Augusta. Harris arrived there on March 17, 1865, and drew his $3,000 annual salary from November 1, 1863, to November 1, 1864, in gold. The salary due for the quarter ending February 1, 1865, $750, he left for Atkins. In addition to the money due him from the state, for which the bank was the depository, Harris had a personal deposit exceeding $20,000 on the books of the bank. While at Greensboro, Harris advised the bank officers that they should make preparations to move its assets across the Mississippi.[53]

In late April, the bank officers resolved to move its assets to Augusta, Georgia, for safekeeping, with a view toward "immediately and quietly" moving them to the Department of Mississippi "for security." Shortly after this determination, however, it was learned that the Confederate authorities soon expected to surrender Augusta. Back in Nashville, Governor Brownlow was doubtless concerned about retrieving the bank and its assets before they were lost in the collapse of the Confederacy. He dispatched a messenger to the bank officers offering safe passage back to Nashville, which was accepted on May 3, 1865. The letter of acceptance, however, said that the movement would be delayed because of inadequate transportation, "and the whole country is filled with returning paroled soldiers," making travel with valuables "very unsafe." Brownlow resolved the situation by asking the Federal army to seize the bank's assets and arrest certain of its officers, as well as the state archives and officers, if found. By mid-May, both the bank assets and the archives were located by Federal troops and eventually dispatched to

52. William C. Davis, *An Honorable Defeat: The Last Days of the Confederate Government* (New York: Harcourt, 2001), 22–25, 31–35; OR 46(2): 1295–96; IGH to Duncan Brown Cooper, December 15, 1888, Cooper Papers.

53. IGH to Duncan Brown Cooper, December 15, 1888, Cooper Papers; "Report of the Joint Committee on School Fund Frauds Made to the General Assembly of the State of Tennessee, May 26, 1870," Appendix to House Journal, 1870–71 General Assembly, 325.

Nashville, along with Dunlap, Battle, Ray, and some of the bank officers. When the gold arrived, Brownlow and his secretary of state mounted the lead wagon, and rode it to the Capitol.[54]

In late March and April, Harris worked his way back through Georgia and Alabama, intending to join Forrest and his staff, carrying with him Forrest's commission as a lieutenant general, a promotion that Harris had solicited for the famed cavalryman. Just after Harris arrived in Greensboro in mid-March, the Army of Tennessee fought its last battle at Bentonville, North Carolina, delaying but not arresting Sherman's march through North Carolina. Lee and his Army of Northern Virginia were forced out of the Richmond and Petersburg lines the first week of April, and surrendered on April 9. At Selma, Alabama, on April 6, Forrest was brushed aside by a massive column of Federal cavalry under Major General James H. Wilson, which embarked on a swath of destruction from Selma to Montgomery, and then on to Columbus and Macon, Georgia. The assassination of Abraham Lincoln on April 14, the flight of Jefferson Davis and the Confederate government, and the surrender of the tattered remnant of the Army of Tennessee on April 26 concluded a cataclysmic month.[55]

With there being little hope for continued resistance, at least on the east side of the Mississippi, Harris took steps to shed himself of his final responsibilities as governor. His last official act was dated May 8 at Grenada, Mississippi, when he dispatched Whitthorne back to Georgia with instructions to Dunlap, Battle, and Ray to return the state archives to the Capitol at Nashville and to advise the officers of the bank that they, too, should return their charge to Nashville, as "the assets of the bank are the property of the people of Tennessee, and I ardently desire that they should be restored to them." It appears that Whitthorne was given safe passage by the Federal commander in south Alabama, Major General E. R. S. Canby, to effect his charge, it being unknown to them that the bank assets and archives were already in Federal hands. Whitthorne was arrested by the Federal authorities, but on account of his friendship with Andrew Johnson, was treated as

54. Hesseltine, ed., *Dr. J. G. M. Ramsey*, 224–26; "Report of the Joint Committee on School Fund Frauds Made to the General Assembly of the State of Tennessee, May 26, 1870," 306–10; OR 49(2):741, 789, 799–800, 824, 884; "Return of the Bank of Tennessee to Nashville," *New York Times*, June 5, 1865.

55. OR 49(2):1144; "The Appeal of the 22nd.," *Macon Weekly Telegraph*, March 24, 1865; IGH to J. Davis, January 3, 1865, 11 *PJD* 268; David J. Eicher, *The Longest Night: A Military History of the Civil War* (New York: Simon & Schuster, 2001), 817–22, 833–35, 837.

a military prisoner under parole at his home in Columbia, and was quickly thereafter pardoned by Johnson.[56]

While Johnston's surrender covered most of the Confederacy east of the Mississippi, Forrest was under the authority of Lieutenant General Richard Taylor, commander of the Confederate Department of Alabama, Mississippi, and East Louisiana. Recognizing the game was over, Taylor surrendered his men on May 4, 1865, at Citronelle, Alabama. During a meeting with Harris, Taylor urged the governor to leave the country for a while, as his enmity with Andrew Johnson, then the new president of the United States, was well known and the governor's presence in Tennessee could only cause trouble. It seems quite clear that Harris at some point determined to go to the Trans-Mississippi to do what he could to help continue the struggle. The hard-bitten Forrest told his men," Men, you may all do as you please; but I'm a-going home." Unbowed, Harris admonished Forrest: "Have you still a command?" But Forrest could count, and told Harris his small command was vastly outnumbered. The cavalryman then said, "Any man who is in favor of a further prosecution of this war is a fit subject for a lunatic asylum, and ought to be sent there immediately." Perhaps chastened somewhat, Harris addressed the Tennessee soldiers of Forrest's command, "counseling them to return to their respective homes and to become, as he felt they would prove, good and loyal citizens of the restored Union, which would, he was assured, give them every protection." For himself, he would seek to join Confederate forces west of the Mississippi and, if unsuccessful, "take refuge in foreign lands."[57]

56. "Yesterday's Speaking," *Knoxville Daily Tribune*, October 19, 1876; J. M. Keating, *History of the City of Memphis and Shelby County, Tennessee* (Syracuse, N.Y.: D. Mason & Co., 1888), 1:598n1; OR 49(2):824; McKellar, *Tennessee Senators*, 420–21. Harris's 1876 speech in Knoxville indicates it was W. C. Whitthorne who was dispatched, although Canby's dispatch indicates the courier was Frank C. Whitthorne, who was attached to Forrest's staff. While it is possible the latter was indeed the courier, W. C. Whitthorne is the more likely.

57. OR 49(2):1283–84; Richard Taylor, *Destruction and Reconstruction: Personal Experiences of the Late War* (New York: D. Appleton & Co., 1879), 223–24; Jason Niles Diary, May 6, 1865, Jason Niles Papers, Southern Historical Collection, UNC; E. T. Sykes (W. H. Jackson staff officer), "A Correction Explained—Gov. I. G. Harris," *Confederate Veteran* 6 (November 1898): 525. Taylor relates that Harris was reluctant to go until the gold of the Bank of Tennessee was returned to Nashville and states that the gold was actually with Harris. Since this contradicts the overwhelming evidence of the sworn testimony of the bank officers and the official reports of Federal officers noted above, I have chosen to keep that aspect of Taylor's account out of the narrative.

7 "BETTER A PENNILESS EXILE THAN TO HAVE VIOLATED PRINCIPLE" 1865–1867

In early May 1865, the new Unionist legislature in Nashville passed a joint resolution "Declaratory of the treason of Isham G. Harris, ex-Governor of the State of Tennessee." The resolution accused Harris of "treason, perjury, and theft" and stated he was "responsible to a great extent for the war, misery, and death of thousands of the citizens of the State and for the desolation of the same from East to West and from North to South." Governor Brownlow was instructed to offer a reward of $5,000 for Harris's apprehension, and to "fully describe" the fugitive governor. The Parson gleefully described Harris as follows:

> This culprit Harris is about five feet ten inches high, weighs about One hundred and forty-five pounds and is about fifty-five Years of Age. His complexion is sallow—his eyes are dark and penetrating—a perfect index to the heart of a traitor—with the scowl and form of a demon resting upon his brow. The study of mischief, and the practice of crime, have brought upon him premature baldness and a grey beard. With brazen-faced impudence, he talks loudly and boastingly about the over throw of the Yankee Army, and entertains no doubt but the South will achieve her independence.

Brownlow also stated Harris chewed tobacco "rapidly," was "inordinately fond of liquor," was "unscrupulous," and would be found "in female society" and "lurking in the Rebel Strongholds of Mississippi, Alabama, or Georgia."[1]

When Harris got news of the price on his head, he was indeed "lurking" in

1. Corlew, *Tennessee: A Short History,* 322–23; "The Tennessee Legislature After Isham G. Harris," *New York Times,* May 8, 1865; White, *Messages of the Governors of Tennessee,* 5:438–40.

Mississippi. With the Confederate surrender in process east of the Mississippi River, Harris was preparing to cross the Mississippi, where he hoped to link up with Kirby Smith's Trans-Mississippi command. From Forrest's headquarters, he went to Grenada, Mississippi, where Marcus J. Wright had his headquarters and where Lieutenant Eugene T. Harris continued to serve as the general's aide. There, the governor saw a Memphis paper with news of the reward being offered. Harris's friend, George Adair, undertook efforts to raise some money for Harris to fund his trip, and even solicited a gambler by the name of Sherman to loan the governor $1,000 in greenbacks, for which Harris gave an order on some friends in Memphis to repay. Harris stayed in a house near Grenada until mid-May, under the assumed name of "Major Green," taking care of last items of business and looking for someone who might be interested in making the journey.[2]

Confederate cavalryman Brigadier General Hylan B. Lyon of Kentucky also did not want to surrender, and Wright told him that Harris was preparing to make the journey. The two conferred, and it was agreed that Lyon would go ahead to Fort Pemberton, near Greenwood, Mississippi, and arrange to have a boat constructed. While traveling to the rendezvous, Harris told the faithful Ran that he was a free man. He explained that he no longer had the means to support him, and that the freedman should go to Memphis where his family lived and do the best he could for himself. Ran was disappointed, and lagged back behind Harris for a while, but then said, "Marse Green, you know that you can't get along without me, and I am going with you." The two got to the departure point, and waited in the bushes until Lyon appeared. Harris and Lyon then departed with Ran and Lyon's servant, and navigated through the flooded back country to a point on the Mississippi River near Island No. 75, itself near where the Arkansas River entered the Mississippi. They proceeded through the backwater on the Arkansas side, and found a loggers camp where they were refused food. They left the waterway on May 22, when Harris was able to procure some mounts for the party, and set out for Kirby Smith's headquarters at Shreveport.[3] Along the way, the party

2. OR 49(2):641–42; "West Tennessee," *Macon Daily Telegraph,* January 18, 1865; Eugene Harris Parole, Eugene Harris Compiled Service Record, NA; "Isham G. Harris as Warrior and Fugitive," *Atlanta Constitution,* August 1, 1897; "How Isham G. Harris Saved His Life," *Atlanta Constitution,* July 29, 1900; "Gov. Harris at the Close of the War," *Confederate Veteran* 5 (August 1897): 402, 404; Coffman, ed., "Memoirs of Hylan B. Lyon," 35, 52.

3. Coffman, ed., "Memoirs of Hylan B. Lyon," 52; *Papers Relating to Foreign Affairs,* 528; "Gov. Harris at the Close of the War," *Confederate Veteran* 5 (August 1897): 404; "Isham G. Harris as War-

rescued a soldier stranded by some compatriots on a log sticking out of the water. The young man, along with the two servants, did most of the rowing work until the party crossed the Mississippi.[4]

Rumors abounded as to Harris's whereabouts. The arrest of Dunlap, Battle, and Ray sparked a rumor that Harris, too, had been apprehended. One newspaper account from Louisville stated Harris had been caught with a woman in Marietta, Georgia, in *"flagrante delicto."* But Federal military authorities received accurate information around May 27, when a person at whose house Harris's party stopped for a half hour later identified the man who was called Major Green as Harris. According to the source, the party was making for Mexico. The Northern press grudgingly conceded that Harris had made his escape.[5]

The party indeed determined to go to Mexico when, on their way to Shreveport, they learned of the disbanding of Kirby Smith's command and his subsequent surrender, which occurred on May 26. The party rode on across southeast Arkansas and northwest Louisiana, heading for Harris's rented farm at Clarksville, Texas, where he had taken some of his slaves and farm stock when the Federals first entered Tennessee in 1862. They arrived at the farm on June 7, and encountered a local Confederate who did not credit news of the surrender. To prove his point, he offered to buy all of Harris's slaves for $500 apiece, but Harris refused, saying his people had been with him too long to part with them. Harris located someone else who was willing to sell their slaves to the man, and the foolish secessionist and his money were soon parted. At the farm, Harris took sick and was confined to his bed for a week, although Lyon apparently questioned the severity of Harris's illness. During the week's delay, some "roughs and bushwhackers" from the next county over heard Harris was at Clarksville, and were

---

rior and Fugitive," *Atlanta Constitution,* August 1, 1897. Lyon's account was written in 1903, while Harris's letter quoted in the latter three sources was written November 12, 1865. The major inconsistency between the two is that Lyon reports that at least two other men and a guide accompanied the party, while Harris said it was he, Lyon, and the two servants.

4. "Harris' Flight to Mexico," *Galveston Daily News,* July 14, 1897; "End of an Eventful Life." Although this is not in Harris's contemporary account, it was a story he told later, and is not inconsistent with his 1865 letter.

5. "The Southwest," *New York Times,* May 23, 1865; "Governor Harris, of Tennessee," *Baltimore Sun,* June 5, 1865; "Isham G. Harris," *Baltimore Sun,* June 5, 1865; "The Louisville Journal," *Macon Daily Telegraph,* May 31, 1865; OR 48(2): 631.

aware of Brownlow's reward offer. Lyon heard of their impending approach, but Harris did not think he could move. Finally, it was reported that the gang was just two miles away, and Harris told Lyon that he would try to leave. With the assistance of Lyon and Ran, Harris mounted his horse, and the party rode four or five miles away and camped in the woods. Lyon wrote that the scare the bushwhacker gang had given Harris "had entirely cured him." Harris's account did not report anything other than the fact that the party departed on June 15 for San Antonio, where they expected to join a large party of Confederates en route to Mexico.[6]

Arriving in San Antonio on June 26, they learned that the party they hoped to join had departed some days before. Accordingly, the next day, they set out for Eagle Pass on the Rio Grande, as the Federals held the other crossings below that point. Along the way Harris and Lyon had a falling out. Ran killed a sandhill crane on the prairie and brought it into camp. Harris told him to throw the bird away, as it was not good to eat. Lyon disagreed, and directed his servant to prepare it, and soon found out that Harris was right—the bird got tougher with every bite. A few days later, the party encountered another traveler who, like Lyon, was a Kentuckian. In the course of the trip, the man offered the opinion that the toughest animal to eat was a monkey. Harris opined it was the sandhill crane, and could prove that fact with Lyon's experience, narrating the previous incident with the bird. Lyon got "furious" and no longer would travel with Harris. Each day he and his servant would ride in sight of the rest of them, but at night Lyon would camp apart from Harris. One night, though, Lyon lost his two mules and rations, and Harris sent Ran to bring him some food. Harris suggested thereafter they ride together, but Lyon did so in a stony silence. Finally, Harris "told Lyon that it was foolish to do it that way, and that they had better make up; but the general would not have it that way."[7]

Harris crossed the Rio Grande at Eagle Pass and entered Mexico at the town of Piedras Negras on the evening of June 30. The next day, Harris and Ran set out for Monterey, leaving the irritated Lyon to go another route. Harris arrived in Monterey on July 9 and found Major General Sterling Price and former Governor

6. OR 48(1):297; OR 48(2):602; "Gov. Harris at the Close of the War"; "Harris' Flight to Mexico," *Galveston Daily News*, July 14, 1897; Coffman, ed., "Memoirs of Hylan B. Lyon," 52–53.

7. "Gov. Harris at the Close of the War"; "End of an Eventful Life."

Trusten Polk of Missouri, who were going to Mexico City with an escort of armed Missourians. Still not well from his illness the previous month and worn out from weeks of travel, Harris felt the necessity of joining the party of Missourians because of the length and danger of the journey. Harris related: "I exchanged my saddle-horse, saddles &c., for an ambulance, put my two mules to it, gave the whip and lines to Ran, and bought me a Spanish grammar and dictionary, took the back seat, and commenced the study of the Spanish language." Traveling about twenty-five miles a day, the party reached Mexico City the evening of August 9, 1865, the trip being "one of the longest, most laborious, and hazardous of [Harris's] life." During the early interval of his sojourn in Mexico, Harris dispatched a Parthian shot back to Tennessee in a satirical letter to the *Memphis Bulletin*, noting that while he and other ex-Confederates had been disenfranchised by the Parson's regime, their right to hold office remained intact. Therefore, he announced that he would be a candidate for governor in 1866. In another humorous incident, Ran dressed up in a Confederate uniform and got drunk one night shortly after they arrived in Mexico City, waving Harris's pistols about. The following day, the incident was forgotten, as Ran seemed entitled to let off some steam after the heavy burdens he had borne on the trip.[8]

Having escaped vengeful Unionists at home, Harris and his compatriots found a volatile situation in Mexico. As the United States descended into civil war in 1861, the Mexican government of President Benito Juarez found it necessary to suspend payment on foreign debts for a two-year period. France, Great Britain, and Spain organized a military force to intervene, which induced the Mexicans to repudiate their repudiation. Napoleon III of France used the opportunity to conquer Mexico, joining with a party of Mexican conservatives who opposed Juarez. A golden opportunity existed as the U.S. government's war against the Confederacy prevented, for practical purposes, the enforcement of the Monroe Doctrine. The Mexican republic was abolished, and the throne of the new "empire" was offered to the Archduke Maximilian of Austria, who was crowned in April 1864. Maximilian understood the importance of the survival of the Confederacy to the survival of his regime, but by the time he took his position, the Confederacy was clearly on the decline. While friendly overtures were made to the United States,

8. "Gov. Harris at the Close of the War"; "End of an Eventful Life"; "Harris' Letter," *Philadelphia Inquirer*, July 10, 1865.

the Lincoln administration's sympathy was with Juarez. With little native support, by 1865 Maximilian's government was propped up on French bayonets.[9]

Given his circumstances, it is not surprising that Maximilian welcomed the influx of political and military talent represented by the exiled Confederates. Harris and the others were invited to an audience at the palace, the famous Halls of Montezuma. Maximilian and his beautiful and intelligent young wife, Charlotte of Belgium, known in Mexico as Carlota, welcomed them with sympathy and expressed "the earnest hope that we might find homes for ourselves and friends in Mexico." Fluent in Spanish, French, German, and English, the talented empress translated for her husband during the meeting. One account states Harris told the couple that he "had just gotten out of a bitter internal strife and did not want another" and that he expected to be "perfectly neutral" in Maximilian's struggle with Juarez. Harris was said to have made a "strong impression" on the emperor, while Carlota was quoted as saying Harris was "the brainiest man she had ever met."[10]

Harris found a plethora of former Confederate talent in Mexico City. In addition to Polk and Price, Harris met Commodore Matthew Fontaine Maury, former Governor Henry W. Allen of Louisiana, Judge John Perkins Jr. of Louisiana, former Governor Thomas Caute Reynolds of Missouri, former Governor Pendleton Murrah of Texas, and General John Bankhead Magruder, along with other former Confederates. On September 5, Maximilian issued a decree opening Mexico to immigration and colonization. Harris, Maury, and others were asked to draft regulations to put the decree into effect, and Maury was appointed the imperial commissioner of colonization, with Price, Perkins, and Harris appointed as agents of colonization.[11]

About two weeks after his arrival in Mexico City, Harris was standing in front of his hotel and saw what appeared to be a familiar figure coming down the street. Harris later related: "I had never in all my life seen a more woe-begone, bedraggled, dirty, foot-worn individual." It was Lyon, who was now glad to see Harris, having had a particularly bad time during his trip. Harris sent him down the

9. James Schouler, *History of the United States of America Under the Constitution* (Cambridge: University Press, 1899), 6:261–69, 428–33; Charles M. Hubbard, *The Burden of Confederate Diplomacy* (Knoxville: University of Tennessee Press, 1998), 161–64.

10. "Gov. Harris at the Close of the War"; "End of an Eventful Life."

11. "Gov. Harris at the Close of the War"; "Decreto Imperial de 5 de Septiembre de 1865 Para Fomentar La Immigracion," John Perkins Papers, Southern Historical Collection, UNC.

street with some money for a bath and a fresh change of clothes, and arranged for a room in his hotel. A few weeks later, Harris was able to arrange a position for Lyon working on the Mexican railroad, as he had an excellent civil engineering education from West Point. Within a few weeks, Lyon repaid the loan with extravagant thanks and departed. The two never would meet again.[12]

In a letter to Adair dated November 12, 1865, from Cordova, Harris said that the colonization group was tasked to examine the lands along the railroad from Mexico City to Vera Cruz to determine their suitability for American colonization. Harris reported that "all things considered, [it was] the best agricultural country that I have ever seen." Harris described the temperate climate, the fertility of the land, and the variety of crops that could be grown, the most lucrative of which was coffee. He also marveled at the tropical fruits and plants and at the view of snow-capped peaks of Orizaba and Pocopatepetel. A hundred years before, Harris wrote, the area was in a high state of civilization, with large, expensive houses, supported by large farms worked by slaves. When slavery was abolished, the owners took their money and moved away, and the property fell into the hands of the Catholic Church, until approximately five years before, when it was taken by the Mexican government. The government was now selling the property to colonists for one dollar an acre, and Harris, Price, Perkins, and General Jo Shelby all planned to settle there. Harris thought that with American energy and industry, the richness of the country would ensure fortune. Harris dismissed the native inhabitants as the "most indolent, lazy and worthless population on earth."[13]

Toward the end of his letter, Harris said that he followed his convictions and had no regrets, except for the failure of the "revolution." Defiantly, Harris thundered: "it is better, far better, for me that I should have lost position, fortune and home and stand here today a penniless exile than to have violated principle and forfeited self-respect for these miserable and paltry considerations. I have been shocked and mortified to see the readiness with which Generals Lee, Johnston, Beauregard, Bragg and many other[s] . . . have bowed the knee and kissed the hand that crushed them." Although the Mexican government was "absolutist," it was "an absolutism that has never sought to injure or degrade me."[14]

Harris's letter also proudly spoke of a new English-language newspaper in Mexico City, the *Mexican Times*. This paper was subsidized by Maximilian's gov-

---

12. "Harris' Flight to Mexico," *Galveston Daily News*, July 14, 1897.
13. "Gov. Harris at the Close of the War," 401–2; *Papers Relating to Foreign Affairs*, 529.
14. "Isham G. Harris as Warrior and Fugitive," *Atlanta Constitution*, August 1, 1897.

ernment and devoted much of its coverage to the activities of Mexico's new American immigrants. Harris, Price, and Perkins were only the agents for the Cordoba region; others were dispatched to Guadalajara, Monterey, Durango, Mazatlan, Merida, and Vera Cruz. On November 24, 1865, Harris, Price, and Perkins submitted their report relative to the Cordoba region, and, as reported in Harris's letter to Adair, the agents found the soil fertile and capable of a number of crops, with pleasant temperatures, abundant timber, and near access to the railroad. The area was "admirably adapted to the purpose of Colonization considering soil climate and variety of crops. We know of no better if indeed we have ever seen so desirable a country for agricultural pursuits." From this and other reports, Maury suggested to the emperor that a string of military colonies be placed along the railroad in this region. The first, named Carlota, in honor of the empress, was "seventy miles west of Vera Cruz, and nine miles southeast of Cordoba, near the present town of Paraje Nuevo."[15]

A number of former Confederates soon made the area their home. At first, their efforts were paid off with fine crops and a very pleasant lifestyle. Price seems to have been recognized as a leader of the colony, but other accounts indicate that Harris was deemed by many as its "alcalde," which translates as either the mayor or its chief judicial official. One of Shelby's veterans described Harris and his influence on the colony:

Ex Governor Isham G. Harris of Tennessee, also a settler, might have been designated as the Alcalde of Carlota. The Confederates looked upon him with a kind of reverence . . . He found penniless asylum at Cordova, poor only in pocket, and courageous and proud to the last. He was a cool, silent, contemplative man, with a heavy lower jaw, projecting forehead, and iron gray hair. In his principles he was an Ironside of the Cromwellian type. Perhaps the intense faith of his devotion gave to his character a touch of fatalism, for when the ship stranded he was cast adrift utterly wrecked in everything but his undying confidence in the success of the Confederacy. He believed in Providence as an ally, and rejected constantly the idea that Providence takes very little hand in wars that come about between families or States, if, indeed, in wars of any kind. With his great energy, his

15. Ibid.; Carl Coke Rister, "Carlota, A Confederate Colony in Mexico," *Journal of Southern History* 11 (February 1945): 33, 40–41 (quote locating Carlota); IGH, Sterling Price, and John Perkins to M. F. Maury, November 24, 1865, John Perkins Papers.

calm courage, his shrewd, practical intercourse with the natives, his record as a governor and a soldier, he exerted immense influence for good
with the soldier-settlers and added much to the strength and stability of
the colony.[16]

Life in exile initially agreed with Harris. Letters trickled back into the United
States from the exiles or from their visitors reporting on the colonization efforts
and indicating that Harris and the former Confederates were in an overall favorable situation. A correspondent encountered the former governor in Mexico
City in mid-December 1865, noting: "He looks better than I ever saw him. His
beard and moustache are cut *a l'imperiale*, he wears a *sombrero* with a brim broad
enough for an umbrella, and swears he never felt happier in his life.—His ranche
near Cordova is already in full blast." Doubtless, by the end of 1865, Harris felt sufficiently comfortable with his situation to summon his family. In March, through
Harris and Andrew Johnson's mutual friend, Frank Dunnington, Eugene Harris
made an application to Johnson that Harris's family, described by Dunnington as
Mrs. Harris, five children, and two former slaves, be allowed to join the former
governor in Mexico. The family departed from Memphis in early April, traveling
to Mexico by way of New Orleans. Questioned by Mexican authorities, Martha
stated that she had a letter from Johnson that no special permission was required.
Eugene, having delivered his mother and siblings, returned to Memphis in June,
reporting that the family was in "excellent health and spirits."[17]

While Harris was departing for Mexico in May 1865, thousands of soldiers and
displaced persons were beginning to return to Tennessee. There, they found large
areas of desolation marked by burned houses, barns, and fences. Roads, bridges,

16. Rister, "Carlota," 45–47; "Village of Carlota," *Atlanta Constitution*, June 17, 1894; "End of an
Eventful Life"; Mary Virginia Plattenburg Edwards, *John N. Edwards: biography, memoirs, reminiscences and recollections; his brilliant career as soldier, author, and journalist; choice collection of his most
notable and interesting newspaper articles, together with some unpublished poems and many private letters. Also a reprint of Shelby's expedition to Mexico, an unwritten leaf of the war* (Kansas City: J. Edwards,
1889), 380 (quote).

17. "From New Orleans," *Philadelphia Inquirer,* October 20, 1865; "Confederates in Luck," *Macon
Daily Telegraph,* October 25, 1865; "Letter from Havana," *Dallas Weekly Herald,* December 16, 1865;
"Ex-Rebels in Mexico," *Farmer's Cabinet* (Amherst, N.H.), January 25, 1866; "The Confederates in
Mexico," *Macon Daily Telegraph,* February 14, 1866; Francis C. Dunnington to A. Johnson, March 1,
1866, 10 *PAJ* 200–202, and n4.

and railroads in disrepair hindered transportation. Between war casualties, loss of slave labor, destruction of farm implements, and scarcity of livestock, food production was at a minimum. Guerrilla bands still infested large areas of the state; their depredations were compounded by an ordinary crime wave. Racial tensions were high, not only from the unaccustomed concentration of the newly freed slaves in the cities, but also because large numbers of the Federal occupation troops were black. Especially in East Tennessee, returning Confederate soldiers faced hostility, and many left the section due to legal and extralegal threats.[18]

Politically, the Radicals were shaken in the summer of 1865, when elections were held for Tennessee's eight seats in the U.S. House of Representatives. Notwithstanding the limited franchise, five conservative Unionists were elected, to only three from Brownlow's Radical faction. Brownlow arbitrarily excluded over 22,000 votes, which changed the result in only one race. A new franchise law was proposed in early 1866 that Conservatives sought to defeat by being absent and then by resigning their seats in the state House of Representatives in order to defeat a quorum. Eventually, Brownlow declared a by-election was necessary, and was barely able to achieve a quorum. The new law, passed in the spring of 1866, transferred the function of determining who was a "qualified" voter from local county officials to commissioners appointed by Brownlow. The split between Radicals and Conservatives widened.[19]

In Memphis, the population, both white and black, grappled with the tensions wrought by a significant demographic change in the population. Contraband camps operated by the Federal army during the war became significant black communities on the periphery of the city, effectively making Memphis a black majority community. The native whites, already unhappy with the war's result, chafed under this new reality, along with continued occupation by white and black Federal troops. Here was tangible evidence of the revolutionary upheaval caused by emancipation. Measures were taken by local and Federal authorities to reduce contact between the races that invariably discriminated against the blacks. An additional level of resentment existed between the blacks and non-native whites, who competed with the freedmen for work. This volatile mix finally exploded in

18. Thomas B. Alexander, "Neither Peace Nor War: Conditions in Tennessee in 1865," *East Tennessee Historical Society Publications* 21 (1949): 32–51; Fisher, *War at Every Door,* 154–71.

19. Eugene Feistman, "Radical Disenfranchisement and the Restoration of Tennessee, 1865–1866," *Tennessee Historical Quarterly* 12 (June 1953): 135–45; White, *Messages of the Governors of Tennessee,* 5:480–503.

early May 1866, and white rioters stormed into the new black community in South Memphis, burning, raping, and pillaging. White Federal troops broke up the initial clash by mass arrests of blacks. Another wave of white abuse occurred, which became so bad that the native whites took steps to bring matters under control. One fairly immediate result of the riots was the ammunition it provided Radicals in their argument that more stringent measures be taken against the former Confederate states.[20]

One of the amenities of Carlota was the still set up by Jo Shelby with Price's and Harris's assistance to manufacture pineapple brandy. Almost thirty years later, Shelby was in Washington and hailed then-Senator Harris, who did not recognize the general. Shelby pointed out that the two had been in business together, and Harris gruffly stated that he would not fail to recognize a former partner. Shelby gently chided Harris, effectively saying that while he might not be proud of the business, he could prove the relationship. Aroused, Harris thundered that he had never been in a business of which he was ashamed. Shelby then mentioned the pineapple brandy operation, and Harris sheepishly acknowledged the business and grasped Shelby's hand. At the time, Shelby was in line for an appointment for a U.S. marshal's position in Missouri, but the other candidates for the job claimed Shelby imbibed too much. Shelby admitted, "I do drink a little, but never to excess." "I drink a little, too," replied Senator Harris, "and I don't care a continental if you do the same as I do in that regard. Your nomination shall be confirmed." And it was. Shelby served as marshal until his death.[21]

While the reports coming out of Carlota back to the states were generally rosy, there were problems that grew as time went on. For starters, the local population that squatted on the government land turned over to the Confederate colony was not happy about being displaced. A visitor in April 1866 found Harris and Price "both living in temporary buildings made of bamboo cane, but very comfortable." But the same man noted "great difficulty in regard to labor, as native labor cannot be relied upon." Harris conceded in a letter that summer that the labor system

20. Bobby L. Lovett, "Memphis Riots: White Reaction to Blacks in Memphis, May 1865–July 1866," *Tennessee Historical Quarterly* 38 (Spring 1979): 9–33; George C. Rable, *But There Was No Peace: The Role of Violence in the Politics of Reconstruction* (Athens: University of Georgia Press, 1984), 33–42.

21. Champ Clark, *My Quarter Century of American Politics* (New York: Harper and Brothers, 1920), 1:265–68; "Joe Shelby in Mexico," *Washington Post*, February 12, 1894.

was difficult to get used to, but that eventually it would be a "cheaper system of labor than that of slavery." A report from October 1866 indicated that the news as to the "situation and circumstances" of Harris, Price, and Perkins was "not favorable." Upon his return to the states, Eugene Harris reported that Price's health was "much impaired," and indeed many colonists suffered from tropical diseases. The Mexican natives never welcomed the colonizers. Because of their apparent connection with the government, the Confederates were considered imperialists by the Juarez opposition.[22]

Toward the end of the summer of 1866, the imperial troops were withdrawn from the area of Carlota, leaving the area in a no-man's land that troops of each side might occupy at any one time. This was, in Harris's view, "a position rendering us liable to be misunderstood by both, which kept us continually in danger, and far from comfortable." Harris eventually went to the local Rebel commander and related that all the colonists wanted to do was quietly cultivate their farms. The commander gave Harris an order directing his men not to disturb the ex-Confederates. This accommodation made the imperial forces suspicious, and they subjected the colonists to a number of annoyances. Harris then went to the imperial commander in the area, explained his contact with the Rebels, and procured a similar order to the imperial troops. The colonists continued to be plagued by "petty annoyances and persecutions," "flimsy charges, followed by occasional arrests," to the point that the colony "became so discouraged that it was impossible to hold them together."[23]

Even as Harris and his fellow Confederates struggled with local problems, Maximilian's regime slowly descended into ruin. Under pressure from the United States, the French government made plans to evacuate its troops from Mexico. Carlota went to Paris to try to convince Napoleon to continue at least a period of support, but failed. She then went to Rome, where she lost her sanity. With the exception of some French Foreign Legion troops and foreign mercenaries, Maximilian's European forces were withdrawn in March 1867. The decline of the im-

---

22. "Letter from Havana," *Dallas Weekly Herald*, December 16, 1865; "Mexico," *Macon Daily Telegraph*, June 6, 1866; "Facts and Rumors," *Georgia Weekly Telegraph* (Macon), June 18, 1866; Rister, "Carlota," 47; "Ex-Confederates in Mexico," *Flake's Bulletin* (Galveston), August 3, 1866; "Isham G. Harris, formerly Governor of Tennessee," *Bangor Daily Whig and Courier*, August 18, 1866; "Mexican Colonization," *Milwaukee Daily Sentinel*, August 20, 1866; "Confederate Exiles," *New York Times*, October 29, 1866.

23. "Mexico," *Milwaukee Daily Sentinel*, March 26, 1867.

perial fortunes signaled a steady departure from Mexico for the former Confederates at Carlota. Maury departed for England in 1866 and never returned. In poor health, Price returned to St. Louis. Harris was stated to have waited "until the last footfall of retreating colonists . . . was heard dying away, then . . . took ship for Havana." With the price still on his head, Harris could not return to Tennessee, but Martha and the boys were dispatched back home to Paris under the protection of the faithful Ran. For his part, Shelby waited until the bitter end, and ironically escaped capture by the vengeful Mexicans by means of a boat flying the U.S. flag. With his support gone, Maximilian was eventually captured and executed.[24]

Thus ended Harris's sojourn in Mexico. While the experience was one he would remember the rest of his life, he left bitter in spirit. Pronouncing colonization a failure, he wrote a friend that Mexico was inhabited by eight million people, seven million of which were "ignorant, indolent, worthless, unprincipled and vicious, ready to oppose any and all government which in any degree restrains their vices or seeks to collect taxes." Harris also condemned a number of the Americans who came to the colony as "mere adventurers," who were not prepared for the life there and "whose rashness or bad conduct in a few instances here did more to injure the American character with the natives than years of good behavior could repair."[25]

On March 8, 1867, Harris boarded a ship at Havana for Liverpool, England, intending to establish a "commission house for the accommodation of Southern trade." He "issued circulars to his friends that he would transact their business for them as a factor and commission merchant." During his passage, he watched as an Englishman repeatedly bested the other passengers at chess. One day, he "grunted" during a move in a particularly close game, and the champion turned to Harris and said, "You seem to know something about this game." Harris played the man seven times the next day, and won six of the games. The next day brought the same results, and Harris and his opponent became friends. The Englishman turned out to be the ship's owner, and after hearing the former governor's story, invited him to stay with him at Liverpool. Harris refused to do so, but promised

24. William Butler, *Mexico in Transition: From the Power of Political Romanism to Civil and Religious Liberty*, 2nd ed. rev. (New York: Hunt & Eaton, 1892), 211–22; Rister, "Carlota," 49–50; "The Family of Ex-Governor Harris," *Flake's Bulletin* (Galveston), February 7, 1867; "Eastern News," *Idaho Tri-Weekly Statesman*, March 12, 1867; "End of an Eventful Life"; Seaton Schroeder, *The Fall of Maximilian's Empire as Seen from a United States Gunboat* (New York: G. P. Putnam's Sons, 1887), 39–42.

25. "Mexico," *Milwaukee Daily Sentinel*, March 26, 1867; "The population of Mexico," *Georgia Weekly Telegraph* (Macon), April 26, 1867.

to pay the man a visit. When he checked into his hotel in Liverpool, Harris fell ill with a serious fever and became delirious. When he finally regained his senses, he found that his friend had called on him at his hotel and discovered Harris in a precarious condition. The man brought Harris to his home, where the Tennessean was nursed back to health. Later, the Englishman gave Harris much useful information of a commercial nature, and Harris was purportedly able to use the same to make himself "a large sum of money" and provide some business for his benefactor.

One account states that while in England, Harris was approached by former Confederate Senator Louis T. Wigfall, who was purportedly in bad financial condition. The account stated that there was a fund of Confederate money in London originally kept in Canada to be used to finance a mass escape of Confederate soldiers held in the Northern states near the Canadian border. Wigfall came to Harris with the name of the man holding the fund, and proposed that they should approach the man and make him divide it with them. According to the account, Harris replied: "I do not know whether or not Mr.—— has any of the money of the Confederacy, but I do know that he has not a d——d cent of my money."[26]

If Harris made a "large sum of money" with his English friend's help, it was insufficient for his needs and that of his distant family. The "low price of cotton and the indebtedness of the southern planters to their home commission merchants precluded [Harris's] success," while Martha and his boys were in some financial difficulty back home in Paris. Between these monetary problems and his own bad health, Harris needed to return home. Governor Brownlow's enmity toward Harris was demonstrated by his reward broadside of May 1865. But as unpleasant as the prospect of seeking the aid of Brownlow was, the thought of approaching the president of the United States, Andrew Johnson, was too bitter to contemplate. John Overton, a prominent resident of Nashville, went to Washington to seek a pardon while the former governor was still in Cordoba, but failed. Later, Harris's aged brother, George Washington Harris, who had survived his imprisonment by the Federals in 1864, wrote Johnson "privately" to ask for a pardon, noting that he was doing so on his own account. There is no evidence that Harris ever asked for or received any pardon from Johnson. Indeed, Johnson issued an amnesty proclamation for a large class of former Confederate officials in the fall of 1867, but

26. "The Havana correspondent," *Savannah Daily News and Herald*, April 3, 1867; "Gov. Harris," *Paris Intelligencer*, February 23, 1867; "Return of Ex-Governor Harris," *Memphis Daily Appeal*, November 26, 1867; "Ex-Governor Harris," *Georgia Weekly Telegraph*, November 22, 1867; "End of an Eventful Life." The identity of Harris's English benefactor is unknown.

Harris, along with a number of other high-ranking Confederate and Confederate state officials, was excluded.[27]

Johnson and Brownlow had troubles of their own. In the first part of his presidential term, Johnson had supervised the reinstitution of civil government in the former Confederacy, along the lines envisioned by Lincoln himself. But the Radicals were fueled by a major Republican victory in the congressional elections of 1866, in which the party won a two-thirds majority in both houses of Congress. Led by the Radicals, the Congress passed Reconstruction acts that placed the South under military rule, made military men and agents the sole authority as to who was qualified to vote, and invalidated the Southern state governments established under the president's authority. With the large Republican majorities in the Congress, these acts were veto-proof.[28]

The Parson, on the other hand, pursued an almost dictatorial course in 1866 and 1867 that maintained Radical control of Tennessee. The wartime spirit of cooperation between him and Johnson evaporated, and their old enmity resurfaced. When the Congress submitted the Fourteenth Amendment to the states for ratification, Brownlow was apprised that ratification by Tennessee would restore the state to full participation in the national government. Therefore, in July 1866, the amendment was submitted to the Tennessee legislature. The state Senate quickly approved it, but enough opponents stayed away in the House to require the arrest of certain members in order to create a quorum. In a session fraught with irregularity, the amendment was passed. A judge who ruled the process illegal was impeached and eventually removed. Brownlow sent a telegram to an ally in Washington announcing his victory, closing the message with: "Give my regards to the dead dog of the White House." Brownlow was vindicated, when on July 26, 1866, Tennessee was readmitted to the Union. Tennessee therefore would not be subject to the Federal Reconstruction acts.[29]

Meanwhile, large areas of Middle and West Tennessee were torn with ex-secessionist lawlessness. Giles County in Middle Tennessee was one of the most

27. "Return of Ex-Governor Harris"; Clark, *My Quarter Century of American Politics*, 1:264; Keating, *History of the City of Memphis and Shelby County, Tennessee*, 1:562n1; G. W. D. Harris to A. Johnson, September 25, 1867, 11 *PAJ* 106; "The Late Amnesty Proclamation," *Flake's Bulletin* (Galveston), October 6, 1867.

28. J. G. Randall and David Donald, *The Civil War and Reconstruction* (Lexington, Mass.: D. C. Heath, 1969), 561–69, 598–609.

29. Feistman, "Radical Disfranchisement and the Restoration of Tennessee, 1865–1866," 145–51; Ben H. Severance, *Tennessee's Radical Army: The State Guard and its Role in Reconstruction* (Knoxville: University of Tennessee Press, 2005), 8; Rable, *But There Was No Peace*, 60, 66.

anarchic counties. It was in Giles County in the late spring of 1866 that six young men founded the Ku Klux Klan to foster their social amusement, rather than to deal with public order. But political events soon turned the mysterious Klan from a harmless social club into a reactionary force of regulators and eventually terrorists. In February 1867, Parson Brownlow and his Radical legislature, fearing that their grip on power might be slipping, passed a law enfranchising the African Americans, and extended the disfranchisement of former Confederates. Continued acts of lawlessness and intimidation of Unionists and blacks such as that seen in Giles County and elsewhere also resulted in the organization of a State Guard, a militia force of "loyal men" under the governor as commander in chief.[30]

The granting of suffrage to the blacks and the creation of the State Guard to protect their exercise of that right necessitated, in the minds of the ex-secessionist opposition, a conservative force to defend "higher white culture and political order . . . against wanton political aggression." Therefore, in April 1867, the Klan was reorganized under Nathan Bedford Forrest as "Grand Wizard." The seminal political event of 1867 was the contest between Radical Brownlow and West Tennessee's Emerson Etheridge for the governorship. Etheridge's Conservative platform did not shrink from the extension of the franchise to the African Americans, but advocated immediate restoration of the full rights of former Confederates. In the ensuing canvass, the Conservative Unionists openly courted the black vote, but the Radicals countered with the falsehood that their opponents wanted to reenslave the blacks. With Brownlow and his allies in firm control of the state's election machinery, Etheridge's defeat was a foregone conclusion. The State Guard was strategically posted to help rigidly enforce the franchise laws excluding former Confederates, defend the lives and property of the freedmen, and suppress ex-secessionist lawlessness or insurrection. It very effectively did so, as the new secret organization failed to make an appearance in the contest.[31]

In these political contests of 1866 and 1867, Johnson, a pro-Southern conservative, was Harris's natural ally, and Brownlow, the Radical Republican, was Har-

30. Allen W. Trelease, *White Terror: The Ku Klux Klan Conspiracy and Southern Reconstruction* (New York: Harper & Row, 1971), 3–10; Severance, *Tennessee's Radical Army*, 9–10, 87; Thomas B. Alexander, "Kukluxism in Tennessee, 1865–1869," *Tennessee Historical Quarterly* 8 (September 1949): 195, 198, 200; White, *Messages of the Governors of Tennessee*, 5:550–51.

31. Trelease, *White Terror*, 14–24; Severance, *Tennessee's Radical Army*, 61–65, 125, 140–44, 230–33; Lonnie Maness, "Henry Emerson Etheridge and the Gubernatorial Election of 1867: A Study in Futility," *West Tennessee Historical Society Papers* 47 (1993): 38, 41–48.

ris's natural enemy. Yet, ironically, Harris trusted Brownlow much more than Johnson. At some point in 1867, Harris wrote former Governor Neill S. Brown, stating: "I wish to return to my home. My family need me; I wish to resume the practice of the law, but I would not feel it safe to do so without a pledge of protection from the President of the United States or the Governor of Tennessee. I would rather die in exile than ask or receive a favor at the hands of Andrew Johnson. I am willing to ask it of Governor Brownlow, confident that he will do whatever he promises to do." No doubt impressed by Harris's confidence in him, and likewise gratified by Harris's distrust of Johnson, whom Brownlow also hated, the Parson told Brown to tell Harris to come home, observing: "Johnson has released many men as reprehensible for the part they took in the war as Harris, without Harris's good qualities." Further, to assist Martha's financial difficulties, Brownlow quietly arranged to have one of the couple's sons appointed to a position with the state's railroad receivers.[32]

While he was privately sympathetic to Harris's situation, Brownlow's message to the General Assembly on October 9, 1867, treated the issue with contemptuous disdain. Advising the "immediate repeal" of the $5,000 reward for Harris's arrest, Brownlow noted that his opinion of the need to punish secessionists had not changed. But not even Jefferson Davis had been punished, and Johnson's "pro-Rebel policy" indicated that none probably would. Further, there had been an election in Tennessee in 1867, and "there were worse men upon the stump than Harris ever was, proclaiming treason and sedition, and inspiring the people with sectional malice." Two other considerations also were at play: humanity toward Harris's family and economy on the part of the state. "The State is liable to be called upon at any day, for this reward, and in return, she would have nothing to show for this outlay." The legislature concurred with the recommendation, repealing the reward resolution on November 11, 1867, and instructing the governor to revoke the offer of a reward for "the apprehension of said Isham G. Harris, *the traitor.*"[33]

32. Clark, *My Quarter Century of American Politics,* 1:264. Clark's quote of the letter from Brownlow's son indicates Brown approached Governor Brownlow on Harris's behalf in 1866, but the context of Harris's situation and that of his family indicates the contact was made in 1867. A similar account in Temple, *Notable Men of Tennessee from 1833 to 1875,* 336–38 relates the story of the Harris son's employment.

33. White, *Messages of the Governors of Tennessee,* 5:587–88, 599; Temple, *Notable Men of Tennessee,* 337 and note. Brownlow's message suggests that a significant motivation for his accommodation of Harris was his own hatred of Johnson. White, *Messages of the Governors of Tennessee,* 5:599.

Upon hearing the news that a price was no longer on his head, on November 6 Harris left Liverpool for New York. Without meeting anyone who knew him, the former governor traveled to Nashville, arriving at midnight on Saturday, November 23. Early the next morning, Harris, accompanied by former Governor Brown, presented himself before Brownlow. The Parson good-naturedly held out his arms and said, "While the lamp holds out to burn, the vilest sinner may return." Harris laughed feebly at the comment, and the discussion turned to the issue of whether Harris would be disturbed by the authorities. Harris expressed the preference that if he were to be arrested, he wanted to go ahead and surrender then and there, as opposed to going home and having his family upset with an arrest there. Even though the price was no longer on his head, Harris thought it possible that a state attorney general might bring charges or that a Federal warrant against him might be executed. Brownlow assured Harris that he had taken steps to make sure that he would not be disturbed by either Federal or state authorities. Gratefully, Harris left Nashville that afternoon on the 4:00 p.m. train for Paris. That night, a Unionist in Henry County telegraphed Brownlow that Harris had come home, and that steps should be taken to quietly arrest him. Brownlow replied that he was "fully informed of Harris' movements, and that he was on a bond for his appearance."[34]

Whether, in the end, Brownlow's kindness toward Harris was based on a desire to aid the Harris family, or for the political reason that Brownlow desired to prove a point to Andrew Johnson, the fact remains that Harris returned to his family and eventually to his law practice undisturbed. Green Harris did not forget his former enemy's kindness. A source for a large part of the foregoing narrative was Parson Brownlow's son, John, who was employed in later years by the Federal government. When Harris once again was on the ascendancy, he was a political patron for John Brownlow. Likewise, in 1886, he took steps to have a claim against the Federal government paid for the Parson's widow.[35]

34. Clark, *My Quarter Century of American Politics*, 1:264–65; Temple, *Notable Men of Tennessee*, 337–38; "Governor Harris," *Memphis Public Ledger,* November 27, 1867; "Return of Isham G. Harris," *Knoxville Whig,* November 27, 1867. The various accounts of Harris's return differ in minor details. The most important deviation from the above narrative is that it was former Comptroller James T. Dunlap who accompanied Harris on his visit with Brownlow rather than Brown. Because Brown originally approached Brownlow, and, like the Parson, had Whig antecedents, it seems more logical to include him in the narrative rather than Dunlap, who, like Harris, was a Henry County Democrat. Ironically, if there were indeed a Federal warrant for Harris's arrest, it would have eventually been rendered a nullity by Andrew Johnson's amnesty proclamation of December 5, 1868, which pardoned "every person who directly or indirectly participated in the late insurrection or rebellion."

35. Clark, *My Quarter Century of American Politics*, 1:264–65; Temple, *Notable Men of Tennessee,*

Reaction to Harris's return was mixed. Harris's old friends at the *Memphis Daily Appeal* gushed that "right cordially will he be greeted by thousands of true and sympathizing hearts who have followed him in sympathy and affection wherever he has wandered." But the *Memphis Evening Post* snidely commented that "it is to be hoped that Mr. Harris is sufficiently wise not to add to the present disturbed state of the public mind." What the former governor thought is unrecorded, although it is unlikely the fervent Confederate sentiments he expressed in his letter to Adair in November 1865 had completely subsided. Likely, Oliver P. Temple very accurately described Harris's feelings when he later observed: "Humiliating as it was to appeal to his enemies for clemency, and revolting as it was to live in a government controlled by hated Yankees, [Harris] determined to submit to both."[36]

337–38; IGH et al. to Green B. Raum, commissioner of internal revenue, May 15, 18??, William G. Brownlow Papers, University of Tennessee; "Harris and Brownlow," *Atlanta Constitution*, June 18, 1886.

36. "Return of Ex-Governor Harris"; "Return of Isham G. Harris," *Memphis Evening Post*, November 29, 1867; Temple, *Notable Men of Tennessee*, 337.

8 "WE OF THE SOUTH HAVE ACCEPTED THE RESULTS IN GOOD FAITH" 1868–1876

On January 29, 1868, an advertisement appeared in the professional cards section of the *Memphis Appeal* for "Isham G. Harris, Attorney at Law." His substantial personal fortune effectively wiped out by the war, Green Harris resumed his life's profession in 1868. There was little other means of making a living, although he appears to have also considered editing a newspaper. In 1865, Parson Brownlow and the Radical legislature passed an act disenfranchising all but "unconditional" Union men, and placing a legal disability on a broad class of former Confederates from holding state office until 1880. Likewise, by operation of Section 3 of the soon to be ratified Fourteenth Amendment, Harris would soon be under a Federal constitutional legal disability from holding any state or Federal office. As a politician, Harris was persona non grata. Still, for a man was living in exile less than four months before, practicing law in Memphis again must have been a welcome change.[1]

Harris resumed his practice with his customary energy. By early April, he formed a partnership with Gideon J. Pillow, who formerly was a law partner of James K. Polk. As Harris & Pillow, the two former Confederates practiced law in an office at Main and Madison and Harris boarded at the now-famous Peabody Hotel. With the hard-working Pillow at his side, Harris rebuilt his practice. Reported cases indicate that Harris litigated complex commercial matters, and on at least one occasion, was called on to sit as a special chancellor on the exclusivity

1. *Memphis Daily Appeal*, January 29, 1868; "The News," *Newark* (Ohio) *Advocate*, January 10, 1868; P. C. Headley, *Public Men of To-Day: Being Biographies of the President and Vice-President of the United States, Each Member of the Cabinet, the United States Senators and the Members of the House of Representatives of the Forty-Seventh Congress, the Chief Justice and the Justices of the Supreme Court, and of the Governors of the Several States* (Hartford: S. S. Scranton, 1882), 164–65; Corlew, *Tennessee: A Short History*, 331; White, *Messages of the Governors of Tennessee*, 5:428–48, 587.

of a franchise granted by the city of Memphis, rendering, in the view of the Tennessee Supreme Court, a "full, clear and conclusive" opinion on the issue.[2]

In Washington, Andrew Johnson's clashes with the Radicals spawned an abortive attempt at impeachment in 1867. The passage of an unconstitutional law that same year requiring the consent of the Senate before a cabinet officer could be removed provided fodder for another attempt in 1868. Secretary of War Edwin M. Stanton's support of Johnson's opponents became intolerable to the president, who suspended, then removed the secretary. The Radicals seized the opportunity, and made this "high misdemeanor" the centerpiece of eleven articles of impeachment. After a trial in the Senate in the spring of 1868, Johnson escaped conviction by one vote, which many attribute to Senator Edmund G. Ross of Kansas, but which could equally be said to have been that of Tennessee Senator Joseph S. Fowler, who defied the wishes of the Brownlow-dominated legislature and voted with his colleague (and Johnson's son-in-law), Senator David T. Patterson, for acquittal.[3]

In Tennessee, the first half of the year saw an outburst of violence against blacks and white supporters of the Brownlow regime under the banner of the Ku Klux Klan. While simple race hatred or leftover wartime animosities likely had much to do with discrete local incidents, the ultimate goal of this wave of violence was to intimidate potential Radical voters. There were hundreds of acts of violence in Middle and West Tennessee. In response, Brownlow called the legislature into special session in July 1868, and obtained passage of measures reviving the State Guard and addressing the Ku Klux violence. Harris's partner Pillow, along with Cheatham, Forrest, and ten other former Confederate generals, sent a memorial to the legislature refuting any attempt at overthrowing the government, denying the need for a state military force, and asking that the franchise be

2. "General Pillow," *Memphis Daily Avalanche*, April 9, 1868; *Edwards Annual Director to the Inhabitants, Institutions, Incorporated Companies, Manufacturing Establishments, Businesses, Business Firms, etc., etc. in the City of Memphis for 1869* (New Orleans: Southern Publishing Company, 1869), 107–8; Hughes and Stonesifer, *The Life and Wars of General Gideon J. Pillow*, 307; *Turbeville v. Gibson*, 52 Tenn. (5 Heisk.) 565 (1871); *Mason v. Pritchard*, 56 Tenn. (9 Heisk.) 793 (1872); *Memphis Gayoso Gas Co. v. Williamson*, 56 Tenn. (9 Heisk.) 314 (1872).

3. Randall and Donald, *The Civil War and Reconstruction*, 601–14; Corlew, *Tennessee: A Short History*, 336–39; Coulter, *William G. Brownlow*, 349–64; White, *Messages of the Governors of Tennessee*, 5:609–24. The Tenure of Office Act was repealed in 1887, and the concept of senate consent to the removal of presidential appointees was ruled invalid by the Supreme Court in *Myers v. United States*, 272 U.S. 52 (1926).

restored. Indeed, the violence abated in July as prominent white citizens became concerned with the consequences of its continuation.[4]

With the presidential election of 1868 approaching, Brownlow oddly did not deploy the State Guard, but instead asked for Federal troops, which the Conservatives actually preferred to the Radical State Guard. A small number of Federal troops was made available, but they did not supervise the elections. The Radical candidate for president, Ulysses S. Grant, carried Tennessee, but the threat of Klan violence significantly reduced the Radical vote over that of the previous year's governor's race. Subsequently, prominent Conservatives such as Neill S. Brown spoke out against Klan violence, and Grand Wizard Forrest issued an order for the organization to disband. Although Brownlow deemed it necessary to call out the Guard for a brief period in 1869, and isolated incidents continued into 1871, the crisis was effectively over.[5]

There is no evidence of Harris's role in these events, if he took any. While Forrest was a high-profile member, by its nature, the Klan was a secret society. Some claimed that every former Confederate in Memphis was a member, but with Harris just recently back from exile at Brownlow's forbearance, it seems unlikely he would have risked his tenuous safety openly supporting or participating in an illegal movement. Further, unlike in other districts of the state, Klan activity in Memphis was minimal, or at least muted. It is likely, however, that Harris counseled with Pillow and the other generals in connection with their memorial to the legislature, and that he approved of the position taken by the socially and politically prominent white Conservatives in 1869 that the Klan at that point was no longer necessary.[6]

Brownlow's control of the state government continued into 1869. In late February, the Parson resigned his governorship and was appointed to a vacant seat in the U.S. Senate. He was succeeded by the speaker of the state Senate, DeWitt C. Senter. Extolled by Brownlow as "a loyal man, capable, tried and trusty," Senter was expected to adhere to the Radical platform. Few men could be as intense in their views as Brownlow, however, and the first part of 1869 saw Senter begin

4. Trelease, *White Terror*, xlvii, 27, 43–44; White, *Messages of the Governors of Tennessee*, 5:607–24; Severance, *Tennessee's Radical Army*, 172–87.

5. Trelease, *White Terror*, 45, 175–77, 179–83, 278–79; Severance, *Tennessee's Radical Army*, 188–89, 193–206, 216–17, 226.

6. Capers, *The Biography of a River Town*, 178–79.

to relax Brownlow's Radical program. Senter planned to run for governor in his own right in 1869, and was opposed by another member of the Radical party, William B. Stokes of Middle Tennessee. The Conservatives, a conglomeration of conservative Unionists and ex-Confederates, wisely chose not to field a candidate, and waited on one or the other of the antagonists to bid for their support. The eventual bidder, and therefore winner of a new term, was Senter, who swept into power with a legislature that quickly restored the franchise to the disfranchised ex-Confederates. The legislature also called for a constitutional convention, which was approved by the newly expanded electorate on December 18, 1869.[7]

Still in political eclipse, Harris kept a relatively low profile in 1869. After Andrew Johnson's presidential term expired in March, the former president embarked on a triumphant tour through Tennessee, acclaimed by the newly enfranchised conservative majority of the state for his stand against the Radicals. In Memphis in mid-April, he was feted at a grand banquet at the Overton Hotel, attended by "many of the principal members of the bar, leading merchants and business men, and citizens of the county most prominent." Harris was conspicuous by his absence. The enmity between the two survived the war with no abatement. While Johnson had not hindered Harris's return to Tennessee, he alluded to his rival "with a sneer as 'I-*sham* G. Harris.'" For his part, notwithstanding Johnson's relatively benign indifference in the aftermath of the war, Harris responded to Johnson's return to Tennessee by venomously rejecting his hero status among conservatives, observing that Johnson, "with a cold-blooded cruelty which at once stamped him as a monster, inaugurated a policy of hate by causing three-fourths of our citizens to be disfranchised, and enfranchising the negroes and endeavoring to place them over their late masters; and now, with an impudence and assurance that is amusing to contemplate, forces himself upon the hospitality of those whose property he has stolen and themselves disgraced." When, in October, Johnson's supporters began bandying about his name as a possible U.S. senator, Harris was reported to have traveled to Nashville "to defeat Andy, and will spare no effort in that direction." A trip to Washington a few weeks earlier may have been in furtherance of the same goal. A strange combination of Radicals, including Parson Brownlow, and former Confederates, including Harris, worked to defeat the ex-president. Johnson was not elected, which must have compounded his ha-

7. White, *Messages of the Governors of Tennessee*, 5:652–53; Bergeron, Ash, and Keith, *Tennesseans and Their History*, 176–78; Thomas B. Alexander, *Political Reconstruction in Tennessee* (1951; reprint, New York: Russell and Russell, 1968), 216–19, 230.

tred for his polar-opposite antagonists. The continued rivalry between Harris and Johnson even extended to control of the *Memphis Daily Appeal,* which was for sale at the end of 1869. Fortunately for Harris, a pro-Johnson group could not be formed, and shortly thereafter, Matthew C. Galloway, a fire-eating former staff officer of Forrest's, became coeditor.[8]

What little public profile Harris presented in those years was mostly limited to the environs of Memphis. A Freemason since his days in Paris, he was elected Grand Orator of his Memphis lodge in 1868. In the first part of 1869, the continued racial tension in Memphis and concern for a reliable labor supply helped bring about a bizarre scheme to import "quiet, orderly, good-natured, docile, cheerful willing" Chinese laborers to work in the cotton fields in the place of the disaffected freedmen. A newspaper article claimed that the freedmen had had their chance to demonstrate their reliability as workers, but that their purportedly unhealthy practices produced a mortality rate to make "African labor" insufficient. It was a common belief at that time that free black labor was unreliable. But just as common was the aversion of whites to contracting with former slaves for labor. A convention was called on the issue of Chinese labor, and it convened in Memphis on July 13. Harris was elected permanent chairman of the convention to the cheers of those there. Pillow, too, had a prominent role in the scheme. The plan eventually came to naught when, in the fall of 1869, Tennessee legislature passed a law by a substantial margin prohibiting importation of Chinese laborers into the state.[9]

As Harris worked to restore his position in postwar society, he did not forget an old friend. In May 1869, he wrote Jefferson Davis, who was then visiting En-

8. "Johnson," *Memphis Daily Appeal,* April 17, 1869; W. F. G. Shanks, "A Political Romance," *Putnam's Magazine* 16 (April 1869): 428, 430; "The Ex-President," *Hagerstown* (Md.) *Herald and Torch,* May 3, 1869; White, *Messages of the Governors of Tennessee,* 6:48–49; "Andy," *Atlanta Constitution,* October 21, 1869; "Andy Johnson," *Atlanta Constitution,* October 26, 1869; "From Washington," *Weekly* (Macon) *Georgia Telegraph,* August 27, 1869; Coulter, *William G. Brownlow,* 393; Robert B. Jones and Mark E. Byrnes, "'Rebels Never Forgive': Former President Andrew Johnson and the Senate Election of 1869," *Tennessee Historical Quarterly* 66 (Fall 2007): 250–69; Saunders to A. Johnson, December 13, 1869, 16 *PAJ* 148; Thomas Harrison Baker, *The Memphis Commercial Appeal: The History of a Southern Newspaper* (Baton Rouge: Louisiana State University Press, 1971), 123–24.

9. Charles Albert Snodgrass, *The History of Freemasonry in Tennessee, 1789–1943* (Nashville: Ambrose Printing Company, 1944), 402; Lennie Austin Cribbs, "The Memphis Chinese Labor Convention, 1869," *West Tennessee Historical Society Papers* 37(1983): 74–77, 81; McKenzie, *One South Or Many,* 155.

gland after finally escaping prosecution for his role in the rebellion. On behalf of the shareholders of the Carolina Life Insurance Company, Harris offered Davis a position in the company managing its office in either Richmond or Baltimore. Harris was careful to note that he had no personal interest in the company. A few weeks later, Davis replied that he had been careful not to get engaged in a business that would be disadvantaged by "our enemy." Davis expressed feelings of warm regards to Harris, and thought that the Baltimore office might be possible. Later, Davis was offered the job by one of the company's principals, and Harris again wrote to encourage the same, noting that to the extent the company could not meet its generous pay offer of at least $12,000 a year, he would personally guarantee up to $15,000. Eventually, Davis was offered the presidency of the company, and moved with his family to Memphis.[10]

Publicly reclaiming his leadership of local ex-Confederates in July 1869, Harris appeared at a meeting of approximately two hundred men, the purpose of which was to reorganize the Confederate Soldiers Relief and Historical Association of the city of Memphis. The objects of the association were "the relief of destitute soldiers, their widows and orphans, the collection of records pertaining to the late war, and to such other matters incident to these that might from time to time arise." Elected president of the group by a large majority, Harris made his influence felt through the course of the meeting, making practical observations relative to the adoption of the group's constitution and admonishing those assembled to avoid matters in the document that "savored of politics." Early in April 1870, Harris chaired a meeting that received a report on Confederate casualties during the war. At the end of the same month, the association met again, with Jefferson Davis himself present. Earlier the same day, Davis, Harris, Patton Anderson, Frank Cheatham, and Pillow appeared in a funeral cortege for their dead comrade, Patrick Cleburne, on his way home to Helena, Arkansas, after sleeping in a Middle Tennessee churchyard for just over five years. In addition to his local affiliation, Harris was also named state vice president of the Southern Historical Association, at that time headquartered in New Orleans. While the Memphis association faded relatively quickly, its meetings and the celebration of Cleburne and other dead soldiers were part of a phenomenon in the South that lionized the Confederate dead as cultural heroes and sought to preserve historical informa-

10. IGH to Davis, May 27, 1869, Davis to IGH, June 22, 1869, Moses Wicks to Davis, July 17, 1869, IGH to Davis, July 20, 1869, IGH to Davis, September 7, 1869, Davis to IGH, September 9, 1869, Davis to Varina Howell Davis, November 23, 1869, 12 *PJD* 359–64, 380–81, 398–99.

tion so that the truth concerning the war, that is, the Southern viewpoint, would be known. Notwithstanding his early conspicuous appearance in these organizations, Harris was not particularly of the Lost Cause mentality. While conservative in his political views, the former governor tended to think and act toward the future.[11]

The principal political event in Tennessee in 1870 was the adoption of a new state constitution, in which the victorious Conservatives restored political rights to ex-Confederates. Properly Tennessee's Redeemers (from Radical rule), this group was made up of several factions: pre-war Whigs with Confederate credentials, such as former Army of Tennessee Major General John Calvin Brown and James D. Porter, a staff officer of Cheatham's; Andrew Johnson and his adherents; and the prewar Democratic secessionists, such as Harris, William B. Bate, and Peter Turney. At this stage, Harris and the other former secessionists were in eclipse, and therefore conspicuously absent from the constitutional convention. Also in eclipse were the Radicals, who were also largely absent; moreover, none of the delegates was black. The suffrage extended to African American citizens in 1867 was preserved in the 1870 constitution, but the new constitution also authorized a poll tax, an implicit threat of disfranchisement.[12]

With Radical power collapsing, blacks and Radical Unionists appealed to the Federal government, claiming fraud and intimidation in connection with the 1869 vote, in hopes that the election would be invalidated and Tennessee placed under military rule, as the other former Confederate states. Neither President Ulysses S. Grant nor the Congress, however, wanted to intervene. In the summer of 1870, an election under the new constitution placed six Conservative judges on the state supreme court, and an election that November resulted in John C. Brown being elected governor and a Conservative majority in the General Assembly. The Conservatives, who soon recognized themselves as Democrats, established a pattern

11. "The Lost Cause," *Memphis Daily Appeal,* July 2, 1869; "The Confederate R. and H. Association," *Memphis Daily Appeal,* April 2, 1870; "Confederate Relief and Historical Association" and "Cleburne," *Memphis Daily Appeal,* April 29, 1870; Hughes and Stonesifer, *The Life and Wars of General Gideon J. Pillow,* 310; "At a meeting of ex-Confederate soldiers," *Galveston Daily News,* April 24, 1875; Gaines Foster, *Ghosts of the Confederacy: Defeat, the Lost Cause, and the Emergence of the New South, 1865 to 1913* (New York: Oxford University Press, 1987), 36–46, 50, 195; Thomas L. Connelly and Barbara L. Bellows, *God and General Longstreet* (Baton Rouge: Louisiana State University Press, 1982), 6–7, 21–25.

12. Roger L. Hart, *Redeemers, Bourbons and Populists: Tennessee 1870–1896* (Baton Rouge: Louisiana State University Press, 1975), 1–10; Alexander, *Political Reconstruction in Tennessee,* 230–33; Bergeron, Ash, and Keith, *Tennesseans and Their History,* 178–79.

that would hold for at least the next decade. Controlling Middle and West Tennessee, they would thereby control the state government. The Radicals, who eventually became the Republicans, held political power in East Tennessee. The Republicans retained a sufficiently strong voice in affairs to take advantage of Democratic political missteps.[13]

The Democratic victory slowed the political progress made by the African American freedmen since 1862. In the interval before 1870, in addition to acquiring the right to vote, a small percentage of the freedmen were the beneficiaries of a rudimentary system of education provided by the Federal government's Freedmen's Bureau, churches and benevolence societies, and, for a very brief time, the state government. These efforts were almost never appropriately funded and local whites were often hostile to these educational efforts, teachers were threatened, intimidated, and assaulted, and schoolhouses were burned. The new Conservative legislature repealed the Radicals' public school law, and further mandated separate schools for the races. Other laws prevented interracial marriage and repealed a provision prohibiting segregation in railroad travel.

In addition to establishing schools, the Freedmen's Bureau also maintained a system of courts to provide a fair forum for the freedmen, but Tennessee's early readmission to the Union resulted in their termination. One of the main functions of the Bureau was to help the freed slaves adjust to their new economic reality by helping them negotiate work contracts. But, at least in Tennessee, the labor contracts it helped facilitate in the early years hindered economic development for the blacks as it helped keep land in control of whites. The Bureau operated in Tennessee until 1870, but its effectiveness diminished with time. In retrospect, African American Tennesseans had reached, for the time being, the apogee of their political power when they helped reelect Governor Brownlow in 1867.[14]

Notwithstanding his low profile, Harris's influence among the ex-secessionists remained strong. In August 1870, the friendly *Memphis Appeal* commented with ap-

13. Bergeron, Ash, and Keith, *Tennesseans and Their History*, 178–79; Joseph H. Cartwright, *The Triumph of Jim Crow: Tennessee Race Relations in the 1880's* (Knoxville: University of Tennessee Press, 1976), 14–16.

14. Lamon, *Blacks in Tennessee*, 37–46; Paul David Phillips, "Education of Blacks in Tennessee During Reconstruction, 1865–1870," *Tennessee Historical Quarterly* 46 (Summer 1987): 98–109; Alrutheus A. Taylor, *The Negro in Tennessee, 1865–1880* (Washington, D.C.: Associated Publishers, 1941), 170–76; Cartwright, *The Triumph of Jim Crow*, 16.

proval on an article lauding Harris in a Clarksville newspaper, noting the unsuccessful attempts of "base deserters of principles and the unholy coalitionists with the hereditary enemies of Democracy" to smear Harris's name. The paper gushed that these "base traitors . . . can no more damage the reputation of Governor Harris than the ragged and wandering Arabs can damage the pyramids."[15]

The ascendancy of the former Whigs was marked by the election of Brown in 1870, although under the new constitution, he had to wait until the expiration of Senter's term before he could take office in 1871. Brown had the strength to resist an effort by ex-Confederate Frank Cheatham to run as an alternative Conservative in 1872. The creation of another statewide office in the form of a special congressional seat brought about by the juxtaposition of the census of 1870 and the need to fill the seat before new districts could be drawn created another opportunity for "Marse Frank," though. Cheatham's primary competition for the seat was Andrew Johnson. Johnson, eventual Republican candidate Horace Maynard, and others expected that the former president would compete for the nomination, not with the ex-general, but with Harris.[16]

A contest for the seat was by then at least a legal possibility for Harris. In March 1872, a small piece appeared in the *New York Times* accusing Tennessee Congressman Robert Porter Caldwell of sneaking ex-Confederate amnesties into a proposed bill, including that of "Isham G. Harris, Ex-Governor and Indian Trust Fund Robber." Actually, the bill was filed on March 18, 1872, by Harris's friend, W. C. Whitthorne. Whitthorne was a congressman in part because his own political disability was removed by congressional action in 1870. Whitthorne's bill included a number of minor Tennessee former Confederates, former Congressman and Harris's self-proclaimed enemy John H. Savage, and Harris. No action appears to have been taken on the bill, perhaps because a general amnesty bill was passed on May 22, 1872, which removed the disability imposed by the Fourteenth Amendment on a large class of former Confederates, including Harris.[17]

With his political rights restored, Harris clearly considered a run for the con-

15. "The Clarksville Chronicle," *Memphis Daily Appeal,* August 9, 1870.

16. Hart, *Redeemers, Bourbons and Populists,* 14–16; Corlew, *Tennessee: A Short History,* 352; Saunders to A. Johnson, June 16, 1872, Netherland to A. Johnson, June 20, 1872, 16 *PAJ* 310–13; "Tennessee Politics," *Memphis Daily Avalanche,* August 26, 1872.

17. "The Smuggled Amnesties," *New York Times,* March 25, 1872; Act of July 15, 1870, ch. 316, 16 Stat. 659; H. R. 2084, 42nd Cong. (1872); Act of May 22, 1872, ch. 193, 17 Stat. 142; "Forty-Second Congress," *New York Herald,* May 23, 1872.

gressional seat, although he remained a controversial figure in the muddled politics of the time. A friend of Johnson's felt that if the race were against Harris, Johnson would easily win. Johnson mockingly told a correspondent that nobody "would make a better subject for dissection before the public than Green Harris." But not all of Harris's detractors displayed such contempt for the former governor. The pro-Johnson *Memphis Avalanche*, criticizing the nomination of former Confederate Senator Landon C. Haynes as the Democratic candidate for the 9th District, said, "if the candidate for Congress must belong to the old class of politicians, then the [choice should have been] one of pluck, brains and vitality, like ex-Governor Isham G. Harris." Nonetheless, Cheatham, who was portrayed as an "intelligent farmer," was "strong" among the delegates to the convention, and seems to have been universally acknowledged as the presumptive nominee. Harris wisely determined to throw his support behind his former comrade, in hopes of heading off his bitterest enemy.[18]

Johnson and his friends had a good idea that Cheatham would be the candidate before the Democratic convention in August, but saw the handwriting on the wall when Harris and Bate were picked to head key committees. As Johnson had already determined to make an independent run, the convention was effectively one of Redeemer Democrats of the former Confederate persuasion, and Cheatham indeed became the nominee. Although Cheatham tried to dissuade Johnson from running, Johnson seems to have had some expectation that the Republicans would not offer a candidate, and indeed expected to win as an independent candidate if they did not. Parson Brownlow's son, John Brownlow, stated that leading Republicans wanted to stay out of the contest, as they did not "want to spoil a pretty fight." Harris feared that a Johnson independent candidacy would "tear up the party so that it would not become healed during this generation."[19]

While the prospect of a Democratic bloodletting must have been attractive for the Republicans, Johnson's split of the Democratic Party made it possible for the Republicans to win a statewide election for the first time since Parson Brown-

18. Hart, *Redeemers, Bourbons and Populists*, 15–16; Netherland to A. Johnson, June 20, 1872, 16 *PAJ* 310; "Interview with Cincinnati Commercial Correspondent," August 20, 1872, 16 *PAJ* 341–42; "The Democratic Congressional Convention," *Memphis Daily Avalanche*, August 9, 1872; Losson, *Tennessee's Forgotten Warriors*, 259.

19. Hart, *Redeemers, Bourbons and Populists*, 15–16; Losson, *Tennessee's Forgotten Warriors*, 258–59; "Interview with Cincinnati Commercial Correspondent," August 20, 1872, 16 *PAJ* 341–42; "Tennessee Politics," *Memphis Daily Avalanche*, August 26, 1872.

low's departure. They therefore nominated old East Tennessee Unionist Horace T. Maynard, who joined Johnson and Cheatham in a series of three-way debates. In a debate at Bristol that September, Cheatham emphasized that he had "no axe to grind, no friends to reward, and no enemies to punish." "Marse Frank" reminded the crowd that it was he, rather than Johnson, who was the "true representative of the democracy of Tennessee." Johnson, for his part, deemed the Democratic convention "packed" and therefore invalid. His harshest words were not for the ex-general, however, but for the man the former president considered the gray eminence behind Cheatham, Isham G. Harris. Harris was stated to be "[a] man who prostituted all that is noble and honorable in human nature, and whose name stinks in the nostrils of honest men, carried off the school fund and the people's money—the money of widows and children. He quitted the city of Nashville like a thief in the night, and he is now one of the supporters of my competitor, Cheatham." In the view of one of Johnson's modern biographers, the fact that Harris was openly against him made Johnson fight all the harder.[20]

Harris worked hard to assist Cheatham, doubtless fueled by his affinity for the general, a prewar Democrat and veteran of the Army of Tennessee, his desire for party discipline in supporting the pick of the nominating convention, and his hatred of Johnson. At a rally for Cheatham that same month, Harris mocked what he deemed to be Johnson's hypocrisy, in that Johnson accused Cheatham of being a military man, while Johnson had held rank as a brigadier general when military governor of Tennessee. He noted that Johnson complained of the convention, yet, in most of the former president's runs for public office, he had been the nominee of a convention. Harris accused Johnson of fostering the harshness of Reconstruction, of treating the states as conquered provinces, and of trampling on the Constitution. Harris's speech was characterized by his editor friend M. C. Galloway's *Memphis Appeal* as "sharp, bright, and as finely tempered as a Damascus sword." The pro-Johnson *Avalanche*, however, deemed it "a bitter assault on Andy Johnson," a sentiment echoed by a Johnson supporter, who transmitted a copy of the account of the *Appeal* to Johnson, noting Harris's "sentiments of hate." Deemed the true opponent in the election by Johnson supporters, Harris stumped the state on Cheatham's behalf.[21]

20. Losson, *Tennessee's Forgotten Warriors*, 259–60; "A Six Hours Political Debate," *New York Herald*, September 25, 1872; Hans L. Trefousse, *Andrew Johnson: A Biography* (New York: W. W. Norton, 1989), 362.

21. "Cheatham," *Memphis Daily Appeal*, September 22, 1872; Logwood to A. Johnson, April 30,

Another irritant Harris faced during this campaign was Arthur St. Clair Colyar, a prewar Whig and former Confederate congressman. In the postwar period, Colyar became an industrial leader and an advocate of both immigration of labor into Tennessee and Northern investment in the state. Colyar was a Redeemer, but he strayed away from the mainstream Democrats on a number of occasions, fearing that the ex-Confederates, who came to be known as Bourbons, would scare away the people and interests he was hoping to attract. In 1872, Colyar started as an independent candidate for governor, but dropped out of the race by early October. Refusing at first to take a stand on the congressional race, Colyar spent much of his time as a candidate attacking Harris and the Confederacy. After he dropped out, he came out openly for Johnson and appeared at Democratic meetings asking for time to speak on behalf of the ex-president. On one occasion in Murfreesboro, he was allowed to speak before Harris, and droned on for two hours in praise of Johnson before Harris had his say. The rest of Colyar's time was spent working on Johnson's behalf and exchanging barbs with Harris in the newspapers.[22]

In the end, Johnson's run as an independent split the Democratic vote, and Maynard beat Cheatham for the seat by almost 17,000 votes. Almost perversely, Johnson's side deemed the result a victory. Colyar wrote Johnson soon after the first of 1873 that all looked well for Johnson's struggle against Harris and the Redeemers. "The fruits of your canvass have already made all the leaders from Harris down quite sick." Colyar predicted if Johnson were to spend some time in Nashville that winter, "there will not be enough of the Harris party left to make a decent show in the next race." For his part, Harris must have at least had the grim satisfaction that even if Cheatham did not win the seat, neither did Johnson. His performance in the Cheatham campaign was another step in the restoration of his political influence, and showed he had lost none of his leadership skills. A short piece in the *Avalanche* two days after the grand Cheatham rally in Memphis

---

1874, 16 *PAJ* 538–39; "Cheatham in Memphis," *Memphis Daily Avalanche,* September 22, 1872; "The Cheatham Demonstration Last Night," *Memphis Appeal,* September 22, 1872; William R. Sevier to A. Johnson, September 24, 1872, 16 *PAJ* 376–77; Orville A. Nixon to A. Johnson, March 31, 1874, 16 *PAJ* 521–22.

22. McBride and Robison, *Biographical Directory of the Tennessee General Assembly,* 2:181–83; Clyde L. Ball, "The Public Career of Colonel A. S. Colyar, 1870–1877," *Tennessee Historical Quarterly* 12 (October 1953): 213, 217–22, 224–27; Hart, *Redeemers, Bourbons and Populists,* 2, 10–12, 15–16.

acknowledged that Harris was "now fairly entitled to the leadership of the Shelby county Democracy."[23]

One theme of Johnson's anti-Harris campaign was his charge that Harris had absconded with the state's School Fund when he left Nashville in 1862, which Harris characterized as a "willful, deliberate and malignant lie." The School Fund issue was before the public eye during this interval as a result of ongoing litigation, as well as the fund's mishandling by a Brownlow administration official, and Johnson and other of Harris's political enemies employed the issue on occasion in an effort to discredit the former governor. The matter was complex, caught up in the difficult constitutional issues created by secession. While Harris emerged from the murk as having acted correctly, the confusing nature of the issue made it fertile ground for continued agitation.[24]

The School Fund was designated by the constitution of 1834 as a perpetual fund, the interest of which was to be expended for the benefit of the common schools. The legislature directed that the fund be deposited in the Bank of Tennessee, which, over the space of twenty years before the war, paid over $2 million in interest for the benefit of the schools. When the war came, and the state issued its various series of war bonds, the Bank of Tennessee voluntarily, and the other two large banks of the state involuntarily, bought the bonds. Much of the cash went out to fund the war effort, in return for what were the eventually worthless state bonds. When Nashville fell, the bank was removed to Memphis, then Chattanooga, and then into Georgia as the fortunes of the Confederacy waned. Legally, the assets of the School Fund were like any other account of the bank, in other words, indistinguishable from the mass of the institution's assets.[25]

Claims were made that Harris had personal charge of the bank's assets during its displacement, a claim that Harris denied. The bank was in the custody

23. Losson, *Tennessee's Forgotten Warriors*, 261; Arthur S. Colyar to A. Johnson, January 21, 1873, 16 *PAJ* 418; "Ex-Gov. Harris," *Memphis Avalanche*, September 23, 1872.

24. "A Six Hours Political Debate"; "Interview with Cincinnati Commercial Correspondent"; "Personal Intelligence," *New York Herald*, October 5, 1872; "The Sacred School Fund," *Memphis Daily Appeal*, November 24, 1868. The difficult legalities of the situation are illustrated to an extent by *State of Tennessee v. President and Directors of Bank of Tennessee*, 64 Tenn. 1 (1875), a lengthy opinion that sought to sort out the enforceability of notes issued by the bank after the May 6, 1861 act by the General Assembly.

25. *State of Tennessee v. President and Directors of Bank of Tennessee*, 64 Tenn. at 7–9, 23; White, *Development of the Tennessee State Educational Organization*, 188.

of its lawful officers, Harris stated, and he was with the Army of Tennessee. Being at headquarters, the governor could tell these officers the safest place for the bank's assets, and could secure military orders and guards for the transportation of the assets and records. As previously discussed, Harris even resisted the Confederate government's efforts to appropriate the specie. Charges were also made at one time or another that Harris illegally drew his salary (and thereby depleted the School Fund) for a year and some months after the expiration of his term, a charge Harris refuted by reference to the provision in the 1834 constitution that provided he would serve until a successor was qualified. As irritating as these charges of dishonesty were at times, there is no evidence that they ever caused Harris much political damage.[26]

While Martha Harris seems to have stayed with Green in Memphis on occasion later in life, she preferred to remain in her hometown, Paris, during this interval, which is not surprising since her husband lived in a hotel. Harris would make frequent visits to Paris, though, to visit his family and keep up his connections there. Years later, a man who was a young store clerk in Paris in 1872 would recall that Harris would "often spend Sunday afternoons with friends, smoking good cigars and relating incidents of the war and some of his experiences while in Mexico, Cuba and England." The former clerk also recalled that Harris "was a good talker, though he could not have been considered a good conversationalist, as he usually selected the topic and did most of the talking."[27]

In 1872, Johnson frustrated Harris's efforts to unite the Democratic Party under the banner of the Redeemers. In 1873, a new issue arose that would prove to dominate debate for much of the next decade, and, in the short term, would provide Johnson fodder to continue the struggle. In January 1873, Governor John C. Brown influenced the passage of a Funding Act to fund the state's debt with 6 percent bonds. While the state first issued bonds in 1832, the substantial debt began in 1852, as Tennessee joined other states in providing public support for transpor-

26. IGH to Duncan Brown Cooper, December 15, 1888, Cooper Papers; "Harris," *Chattanooga Times,* October 17, 1876. The Bank of Tennessee was liquidated in 1866. Except for the specie that was preserved, the School Fund, in the roundabout fashion discussed above, went to support the unsuccessful war effort. White, *Development of the Tennessee State Educational Organization,* 188–89. Harris's enemies would dredge up the issue on occasion, to little avail, even close to the end of his life. See "According to Col. John H. Savage," *Chattanooga Daily Times,* July 3, 1894.

27. McLeary, "The Life of Isham G. Harris," 8–9; "Gives Sidelights on Isham G. Harris' Life," *Memphis Commercial Appeal,* February 5, 1922.

tation projects. Other projects included money for completing the state Capitol, for purchasing Andrew Jackson's home, the Hermitage, and for erecting buildings on the state fairgrounds. By 1860, the debt was at $20,898,606, almost 70 percent of which was borrowed for railroad construction since 1852.[28]

The war intervened. Its adverse economic consequences almost halved the value of taxable property in Tennessee, value that was not fully restored until 1892. Instead of taking steps to ameliorate the situation, Brownlow and the Radical legislature ran up another $14 million in railroad debt. The state suffered not only from a decline in values, but also delinquent taxes and inefficiencies in the system, the default on the railroad bonds caused by the war, the expense of Brownlow's Tennessee State Guard, and legislative sessions of record length. Additionally, there were substantial issues of bribery and fraud in those tumultuous years. Fed up, the delegates to the constitutional convention in 1870 inserted a clause that prevented the credit of the state from being used for private enterprise.[29]

It was an issue that demanded attention. Most of the debt was held by investors outside the state, many from New York. When Brown's funding legislation was passed, much of the resistance to the measure was from largely agrarian West Tennessee, where opponents argued that full funding of the debt would drag taxpayers down. Many also resented the legal recognition of the debt that it was felt the Radicals had fraudulently and illegally incurred. Those in favor of Brown's legislation saw it as "vital to the encouragement of economic growth and development in Tennessee." The proposal that passed was based on an optimistic view of the state's economic future, a view that dissipated late that year with the effects of a severe national economic downturn started by the Panic of 1873.[30]

Already fractured by Johnson's rogue candidacy, the Democrats also split on this issue. The two factions eventually became known as the "low-taxers" (who opposed full funding of the debt) and "state credit men," most of whom were also Redeemers, who supported Brown's position toward funding the debt. Johnson seized upon the dissatisfaction with the Funding Act as the issue to carry him through the 1874 political campaign, in which legislators would be elected who in

28. Hart, *Redeemers, Bourbons and Populists*, 19; Robert B. Jones, *Tennessee at the Crossroads: The State Debt Controversy 1870–1883* (Knoxville: University of Tennessee Press, 1977), 4–6, 23; Corlew, *Tennessee: A Short History*, 356.

29. Jones, *Tennessee at the Crossroads*, 6, 9–12, 15–16.

30. Ibid., 13, 26–28, 32–33; Corlew, *Tennessee: A Short History*, 356–57.

turn would select a U.S. senator in the place of Parson Brownlow. John C. Brown wanted the seat, too, and remained in favor of the financial settlement embodied by the Funding Act. While Johnson argued the Jeffersonian principle that debt should not be passed down from one generation to another, Brown ridiculed his opponent, noting that at one time Johnson had been in favor of the measure, and that as governor and president, condoned the state's incurring the debt.[31]

While most of the state credit men were former Whigs, they could count Harris and former Confederate generals William B. Bate and William A. Quarles among their ranks. Unlike other issues the Redeemers contested with Johnson, Harris stayed somewhat in the background on the funding controversy. The reason for this is unknown, although there are a number of possibilities. First, Harris was governor when a portion of the debt was incurred. Already, Johnson was being skewered with the inherent contradiction of once being for the debt and now being against it. Second, Harris deemed party unity to be of primary concern, and the majority of the Redeemer Democrats were in the state credit wing. On the other hand, his enthusiasm for the state credit position must have been tempered by the fierce opposition to it in his West Tennessee power base and the inconvenient facts that the legitimate aspect of the debt was basically incurred for internal improvements, and the arguably illegitimate aspect incurred by the Radicals. Finally, there is the strong possibility that Harris did not at that time deem it to be a significant issue, as his later stance on the issue indicates.[32]

Even if Harris would not take a strong position on the debt controversy, he continued to be concerned with party unity and to oppose Andrew Johnson. One of Johnson's supporters in Memphis got wind of a caucus between Harris, Quarles, Bate, Brown, Galloway, and others relative to the 1874 political season. According to Johnson's friend, Harris opined that if a former Confederate soldier were put forward as a candidate for governor, he would be beaten. It was decided that a Union man should be the party's candidate and an ex-Confederate should succeed Brownlow. Johnson and his adherents naturally preferred the reverse, as the ex-president had his sights set on returning to Washington. Johnson was an open candidate for the seat, and made a speaking tour of the state in the fall of 1874. While the Bourbons did all they could to defeat Johnson, when the new General Assembly took up the issue of the Senate seat in early 1875, Johnson was elected

31. Jones, *Tennessee at the Crossroads*, 35–40, 52; Hart, *Redeemers, Bourbons and Populists*, 19–21.

32. Jones, *Tennessee at the Crossroads*, 54; "Yesterday's Speaking."

on the fifty-fifth vote, defeating Brown and Bate, among others. Johnson must have been aided by the sentiment, no doubt founded in the events of 1872, that it was better to "get him out of the way," as some feared "he will break up the party if he is defeated." In the gubernatorial election, James D. Porter of Henry County, a prewar Whig and Confederate officer, was elected, completing the reverse of Harris's plan.[33]

Back in Memphis, there were some distractions in the late summer and early fall of 1874. Agitation over civil rights legislation threatened a riot in nearby Somerville. In Gibson County, between Memphis and Paris in West Tennessee, night-riders clashed with African Americans, resulting in the predictable arrest of sixteen blacks. A group of disguised white vigilantes succeeded in breaking the prisoners out of the jail and lynched them, resulting in the deaths of five of the prisoners and the wounding of others. While Klan violence had abated, blacks still faced terrorism intended to suppress their voting rights. A mass meeting was held in Memphis to denounce the killings. The crowd called for speeches by Harris, Jefferson Davis, and Forrest, an assembly of ex-Confederates that was viewed with disdain by one of Johnson's friends. Harris stated that the assembled citizens "owed it to themselves to vindicate the law and rebuke crime and lawlessness; to vindicate the rights of citizens regardless of color, nation or condition." Soon after coming off well in the midst of such public unrest, Harris suffered a private reverse, as his partnership with Pillow came to an end in October 1874. Matters with Pillow eventually soured, doubtless in part because Pillow later collected a fee without Harris's knowledge in the course of winding up the partnership. Not only did Harris not get his share of the fee, but the whole affair ended up costing Harris another $500 besides.[34]

Still one of the finest lawyers in Tennessee, upon dissolving his partnership with Pillow, Harris became the senior partner of what eventually became Harris, McKisick & Turley, an association he continued in one form or fashion to the

33. Thomas H. Logwood to A. Johnson, April 30, 1874, 16 *PAJ* 538–40; Hart, *Redeemers, Bourbons and Populists*, 19–23; White, *Messages of the Governors of Tennessee*, 6:408–11; "Telegraphic," *Chattanooga Daily Times*, January 13, 1875.

34. Keating, *History of City of Memphis*, 1:624; Andrew J. Kellar to A. Johnson, September 4, 1874, 16 *PAJ* 580; "The Tennessee Massacre," *Atlanta Constitution*, September 4, 1874; U.S. Senate, *The Executive Documents Printed by Order of the Senate of the United States for the Second Session of the Forty-Third Congress, 1874–75 and the Special Session of the Senate in March, 1875* (Washington, D.C.: Government Printing Office, 1875), Ex. Doc. No. 12; *Williams v. Whitmore*, 77 Tenn. 262 (1882); Hughes and Stonesifer, *The Life and Wars of Gideon J. Pillow*, 319.

end of his life. Harris continued to handle a number of significant and complex cases. His practice earned him about $20,000 a year, a figure, for the day, which was "exceedingly lucrative." Among the cases he litigated in this latter portion of his career included a criminal case in which the defendant was charged with embezzlement and conspiracy, a tax matter between the city of Memphis and Union Planters Bank, a case involving the bonded indebtedness of the cash-strapped city of Memphis, and a case relating to licensing a patent. The latter two cases eventually made their way to the U.S. Supreme Court.[35]

Harris also had a role in a moving the city of Memphis toward a significant and necessary change in its form of government in this period. The city's prewar debt was funded in a disadvantageous manner by the Reconstruction government. Efforts to raise taxes drove away businesses, lessening tax collections and thereby contributing to a downward spiral. The local Chamber of Commerce, the Memphis Cotton Exchange, and a "People's Protective Union," the latter of which was formed in reaction to the crisis, commissioned a group of lawyers, Harris among them, to draw up a resolution and recommendations for dealing with the problem. The problem was an electorate with no stake in the economic welfare of the city, and, in consequence, the election of a class of municipal officers who were interested only in catering to that electorate. The proposed solution was to dissolve the city government and have it run by appointees from the state government. While too drastic for 1874, by 1879 Memphis had surrendered its charter and was officially not a city, but a state "taxing district" along the lines suggested by Harris and the others.[36]

Triumphant Andy Johnson returned to Washington in March 1875. Not only did Johnson's election to the Senate vindicate his fight against the Bourbons at home, but it also challenged the Radicals in Congress who had almost removed him from the presidency in 1868. Johnson even had the additional satisfaction of replacing Parson Brownlow. His victory was short-lived, as on July 31, while on a visit to his daughter's home in upper East Tennessee, Johnson died from the effects of a stroke.[37] The ex-president's death not only removed Harris's bitterest and

35. "End of An Eventful Life"; "Spirit of a Great Man"; *Loudon v. Taxing District,* 104 U.S. 771 (1881); *Oliver v. Rumford Chemical Works,* 109 U.S. 75 (1883).

36. Keating, *History of Memphis,* 1:628–29; Capers, *The Biography of a River Town, Memphis,* 200–203.

37. Coulter, *William G. Brownlow,* 395; "Andrew Johnson," *Chattanooga Daily Times,* August 1, 1875. The *New York Times* published a short piece in 1884 to the effect that Johnson suffered a fatal stroke when writing a letter to dispute something Vice President Henry Wilson had told Harris about

greatest rival within the Democratic Party, but it also opened up Johnson's seat in the Senate. Various newspapers across the state floated candidates, ranging from the man Johnson defeated for the seat, General William B. Bate, to Harris's un-inaugurated successor as governor, Judge Robert L. Caruthers, to Judge David M. Key of Chattanooga. One paper even nominated Jefferson Davis, who was still living in Memphis. The *Appeal* loyally floated Harris's name at the head of five possible candidates, stating that "friends and foes alike have had the most implicit confidence in his honor and integrity."[38]

In the end, Governor Porter appointed Judge Key. Born in Andrew Johnson's hometown of Greeneville, Key had solid Democratic credentials and served the Confederacy as lieutenant colonel of the 43rd Tennessee Infantry. Notwithstanding these credentials, Key portrayed himself as a moderate Redeemer, and sought to keep distance between himself and the Bourbons. A friend of Johnson's, Key seemed to some to be the dead senator's successor as a counterweight to Harris and the other Bourbons. But unlike Johnson, Key was a state credit man, an issue that still smoldered as the state had defaulted on its interest payments that July. The reaction to Key's appointment from the state's newspapers ranged from the *Jackson Whig and Tribune*'s disappointment a West Tennessean was not appointed to the gloating of Key's hometown *Chattanooga Daily Times*, which mocked the *Appeal*'s disappointment that Harris was not appointed. Some felt that Porter was attempting to cater to the former Union men that had been Johnson's core group of supporters, others that since the next appointment should logically go to a West Tennessean, that Porter, himself from Henry County, was positioning himself for that next seat. The *Memphis Ledger* said it best, however, when it observed: "all candidates will have an equal chance next time, and they have seventeen months to lay pipes and court the favor of the dear people."[39]

Abraham Lincoln's postwar policy, but given the account of Johnson's death and the purported date of the letter, it seems unlikely that writing of an incident involving Green Harris brought about Andy Johnson's fatal stroke. See "Andrew Johnson's Last Written Word," *New York Times*, February 24, 1884.

38. "Who Shall Be the Next Senator?" *Chattanooga Daily Times*, August 7, 1875 (publishing the views of a number of other Tennessee newspapers).

39. David M. Abshire, *The South Rejects a Prophet: The Life of Senator D. M. Key, 1824–1900* (New York: Frederick A. Praeger, 1967), 18, 29–34, 66–67, 74, 130; Jones, *Tennessee at the Crossroads*, 49–50; "The New Senator," *Chattanooga Daily Times*, August 24, 1875 (publishing the views of the other newspapers); "Andrew Johnson's Successor," *Chattanooga Daily Times*, August 25, 1875; "The Memphis Appeal says," *Chattanooga Daily Times*, August 21, 1875.

The *Appeal's* floating Harris's name in the fall of 1875 was a strong indication that the former governor had decided at least at that time to make a run for one of Tennessee's seats in the U.S. Senate, both of which would be selected by the General Assembly in early 1877. Harris confirmed such was the case in February 1876. In a letter on a legal matter to North Carolina lawyer and politician Kenneth Rayner, Harris disclosed his plan to canvass the state in the coming summer, and indicated he would be a candidate "before the next Legislature." Harris counted on the support of the *Appeal* and the *Memphis Ledger,* but expressed the view that the *Avalanche* would probably "bitterly" oppose him.[40]

Key's assumption of Johnson's mantle as a conservative counterweight to the Bourbons necessarily brought him into conflict with Harris. Key's biographer portrays Key as an idealistic conservative who sought to bridge the conflict that remained between the two sections of the country, and Harris as the virtually dictatorial leader of a monolithic political machine that opposed Key's noble efforts at reconciliation.[41] Modern scholarship has done much to refute this view of Harris. While Harris's influence at this time was significant, and his prestige, especially in the Bourbon faction, was great, he was not so much a political "boss" as what he had always been, "a remarkably skillful politician."[42] This was especially true in 1876, when Harris, with no patronage to dispense, had little but his influence, prestige, political skill, and force of will to exercise in the political contest of that year.

However well-intentioned he may have been, Key was not the politician Harris was, nor what his friend Andy Johnson had been. Late in 1875, Senator Oliver P. Morton, the "war governor" of Indiana, sought an investigation of an election that year in Mississippi, as an apparent Republican victory became a win for the Democrats. Naturally, the senators picked sides based on party lines. For over three months, debate on the issue raged in the Senate, until the time, late in March 1876, Senator Key rose to give his views on the subject, and announced that he would vote to support Morton's proposal, although he did not believe the allegations. As events transpired, Key was the only Democrat to support Morton, and his speech touched off a renewed war among the newspapers loyal to either faction of the party. The pro-Johnson Democratic papers proclaimed Key a patriotic senator

40. IGH to Kenneth Rayner, February 4, 1876, Kenneth Rayner Papers, Southern Historical Collection, UNC.

41. Abshire, *The South Rejects a Prophet,* 74–75, 126–32.

42. Hart, *Redeemers, Bourbons and Populists,* 55.

with the interests of the entire country at heart, "unbiased by party checks, un-trammeled by provincial interests." The Bourbon-leaning *Memphis Appeal* and *Nashville American*, among others, blasted Key's defection from the position of the Democratic Party and his willingness to perpetuate the sectional hate Morton was deemed to be preaching. The *Chattanooga Daily Times* accused the Bourbon papers of speaking for the "selfish ambition of cliques and rings" and wanting Key "killed off." Without naming names, the *Times* spoke in terms of the two Bourbon papers seeking to "hoist this or that demagogue to place," and of attacking "any man or party which fails to contribute to the glory and greatness of the Mogul." It is likely the newspaper had Green Harris in mind. Key's mistake, at least for a man with political ambitions in Tennessee, was certain. A Northern Republican paper essentially agreed with the Bourbon view of Key's stance, when it predicted that Key "has made a political mistake that will cost him his official head."[43]

In contrast to Key, Green Harris moved forward in a sure fashion, appearing as a speaker at a Democratic meeting on July 1, 1876, called to "ratify" the national party's nomination of Samuel J. Tilden for president and Thomas A. Hendricks for vice president of the United States. Addressing the crowd, Harris described the Democratic ticket as part of a national effort to reform the Federal government. As would be his practice for years to come, Harris attacked the tariff policies of the Republicans as having the purpose of "enriching a few pampered and favored manufacturers." He condemned the opposition's appeal to sectional feelings (waving the "bloody shirt"), noting that "we of the South have accepted the results in good faith, recognize the issues settled by the war as finalities, and look only to the present and the future to secure to us a political existence in the Union . . . animated by sentiments of fraternity, devotion to the old flag, and an ardent desire for the peace, prosperity and happiness of the whole country."[44]

On schedule, the *Appeal* and other newspapers began to endorse Harris for U.S. senator.[45] Harris's satisfaction with the favorable course of events doubt-

43. Abshire, *The South Rejects a Prophet*, 82–87; "Senator Key's Speech," *Memphis Avalanche*, April 6, 1876; "The Press on Senator Key," *Chattanooga Daily Times*, April 6, 1876; "Senator Key and the Bloody Shirt," *Chattanooga Daily Times*, April 21, 1876; "The Late Style of Assault on Senator Key," *Chattanooga Daily Times*, April 28, 1876; "Our Sweet Central Organ," *Chattanooga Daily Times*, May 27, 1876; "Senator Key," *Decatur* (Ill.) *Republican*, May 4, 1876; see also "Senator Key's Blunder," *Atlanta Constitution*, April 8, 1876.

44. "Our Ticket Ratified," *Memphis Daily Appeal*, July 2, 1876.

45. "The Art. from the Morristown Gazette" and "Isham G. Harris," *Memphis Daily Appeal*, July 22, 1876; "The Memphis Appeal has taken decided ground," *Knoxville Weekly Age*, July 27, 1876.

less was shattered on July 22, when his oldest son, Eugene, died at his parents' house in Memphis. After a Methodist funeral, Eugene was laid to rest next to his younger brother, George, at Elmwood Cemetery in Memphis.[46] Overcoming his grief, the ex-governor went to the state Democratic convention in August with the expectation that he would be named one of the two electors at large for the Tilden campaign, which in turn placed him before the people voting for the legislative candidates who would be making the senatorial selection. But, as the delegates gathered for the convention, it was made known that delegates from the Knoxville area feared that a prominent role for the Confederate war governor of the state would injure the party's cause in East Tennessee and in the North as well. The *Appeal*'s correspondent suspected that the opposition came from friends of Senator Key's, who were "jealous" of "Harris' future candidacy for the United States senate." The *Appeal* loyally condemned this "base attempt" to defeat "the ablest statesman in Tennessee."[47]

When the convention opened on August 9, Bate was the first nominee for elector at large, with Harris and two Knoxville delegates nominated after a short speech by Mrs. Napoleon Cromwell, who "spoke for female suffrage and the rights of her sex." It soon became apparent that there was substantial opposition to the former governor from East Tennessee delegates, and Bate was elected. Then, a dramatic scene occurred, as Harris "was enthusiastically called for and addressed the convention." Harris said he agreed with the action of the convention, and understood the objections against him. He loyally remarked that "he was always, and always will be, a Democrat; would do all he could for the party, irrespective of their action." The effect on the convention was all Harris could want, as those in attendance "became all the more enthusiastic, members saying 'no,' 'no,' to Governor Harris' utterance, that the majority opposed his nomination and he would decline." One of the Knoxville candidates was again nominated, along with Chattanoogan E. A. James. There were calls for Harris, who asked not to be considered. He was drowned out with "lusty" cheering, and Harris was elected by a large majority, although most of the East Tennessee counties voted for James.[48]

As the East Tennessee Democrats feared, though, the Republicans of that section seized upon Harris's reappearance in an official role for the Democracy to

46. "Died," *Memphis Avalanche,* July 23, 1876; Eugene T. Harris tombstone at Elmwood Cemetery, Memphis, viewed by author on June 15, 2006.

47. "Platform of Our Delegates," *Memphis Daily Appeal,* August 5, 1876; "Nashville" and "Our special and the letter of our correspondent," *Memphis Daily Appeal,* August 8, 1876.

48. "Nashville," *Memphis Daily Appeal,* August 10, 1876.

wave "the ensanguined undergarment" with renewed vigor. At a meeting at Knox-ville, Republican speakers spoke of a Democratic plot to "resurrect" the Confed-eracy and re-enslave the freedmen, and of Harris's taking the state out of the Union "at the point of the bayonet" and of stealing $11 million of state funds. The *Appeal* countered with a charge of "slander," "appealing to sectional preju-dices," and by trying to obscure the truth "by din of uproar and confusion." No doubt sensing that his political future required a concession to the conservative Union Democrats in East Tennessee, Harris wrote a long, conciliatory letter to the party's executive committee on August 18, declining to continue as elector. The letter stated that Harris never had a political aspiration that he "did not hold subordinate to the success of the principles which were, in my opinion, impor-tant to the public welfare." Rather than being a "conspicuous leader," he would take his place in the ranks as a private in the coming campaign, promised to vin-dicate the constitutional rights of all, regardless of "race, nationality or color," and condemned the attempt to stir up sectional prejudices. Continuing his mes-sage of sectional reconciliation, Harris wrote that from the time of the Confed-erate surrender, "every intelligent citizen of those States has regarded the issues of the war as settled forever, and has endeavored to make himself a law-abiding and good citizen, deeply interested in the peace, prosperity and happiness of not only his state, but of all the States of the Union." Fortunately, no one seems to have pointed out the contradiction between the last statement and Harris's own bitter-end exile.[49]

The state executive committee met a few days later and replaced Harris with James. Harris's friend, Luke E. Wright, on behalf of the Shelby County delegation, noted with regret that Harris's nomination "was not satisfactory to what may be termed the Union element of our party," which was due to a "misapprehension of Gov. Harris and his principles." Harris, therefore, withdrew in order "to prevent even the possibility of dissention" in party ranks, and in the "same spirit," James, "an original Union man," was placed in nomination by Wright and was selected as the second elector at large. Through a mutual friend, James made it known that he regretted Harris's withdrawal very much, and had intended to give the ex-governor his "warmest support."[50]

Kellar's unfriendly *Avalanche* contested the *Appeal*'s claim that Harris removed

49. "A Campaign of Slander," *Memphis Daily Appeal*, August 17, 1876; "Governor Harris," *Memphis Daily Appeal*, August 19, 1876.

50. "The Democracy," *Chattanooga Daily Times*, August 26, 1876; "Hon. E. A. James," *Memphis Daily Appeal*, September 1, 1876.

himself because of the Republican opposition, noting that he was "not disposed to yield to his political enemies." Instead, Harris's "uncompromising personal and political opposition to Andrew Johnson is the cause of his unpopularity with East Tennessee Democrats." In the same vein, Parson Brownlow's *Knoxville Weekly Whig and Chronicle* gleefully mocked that Harris's name was "so obnoxious that East Tennessee Democrats were frightened out of their boots, and they demanded that he should step down and out."[51]

Conversely, the loyal *Appeal* and the *Nashville Daily American* deemed Harris's withdrawal as the sublimest expression of party loyalty and patriotism. Whether by wishful thinking or with unusual political insight, the *Appeal* predicted that Harris became stronger by his timely move, stating the "revolution in his favor will be instantaneous and overwhelming." Indeed, in the eyes of many Unionist Democrats, Harris ceased to be a machine politician and became "a truly great and patriotic citizen." The previously unfriendly editors of the *Chattanooga Daily Times* wrote that Harris was unfairly misunderstood as a "malignant Bourbon," but was in reality an actor of "statesmanship and broad patriotism." The only fault that could now be found with Harris was "unswerving, relentless enforcement of the political principles he adopted and believed." Observing that Harris had "more ability, more nerve, more influence, more courage of all sorts, than are generally portioned out to the sons of men," the paper noted that men with Harris's gifts did not "inspire love." "Their partisan followers fear or admire them at a distance. Their enemies pay tribute to their great qualities by hating them with the very essence of bitterness." The pro-Key (or latently anti-Harris) editors of the *Daily Times*, however, hoped to bury Caesar in the midst of their praise, observing, "But it seems as if he is one who will have to be content with the vindication of impartial history, when the passions of this generation shall have died with it. And this he can afford to do. Especially can Governor Harris *not* afford, in this of all the years since the war, to permit his name or his acts to embarrass the conservative party of the nation to relieve the people of the incubus of Grantism."[52]

Clothed, for the moment, in the raiment of a selfless statesman, Harris began his speaking tour as a "private soldier," starting in Clarksville in late August and swinging through West Tennessee in the first weeks of September. The message

51. "Ex Gov. Harris acted promptly," *Memphis Avalanche,* August 20, 1876; "Isham G. Harris," *Knoxville Weekly Whig and Chronicle,* August 23, 1876.

52. "Governor Harris Declines," *Memphis Daily Appeal,* August 19, 1876; "Gov. Harris Declines," *Nashville Daily American,* August 19, 1876; "The Vacant Electorship," *Chattanooga Daily Times,* August 20, 1876; "Concerning Gov. Harris," *Chattanooga Daily Times,* August 28, 1876.

in Clarksville was of the foibles of the Grant administration, the relative unimportance of the state debt issue, the need for mutual reconciliation of the sections, and the necessity of good will toward the freedmen. In late September, Harris was at a massive Democratic rally at Franklin, although he was too sick to give a speech. Later, he held a "levee" at a private residence, and was welcomed by a large number of citizens. The local newspaper noted: "Evidently there has been a tremendous revolution in this county in his favor." The ex-governor went on a month-long speaking tour in October through the middle of the state, stopping also in Knoxville, Cleveland, and Chattanooga. At Chattanooga on October 16, Harris more directly addressed the issues raised by the Republicans in August. He spoke of the importance of the state and national elections that lay ahead, attacking the Republicans on their expenditures, their anti-silver money policy, and the continued interference of the Federal government in the Southern states, including the Mississippi issue of the previous year. Harris also defended himself on the issue of the School Fund, once more dredged up by the Republicans, and referred to Senator Key as a witness to his efforts to protect the rights of Union men under the Confederate government. As for the charge that he had carried the state out of the Union at bayonet-point, although Harris thought each citizen had voted his own "honest" view, he thought it a "compliment, in that it would be a great power or influence that would enable a single individual to influence so many."[53]

Harris stopped in Cleveland next, and then went on to Knoxville, the very heart of enemy country. In anticipation of Harris's visit, Parson Brownlow's *Knoxville Daily Chronicle* dedicated much of its editorial page to recalling Harris's approval of opening mail in 1861, mocking E. A. James for the tepid reception he received in Knoxville in contrast to what was planned for Harris, and calling Harris "King" once more. Seeking to exploit the discomfort that caused Harris to withdraw as elector, the *Chronicle* wrote: "We regret that every Union Democrat in East Tennessee can not be here to-night and witness the grand ovation to 'King Harris.' The ovation is personal to him and intended to advance his prospects for election to the United States Senate." The *Chronicle* sneered that while the Democratic *Knoxville Weekly Age* wanted Harris to give up the electorship, he now was

53. "Governor Harris" and "The State Canvass," *Memphis Daily Appeal,* August 29, 1876; "The Barbeque at McGavock's House," *Franklin Review and Journal,* September 18, 1876; "State Political News," *Chattanooga Daily Times,* September 30, 1876; "Harris," *Chattanooga Daily Times,* October 17, 1876; "The Commercial Charges Gov. Harris," *Chattanooga Daily Times,* August 28, 1876. By the first of October, the *Times* was under friendly new management for an interval.

their "favorite," and urged Democrats to question their legislative candidates on the issue of their support for Harris for senator.[54]

In Knoxville, Harris made much the same speech as made in Chattanooga earlier that week. To repudiate the charges relating to violating the rights of Union men in the Knoxville area, Harris gave several examples of positive steps he had taken to make sure they were treated fairly, and one of the examples in the audience confirmed what was stated relative to his personal experience to be the case. The Democratic *Knoxville Daily Tribune* deemed the speech "truly a great one," as it was "argumentative, logical, eloquent, and characterized by a most patriotic spirit." That night, a torchlight procession of 1,200 persons, complete with bands, flags, fireworks, and portraits of Tilden and Hendricks, snaked to the Lamar House, where they cheered Harris and other dignitaries on a balcony.[55]

Not for the first time in his public career, Harris's canny political instincts had served him well. Better received in East Tennessee than he could have dared hope, he returned to Middle Tennessee in the weeks before the election, speaking to "a large and enthusiastic crowd at Murfreesboro." Harris's "grand display of oratory" was, to the local newspaper correspondent, a "masterly . . . speech of a statesman." The Murfreesboro paper not only endorsed Harris for senator, but for the "long term," that is, the six-year term of Senator Henry Cooper that expired early the next year, not the unexpired term of Johnson, held for the moment by Key, but which was also at issue. As the Hayes–Tilden election hung in the balance for weeks after the November ballot, support grew for Harris's election to the long term, to the point that by the time the General Assembly convened in early January, Harris's election was a foregone conclusion. He easily captured a majority of both houses of the legislature in the voting on January 9, 1877. In the House, Harris captured 56 of the 75 votes, with 15 Republicans voting for Representative Lucian L. Hawkins of Carroll County, Hawkins himself modestly casting a single vote for another Republican. Bate got two votes, one from a fellow Democrat and one from an Independent, Representative Frank M. Lavender, who served under Bate's command during the war. Governor Porter got a vote from the tirelessly hostile John H. Savage.[56]

54. "It would add variety," "When Eb. James," "Gov. Harris will probably have something to say," and "We regret that every Union Democrat," all in *Knoxville Daily Chronicle*, October 18, 1876.

55. "Yesterday's Speaking," "Ex-Governor Harris at the Opera-House Yesterday," and "Democratic Jollification," *Knoxville Daily Tribune*, October 19, 1876.

56. "Governor Harris in Rutherford," *Memphis Daily Appeal*, October 24, 1876; "Ex-Governor

Senator Key's effort to succeed Andy Johnson collapsed on the seventy-third ballot, after Kellar tried and failed to forge an alliance with the Republicans. Former Whig James E. Bailey, a Redeemer ally of John C. Brown from Montgomery County, was elected to the second seat, a "short term" that ended in 1881. A disappointed Kellar later arranged for Key's appointment to eventual new President Rutherford B. Hayes's cabinet as postmaster general, a move that in Harris's words "killed himself" politically.[57]

Harris's skill in engineering his election not only confounded those who opposed him, such as Kellar, Key, and Colyar, but also left at least one fellow Bourbon perplexed. Shortly after the election, William B. Bate wrote a friend in Memphis expressing his surprise at not being elected. Bate felt that in a head-to-head popular vote, he would beat Bailey by a substantial portion, and complained that he "never could get a vote (when it would do me any good) from any of your Memphis delegation." Bate also reported that some of his friends thought he might have been able to beat Harris for the full-term seat, although Bate confessed: "How this would have been I cannot say with certainty." Counting votes, Bate felt he would have had a certain number of Democratic votes. Bate went on: "Perhaps I was over-sensitive about receiving Republican votes—especially as Govr H's friends after his election, went back on me almost to a man. Of course with their constituents for me I had reasonable grounds to expect a large share of West Tenn vote—Harris being provided for. In that I was woefully disappointed. As to who caused it & why—you can form your own opinion."[58]

The night of his election, Senator-elect Harris was serenaded by a military company and a band at the famous Maxwell House in Nashville. Harris expressed his deep humility and gratitude to the people of Tennessee, and promised to con-

---

Harris for the U.S. Senator for the Long Term," *Memphis Daily Appeal*, December 6, 1876; "Isham G. Harris" (quoting *Columbia Journal*), *Memphis Daily Appeal*, December 17, 1876; "At a meeting of the people of Overton," *Memphis Daily Appeal*, December 21, 1876; "Nashville," *Memphis Daily Appeal*, January 3, 1877; *House Journal* (First Session) 1877, 66–75; "The Senatorial Election," *Nashville Daily American*, January 10, 1877; McBride and Robison, *Biographical Directory of the Tennessee General Assembly*, 2:512. Disproving to an extent David Key's biographer's contention that Key was in a struggle against the Harris "machine," Key's brother, Summerfield A. Key of Hamilton County, was among the Democrats voting for Harris. See ibid., 2:494–95.

57. *House Journal* (First Session) 1877, 67–201; Hart, *Redeemers, Bourbons and Populists*, 24–25; Abshire, *The South Rejects a Prophet*, 132–52, 155–60, 195.

58. William B. Bate to J. H. Erskine, February 7, 1877, University of Tennessee Special Collections.

tinue to work for the good of each section of the country, as Tennessee's interests were on the whole commensurate with the country at large. "As one of the representatives of Tennessee in the American Senate, I can only promise that the Constitution shall be my chart; and the controlling motive and object which shall prompt my action shall be: first, the interests of the State of Tennessee in common with *all* the other states that compose the Union." The editors of the *Nashville Daily American* noted that, in the end, the sweeping nature of Harris's victory "as a triumph perhaps beyond anything expected by his most sanguine friends." Although the loyal *Appeal* gloated about Harris's vindication over the perfidy of the Radicals who made him a "scapegoat," it keenly observed that the ex-governor had "learned the great lesson of knowing how to wait."[59]

Harris's political victory of 1876–77 was not an indicator of his control of a "machine" or of any other monolithic party organization. Harris's election as senator was purely a reflection of his political acumen, which generated a message focused on party loyalty and unity, sectional reconciliation, the alleged villainies of the Republicans, and traditional Democratic values. While he stood unashamed of his role in the Confederacy, he let it be known that he abided by the result of the war and intended to move his party forward on that basis. Thereby, he retained the influence he had always had among ex-Confederates. Other factors were his apparent willingness to subordinate his personal ambition to the good of the party and the unmistakable force of his intelligence and personality. Clearly the state's senior Democrat after Johnson's death, he skillfully maneuvered himself back to the top after years of being too controversial to hold statewide office, trampling, when necessary, on other Democrats to do so. It now remained for him to assure that his party finally regained its preeminence as well.

59. "Isham G. Harris" and "Senator Harris," *Nashville Daily American*, January 10, 1877; "Rebel Felicitations, A Memphis Democratic Paper on the Election of Isham G. Harris to the United States Senate," *New York Times*, January 13, 1877.

9 "STAND BY YOUR TIME-HONORED PRINCIPLES"
1877–1883

Although the previous Congress had numerous ex-Confederates in its ranks, the prospect of Confederate war governor and Mexican exile Isham Green Harris in the Senate seems to have been particularly obnoxious to his former enemies. The *New York Times*, crediting the School Fund slander, recalled Andrew Johnson's hatred of Harris, and that every time the former president mentioned his rival's name, it was with "bitterness and loathing." In the view of the *Times*, Harris was "not only an unrepentant and irreconcilable rebel, but a plunderer, who should be outlawed from honest politics." Of the new senators, one paper observed, Harris alone was to do no credit to the venerable institution, and another suggested that the possibility that the Tennessean was a Mexican citizen should be investigated. Harris's 1876 campaign theme of reconciliation had not touched many hearts in the North.[1]

Whether his former enemies in the North liked it or not, Green Harris returned to Washington, albeit a much different city from the one he had left in 1853. From the completed Capitol, one could see improved streets extending to areas that had been open ground in 1853. The population of the city had increased by approximately a hundred thousand, and although the wartime hospitals and fortifications were largely gone, a large portion of the extensive earthworks remained, a stark reminder, no doubt, of Harris's efforts fifteen years before to subvert the government of which he was now a part. Many senators of the day found that their $5,000 salaries were hardly enough to bear the expense of living in the

1. "Ex-Rebel Officials in Congress," *Athens* (Ohio) *Messenger*, October 26, 1876; "Harris," *New York Times*, January 13, 1877; "The commencement of the extra session of the senate," *Williamsport* (Pa.) *Daily Gazette and Bulletin*, March 8, 1877; "Here is a chance for an investigation," *Oakland Evening Tribune*, January 25, 1877.

city, and the accommodations that could be had even at the highest-priced hotels were uncomfortable, especially in the summer.[2]

Sectional feelings still ran high in 1877, as the uncertain result of the presidential election between Republican Rutherford B. Hayes and Democrat Samuel J. Tilden and the resulting dispute between the two parties and the two sections dragged on for weeks. A commission was appointed to settle the issue of the electoral votes of four states, three of which were formerly Confederate. Questioned on the matter in late January 1877, Senator-elect Harris agreed with the creation of the commission, but would have preferred the matter be settled by the Supreme Court. Harris made it clear that "the peaceful settlement of the present difficulties is a matter pre-eminently more important than the question as to which party shall administer the government." Harris attended a short special session of the Senate in March 1877 called to deal with aspects of the crisis. The contest was effectively resolved on March 2, 1877, when Hayes was declared the winner. In return, Federal support of the Republican state governments in South Carolina and Florida was withdrawn, restoring control to local conservatives.[3]

Although Harris was new to the Senate, he was among his peers. He would have been previously acquainted with Benjamin Hill of Georgia, who had served the Confederacy too as a senator, and Francis Marion Cockrell, who had commanded the Army of Tennessee's famous Missouri Brigade. Approximately seven out of ten of the senators of the day were, like Harris, lawyers. Like Harris, over half had significant experience as politicians on either the national or state level. If, by origin, Harris was in the minority, it was in his family's original near-subsistence existence, which, of course, Green and his brothers did a fine job of overcoming by their own hard work. The Senate of 1877 was divided by party into forty-one Republicans and thirty-eight Democrats (with one independent), but neither party had the structure to dominate the body, nor would that be the situation for another decade or so. Each party had its factions favoring this proposal or

2. Wilhemus Bogart Bryan, *A History of the National Capital from its Foundation through the Period of the Adoption of the Organic Act* (New York: The Macmillan Company, 1916), 2:539–40, 587–90, 601; David J. Rothman, *Politics and Power: The United States Senate, 1869–1901* (New York: Atheneum, 1969), 138–39.

3. Brooks D. Simpson, *The Reconstruction Presidents* (Lawrence: University Press of Kansas, 1998), 192–96; William H. Rehnquist, *Centennial Crisis: The Disputed Election of 1876* (New York: Knopf, 2004), 163–79; "U.S. Senator Elect, Isham G. Harris, Urges the Passage of the Bill," *Atlanta Constitution*, January 25, 1877; *Cong. Record*, 45th Cong., Sp. Sess., 1–46.

that policy, and as senatorial historian David J. Rothman notes, "variation was the rule, not the exception."[4]

No stranger to hard work, Senator Harris must have found his increased workload taxing. His first committee appointments reflected his lack of seniority. As a member of the standing Committee on Claims, he would have shared the responsibility of investigating claims made by citizens asserting some injury or other entitlement from the Federal government. Harris also was appointed to two select committees, the Committee on Levees of the Mississippi River and the Committee on Transportation Routes to the Seaboard. The drudgery of these mundane assignments would not have been offset by an opportunity to give a speech in the Senate chamber. By tradition, that privilege was not accorded new members during their first session.[5]

The first session of the 45th Congress was called back a few weeks early in mid-October 1877, in order to correct an oversight in the previous Congress relative to the funding of the army. Just over two weeks later, Harris submitted his first bills, asking for relief for certain veterans from Tennessee. He later introduced another bill of a local nature, seeking authorization to build a marine hospital at Memphis. Harris's only bill of national importance, a proposal to amend the law to expand the right of appeal in *habeus corpus* cases, seems to have died in committee. Harris also used his new position to seek help for an old friend, writing President Hayes in favor of Marcus J. Wright's application for the post of secretary of state of New Mexico. Wright did not get that post, but was appointed the following year as agent for the collection of Confederate records for inclusion in the War Department's *Official Records* of the Civil War.[6]

Harris's fortunes changed to a small, but eventually significant degree when the second session began in early December 1877, when he traded his post on the Select Committee on Transportation Routes to the Seaboard to the standing Committee on the District of Columbia. As a member of the committee that session,

4. Rothman, *Politics and Power,* 35–37, 115, 128; "The New United States Senate," *Stevens Point* (Wis.) *Journal,* March 10, 1877. An exhaustive analysis of Harris as a U.S. senator may be found in John Thomas Looney, "Isham G. Harris of Tennessee: Bourbon Senator, 1877–1899" (M.A. thesis, University of Tennessee, 1970).

5. Rothman, *Politics and Power,* 145–47; *Cong. Record,* 45th Cong., 1st Sess., 1877, 39; Looney, "Isham G. Harris," 15–18.

6. *Cong. Record,* 45th Cong., 1st Sess., 1877, 1, 50, 201, 341, 361, 548, 767; IGH to R. B. Hayes, October 10, 1877, Marcus J. Wright Papers; "General Marcus J. Wright," *Atlanta Constitution,* July 18, 1878.

Harris advocated a number of measures relating to the government of the District. In a debate in late April 1878, Harris explained the intricacies of a bill to correct illegal or excessive tax assessments in the District. He later warned against a proposal seeking to unduly limit the power of the District Commission to tax property, noting that it would likely result in a deficit the District would ask Congress to make up. In April, and again in May, he advocated a bill reported by the committee to incorporate a street railroad company to serve the city, adroitly answering a number of questions as to the application of the measure. He demonstrated a satirical sense of humor when Senator James B. Beck of Kentucky attempted to insert an amendment prohibiting the carrier from conveying more passengers than could be comfortably seated. Harris replied that someone who would prefer standing and riding rather than waiting would have the conductor say to him, "You shall not enter at all; you shall remain here or walk." Other senators agreed with Harris's point, and one invoked laughter by suggesting an amendment that a passenger seeking to stand might be fined and imprisoned.[7]

Harris also continued efforts on behalf of his constituents. In the first weeks of the session, he pushed the use of East Tennessee marble to build a custom house at Memphis, prevailing on his senatorial colleagues to note the building an exceptional case to justify the additional expense. He also submitted a claim on behalf of the Odd Fellows in Pulaski. A serious illness in February 1878 caused Harris to miss votes on silver and other monetary policy. At one point newspapers reported Harris was serenely facing death from Bright's disease. Fortunately, by the time these stories hit the newspaper, he was already back in the Senate introducing petitions on behalf of constituents, and retractions were quickly published. Again looking homeward, he closed the session passing a measure to provide for the reimbursement of the state of Tennessee for keeping Federal military prisoners.[8]

Even as Harris finished his second session of Congress in June, a disaster was brewing that would dominate his time when he returned to the Senate in December. Memphis's bankrupt and inefficient government, coupled with its swampy location near the Mississippi, made sanitary conditions in the Bluff City "perhaps no better than those of the poorest medieval borough." That month, word came

7. *Cong. Record*, 45th Cong., 2nd Sess., 1877, 1, 40, 1878, 2838–41, 2847–49, 3507–15, 3701, 3744–51, 1879.

8. *Cong. Record*, 45th Cong., 2nd Sess., 1878, 57, 81, 547–49, 1076, 1084, 1112, 1230, 1289, 4472; "A Hero's End," *Washington Post*, February 23, 1878; "City Personals," *Washington Post*, February 25, 1878.

of an outbreak of yellow fever in New Orleans, a fact confirmed by the end of July. While the local government took steps to quarantine Memphis, on August 13, the first confirmed death from the contagion occurred. Between mid-August and the end of October 1878, it is estimated 25,000 residents fled the city, leaving 20,000, mostly poor whites and Negroes, of whom 17,000 contracted the fever and 5,150 died. Nationwide, the epidemic killed almost 20,000 people, with resulting economic loss and disruption.[9]

By the first week of September, the city government and the public health authorities were no longer functioning. That week, Episcopal priest Charles C. Parsons, a former Federal soldier who had survived the worst of the fighting at Perryville, described the contagion in apocalyptic terms to his bishop, Harris's friend Charles Todd Quintard: "Go and turn the Destroying Angel loose upon a defenseless city; let him smite whom he will, young and old, rich and poor, the feeble and the strong, as he will, silent, unseen, unfelt, until his deadly blow is struck; give him for his dreadful harvest all the days and nights from the burning mid-summer until the latest heavy frosts, and then you can form some idea of what Memphis and all this Valley is." Like a number of others seeking to minister to the stricken, Parsons did not survive. The fever lingered until the first frosts of the late fall killed the disease-bearing mosquitoes.[10]

Just as the first deaths were occurring in mid-August, Senator Harris was at the state Democratic convention in Nashville, where the attention of the delegates was focused on the state debt issue. But when the convention ended, like so many others, Harris stayed out of the Bluff City. He had remained in Memphis during an earlier outbreak of yellow fever in 1873, nursing sick family members. Accustomed to spending much of the summer in Paris at any rate, it is possible that the grim experience of 1873, along with his serious illness in February 1878, contributed to keep him from the stricken city in 1878. Personal business also had a role in his absence, as, in mid-October, he was in Callahan County, Texas, apparently

9. Capers, *Biography of a River Town,* 188 (quotation); John H. Ellis, "Disease and the Destiny of a City: The 1878 Yellow Fever Epidemic in Memphis," *West Tennessee Historical Society Papers* 28 (1974): 75–78, 80–88. Ellis notes that while most of the people left in the city were African American, the death rate was much greater for whites. Ibid., 87.

10. Ellis, "Disease and the Destiny of a City," 83; Parsons to Quintard, September 1, 1878, in John Henry Davis, "Two Martyrs of the Yellow Fever Epidemic of 1878," *West Tennessee Historical Society Papers* 26 (1972): 20, 34–35.

looking at farmland. On September 22, 1879, Harris bought 640 acres southwest of Belle Plain.[11]

When Congress resumed in December, Harris immediately offered a resolution that created a select committee "to investigate and report the best means of introduction and spread of epidemic diseases." Harris pushed the resolution forward, arguing "the importance of the investigation provided for by the resolution . . . is so obvious as not to require either explanation or argument." The Senate agreed, and on December 5, 1878, a select committee was appointed with Harris as its chair. The committee met the next day, hearing a report from a government doctor and discussing the scope of the inquiry. Subcommittees were appointed to inquire as to the power of Congress to legislate on epidemic prevention, to prepare a plan of investigation, and to select experts to be employed by the committee. Eventually, the cooperation of the House made the committee a joint effort, and funds were appropriated and staff hired, giving Harris additional patronage to dispense.[12]

Members of the committee, along with staffers and a bevy of medical experts, embarked on a Southern tour during the holidays. It was determined that the various inquiries would include the origin of the disease, the season of the year and atmospheric conditions favorable to it, the means by which the pestilence came into the country, the method of preventing propagation, and the number of deaths and economic impact caused by the disease. The hearings first took place in late December 1878 in Memphis, where Harris was lauded for quick congressional action on the issue, and in New Orleans. Having escaped the yellow fever itself, the senator was fortunate in that it did not kill him in an indirect way while he was traveling by rail back to the North from the hearings. Near his home in Paris, a broken rail caused the sleeping car he was in to overturn, leaving Harris and another passenger "badly shaken up."[13]

11. "Nashville," *Memphis Daily Appeal*, August 16, 1878; IGH to Grover Cleveland, n.d. 1884?, Grover Cleveland Papers, LC; "Gives Sidelights on Isham G. Harris' Life," *Memphis Commercial Appeal*, February 5, 1922; IGH to J. D. Porter, October 22, 1878, James D. Porter Papers, TSLA; Deed from Texas & Pacific Railway Company et al. to Harris, Deed Book C, Page 88, County Clerk of Callahan County, Texas.

12. *Cong. Record*, 45th Cong., 3rd Sess., 1878, 2, 30–31, 35, 48, 275; "Notes from the Capital," *New York Times*, December 7, 1878; "Senator Isham G. Harris," *Memphis Daily Appeal*, December 15, 1878.

13. "The following are the yellow-fever experts," *Memphis Daily Appeal*, December 24, 1878; "The Yellow Fever Commission," *Atlanta Constitution*, December 27, 1878; "Yellow-Fever," *Memphis Daily Appeal*, December 28, 1878; "Senator Harris's Resolution," *Memphis Daily Appeal*, December 6, 1878;

The committee's experts collected data and submitted their findings at the end of January. On February 3 and again on February 7, Harris and his co-chair, Senator Stanley Matthews of Ohio, proposed a bill "to prevent the introduction of contagious or infectious diseases into the United States, and to establish a bureau of public health." Based upon the findings of the experts, the committee determined that "the great majority, if not all, of the epidemics of [yellow fever and cholera] have resulted from importation." It proposed procedures that vessels coming from areas of contagious disease would have to perform before coming to American ports, and "inspection, and if necessary, disinfection and detention of vessel, cargo, passengers and crew before entering any port of the United States." A Bureau and Board of Public Health were to be established to help formulate these regulations.[14]

Debate on the measure started on February 24, 1879. Given Harris's views on the limited power of the national government, there is some irony in his being forced to defend the measure against objections that the new Federal enforcement structure would interfere, on a practical basis, with state quarantine regulations. But Harris argued that his measure "did not seek to interfere with any law, or the functions or the power of any officer . . . of any . . . State in this Union; but exercising the power that Congress has to so regulate commerce as to prevent the importation of disease that decimates a whole people, we claim that it should be so regulated as to prevent the importation into the United States at all, whether it be the port of New York, the port of Boston, the port of Mobile, the port of New Orleans, or any other port." Eventually, the bill was passed, but with a time limit of four years.[15]

On March 1, debate then moved to the House, where Representative Casey Young of Memphis, who had stayed in the city and witnessed the terrible effects of the contagion the previous summer, pushed a weaker version of the measure adopted by the Senate, hoping to get it quickly to conference between the two houses. Other congressmen, including former Confederate General James B. Chal-

---

"A National Health Bureau," *New York Times*, February 8, 1878; "Badly Shaken Up," *New York Times*, January 5, 1879.

14. Looney, "Isham G. Harris," 73; *Cong. Record*, 45th Cong., 3rd Sess., 1879, 929, 1072; "Notes From Washington," *New York Times*, February 4, 1879; "A National Health Bureau," *New York Times*, February 8, 1879.

15. *Cong. Record*, 45th Cong., 3rd Sess., 1879, 1826–58.

mers of Mississippi, preferred the Senate bill. Eventually, the House passed neither, and a quick compromise measure was cobbled together that created a relatively toothless National Board of Health. As the 45th Congress neared its end,
Harris rushed the House bill through the Senate, making sure that at least something was done before adjournment.[16]

An unintended consequence of Rutherford B. Hayes's efforts to reconcile the
South was the reemergence of the Democratic Party in the South, which in turn
resulted in the Democrats' regaining control of Congress after the elections of
1878. Harris not only retained the chairmanship of the Select Committee on Epidemics, but he also became chairman of the District of Columbia Committee. As
chairman, he was able to appoint a fellow Memphian, Charles Stone, clerk of the
committee. Democratic control of the Senate also gave Harris an opportunity
to install a Tennessean as secretary of the Senate, Colonel John C. Burch, a former staff officer of Pillow's, Nashville newspaper editor, and comptroller of Tennessee. The New York Times published a story that claimed Burch was not trusted
in Tennessee, and intimated that Harris had misled his colleagues in having him
appointed. The Washington Post countered with a number of testimonials from
Tennessee politicians, dignitaries, and newspapers as to Burch's "fitness and integrity." While Harris denied the claims against Burch, it seems that the appointment, and the much more dubious naming of Richard J. Bright as sergeant at arms
at the instance of another senator, caused Harris's fellow Democrats some discomfort. Burch would serve as secretary of the Senate until his death in 1881, and Harris would ask that the government grant his widow a year's salary.[17]

Harris was poised to revisit the epidemic issue early in the first session of the
46th Congress. The Senate confirmed the nominations of the five members of
the National Board of Health, including Dr. Samuel Bemiss of New Orleans, the
former assistant medical director of the Army of Tennessee, and Dr. Robert W.
Mitchell of Memphis, a survivor of the previous summer's epidemic. Harris in-

16. Ibid., 2260–73; Looney, "Isham G. Harris," 75–76.

17. Simpson, The Reconstruction Presidents, 218; "By Telegraph," Chattanooga Daily Times, March
16, 1879; Cong. Record, 46th Cong., 1st Sess., 1879, 15; "The New Committee Clerks," Washington
Post, March 31, 1879; McBride and Robison, Biographical Directory of the Tennessee General Assembly,
1:100–101; "The New Senate Officers," New York Times, March 26, 1879; "Mr. Gorham's Successor,"
Washington Post, March 27, 1879; "The Election of Col. John C. Burch," Chattanooga Daily Times,
March 21, 1879; "Burch and Bright," New York Times, March 29, 1879; "Congressional News Notes,"
Washington Post, December 20, 1881.

tended to introduce a new and tougher quarantine bill, similar to his previous proposal, which gave the newly created board sweeping powers. Surprisingly, the board did not want to assume such powers, advising Harris in a letter that its view of its duties did not match what Harris intended in his new legislation. Harris made it clear that they needed his support to perform at all, which resulted in the board's endorsement of the legislation. The bill was not without its faults, and included a provision that U.S. officials would inspect vessels coming from any port where infectious and contagious diseases existed, as well as Havana, which must have been presumptively a source of pestilence.[18]

In the opening days of the session that March, Harris introduced his new quarantine bill, and also a bill to authorize the construction of a refrigeration ship "for the disinfection of vessels and cargos." The latter measure stemmed from the observations of the time that "cold destroys the germs" of yellow fever. An appropriation of $200,000 was to be made for a steel ship "fitted with refrigerating machinery, devised by an Englishman, Prof. John Gamgee." It was contemplated the ship would be stationed at New Orleans and other Southern ports and be used to disinfect, by "freezing out the fever germs," ships arriving from disease-suspect climes. Gamgee's plans and models were examined by the now compliant Board of Health, which unanimously made a favorable report. The measure was approved by both houses of Congress and signed into law by the president on April 21. Ultimately, the refrigeration ship idea sank. The Treasury Department proposed to take Gamgee's designs and use them as specifications for a competitive bid on the project, to which Gamgee naturally objected. Harris's efforts to resolve matters came to naught, and the project eventually died.[19]

Debate in earnest began on the new quarantine bill on April 30, 1879. Objections, principally on the grounds of the scope of expanded Federal power, contributed to the measure being recommitted to Harris's committee. Harris was back the next day with a slightly amended version, lecturing the bill's opponents on the powers conferred by the commerce clause of the Constitution and citing Supreme

18. "By Telegraph" and "Memphis *Avalanche* of Wednesday," *Chattanooga Daily Times*, March 28, 1879; Glenna R. Schroeder-Lein, *Confederate Hospitals on the Move: Samuel H. Stout and the Army of Tennessee* (Columbia: University of South Carolina Press, 1994), 187; Looney, "Isham G. Harris," 77–78; "The Nation's Health," *Washington Post*, April 10, 1879.

19. *Cong. Record*, 46th Cong., 1st Sess., 1879, 33, 44, 593; "A New Yellow Fever Bill," *New York Times*, March 24, 1879; "Current News at Washington," *New York Times*, March 31, 1879; "The Bill of Senator Harris," *Washington Post*, April 1, 1879; Looney, "Isham G. Harris," 83–84.

Court precedent in response to an argument made by Roscoe Conkling of New York. Harris noted that if Congress had the power to adopt safety regulations for ocean-going ships, it certainly "has the power under the same clause of the Constitution to so regulate commerce as to strip it of that contagion which so seriously threatens human life and health and the prosperity of the country."[20] Harris addressed concerns about the rule-making authority of the Board of Health in executing its mandate, and with the irregularity and inefficiency of state quarantine regulations in the past. Referring to Morgan's comment that there had never been such a law proposed and that Congress had previously relied on the states for such measures, Harris conceded such to be the case. "It is a sad and a melancholy fact that Congress has so relied, and the results that have followed that reliance are more eloquently announced by the appalling death-toll of the yellow-fever epidemics of 1867, 1873 and 1878."[21]

On May 5, debate resumed with Harris proposing an amendment to the effect that nothing in the bill "would supersede or impair the operations of the sanitary or quarantine laws of any State" within that state's territorial limits. Again, though Conkling and others objected on essentially states' rights grounds, this position was deemed hypocritical by a Tennessee newspaper in light of Conkling's previous positions on national authority. Again, the bill was sent back to the committee, doubtless much to Harris's frustration.[22] In Memphis, a political enemy blamed the failure of the measure on jealousy between Harris and Congressman Young, to which Harris responded in a letter to the *Appeal*. Noting the incident, the *Chattanooga Times* stated that Harris and Young had been "most effective" and that there should be no "censure where the highest praise is due." On May 22 and 23, debate resumed, and the measure finally passed, with Morgan offering one last amendment that limited the life of the new law to four years. But Morgan and others felt the pressure of the fast-approaching yellow-fever season, and the bill was eventually passed on May 23, as amended, 34–12. It also gained the approval of the House, and was signed into law by the president on June 2, 1879.[23]

The new law slowly sank into oblivion. The summer of 1879 brought no new epidemic, and as the memory of the terrible outbreak of 1878 faded, Congress's in-

20. *Cong. Record*, 46th Cong., 1st Sess., 1879, 987–93; 1002–3 (quote on 1003).

21. Ibid., 1879, 1005.

22. Ibid., 1044–48.

23. Ibid., 1507–20, 1539–52, 1716; "Senator Isham G. Harris," *Chattanooga Daily Times*, May 20, 1879; "By Telegraph" and "Senator Conkling," *Chattanooga Daily Times*, May 23, 1879.

terest in the issue likewise grew dim and funding to the National Board of Health was severely cut. Events proved that the provision for inspections in foreign ports was unworkable. The board responded by suggesting an international sanitary conference, which Congress approved in 1880. Held in early 1881, the conference adopted resolutions relating to disinfection in foreign ports, but no treaties were adopted to put the conference's work into practice. Eventually, despite Harris's best efforts, the four-year expiration date for the 1879 quarantine act brought about the demise of the National Board of Health.[24]

Harris's willingness to expand the power of the Federal government on the overarching issue of quarantining yellow fever and other epidemic diseases did not extend to other issues. At issue late in the spring of 1879 was Senator Joseph E. McDonald's proposal to repeal Reconstruction-era legislation authorizing the use of Federal power in connection with state elections. Harris characterized opposition to the repeal as mere appeals to "passion, sectional prejudice, and hate." Indeed, "there [was] scarcely a section of this election law which does not contain gross and alarming usurpations of the rights and powers of the States, scarcely a section that does not bristle with insult to the States and people by the plainly implied distrust in the honesty of the administration of the States and in the integrity and patriotism of the people." The pettiest of Federal officials had the power to challenge state elections, he argued, and demonstrated that a number of such officials in New York were criminals and drunkards. Harris deemed the law a means of perpetuating Republican rule, not of a government of peace and prosperity. The *Washington Post* approved, noting that Harris had "few equals" on matters of constitutional law.[25]

That spring, Harris also leapt to the defense of an old friend. When the Senate was considering a bill providing for the payment of military pension arrears, Senator Hoar of Massachusetts proposed an amendment excluding Jefferson Davis from benefiting from the bill for his Mexican War service. Harris was among the Southern senators who spoke in Davis's favor, defending him "from the wanton and malicious attack" motivated, in his words, by politicians seeking "to perpetuate the memories of the war for partisan purposes." Northern senators replied with equal fervor, and, in the end, Hoar's amendment was approved along party

24. Looney, "Isham G. Harris," 85–93.

25. *Cong. Record*, 46th Cong., 1st Sess., 1879, 1862–67; "An Abject Surrender," *Washington Post*, June 10, 1879; "By Telegraph," *Chattanooga Daily Times*, June 10, 1879; "The Forty-Sixth Congress," *Atlanta Constitution*, June 10, 1879.

lines. Months later, when asked to intervene in a dispute over Beauregard's role at Shiloh, Davis wrote of Harris: "Harris has been a personal friend of mine, manifesting always much interest in my welfare, I am therefore, unwilling to press him for a statement which he does not appear to have been willing to make to Preston Johnston [Albert Sidney Johnston's son and biographer]. He is a fearless and a truthful man, would not prevaricate or mis-state, but might refuse to answer."[26]

Harris's membership on the District of Columbia Committee required significant attention during his first years in the Senate. The minutiae of governing the District included the consideration of measures relating to health ordinances, recruiting and increasing the District police force, taxes and finances, the incorporation and taxation of rail lines, bridging the Potomac, establishing hospitals, and the enactment of a new municipal code.[27] Harris considered the people of the District a constituency, as they had no representation in Congress except through the House and Senate committees.[28] Accordingly, he presented petitions on their behalf, and fought for protective measures such as a higher business license rate for outside salesmen. In an ironic exchange of positions on protectionism, Senator Hoar of Massachusetts opposed the protective measure, while Harris supported the higher fee. It was noted that District merchants recalled that lighter duties in the past resulted in the District being overrun by "drummers" from Baltimore, "who went from house to house seeking orders for groceries, dry goods and even meats."[29] The Tennessean's efforts were appreciated by his District "constituents," to the extent that the *Washington Post* expressed the hope that he would be reelected in his bid for a second term: "Certainly, every friend or well wisher of the

26. "The Last Night," *Hagerstown Herald and Torch,* March 12, 1879; "A Republican's Opinion," *Chattanooga Daily Times,* March 11, 1879; Davis to Northrop, January 14, 1880, in *Jefferson Davis, Constitutionalist: His Letters, Papers and Speeches,* ed. Dunbar Rowland (Jackson: Mississippi Department of Archives and History, 1923), 8:437–38.

27. "Outside Capitol Matters," *Washington Post,* January 30, 1880; "District Matters in Congress," *Washington Post,* March 9, 1880; "The Street Railroad Taxes," *Washington Post,* March 11, 1880; "Mr. Gilfillian Answered," *Washington Post,* March 31, 1880; "The District in Congress," *Washington Post,* May 18, 1880; "City Talk and Chatter," *Washington Post,* January 13, 1881; "The District in Congress," *Washington Post,* January 21, 1881; "District Matters in Congress," *Washington Post,* May 25, 1880; "The Proposed License Laws," *Washington Post,* February 15, 1883; "A Code of District Laws," *Washington Post,* January 30, 1884.

28. "The District in Congress," *Washington Post,* December 22, 1883.

29. "District Measures in Congress," *Washington Post,* June 15, 1880; "Drummers in the District," *Washington Post,* October 26, 1881.

National Capital would regard Mr. Harris's defeat as a personal loss if not a personal calamity . . . Ten men such as Senator Harris can in either House effect more practical good for the country in a common-sense business-like way than a hundred mouthing sound and sense dispensers."[30]

The District's greatest challenge during Harris's era was its wholly inadequate water supply. The last time the District had enough water was probably 1831, when water was brought in from a spring two miles from the Capitol. By the early 1850s, the city's population had doubled, but its water supply remained the same. Parched citizens resorted to tapping into pipes going into public buildings. A study commissioned in 1853 recommended drawing water from the Great and Little Falls areas of the Potomac, a project that was finally completed in 1863.[31] When the new works first went into operation in 1859, it had 354 customers. By 1882, there were 10,000. The shortage was so bad that the government had difficulty in keeping the vegetation on the Capitol grounds watered. In the hot weather of the summer of 1881, a District school building serving 700 children did not have water flow in the water closets or the urinals. It was necessary to shut down all the public fountains to make sure enough water got to the schools.[32]

Several plans were proposed to deal with the problem, but by the summer of 1879, nothing was pending. Harris spent many hours investigating and inspecting the District water supply and water works in the course of his work on a subcommittee tasked with the water issue, staying in Washington after the end of the congressional session in 1879 for that purpose. After a break on his new Texas ranch, he returned to complete his work in early October. The subcommittee found that water was wasted in huge quantities. In the absence of a complete remedy, as a "temporary expedient," it was suggested that the District authorities have wide-ranging powers to enter private premises to inspect for wastage. While Harris deemed the proposal a "harmless little bill," the constitutional implications of the proposed inspections disturbed enough senators to defeat the proposal.[33]

30. "It is greatly to be hoped," *Washington Post*, July 29, 1882; see also "Tennessee will return Senator Harris," *Washington Post*, December 8, 1882.

31. Bryan, *A History of the National Capital*, 305, 396–97.

32. "Washington's Water Supply," *Washington Post*, June 12, 1882.

33. "The Water Investigation," *Washington Post*, August 9, 1879; "In General," *Atlanta Constitution*, October 7, 1879; "Inspecting the Water Works," *Washington Post*, October 9, 1879; "The District in Congress," *Washington Post*, December 9, 1879; *Cong. Rec.*, 46th Cong., 1st Sess., 1879, 1715, 1736–39; *Cong. Rec.*, 2nd Sess., 1880, 3167–72; *Cong. Rec.*, 3rd Sess., 1880, 178.

In 1882, a comprehensive proposal was submitted, which called for a dam, the extension of an aqueduct, the construction of a reservoir, and other features. The *Post* observed that Harris's measure would "furnish a complete and adequate remedy, and nothing less will."[34] The bill was passed, and work began. But the engineer officer originally assigned to the project was reassigned, notwithstanding Harris's protests to the chief of engineers, the secretary of war, and the president of the United States. The new officer in charge defrauded the government in the course of the work, and an incensed Senate at the instance of the Appropriations Committee conferred the investigation on a special commission, depriving the District of Columbia Committee of jurisdiction. In the end, the project went nowhere. In 1895, Senator Eugene Hale of Maine, a member of the Appropriations Committee, arose to question why the District Committee had not adequately provided for the water supply. Harris rather tersely recounted how the matter had been taken out of his committee's hands by Hale's committee. A serious flap was averted by Senator Arthur P. Gorman's summation of the affair in a manner complimentary to the District Committee. In the end, nothing was done until after the turn of the century. Harris's efforts to improve the District's sewer system met a similar fate.[35]

Unsettled politics on the Republican side in the early 1880s had the odd effect of creating both an opportunity and a problem for Harris. While the Democrats hoped to reverse the bitter result of the election of 1876, the unfortunate Tilden was not chosen as the party's standard-bearer in 1880. Harris initially thought the Democratic candidate would be New York's Horatio Seymour, but Federal Civil War hero General Winfield Scott Hancock was the party's nominee, and Harris boldly predicted that his former enemy in blue would win. Harris attended public functions in the North with Hancock, and campaigned in Tennessee for the Democratic ticket. Hancock was eventually defeated by Republican James A. Garfield.[36]

---

34. "The District in Congress," *Washington Post,* March 10, 1882; "The District in Congress," *Washington Post,* April 18, 1882; "The Water Supply Bill," *Washington Post,* May 25, 1882; "Washington's Water Supply," *Washington Post,* June 12, 1882.

35. *Cong. Rec.,* 53rd Cong., 3rd Sess., 1895, 1621–22; "With Slow Progress," *Washington Post,* February 2, 1895; Looney, "Isham G. Harris," 20–22.

36. "Views of the Congressmen," *Washington Post,* January 17, 1880; "Our Young Hickory," *Atlanta Constitution,* June 25, 1880; "Hancock's Callers," *Washington Post,* July 25, 1880: "Senator I. G. Harris was called out," *Paris Weekly Intelligencer,* September 9, 1880; "Notes of the Campaign," *Washington Post,* October 20, 1880.

In May 1881, powerful New York Senator Roscoe Conkling suddenly resigned his seat, followed by his colleague, Thomas ("Me, Too") Platt, in the course of an intra-Republican spat over the appointment of the collector of customs at New York. Conkling assumed that he would be speedily reelected by the New York legislature, expecting, in Harris's view, to secure a mandate from his constituents in his dispute with the administration.[37] Conkling's stupendous miscalculation in that regard suddenly gave the Democrats control of the Senate, and the office of president pro tem of the Senate was unexpectedly fair game. As the session ended on May 20, 1881, Republicans made it known that they would deem Harris "an acceptable choice for the position and will cheerfully acquiesce in his election."[38] During the course of his relatively short time in the Senate, members from both parties came to acknowledge Harris's mastery of the arcane parliamentary procedures that governed that body. Therefore, while the nomination was likely premised on Harris being considered the best presiding officer on the Democratic side, there were no doubt those who recalled a rumor that had briefly flared up two months previously.[39] Then, the *Washington Post* reported that it was "whispered" that one or two Democratic senators would make a party switch. Harris was rumored to have visited Garfield. Next day, the previous day's report was based on "misapprehension." Harris did not visit Garfield, and if there was a senator considering a switch, "it is certainly not Mr. Harris," who steadfastly adhered "to the principles of the Democratic party."[40] Apparently, Vice President Chester A. Arthur was not warm to the idea of Harris's election to the post, as he remained in the chair to the end of the session, seen by some as "an indirect and indelicate attack on Senator Harris."[41]

Harris was approached by "a number of senators, both democratic and republican, with the proposition to elect [him] president pro tempore of the senate." Harris asked the Democrats if they had talked to Senator Thomas F. Bayard of Delaware, the senior Democrat in the Senate. When they indicated that they had not, Harris undertook to do so "and stated the case to him" in the cloak room.

37. Zachary Karabell, *Chester Alan Arthur* (New York: Times Books, 2004), 55–58; "What the Senators Think," *Washington Post*, May 17, 1881.

38. "Eating Crow," *Atlanta Constitution*, May 17, 1881; see also "The Republican Senators" and "Republicans in Caucus," *Washington Post*, May 17, 1881.

39. "A Noble Tribute," *Galveston Daily News*, September 30, 1881.

40. "What Says Mahone," *Washington Post*, March 13, 1881; "Senator Harris and His Record," *Washington Post*, March 14, 1881; "Death of Isham G. Harris," *New York Times*, July 9, 1897.

41. "Senator Beck's Version," *Atlanta Constitution*, July 21, 1881.

Bayard said, "I will think of it," but never mentioned it again. Harris said "to the end of that congress I refused to entertain any proposition looking to my election to that position, and the congress adjourned without the election of a president pro tempore." Harris noted Bayard was a "warm personal friend" of the other Tennessee senator, Howell Jackson, and had been in "full sympathy" with Jackson in instances where Harris and Jackson differed on appointments.[42]

Events that summer precipitously made the office of the president pro tem much more significant than normal. In June, after calling at the White House with such diverse visitors as James Longstreet and Robert Lincoln, Harris departed for his ranch in Texas.[43] It was likely the last time Harris saw President Garfield alive, as he was shot by an assassin on July 2, 1881. Garfield lingered most of the summer, but died on September 19. Returning to Memphis, the senator addressed the Memphis Bar Association, speaking of his respect for the president's "splendid talent." While Harris felt Garfield's conduct was "inconsistent" because he tried to "honestly accommodate the views of those who appealed to him . . . I have always awarded to him the same honesty of sentiment and integrity of purpose that I have claimed for myself." Harris assured the assembled lawyers that Arthur was a man of conviction and frankness, and the "great business interests" had nothing to worry about in regards to him.[44]

Under the Succession Act of 1792, still in effect, should anything happen to Arthur, the president pro tem would become the president of the United States.[45] Because the issue was not solved in May, the Senate was called into special session on October 10 to elect a president pro tem. Like the departed Conkling, Bayard was noted to have tendencies of "bossism," but without Conkling's ability. Bayard managed to secure election for a period of three days, but, without the Republican acquiescence that Harris would have certainly enjoyed, lost it to Illinois Senator David Davis, a friend and political advisor of Abraham Lincoln's. The portly independent from Illinois managed to secure the office because of the even split be-

42. "Harris and Bayard," *Atlanta Constitution*, May 2, 1885; see also "Organizing the Senate," *Washington Post*, October 1, 1881. It should be noted the comment relative to Jackson was made in 1885, after the bitter canvass of 1882 in Tennessee.

43. "Callers at the White House," *Washington Post*, June 17, 1881; "Personal," *Washington Post*, June 29, 1881; "Social Intelligence," *Washington Post*, October 16, 1881.

44. "Legal Grief," *Memphis Daily Appeal*, September 23, 1881.

45. Succession Act of 1792 (1 Stat. 240). The Succession Act of 1886 (24 Stat. 1) eliminated the president pro tem and the Speaker of the House in favor of cabinet officers. Current law makes the president pro tem third in line of succession behind the vice president and Speaker of the House. 3 U.S.C.§ 19.

tween the two parties caused by the resignations of Conkling and Platt. Ironically, Lincoln's friend and the ex-Confederate from Tennessee became good friends, and during his tenure as president pro tem, Davis would often call Harris to the chair. Two years later, when Davis left the Senate, he was heard to say, "Harris! Harris! When I get out of here I won't have to listen to old Bayard any more!" When the special session of 1881 ended, Harris visited the president, and then departed on a trip to Paris, France. As he sailed away, Green Harris, last in Europe as a fugitive from the vengeance of Parson Brownlow, must have contemplated that he had gotten closer to the presidency of the United States than any other ex-Confederate or, for that matter, any former Mexican alcalde.[46]

With his reelection at issue in 1882, Harris spent significant time in the first regular session of the 47th Congress on issues of federal patronage in Tennessee. He started the session trying to get Neill S. Brown Jr., the son of his opponent in the 1856 debate and proponent with Brownlow in 1867, appointed to the chief clerkship of the Senate. Brown was formerly reading clerk in the House of Representatives. Harris introduced a resolution to appoint Brown on February 9, 1882, which resulted in a tie vote 25–25, independent David Davis voting for it, independent William Mahone of Virginia against. Georgia Senator Joseph E. Brown, a fellow Southern Democrat, also voted against Brown. Brown explained as his reasons that there was an effective truce in the Senate because of the even split, with the Republicans in control the committees and the Democrats the offices: "I should like very much to see Mr. Neil Brown get the position he deserves, but as Tennessee already has about twice as much as patronage as Georgia, I do not feel called upon to risk what we now have and what the other democrats now have, simply to give a place to Mr. Brown." Brown's comment was compelling testimony on the efficacy of Harris's patronage efforts. During the course of the year, Harris also stood up for the Republican postmistress of Memphis, and took an excursion party from Tennessee to visit the White House.[47]

46. "The Senate Begins Work," *New York Times*, October 11, 1881; "Bayard as a Boss," *New York Times*, July 22, 1881; "It is greatly to be hoped," *Washington Post*, July 29, 1882; "Sat Upon by David Davis," *Washington Post*, October 14, 1881; "The President's Callers," *Washington Post*, October 29, 1881; Shelby M. Cullom, *Fifty Years of Public Service* (Chicago: A. C. McClurg & Co., 1911), 38; "Telegraphic Summary," *Atlanta Constitution*, November 8, 1881.

47. "The Chief Clerkship of the Senate," *Washington Post*, December 20, 1881; "Monday in Congress," *Washington Post*, February 7, 1882; "In the Capital," *Atlanta Constitution*, February 10, 1882; "The Topics Discussed," *Atlanta Constitution*, February 21, 1882 (Senator Brown's quote); "Senator

The story of Harris's reelection to a second term in the Senate in 1883 is closely tied to the story of the continuing agitation over the state debt controversy within the Tennessee Democratic Party. Just as Harris was named elector at large in early August 1876, A. J. Kellar and the *Avalanche* sought to force his hand on the issue by dragging out the report condemning high taxes the former governor made with other members of the Memphis bar to the Protective Union in 1874. But during his 1876 speaking tour, Harris almost ignored the state debt and taxation issue, emphasizing the enormity of the Federal government's financial problems under the Republicans, stating that in contrast, the "burden of State taxes was a mere bagatelle, and no more to be compared to it than a wad from a pop-gun to the shot of a seventy-four pounder." Ignoring the issue likely facilitated Harris's election, but it did not make the problem go away. When the legislature met in 1877, the vexatious issue remained unsolved. Newly reelected, Governor Porter proposed that a commission go to New York to negotiate an equitable settlement of the debt. The issue, then, was no longer full repayment, but a scaled-back settlement. Out of the conference came a proposal to pay the debt at 60 cents on the dollar, and at 6 percent interest. While Harris and other leading Democrats supported the proposal, the legislature rejected it, and, when called into two special sessions later in 1877, rejected similar proposals. In connection with one of the special sessions, Harris wrote a letter to Governor Porter that was obviously intended for publication, urging acceptance in order to avoid the evils of repudiation. The stage was set for a battle during the state Democratic convention of 1878.[48]

Harris retained the enmity of Andrew Johnson's friend and the low-taxer's champion, A. S. Colyar. The politically mercurial Colyar ran as an independent candidate for the legislature in 1876, and let it be known during the campaign that in his view, Harris deserved "a thousand years in Hell," and that he would vote for Bate as senator only if it would help beat Harris. Harris replied that Colyar was "the most chronic case of *independent candidate* I ever saw," which, to

---

Harris and a Lady Postmaster," *New York Times*, March 6, 1882; "Current Capital News," *Washington Post*, August 10, 1882.

48. "Ex-Gov. Isham G. Harris," *Memphis Avalanche*, August 8, 1876; "Yesterday's Speaking" (a "bagatelle" is a mere trifle); Jones, *Tennessee at the Crossroads*, 89–91; Hamer, ed., *Tennessee: A History, 1673–1932*, 2:683; Hart, *Redeemers, Bourbons and Populists*, 29–31; "State Politics," *Chattanooga Daily Times*, August 22, 1882.

Harris's party-loyal mind, must have been the keenest of insults. In 1878, Colyar was joined in his leadership of the low-tax element of the party by Colonel John H. Savage of Warren County. As much as Colyar disliked Harris, Savage hated the new senator with all the fervor that his last name might imply.[49]

As previously discussed, Savage blamed Harris for opposing his promotion to brigadier general in the Confederate army in 1863, an accusation Harris denied. Savage was an unsuccessful candidate for Confederate Congress in 1863, and again blamed Harris, this time for purportedly fixing the election. He openly wished Harris would challenge him to a duel, and made many disparaging remarks about Harris's role in the war and lack of military service, disputed his account of what occurred at Shiloh, and even claimed Harris had lied about his age. Savage claimed that he had rejected a postwar effort by Harris to bury the hatchet, and that Harris's reconciliatory tone in his 1876 campaign speeches "did more for the Republican party in Tennessee than Maynard and others could have done in ten years."[50]

With his best efforts at solving the debt question lost in futility, Governor Porter declined a third term. The Democratic convention in August 1878 boiled down to a fight between the two factions for control of the party. Both senators addressed the convention, and Harris exhorted both sides to find a place to compromise the issue; "other questions are pending which must not be jeopardized by your divisions on this question." Savage and Colyar both sought the gubernatorial nomination, along with John A. Gardner of Weakley County, while the pro-credit Redeemer coalition supported John M. Flemming of Knoxville. Harris implored the delegates to suborn their views on the debt question to party unity, but whatever good that did soon dissolved into further infighting.[51]

The party's platform bowed to both sides, calling for an equitable adjustment of the debt, and for a referendum on "any adjustment of the State Debt which may be made by the Legislature," and until then, no greater taxes than necessary should be assessed. The drafter of the platform, Chancellor Albert S. Marks of Winchester, addressed the convention and then returned home. On the twenty-second ballot, the convention, which had been hopelessly deadlocked to that

49. Ball, "The Public Career of Colonel A. S. Colyar," 235.

50. IGH to Wright, February 12, 1863, Southern Historical Collection, UNC; Savage, *The Life of John H. Savage*, 73–77, 144–47, 161–67.

51. "Senator Harris," *Memphis Avalanche*, October 8, 1882; Hamer, ed., *Tennessee: A History, 1673–1932*, 2:683; Hart, *Redeemers, Bourbons and Populists*, 30–31.

point, suddenly switched to Marks as a compromise candidate for governor, who was then nominated. Harris deemed Marks, a Confederate veteran who had lost a leg at Murfreesboro, both "able" and "available," and told a reporter for the *Washington Post* that while there was "a difference of opinion" on the state debt issue, it was "purely a local question" that would not split the party. True to Harris's prediction, Marks won the election over Republican Dr. E. M. Wight of Chattanooga and R. M. Edwards, the small Greenback Party's candidate.[52]

Dutifully, Marks set out to settle the debt issue, but the General Assembly could not reach agreement on a bill dealing with the matter. As the 1879 session neared an end in March, an exasperated governor sent the legislators a message that "the public welfare imperatively demands that this question be eliminated from the politics of the State, as speedily as possible." If they were unable to do so, Marks suggested a constitutional convention could be called to finally settle the matter. Eventually, the two houses settled on a referendum providing for a settlement of 50 cents on the dollar at 4 percent interest. Prior to the election on the question in August 1879, a number of prominent Democrats urged acceptance of the measure, including former governors Brown and Porter, Marks, Senator Bailey, Bate, and even Colyar. Harris wrote a tepid letter quoted in the *New York Times* urging that the matter be ratified, but which also stated that "Tennessee can much better afford to undertake to pay the whole debt than take upon herself the manifold evils which must result from repudiation." The measure was defeated by a margin of almost thirty thousand. Most of the negative votes were cast in the Democratic strongholds of Middle and West Tennessee.[53]

The unburied corpse of the state debt issue did the Democrats the maximum possible damage in 1880, as the bitter division in the party finally had an effect on the party's control of the state government. Although Harris warned that the party could not afford to split on the issue, in June the state credit wing seized control of the convention called to nominate candidates to the national convention. A vote unfavorable to Marks demonstrated that the state credit faction could deny him the nomination for a second term, and he withdrew as a candidate for reelection. At the regular convention in August, John V. Wright of Columbia was

52. White, *Messages of the Governors of Tennessee*, 6:560–61, 563–64; Hart, *Redeemers, Bourbons and Populists*, 31–35; "Senator Harris Talks," *Washington Post*, August 20, 1878.

53. White, *Messages of the Governors of Tennessee*, 6:607–13; Hart, *Redeemers, Bourbons and Populists*, 35–37; "Senator Harris on the Tennessee Debt," *New York Times*, July 26, 1879.

nominated as the party's candidate for governor. Frustrated by the state credit wing's control of the regular convention, more than a hundred low tax delegates bolted the convention and nominated their own candidate, S. F. Wilson of Sumner County, for governor.[54]

Harris campaigned for Wright and for General Hancock, the Democratic presidential candidate. But John H. Savage, at the height of his power during this time, attacked Wright as a candidate of the urban elite. Curiously echoing Andy Johnson's common man line, the Savage/Wilson alliance brought about a result that was essentially the same as that wrought by Johnson in the congressional race of 1872—the Democratic vote was sufficiently split to enable the Republicans to elect their candidate, West Tennessean Alvin Hawkins, as governor. Additionally, the legislature was evenly divided, 37 to 37, with a fusion Republican/Greenbacker as a single third-party legislator. Savage's claim that Harris had advanced the Republican cause with his conciliatory tone in 1876 rang hollow in light of his assistance to the Republicans in 1880.[55]

The dispute affected Senator Bailey's seat, which cannot have avoided Green Harris's keen political eye. Being the seat originally filled by Andrew Johnson in 1875, Bailey's position was subject to election in 1881. Bailey remained the candidate of the regular Democrats, and Savage became the candidate of the low-taxers. Try as they might to unite behind a single man, the Democrats could not settle on a candidate, as Savage withdrew in favor of Bate. Thereafter, both Bate and Bailey declined in favor of party unity. Meanwhile, the Republicans attempted to put the trusty Horace Maynard in the seat, but the Democrats succeeded in blocking him. Finally breaking the ice, a Republican announced that since a Republican could not be elected, he was voting for Democrat Howell E. Jackson of Middle Tennessee, the brother of former Confederate General William H. "Red" Jackson. A first-term legislator who was in the right place at the right time, Jackson, a Redeemer of the prewar Whig persuasion, was chosen, to the delight of Democrats who

54. "Senator Harris," *Memphis Avalanche*, October 8, 1882; Hamer, ed., *Tennessee: A History, 1673–1932*, 2:687–89; Hart, *Redeemers, Bourbons and Populists*, 40–42.

55. Hart, *Redeemers, Bourbons and Populists*, 43–49; "Senator Harris," *Memphis Avalanche*, October 8, 1882; "Gov. Isham G. Harris, 1857 vs. 1882," *Nashville Daily American*, August 30, 1882; Harvey Gresham Hudspeth, "Seven Days in Nashville: Politics, the State Debt, and the Making of a United States Senator; January 19–26, 1881," *West Tennessee Historical Society Papers* 52 (1998): 81–82.

feared Maynard's election would make the Senate incontestably Republican that March. Harris was quoted as saying Jackson was "young," "but an able lawyer and a man in every way qualified to represent the State in Senate."[56]

Although the low-tax Democrats were able to prevent state credit advocate Bailey from securing a second term, they were definitely in the minority when the state credit Democrats and the Republicans joined forces. A law was passed in 1881 that funded the debt at 100 cents on the dollar at 3 percent interest. It also provided that interest coupons could be used to pay state taxes. Outvoted in the legislature, the low-tax Democrats resorted to the courts, obtained an injunction, and eventually secured a ruling from the Tennessee Supreme Court that the 100–3 funding law was unconstitutional on the grounds of the coupon tax payment provision. The General Assembly then passed a measure calling for payment at 60 cents on the dollar at 3 percent for 2 years, 4 percent for 2 years, 5 percent for 2 years, and 6 percent until maturity. The 60–3–4–5–6 solution was again supported by a coalition of state credit Democrats and Republicans, but the issue of the state debt remained unresolved entering the 1882 election cycle.[57]

In late December 1881, the *Memphis Avalanche* called for Harris to resign from the Senate and return home to "become, as he may for the asking, the Governor of Tennessee, and as such, with a Legislature elected to follow him, put the public debt of Tennessee on the right basis of financial stability."[58] Indeed, there was speculation early in 1882 that the state debt issue would be the issue that would keep ex-governor from returning to the Senate, as it was predicted that "Tennessee would fall into the close clutches of the low tax men" who had "no love" for Senator Harris.[59]

During much of the debate, Harris was a state credit proponent, following the party line of the regular Democrats who led the Redeemer coalition. But the issue was never one of which Harris took ownership, minimizing the issue as a "mere bagatelle" in favor of party unity. But, in the late spring of 1882, observers felt that the low-taxers would gain control of the state Democratic convention that June. The Republican/state credit Democrat–passed 100–3 and 60–3–4–5–6 measures

56. Hart, *Redeemers, Bourbons and Populists*, 48–51; Hudspeth, "Seven Days in Nashville," 82–90; "The News in Washington," *Washington Post*, January 27, 1881.

57. Hart, *Redeemers, Bourbons and Populists*, 52–54, Hamer, ed., *Tennessee: A History, 1673–1932*, 2:689; "Politics in Tennessee," *New York Times*, July 6, 1882.

58. "Current Comment," *Washington Post*, December 10, 1881 (quoting *Memphis Avalanche*).

59. "The Topics Discussed," *Washington Post*, February 21, 1882.

caused substantial discontent among an electorate that had decisively rejected the 50–4 settlement less than 3 years before. Harris discreetly kept his counsel during this interval, but with his Senate seat on the line and the threat of the state credit Democrats joining with the Republicans on a long-term basis, some action was necessary to master the situation. Indeed, within the party, many saw Harris "as the Moses who is to lead the party out of the wilderness."[60]

Three weeks before the Democratic convention of June 1882, the *Nashville Daily American* published a short biographical sketch of Harris, which described his ability in this time of party turmoil, noting that among Harris's gifts was an "almost intuitive insight into the motives of men" and the "singular power to see through a subject or its surrounding circumstances almost at a glance," powers that Harris almost certainly used in 1882. As true as these observations were, though, the piece also mentioned that Harris's strong sense of duty meant "his course . . . never excites surprise, nor creates a feeling of disappointment among his associates."[61] Harris was indeed about to spring a surprise that would disappoint some of his associates, a change brought about by his constant sense of duty to his party.

As suggested some months before, there was talk that Harris would resign his seat in the Senate and run for governor on "an all comprehensive platform." But Harris had little or no interest in doing so. No one, in Tennessee or elsewhere, very often considered leaving the Senate for the governor's chair a promotion. When Harris was actually nominated at the convention, a friend on the floor announced that he "was absolutely directed by Mr. Harris to decline the nomination."[62] But Harris did not need to be the party's candidate for governor to move decisively. In a speech to open the convention, he acknowledged that the taxation (debt) issue was the "rock" that split the party in 1880. Shifting his position on the issue, he stated he preferred "to split the rock to allowing it to split and destroy the party."[63]

60. "Under the caption 'The Outlook' the Athens *Post* says," *Chattanooga Daily Times*, June 3, 1882; Hart, *Redeemers, Bourbons and Populists*, 53–55; Jones, *Tennessee at the Crossroads*, 138; "End of an Eventful Life"; "Tennessee Political Gossip," *Chattanooga Daily Times*, June 1, 1882.

61. "Representative Tennesseans," *Nashville Daily American*, May 26, 1882.

62. "Harmony at Nashville," *Washington Post*, June 21, 1882; Rothman, *Politics and Power*, 154–55; "The New Senator," *Nashville Daily American*, January 26, 1887; "Night Session," *Chattanooga Daily Times*, June 22, 1882.

63. "The Democrats," *Chattanooga Daily Times*, June 21, 1882; "Democratic Councils," *Nashville Daily American*, June 20, 1882; "End of an Eventful Life."

So far as I am concerned, I can say that I have as well defined opinions and as profound convictions as anyone who hears me; but profound as these convictions are, if a majority of the delegates, fresh from their respective constituencies, shall decide to settle at any reasonable figure other than the present act, I shall subordinate this to the many more important questions, and stand by the organization and battle for its success. Upon the slight difference between fifty and sixty, I cannot afford to turn from or desert that old time-honored Democratic banner. I am a Democrat from principle, have always been a Democrat, and expect to live and die a Democrat, and I appeal to you as Democrats to sacrifice the less in order that you may preserve the greater interest. Stand by your time-honored principles; you are the majority, the controlling element in the State; you must, as you alone can finally settle this issue.[64]

The convention nominated Bate for governor, and adopted a platform that rejected the 60–3–4–5–6 measure as "unwise, because it is, in our opinion, not in the accord with the views of the people." The platform called for the full payment, with accrued interest (less war interest) of the "state debt proper," defined as "the bonds, issued for building our capitol, for the purchase of the Hermitage, capitol, etc." It was proposed that the remainder of the debt be paid at 50 cents on the dollar, at a rate of 3 percent for 10 years, and 4 percent thereafter.[65]

Unhappy with the platform, one-fifth of the delegates walked out. These "Sky Blue Democrats," as they came to be known, were largely professional men of significant social status, who historian Roger L. Hart determined had a "genealogical relationship to each other, to other prestigious persons, and to leaders of previous generations."[66] Among the Sky Blues were Senator Jackson, ex-Senator Bailey, Cheatham, James D. Porter, future U.S. Supreme Court Justice Harold H. Lurton, and Campbell Brown, Harris's confidant of 1868. Holding a convention on July 11, the Sky Blues stated they were against repudiation, but were in favor of the 60–3–4–5–6 settlement. They nominated Joseph H. Fussell, a Maury County lawyer, as their candidate for governor.[67]

As would be expected, state credit proponents expressed disappointment with

64. "The Democrats"; "Democratic Councils."

65. White, *Messages of the Governors of Tennessee*, 7:7–9.

66. Hart, *Redeemers, Bourbons and Populists*, 61–63; "Politics in Tennessee."

67. Hart, *Redeemers, Bourbons and Populists*, 62n14; White, *Messages of the Governors of Tennessee*, 7:12–13.

Harris's switch. The *Nashville Banner* warned of a "Waterloo," and lectured the senator that "it is easy to plead the cause of the crowd, and to go with the tide." Harris's hometown *Paris Weekly Intelligencer*, however, chided the *Banner* by mocking that "a man could be a good and glorious Democrat for 40 years, and then if he fails to endorse a Republican settlement it is good bye." The *Nashville Daily American* felt that Harris had "the good sense to believe it is better, and indeed sounder State credit doctrine to pay what the people can be got to pay, than to brag about being for State credit and paying nothing." Effectively seeing matters in the same light as Harris, one outside observer was mystified by the dispute, noting that "the split has passed beyond argument or common sense, and the fight is to go on to the great delight of the republicans both at home and in Washington."[68]

In early July, Harris's prospects were pronounced dubious by the Nashville correspondent of the *New York Times*. On the one hand, an alliance between the Republicans and the state credit Democrats as occurred in 1881 would likely spell the end of his senatorial career, now that he was joined with Bate on the "state debt proper" ground. On the other, since on the grounds of party harmony Harris had joined the ranks of what the Sky Blue press called "repudiationists" or "Readjusters," he was now not only an ally of his old enemy Colyar, but operating on Savage's playing field. Savage felt that he had given Bate the nomination, and claimed that the platform of the June convention proved that the party had "come to him." Likewise, a Republican observer felt that while, as always, Harris marched under the banner of his party, "for the first time in his life he marched behind and not at the head of the column." The *Times's* correspondent reported that Harris again held out the olive branch to Savage, asking for his support in the upcoming Senate race. With some vehemence, Savage made it clear that he was a candidate for Harris's seat, thundering that "you have done little good for Tennessee during your stay in Washington and I would advise you to retire to your Texas farm and allow a better man to be chosen as your successor." The *Times's* correspondent felt that while it was unlikely Savage could win, he could prevent Harris's reelection.[69]

68. "Let Senator Harris beware" and "A Modest Contemporary on Senator Harris," *Nashville Banner*, June 21, 1882; "A Good-Bye," *Paris Weekly Intelligencer*, June 22, 1882; "Senator Harris and his Critics," *Nashville Daily American*, July 1, 1882; "Tennessee and Her Debt," *Atlanta Constitution*, July 13, 1882.

69. "Politics in Tennessee"; "Savage Says" and "John H. Savage," *Chattanooga Daily Times*, November 7, 1882; Temple, *Notable Men of Tennessee*, 449; see also Savage, *The Life of John H. Savage*, 165.

As proven by events, Harris had formulated his strategy with his usual political skill, although the campaign started with a misstep. The low-tax *Nashville World*, doubtless with the tacit if not actual approval of the Harris/Bate camp, issued a challenge that Jackson appear at Harris's appointments across the state and debate the issue. It appears Jackson desired to take up the challenge, ignoring warnings by a friend that such a course could damage the party. On August 27, Jackson wrote Harris a letter to the effect that if his colleague thought that the debate would injure his chances for reelection, they could "annul the arrangement." Harris somewhat stiffly replied the following day that it was for Jackson to determine what effect the debate would have.[70]

The debates therefore proceeded. A debate in Erin, in western Middle Tennessee, got nasty as each senator made reference to a letter written by the other in the past that undermined their present position. Jackson was confronted with a letter that endorsed the position Governor Marks took on the debt in his inaugural address, proving, to the *Appeal,* that he was "inconsistent as a bushwacker." For his part, Harris endured the production of his November 1877 letter to Governor Porter that condemned repudiation and hoped for the acceptance of a compromise of 60 cents on the dollar that was then a possibility. The Sky Blue press hammered Harris with the inconsistency. No friend of Harris in the best of times, Adolph S. Ochs of the *Chattanooga Daily Times* wrote: "How can he explain the letter here referred to, and make its bold, manly utterances consist with the shabby, shuffling, cowardly, dishonest Readjuster resolutions? Fine lawyer, debater and orator that he is, the Senator is not equal to convincing the dullest clodhopper that black is white, or that open and defiant robbery can be based on sound, legal or moral principles."[71]

With each side likely stung by reference to previous contradictory stands on the issue, the confrontation moved into West Tennessee and the antagonists traveled to Trenton, Troy, and Dyersburg. At Trenton, while each senator sought to ex-

70. "The Readjuster swaggering," *Chattanooga Daily Times*, August 29, 1882; "Why the Settlement Should Stand," *Chattanooga Daily Times*, September 4, 1882; B. M. Estes to Howell Jackson, August 28, 1882, Jackson to IGH, August 27, 1882, IGH to Jackson, August 28, 1882, Harding and Jackson Family Papers, Southern Historical Collection, UNC.

71. "Erin, Tenn," *Nashville Daily American*, September 3, 1882; "The State Canvass," *Memphis Daily Appeal*, September 3, 1882; "Our readers will find," *Memphis Daily Appeal*, September 9, 1882; "State Politics"; "Who's Afraid," *Chattanooga Daily Times*, August 23, 1882; "The Senatorial Debate" and "Writing Governor Porter," *Chattanooga Daily Times*, September 6, 1882.

plain his previous inconsistency, matters got a little nastier, as Jackson held that surrender of honest convictions in deference to party dictate was "base abandonment of the right of thought." For his part, Harris thundered that if Jackson had been in the military rather than in a political organization, he "would be shot for giving aid and comfort to the enemy." In keeping with his view of the state credit issue, Harris spent a great deal of time on tariffs, producing figures that it affected the economy much more profoundly than the trifle involved with the debt. Jackson stated he agreed with Harris on the tariff issue, but argued that the lack of trust engendered by repudiation might indeed affect the party nationally. At Dyersburg, Harris made his most telling point when he sneered that Fussell had "no more chance for election than he had to pluck the sun from the firmament and crush it under his little heel," and expressed his regret that Jackson "was engaged in an earnest effort to draw votes enough from the Democratic candidate to secure the triumph of Republicanism in Tennessee."[72]

Not surprisingly, evaluations of the effect of the speeches depended on the political sympathies of the newspapers reporting the same. Sky Blue papers held that Jackson was the better speaker and made the more logical points. In reporting on the debate at Trenton, the *Avalanche* stated that as Jackson laid down one argument after another, "Harris felt their effect and was considerably worried." The pro-Harris *Appeal* observed that the two speeches at Trenton were "widely different." The *Appeal* crowed, "Senator Harris's was electric, masterly and conclusive, and produced grand outbursts of applause from a delighted audience. Senator Jackson's speech was cold, lifeless and failed to produce a single utterance of applause or approval." In the view of the *Appeal,* "Harris is the greatest man on the stump in the South. Every gray hair upon his head seems to shake with eloquence."[73]

There was no speaking at Ripley on September 7, "owing to the sore lungs and hoarseness of both senators." On September 8, only Harris spoke at Covington, as it was reported Jackson's physician "strongly advised" him not to speak. Suddenly, on September 9, at Milan, the parties issued a joint statement that both concluded that their "joint discussion tends to so embitter the issue as to make difficult, if not impossible, to unite the party hereafter, and, therefore, we mutually agree

72. "Senator Harris," *Memphis Daily Appeal,* September 4, 1882; "Humboldt," *Memphis Avalanche,* September 14, 1882; "Trenton," *Memphis Avalanche,* September 5, 1882; "Senator Harris," *Memphis Daily Appeal,* September 7, 1882.

73. "Trenton," *Nashville Daily American,* September 5, 1882; "Senator Harris," *Memphis Daily Appeal,* September 4, 1882; "Howell E. Jackson," *Memphis Daily Appeal,* September 5, 1882.

to have no more joint discussions." Matters had gotten so acrimonious that each side suggested that the other had thrown in the towel. According to the Sky Blue press, Harris realized that continuation of the debates might injure his efforts at reelection, and asked Jackson, as a "brother and a friend," to agree to cancel. Harris "denounced" the account as "basely false." Harris's main political organ, the *Memphis Daily Appeal*, stated that Jackson was "so punished that he threw up the sponge."[74]

Thereafter, Harris proceeded across Middle and West Tennessee, giving his speech on tariffs and other national issues to enthusiastic crowds. Harris's strategy restricted his speaking engagements to traditionally Democratic Middle and West Tennessee. The senator kept an ambitious schedule until late October, when he finally was stopped by an illness. The strain of the canvass was enormous, as a correspondent who saw Harris three years later said he looked ten years younger than he did in 1882. Having ended his debate with Jackson, Harris was not interested in debating Savage, who was openly running against him for senator as they both stumped for Bate. Harris basically ignored Savage, in expectation that the extreme nature of "the old war horse of the mountain" would prove to be his undoing. In one article, after begrudgingly acknowledging Harris as a man of "ability" and "respectable and honorable as a gentleman," Sky Blue Chattanooga editor Ochs characterized Savage "as a gambler by nature and training, a fraud in every sense, a pigmy in intellect, and totally destitute of moral sense."[75]

The Sky Blues were horrified by a political arrangement forged in Memphis

74. "The Senators," *Nashville Daily American,* September 8, 1882; "Tipton Aroused," *Memphis Daily Appeal,* September 9, 1882; "Joint Discussion," *Memphis Daily Appeal,* September 10, 1882; "Political," *Nashville Daily American,* September 10, 1882; "Harris Growing Weary," *Chattanooga Daily Times,* September 14, 1882; "The Readjuster organs," *Chattanooga Daily Times,* September 15, 1882; "The Outlook," *Paris Weekly Intelligencer,* September 28, 1882; "Senator Jackson as a Leader," *Memphis Daily Appeal,* September 14, 1882.

75. White, *Messages of the Governors of Tennessee,* 7:18; Hart, *Redeemers, Bourbons and Populists,* 69; "Senator Harris," *Memphis Daily Appeal,* September 12, 1882; "Senator Harris," *Nashville Daily American,* September 16, 1882; "Senator Harris," *Memphis Avalanche,* October 8, 1882; "Senator Isham G. Harris," *Chattanooga Daily Times,* October 6, 1882; "Illness of Senator Harris," *New York Times,* October 31, 1882; "The Senior Senator," *Nashville Daily American,* September 9, 1885; "Senator Harris" and "Harris' committee and Harris are both 'afraid,'" *New York Times,* October 27, 1882; "Meanwhile Savage, the old war horse of the mountain" and "Harris and Savage," *New York Times,* August 28, 1882; Savage, *The Life of John H. Savage,* 165; Jones, *Tennessee at the Crossroads,* 138–39; "The Hon. John H. Savage," *Chattanooga Daily Times,* October 13, 1882.

between the Harris/Bate Bourbons and Edward Shaw, an influential political leader of Memphis's African American community. While Shaw, like most of his race, was Republican, he had a history of taking an independent course when he deemed that party was taking his people for granted. Harris paternalistically recognized Shaw as "a very bright and able colored man." Coming out for the low-tax Democrats in October, Shaw's price was a place for two black candidates in the legislature on Bate's ticket. While the deal was billed by the *Appeal* as uniting "low-tax Republicans" with "low-tax Democrats for Bate and Senator Harris," the Sky Blue *Chattanooga Daily Times* sniffed that the deal was another example of "substituting expediency for principle," and the *Memphis Avalanche* deemed the new coalition "an unholy alliance."[76]

Black political power had been on the wane since the fall of the Radical regime, although in the 1870s an African American was actually elected to the General Assembly. But the election of Hawkins in 1880 and the Republicans' failure to respond to black demands for patronage and education improvements irritated Shaw and others. Shaw saw in the state debt controversy an opportunity to cut a deal with the Harris/Bate faction of the Democratic Party for a fusion ticket in Shelby County. While, in the end, Shaw was able to shift about a thousand votes Harris's way, the two black "fusion" candidates were defeated. The senator's relationship with Shaw was deemed by his opponents as a gross example of "machine" politics. Harris, to whom one of the African American members of Shaw's faction felt the "warmest ties," later nominated Shaw for a Federal customs post at Memphis. This resulted in more criticism than even Harris could handle, and eventually the senator withdrew his support for the nomination, lamely observing that qualified blacks were needed for such government posts.[77]

In the end, Shaw's support had little positive effect for his race, except that it did stimulate their participation in political activity. In the 1880s, a few black legislators were elected to the General Assembly, but white attitudes began to change from paternalism to hostility, and the most vocal of the black legislators eventually had to leave the state. The legislature elected in 1888 was solidly under Democratic control, and it began a systematic effort to disfranchise and segregate the blacks from politics and white society. Literacy tests that only applied to the

76. Bergeron, Ash, and Keith, *Tennesseans and Their History*, 171–72; Jones, *Tennessee at the Crossroads*, 139; Cartwright, *The Triumph of Jim Crow*, 25; "A Political Medley," *Chattanooga Daily Times*, October 12, 1882; "An Unholy Alliance," *Memphis Avalanche*, October 5, 1882.

77. Cartwright, *The Triumph of Jim Crow*, 23–51.

urban areas and poll taxes suppressed the right to vote. Segregation in the schools was already a fact; to it was added segregation on the railroads. Lynchings helped make segregation a de facto code in matters where an actual statute was not involved. By 1890, Harris and the Democrats no longer had to include black voters in their political calculations.[78]

The results of the election of 1882 confirmed the soundness of Harris's political judgment. In speeches, he accused the Sky Blues of "bolting" over difference of one "poor little copper cent." Contrasting the low-tax "bolt" in 1880 to the Sky Blue "bolt" in 1882, Harris said the former was "a large bolt to the people" while the latter was "a small-sized bolt to the bondholder." This said it all. The senator was able to read the political tea-leaves and ascertain that for the typical Democrat, the small percentage difference in the low-tax Democratic platform and the 60–3–4–5–6 solution espoused by the Republicans and Sky Blues was not worth further fracturing the party or keeping the Republicans in power. In the November 1882 election, Bate defeated Governor Hawkins by over 28,000 votes. The Sky Blue candidate, Fussell, received only 4,599 votes, more than 4,000 less than the Greenback candidate, John R. Beasley. Furthermore, not a single Sky Blue candidate was elected to the legislature. The *Appeal* crowed the result was "complete, decisive, grand and glorious." Having perceived in September that Harris's fence-mending in 1876 had won the decisive allegiance of the old Unionist Democrats, the *Avalanche* begrudgingly gave the senator credit for tipping the balance in the struggle with the Sky Blues, and discerned "an implied instruction" by the electorate to return him to the Senate, as "he is the best man for it by all odds and there should be no nonsense about this business."[79]

The overwhelming victory of the low-tax wing seems to have misled some observers into thinking that Savage had gained decisive leverage in his personal crusade against Harris. Savage worked hard to give the impression that he had a significant chance, claiming he had thirty votes in the legislature with him to the

78. Ibid., 40–41, 161–76, 255; Bergeron, Ash, and Keith, *Tennesseans and Their History,* 194–99.

79. White, *Messages of the Governors of Tennessee,* 7:21; "Senator Harris," *Memphis Avalanche,* October 8, 1882; "What Democrats Would Have Consented to in June," *Chattanooga Daily Times,* September 6, 1882; "Sky-Blew," *Memphis Avalanche,* November 8, 1882; "The Fussellites Fail," *Chattanooga Daily Times,* November 11, 1882; Hart, *Redeemers, Bourbons and Populists,* 69–70; Jones, *Tennessee at the Crossroads,* 140; "It is astonishing that the Appeal," *Memphis Avalanche,* September 8, 1882; "The Avalanche will keep its weather eye," *Memphis Avalanche,* November 9, 1882.

bitter end, "eternally against a caucus." He convinced the correspondent of the *New York Times* that the election would be "close and bitter." Always a good interviewee, Savage told the correspondent that he felt both Jefferson Davis and Harris should have been hanged for their "d——d foolishness" during the war, and once more accused Harris of impeding his promotion, claiming Harris stated he had his "foot on [Savage's] neck." As an outsider sizing up the senatorial field, however, the *Times* correspondent recognized that Harris was "undoubtedly the shrewdest politician among [the candidates] and will leave nothing undone to outgeneral his opponents."[80]

The General Assembly voted for senator on January 16, 1883. Harris outpolled Savage 17–5 in the Senate and 59–9 in the House, and outpolled the nearest Republican candidate by a substantial margin, and was thereby for the second time elected senator on the first ballot.[81] That night, Harris appeared at Nashville's Maxwell House and expressed satisfaction that the position he had taken on the debt the previous June had been vindicated. Grateful for the honor, he stated that once he finished the term to which he was elected, he would "step down and out of the political arena and into private life."[82]

The state debt controversy fractured the postwar Redeemer coalition in 1878, and the intervening four years were a time when the disunity of the Democratic Party made it possible for both black and white Republicans, by playing one faction against the other, to assert more influence than they would for the rest of the century. The election of 1882, which returned Green Harris to the Senate with a renewed mandate and put General William B. Bate in the governor's chair, brought Tennessee's Bourbons into control of the state's majority party. The term *Bourbon* had a different meaning in Tennessee than it did on the wider national stage. Historian Roger Hart has noted the difference between the "ingrained conservatism" of Tennessee's Bourbons and the more expansive view of the term as it was used nationally, which included a pro-business component.[83]

Modern historians of this era in Tennessee politics give Harris significant credit for disposing of the irksome debt question and restoring Democratic unity

---

80. "It is said Savage has counted," *Chattanooga Daily Times*, December 16, 1882; "The Tennessee Senatorship," *New York Times*, December 30, 1882; "Harris Favored in Tennessee," *New York Times*, January 11, 1883.

81. "Isham G. Harris," *Chattanooga Daily Times*, January 17, 1883.

82. "Speaking Last Night," *Nashville Daily American*, January 17, 1882.

83. Hart, *Redeemers, Bourbons and Populists*, 31, 48–56.

and therefore party dominance in the state.[84] There is no reason to question that conclusion. A Democrat from first to last, Harris saw the adverse results of party disunity in the election of Maynard as congressman in 1872, Hawkins as governor in 1880, and the near election of Maynard as senator in 1881. The passage of the 100–3 and the 60–3–4–5–6 measures came from the unholy alliance of state credit Democrats with Republicans. Like others, Harris saw the overwhelming rejection of the 50–4 proposal in Governor Marks's 1879 referendum as a strong indication that some degree of repudiation was the only way to settle the issue once and for all. Accordingly, Harris switched sides, minimized the extent of his change of heart ("one poor little copper cent"), and focused on the practical consequences of the dispute—disproportionate Republican influence, if not continued Republican rule. He cannot be faulted for recognizing, as did others, that loss of party unity over the debt question meant his senatorial career was placed in jeopardy by the ongoing dispute. In the midst of the 1882 campaign, he withstood the bitterest attacks from his natural allies, the Sky Blue men of the party, as well as the shrill Savage. Having shrewdly "outgeneraled" the opposition on both sides, Harris built a new Bourbon coalition that was the basis for Democratic unity in the following years. Green Harris was therefore entitled to his restored preeminence in the Tennessee Democratic Party, a preeminence he was able to retain, along with his Senate seat, to the end of his long life.

84. Ibid., 54–55 ("If any one man saved the Democratic party in 1882, it was Senator Harris"); Corlew, *Tennessee: A Short History*, 360 ("Isham G. Harris and other Bourbons welded the party together sufficiently to elect Bate"); Jones, *Tennessee at the Crossroads*, 138, 143–44 (Harris's "easy re-election was a manifestation of Democratic unity based on the debt plank shaped at the June convention"); Bergeron, Ash, and Keith, *Tennesseans and Their History*, 205 (the Democratic Party was reunified "under Isham Harris's leadership").

10 "THE OLD MAN INVINCIBLE"
1883–1897

In a letter to a friend in early 1884, Harris complained that he was becoming increasingly "disgusted with modern politics and modern politicians." Lamenting that neither party adhered "to the old landmarks," Harris felt that the Democrats were almost no better than the Republicans in observing the constitutional limits on the powers of Congress, and that he was a minority in his own party. He hoped that the election of his friend, Senator Joseph E. McDonald of Indiana, would result in a return to "sound democratic cardinal principles."[1] These two "cardinal principles . . . [which were] of paramount importance to all others" were described to a newspaper as "the doctrine of strict construction which should confine the action of Congress solely to the powers intrusted to it by the Constitution." Not surprisingly, Harris's other principle was "the doctrine of a tariff for revenue, and for such an amount of revenue only as may be necessary to support the Government, economically administered, when added to the legitimate internal revenue from whiskey and tobacco."[2] Much of Harris's second term was spent vindicating these two principles, sometimes putting him in the minority even among Southern senators, and extending, for a time, his conflict with the Sky Blue faction at home.

One of the hallmarks of the Blue Sky faction was the advocacy of many of its members of the "New South" ideal. Under this concept, which started in the 1870s and gained momentum in the 1880s and 1890s, the South's ample natural resources and cheap native white laborers would be combined with favorable government policy to achieve economic growth through industrialization. One of the principal proponents of the concept in Tennessee was Harris's occasional rival,

1. IGH to Jonathan S. Claybrooke, February 29, 1884, Claybrooke–Overton Papers, TSLA.
2. "Two Cardinal Principles," *Washington Post*, May 20, 1884.

Arthur S. Colyar, who owned significant coal and iron interests. Although Colyar's industrial interests were on the Cumberland Plateau in the southeastern part of Middle Tennessee, the primary area targeted for such development was in East Tennessee, where timber, coal, and water power combined with suspected deposits of iron ore. Indeed, the two main cities of that section, Knoxville and Chattanooga, became centers of speculative economic activity. Although Harris was generally opposed to the politicians advocating the New South concept, he retained a streak of entrepreneurship from his younger days. In 1891, he invested in a Georgia gold mine and was active in an effort to build a "manufacturing city" at Elizabethton, Tennessee.[3]

While New South industrialization did not change the fact that most Tennesseans during the era made their living from farming, just as their ancestors did, many worked in cotton mills, flour mills, iron production, coal mining, and timber operations. Cities with such operations, such as Nashville, Chattanooga, and Knoxville, grew and encouraged Northern or even foreign investment. But the fact of Northern investment meant that Tennesseans in industry were generally working at low wages for outsiders, who did little to keep the money they earned in the state there to foster further development. The state government did little to help its industrial working class. In 1891, coal miners in Anderson County in East Tennessee protested against the use of convict labor in the mines, which threatened their livelihood. Armed miners sent the convicts and their guards to Knoxville. The state government, which made good money off of leasing convicts, sent in troops to disperse the miners. When the miners refused to back down, a special session of the legislature was promised for August 1891 to deal with the issue of convict leasing.[4]

While the Republicans were typically for industrial interests, in the special session they recognized that the miners were among their constituents. Few in

3. Hart, *Redeemers, Bourbons and Populists*, 56, 79, 84–85, 95, 100–101; Bergeron, Ash, and Keith, *Tennesseans and Their History*, 182–84; Constantine G. Belissary, "The Rise of Industry and the Industrial Spirit in Tennessee, 1865–1885," *Journal of Southern History* 19 (May 1953): 193–215; Ronald D. Eller, *Miners, Millhands, and Mountaineers: Industrialization of the Appalachian South, 1880–1930* (Knoxville: University of Tennessee Press, 1982), 41–45, 52–53; Ball, "The Public Career of A. S. Colyar, 1870–1877," 216–17; Karin A. Shapiro, *A New South Rebellion: The Battle Against Convict Labor in the Tennessee Coalfields, 1871–1896* (Chapel Hill: University of North Carolina Press, 1998), 21–23; "Georgia Gold," *Atlanta Constitution*, March 13, 1891; Advertisement for The Cooperative Town Company, *Washington Post*, August 2, 1891; "Town Site Selected," *Washington Post*, November 7, 1891.

4. Eller, *Miners, Millhands, and Mountaineers*, 85; Bergeron, Ash, and Keith, *Tennesseans and Their History*, 186–94, 199–202.

the Democratic Party, including Harris's faction, had much sympathy for the Republican-voting miners. The legislature actually passed legislation that made it illegal to interfere with convict leasing. But the miners again refused to back down, and by 1893, convict leasing, which was supposed to save the state money housing and feeding the prisoners, actually cost it more in money spent to pay and maintain the militia in the disaffected area. Convict leasing was voted out, and the last lease expired in 1896. To the miners, at least, the New South concept meant privilege for outside corporate interests and unequal relations between capital and labor.[5]

The early part of Harris's second term was of little import. Things in Tennessee were quiet, for the time being, and the final months of Chester Arthur's administration brought few initiatives that stirred Harris to action. Because he was the leading Democrat of Tennessee, national newspapers sought his opinion on the party's potential candidates in the 1884 election. As indicated, Harris favored his former Senate colleague, Joseph E. McDonald, stating that regardless of the injustice done to Tilden, there was little support for him in Tennessee. Harris was not in New York Governor Grover Cleveland's camp, "for he is too little known in the politics of the country. A candidate should be taken from among persons sufficiently identified with the politics of the country for their principles to be well and generally understood."[6]

Harris's support of his friend McDonald was fruitless. Although the senator went to Tennessee to work for McDonald the summer of 1884, the Democratic nomination went to Grover Cleveland, who eventually won the election. Harris was not in Tennessee enough during the fall campaign season to satisfy some Democrats; indeed, Bate was in a closer election than must have been anticipated, receiving fewer votes in the general election in the state than did Cleveland.[7] Even though Harris's support for Cleveland was lukewarm, he lost no time in contacting the president-elect to recommend Senator Augustus Hill Garland of

5. Bergeron, Ash, and Keith, *Tennesseans and Their History*, 199–202; Shapiro, *A New South Rebellion*, 91, 122–23, 126–27, 130–32, 246.

6. "The Political Outlook," *Washington Post*, May 29, 1883. See also "The Presidential Candidates," *New York Times*, July 10, 1883; "Tennessee," *New York Times*, July 16, 1883.

7. "Tennessee Democrats" and "Cleveland's Great Boom," *New York Times*, June 17, 1884; "Hon. Isham G. Harris," *Paris Post Intelligencer*, July 20, 1888; Hart, *Redeemers, Bourbons and Populists*, 80; "The President's Mot," *Washington Post*, March 22, 1885; "The Tennessee Muddle," *Washington Post*, April 5, 1885.

Arkansas for attorney general, and in gathering testimonials in support of an unsuccessful effort to have Whitthorne appointed secretary of the navy.[8] At Maryland Senator Arthur Pue Gorman's suggestion, Harris was considered with other Southern senators as a possible cabinet candidate by Cleveland, who eventually selected Mississippi's L. Q. C. Lamar to serve as secretary of the interior.[9]

The four thousand-vote difference between the votes garnered by Cleveland in Tennessee and those received by Bate in his close race in 1884 illustrated that in a tight race, the remnants of the Sky Blues had disproportionate influence. After the election, the split in the Tennessee Democracy made national news when James D. Porter was nominated as first assistant secretary of state. Members of the Bourbon faction grumbled that Porter had not "worked for the regular party nominees" in the last election, calling national attention to the political fallout from the state debt controversy. While there was some speculation that Harris would make this an issue in connection with the nomination, in the end he did not oppose Porter's confirmation. While publicly Harris let Porter pass, his true views were likely reflected by Whitthorne, who commented that both Porter and Senator Jackson were not part of the true Democracy of Tennessee. Porter replied that Whitthorne's "malevolence . . . was without influence" in Tennessee. The episode ended with Whitthorne sending a challenge, which was declined.[10]

It is difficult to ascertain whether the Porter incident damaged the relationship between Tennessee's senior senator and leading Democrat and the president. Certainly, Cleveland consulted Harris on matters of patronage in Tennessee, although Harris protested that the choices were not his but those of the "Tennessee Democracy." And Harris made sure it was known that he admired the president, stating that "while the conditions were initially not very favorable to mutual friendship, . . . the more I see of his unwavering honesty and good faith, the better I like him." But the Porter appointment and a later one involving the appoint-

8. IGH to Grover Cleveland, November 25, 1884, George Morgan to IGH, December 20, 1884, enclosing Morgan to Grover Cleveland, December 20, 1884, S. P. Carter to IGH, December 31, 1884, B. B. Lewis to IGH, January 20, 1885, all in Grover Cleveland Papers.

9. Allan Nevins, *Grover Cleveland: A Study in Courage* (New York: Dodd, Mead & Co., 1933), 193–94; John R. Lambert, *Arthur Pue Gorman* (Baton Rouge: Louisiana State University Press 1953), 115; see also "Original and Otherwise," *Washington Post*, December 13, 1884.

10. "The President's Mot"; "The Office Seekers Going Home," *New York Times*, March 21, 1885; "Sent to the Senate," *Washington Post*, March 21, 1885; "The Tennessee Muddle," *Washington Post*, April 5, 1885; "The Dissentions in Tennessee," *Washington Post*, April 18, 1885; "Mr. Porter Challenged," *Washington Post*, April 23, 1885.

ment of J. H. Wagner of Knoxville, a member of the 1865 Tennessee legislature who voted to disenfranchise Confederates and outlaw Harris, illustrate that while publicly and ceremonially Cleveland and Harris maintained cordial relations, they did not always see eye to eye. As a New Yorker, Cleveland likely had a dim view of Tennessee's debt readjustment, and therefore favored Sky Blues such as Porter and Senator Jackson. But Jackson, likely anticipating that his seat was targeted by Bate in 1887, decided to accept an appointment to the Federal bench in 1886. Governor Bate appointed the loyal Whitthorne as a place holder for the remainder of Jackson's term. While Harris protested he had nothing to do with Whitthorne's appointment, it certainly cemented his control of Federal patronage in Tennessee. A hostile article in the *New York Times* that August described the extent of Harris's influence, noting the various government employments of Harris's sons and nephews. Harris purported high-handedness was denounced as "not only bad policy but bad politics, and has increased the popular sentiment against King Harris."[11]

One of the obvious benefits of patronage was the ability to confer Federal positions on various relatives. At various points during his twenty years in the Senate, three of Harris's four remaining sons were employed by the government. Harris's eldest surviving son, James E. H. Harris, was the assistant postmaster of Memphis. Sons Charles and Edward were employed by the Senate bureaucracy, one or the other being employed by Harris's man John C. Burch as a clerk and the other working for the Committee on Epidemic Diseases. When the Republicans regained control of the Senate, employment by the body's bureaucracy became problematic, occasioning an effort to secure a son's employment, probably Edward's, as an auditor in the Treasury Department. Cleveland balked at the idea of government employment for senators' sons, but it is likely Harris found other employment for the young man. Eventually, Charles ended up as his father's private secretary. Harris even managed a place for nephew Warren F. Travis, who was appointed to a position in California, and other nephews had political aspirations in West Tennessee thanks to their connection with the senator. Only young Isham was in a private endeavor, running the Texas sheep ranch. Harris was not alone

11. IGH to Grover Cleveland, May 2, 1893, Cleveland Papers, LC; "The Senior Senator," *Nashville Daily American*, September 9, 1885 ; "The Man Senator Harris Indorsed," *New York Times*, October 24, 1886; "Secretary Lamar's Stand," *Washington Post,* October 24, 1886; "Cheer from Tennessee," *Atlanta Constitution*, April 7, 1885; "The President Will Attend," *Washington Post,* July 25, 1885; "Mr. Whitthorne's Appointment," *Washington Post,* April 19, 1886; "Senator Whitthorne," *Washington Post,* April 17, 1887; "Buying the Negro Vote," *New York Times*, August 24, 1886 (King Harris).

in his nepotism, as Senators Mahone, McMillian, Lapham, and George also found employment for their sons in Senate offices.[12]

Another point of conflict in the maneuvering between the Bourbons and the Sky Blues in Tennessee in the mid-1880s was the issue of railroad regulation. Businessmen in the smaller towns of Tennessee paid more to ship a barrel of flour to Nashville than a merchant in Nashville did to a point far out of state. Harris's allies in the Tennessee legislature passed a law establishing a railroad commission, headed by, of all people, John H. Savage. But the railroads had powerful adherents among the Sky Blues, such as Porter and Colyar, and with Republican assistance the railroad interests frustrated Savage's efforts.[13]

While railroad regulation was a partisan issue in Tennessee, it was effectively nonpartisan in the U.S. Congress. In 1884, an interstate commerce bill was introduced by Republican Senator Shelby M. Cullom for the purpose of regulating the railroads. A similar bill with significant differences was passed by the House, and when the conference committee could not agree, Cullom engineered a resolution appointing a committee to take evidence on the proposed legislation. Cullom and two other Republicans, and Gorman and Harris, representing the Democrats, traveled about the country in 1885 taking evidence relative to railroad practices and rates, and how they affected the business community. By the time of the last stop in Atlanta, Harris was the only member still on the trail, as Cullom, who was scheduled to be there, was absent. Interviewed by a reporter for the *Atlanta Constitution*, Harris opined that he thought a national commission with no power to fix rates, but with power to address discrimination, should be created. Each railroad should be compelled to post its rates at stations to put the public on notice of the rates. Harris also advocated prohibiting charging more for short hauls than long ones, but he doubted he could get the committee to agree. The need, in the Tennessean's mind, was a practical remedy. Questioned closely about the states' rights implications, Harris wryly answered that he had been "accounted an extremist in that regard" but this legislation was "clearly within" the interstate com-

12. "The News at Washington," *New York Times*, June 7, 1881; "Current Capital Notes," *Washington Post*, June 21, 1883; "The Senate Rules Committee," *New York Times*, July 10, 1883; "Senator's Sons Barred Out," *New York Times*, October 17, 1886; "About Senator's Sons," *New York Times*, January 11, 1884; "Buying the Negro Vote," *New York Times*, August 24, 1886; Hart, *Redeemers, Bourbons and Populists*, 157; "Political Gossip," *Washington Post*, December 2, 1896; "Grim Death Claims a Great Statesman," *Chattanooga Daily Times*, July 9, 1897.

13. Hart, *Redeemers, Bourbons and Populists*, 72–79.

merce powers of the Congress. The legislation was enacted in early 1887, and had a promising start in the remaining years of Cleveland's first term. The effectiveness of the Interstate Commerce Commission began to decline under President Harrison, and was not to be revitalized until early in the 1900s.[14]

Although Harris's concept of limited Federal power was not offended by the Interstate Commerce Act, he remained jealous of states' rights, especially when this political touchstone became enmeshed with the Tennessean's other "cardinal principle." From the very start of his political career, Green Harris opposed tariff policy that raised prices on imported goods to protect Eastern business interests at the expense of his constituents. He campaigned against tariffs in 1876 and made it a central theme of his 1882 canvass. Indeed, by the mid-1880s, high tariffs created an embarrassing, if not economically unhealthy, surplus for the Federal government. Seeking to address the issue, on December 3, 1883, Senator Henry W. Blair of New Hampshire introduced a bill to "aid in the establishment and temporary support of the common schools." The tariff surplus would be spent aiding education in the various states in proportion to their degree of illiteracy.[15]

Positions taken for or against the bill transcended party lines. In the Senate of 1884, 75 percent of the Republicans and 60 percent of the Democrats supported the measure. Southern Democrats supported the bill on the grounds that the increased burden of educating the newly enfranchised African American segments of their population justified the expenditures. Republicans who opposed it thought it unfair, among other reasons, that so much of the money would go to the Southern states. A Northern Democrat opposed the bill on the grounds that it was a device to sugarcoat the tariff.[16] While the bill was proposed in each Con-

14. Rothman, *Politics and Power,* 84; "Interstate Commerce," *Atlanta Constitution,* November 19, 1885; "Interstate Commerce," *Atlanta Constitution,* November 20, 1885; Nevins, *Grover Cleveland,* 355–57; James Ford Rhodes, *History of the United States from Hayes to McKinley, 1877–1896* (New York: Macmillan, 1919), 291–92; Lambert, *Arthur Pue Gorman,* 129–31. Harris's view relative to the power of Congress to regulate interstate commerce in this instance was effectively confirmed a year later in *Wabash, St. L. & P. Ry. Co. v. Illinois,* 118 U.S. 557 (1886), when the Supreme Court struck down an Illinois law seeking to regulate interstate railroad rates.

15. Dan M. Robison, "Governor Robert L. Taylor and the Blair Educational Bill in Tennessee," *Tennessee Historical Magazine* Series II, vol. 2 (October 1931): 28, 29.

16. Rothman, *Politics and Power,* 86; Robison, "Governor Robert L. Taylor and the Blair Educational Bill in Tennessee," 33–34.

gress from 1883 to 1893, and passed the Senate several times, it never passed the House.[17]

Harris was among the relatively small minority in the Senate to oppose the bill, first on the constitutional ground that the Federal government had no power to tax for the purpose of appropriating money "to this purely State purpose of maintaining a system of common schools." Second, Harris maintained that the money was collected from tariffs that he considered to be unfair, "the practical operation of which, to get $1 into the Treasury they are compelled to pay many dollars in the way of bounty to the protected home manufacturers, and the poorest man often compelled to pay as much as the most wealthy." Harris deemed it the "most dangerous political heresy of the day," as it involved "principles of centralization and so-called paternal government." He reminded those who deemed his position as adverse to education that it was he who had struggled to keep the School Fund intact during the war. At one point, Harris moved to amend the bill's title to "A bill offering a bribe to the States to relinquish the rights of local self government." Senator Jackson, on the other hand, spoke in favor of the measure, indicating that the issue was the next threat to the unity of the Tennessee Democracy, a conclusion buttressed by the fact that in 1885, the Tennessee Senate voted to instruct Harris and Jackson to support the Blair bill, while a similar resolution failed by only one vote in the Tennessee House.[18]

An effort to help out an old friend started a cycle of bad publicity, lawsuits, and a congressional investigation, even as the Blair bill issue simmered. Dr. J. W. Rogers of Memphis, whom Harris had known for over thirty years, had a son, J. Harris Rogers, who developed patents relating to the newly developing telephone technology. The elder Rogers was something of a character, being both an Episcopal priest and a poet, and was considered by some as visionary and by others a crank. Having failed at an initial effort to gain financing on Wall Street, Dr. Rogers turned to his old friend the senator, who thought the inventions had promise. Rogers suggested J. D. C. Atkins as a participant, and Harris said he would have to have control over who else was involved. Rogers concurred, and Harris agreed to

17. Watters, "Isham Green Harris," 161–62.

18. "At the National Capital," *New York Times,* March 8, 1886; *Cong. Record,* 49th Cong., 1st Sess., 1886, 1644; *Cong. Record,* 50th Cong., 1st Sess., 1888, 1221; "The Senior Senator," *Nashville Daily American,* September 9, 1885 (heresy); "Senator Jackson's Position," *Nashville Daily American,* September 10, 1885; Hart, *Redeemers, Bourbons and Populists,* 93–94; Robison, "Governor Robert L. Taylor and the Blair Educational Bill in Tennessee," 38.

Atkins and General Joseph E. Johnston. Atkins later suggested Senator Augustus Hill Garland of Arkansas and Rogers's former congressman Casey Young.[19]

The Pan-Electric Telephone Company was organized on March 13, 1883, with Johnston as president and Young as secretary-treasurer. The nominal capitalization of the company was young Rogers's patents, which were assigned an arbitrary value of $5,000,000. Although it was intended the company would be chartered in New York or New Jersey, the lack of paid-in capital resulted in the charter being obtained in Tennessee. The company began to sell territorial rights, and in at least one instance, guaranteed to defend any suits for infringement by Bell Telephone. Several newspaper articles appeared in the spring of 1884, noting the new territories, a line between Washington and New York, and the company's first dividend.[20]

Difficulties arose when Bell challenged the company over patent rights. They were compounded when the mercurial Rogers filed a suit against Garland, Harris, Atkins, Johnston, and Young, seeking a judicial dissolution of the business and an accounting. Meanwhile, there were efforts to have the government bring suit to invalidate certain of Bell's patents, and Rogers suggested as much to Garland, who, by that time, was attorney general. Rogers also wrote Harris a letter urging that he use his influence in that regard dated May 23, 1883, but Harris received the letter and quickly discarded it, attaching, he claimed, no importance to it.[21]

Depending on a newspaper's party affiliation, the actors, including Harris, were either pummeled or supported in the uproar that followed. Eventually, the government did bring suit, in fact, more than once, but Bell ultimately prevailed. On account of so many highly placed personages being involved, a congressional investigation ensued, and all of the principal actors, including Harris, testified, although Harris seems to have been accorded considerable deference by the committee. Harris specifically denied any intention or action to use his official position to profit the company. Eventually, on June 30, 1886, a majority of the committee issued a finding that exonerated Harris and the other official or ex-official actors

19. "Senator Harris as a Witness," *New York Times,* April 1, 1886; Frank B. Williams, "The Pan-Electric Telephone Controversy," *Tennessee Historical Quarterly* 2 (June 1943): 144–45.

20. Williams, "The Pan-Electric Telephone Controversy," 145–46; "New Telephone Company," *Washington Post,* March 7, 1884; "Telephoning Between Washington and New York," *Washington Post,* May 12, 1884; "The Pan Electric Company's Dividend," *Washington Post,* July 27, 1884.

21. Williams, "The Pan-Electric Telephone Controversy," 148–49; "The Pan-Electric Case," *Washington Post,* December 18, 1888; "Senator Harris as a Witness," *New York Times,* April 1, 1886.

from anything "dishonest, dishonorable, or censurable." In the end, while the episode must have been highly disagreeable, it did Harris little political damage.[22]

With Harris's support, Bate was elected to Tennessee's second seat in the Senate upon the expiration of his second term as governor in early 1887. The former
general was succeeded as governor by Robert Love Taylor, a charismatic young
Democrat who had been born in 1850. While he came from a political family,
its East Tennessee roots helped keep him independent of the struggle between
Sky Blues (or "mugwumps") and the Bourbons. He was able to win the Democratic nomination for governor in 1886 over former Confederate General and
ex-Congressman George G. Dibrell, Harris's favorite, Robert F. Looney of Memphis, and T. M. McConnell of Chattanooga. Looney likely suffered from the adverse publicity of the Pan-Electric mess. Taylor won the governor's race against his
brother, future Governor Alfred A. Taylor, in one of the most colorful campaigns
in Tennessee history, known thereafter as the "War of the Roses."[23]

During the 1886 campaign, a frustrated Sky Blue Democrat wrote the *New
York Times* making it clear that Taylor was not part of Harris's faction, but was
"one who has advocated unceasingly the preservation of the State's honor, and
has had the courage to proclaim openly against the antiquated heirloom of antebellum Bourbonism, Isham G. Harris, the *bete noir* of Tennessee politics."[24] Taylor
straddled the issue of the Blair bill during the election, even to the point of fool-
ing the Bourbon organ the *Nashville Daily American,* but tepidly came out for the
funding afterward, which, with certain of his political appointments, proved he
was independent of Harris and the Bourbons. With Taylor in power, the Bourbon
dominance of state politics established in 1882 appeared in danger. While the
Bourbons were able to make his nomination difficult in 1888, Taylor was eventually the nominee and was reelected that year. But notwithstanding his individual

22. Williams, "The Pan-Electric Telephone Controversy," 149–61; "Senator Harris as a Witness,"
New York Times, April 1, 1886; "The Telephone Hearing," *New York Times,* March 14, 1886; "Rogers
Tells His Story," *Washington Post,* March 18, 1886; "Col. Young Denies It," *Washington Post,* March 21,
1886; "Complete Vindication," *Washington Post,* July 1, 1886; "The Telephone Inquiry," *New York
Times,* July 1, 1886.

23. "Tennessee's Next Senator," *New York Times,* January 1, 1887; "Tennessee's Senator-Elect,"
New York Times, January 26, 1887; "The Two Taylors," *Atlanta Constitution,* September 10, 1886; Hart,
Redeemers, Bourbons and Populists, 84–92; Daniel M. Robison, "The Political Background of Tennes-
see's War of the Roses," *East Tennessee Historical Society Publications* 5 (1933): 125.

24. "Tennessee Democrats," *New York Times,* August 16, 1886.

ability to defy the Bourbon mainstream, Taylor was never able to establish a permanent new coalition to threaten Harris.[25]

Harris's opponents characterized his influence as that of a "machine," against which Governor Taylor struggled to maintain independence. But a machine, like other politicized concepts, is often in the eye of the beholder. To Harris's supporters, what was characterized as a machine was the normal party organization to which every Democrat should adhere. To them, the true "machine" was a group "backed by corporate money and influence; its methods are dark and devious, and its success depends upon the power of wealth and cunning . . . which is desperate, unscrupulous and selfish, and utterly without sympathy for the needs and wishes of the people." To the Bourbon, Taylor, in repudiating sound Democratic doctrine, did not fight against a "machine," but against the sound doctrine that he previously affirmed on the stump to get elected.[26]

Disproving the concept of a Harris "machine," as the 1888 election season approached, a number of names were floated as possible opponents to the senator, some realistic, some not. Ex-Governor Marks was in the latter category. So was Whitthorne, who would return to the House of Representatives after his short term as a senator, and die in office while at his home in Columbia in September 1891. In the former category were ex-Governor Porter and Commissioner of Indian Affairs J. D. C. Atkins, both of whom, like Harris, claimed Henry County as home. Indeed, it was noted that Atkins made no secret of his desire for the post. The *Atlanta Constitution* waggishly noted that Harris thought Atkins's candidacy "the height of ingratitude," as Atkins owed his position with the government to Harris's influence, but observed that if Atkins won, he could return the favor.[27] While the Atlanta editor was enjoying the joke, Harris, pummeled for years after the war over the money he took in pay at the end of the war and loaned, in part, to Atkins, doubtless would have echoed the sentiment of Atkins's ingratitude.

25. Robison, "Governor Robert L. Taylor and the Blair Educational Bill in Tennessee," 40–46; Hart, *Redeemers, Bourbons and Populists*, 93–104; "Robt. L. Taylor's Letter," *Nashville Daily American*, August 30, 1886; Looney, "Isham G. Harris," 27–29.

26. "Tennessee Democrats," *New York Times*, August 16, 1886; "What is the Machine?" *Nashville Daily American*, February 15, 1887. As noted above, historian Roger Hart concludes that Harris was not a "boss," but a skillful and intuitive politician. Hart, *Redeemers, Bourbons and Populists*, 55.

27. "The Supreme Bench," *Atlanta Constitution*, April 13, 1888; McKellar, *Tennessee Senators*, 422; "In the Senate Next Year," *Washington Post*, April 16, 1888; "Mr. Atkins," *Atlanta Constitution*, May 10, 1888.

Some naturally inclined to support Harris turned on him at this point. Atkins in reality had closer ties to Henry County and its congressional district than Harris, who only spent a period of weeks there each year, splitting time between Washington, Memphis, Texas, and Paris. Already having endorsed Atkins, the Paris newspaper criticized the senator for not being in Tennessee much during the 1884 election, since "Tennessee was a close state in 1884 and needed his powerful eloquence." The paper was glad to see him around in 1888, "even if self-promotion as some suggest, is the chief incentive." Unfortunately for Harris, on July 21, the day after that piece was published, he was called back to Washington to deal with the tariff measure then before Congress, and was unable to return until mid-October.[28]

Atkins pressed forward, hinting at the machine angle by arguing "it was a good time for the people to have a choice in the selection of a senator." He noted that he was in line with the Democratic Party and the president. Opponents jumped on a published letter that Harris wrote to a friend in Montgomery County explaining why his business in Washington kept him from canvassing Tennessee. Harris complained "that I have enemies in Tennessee, who are active and earnest, and some of them perhaps bitter, who would seek my defeat, I should like to put their arguments and suggestions before the people." While not a political misstep on the level of debating Jackson six years before, publishing the letter provided fodder for Atkins's supporters, who protested that the position was not Harris's personal property and that just having the opinion someone else should be senator did not make one Harris's enemy. Not surprisingly, Harris's remark after his last election that he would not run again was used against him, as was his advanced age. On the latter point, an opposition Clarksville paper stated since Harris was "fast approaching senility," a younger man should be elected.[29]

Harris's absence from Tennessee, however, did not mean he was out of touch with events in the state. While he had no particular campaign manager, he had a number of people working for him, and wrote letters to at least a hundred men across the state "with equal confidence and at equal length," and had a good idea of the votes on which he could rely. Harris, a master political organizer, had a

28. "Hon. Isham G. Harris," *Paris Post Intelligencer*, July 20, 1888; "Senator Harris," *Nashville Daily American*, August 31, 1888.

29. "J. D. C. Atkins," *Clarksville Semi-Weekly Tobacco Leaf*, August 24, 1888; "In a long article," *Clarksville Semi-Weekly Tobacco Leaf*, August 28, 1888 (commenting on the letter); "Senator Harris," *Paris Post-Intelligencer*, September 14, 1888 (fast approaching senility).

network of two to five of the most influential men in each of the state's counties, allowing him to keep a finger on the pulse of the electorate. Finally able to leave Washington in mid-October, Harris returned to Middle Tennessee, giving a lengthy speech in Springfield and then at Nashville focusing on the tariff and other economic issues. Responding to criticism that he had not pushed through enough funding for improving navigation on the Cumberland and other Tennessee rivers, Harris demonstrated such was not the case, and found it interesting that this issue was all of a sudden of importance, whereas months ago it was not. To the senator, his opponents were more interested in "damning me than damming the Cumberland." After calling for the voters to support Cleveland and Taylor, he closed with his tried and true exhortation for all Democrats to support the party ticket, as that was the key to assuring that Democratic principles would prevail.[30]

As the Democratic members of the General Assembly met in preparation for their caucus in early January 1889, Harris set up in Andrew Johnson's old quarters in Room 5 of the Maxwell House Hotel in Nashville, while Atkins settled in Room 14, which had been occupied by Bate during his last election. With Atkins his most serious threat in years, Harris was all business, and placed matters under his personal supervision. Both candidates conducted hourly meetings, and talked with "persuasive eloquence." Harris was reported to think he had fifty-seven votes, while Atkins's supporters thought the total was about forty each, with the crusty Savage having a little support. Under the rules then prevailing, a candidate needed a two-thirds majority in the caucus to receive the party's nomination.[31]

Harris's count of the votes proved much more accurate. The caucus's first ballot on January 11 showed the senator had 47 votes, Atkins 27, Savage 9, with 9 absentees. While some thought the two-thirds rule a waste of time under the circumstances, another vote was necessary on January 14. This time, Harris received not only more votes as the absentees came in, but Savage's voters began switching over to him as well, which must have chagrined the "old man of the Mountain." Finally, the motion was made to make the nomination unanimous, and Harris

30. "Outlook in Tennessee," *Washington Post*, October 1, 1888; "End of an Eventful Life," *Memphis Commercial Appeal*, July 9, 1897; "Harris and Marks," *Nashville Daily American*, October 17, 1888; "A Senator Welcomed" and "Senator Harris' Speech," *Nashville Daily American*, October 18, 1888.

31. "The State Legislature," *Memphis Daily Appeal*, January 3, 1889; "Gen. J. D. C. Atkins," *Nashville Daily American*, January 4, 1889.

made a short speech of gratitude. A few days later, the Democratic majority in the Legislature confirmed the result in the caucus, and Harris was elected to a third full term, the first time that any Tennessean received that honor. He returned to Washington in triumph in mid-January, to the congratulations of his colleagues in the Senate and his fellow Tennesseans in the capital.[32]

At the time of Bate's election in 1887, the *Nashville Daily American* gushed that "the United States Senate was the most honorable body of men in the world." But by the 1890s, the senators were not viewed with the same national awe as those who inhabited the Capitol when Harris was a congressman. Indeed, the constitutional theory behind the creation of the Senate, to act as a brake on runaway popular passion, often made it an unpopular institution. One observer acidly wrote, "On the senate stage, which was once used for tragedy, there is now enacted comedy and farce." Instead of attentively debating the great issues of the day in dark suits, the senators sprawled about without shoes, wearing bright colors, often napping, among them Harris, who snored "in a high tenor with a tremolo effect." It was probably after reading a story of this nature that Harris made the remark that he wanted to melt all the newspaper type into bullets, turn all the paper into wadding, transform the presses into guns, and shoot the head off of every editor in the country.[33]

Although an old man, Harris was at his height as a senator in his final full term. Senator Horace Chilton of Texas described Harris in those years:

> I have often watched him, in the cloakroom, in his Senatorial seat, in the chair of the presiding officer, and he always seemed the same. I do not remember ever to have heard him laugh aloud. There was the twinkle in the eye, the manifest enjoyment in the general merriment, but he would never appear to "turn himself loose."

32. "Democrats Caucus," *Nashville Daily American,* January 12, 1889; "The Senatorial Contest," *Nashville Daily American,* January 14, 1889; "The Battle is Over," *Nashville Daily American,* January 15, 1889; "Await His Coming," *Nashville Daily American,* January 17, 1889; "The Capital City," *Nashville Daily American,* January 19, 1889; "The Pace Grows Hot," *Nashville Daily American,* January 23, 1889; "General Gossip," *Washington Post,* January 22, 1888.

33. Rothman, *Politics and Power,* 243–46; "The New Senator," *Nashville Daily American,* January 26, 1887; "Senate Vaudeville," *Atlanta Constitution,* November 8, 1894 (quotes); "Senator Harris Dead," *Washington Post,* July 9, 1897.

I picture him as he would come into the Senate Chamber. There, in his familiar place on the right of the Vice-President, in the front row, he would take his seat. He hardly seems to say anything as if by previous design. He seems never to make an occasion, but to find it in the current proceedings as set on foot by others. He seems to spy out that something is taking an irregular direction and that he must set it right. He first asks a question or calls for the reading of some document, as if he imperfectly understood it. Then he proceeds to clear up all doubts. First emphasis, then gesticulation—no, not in succession, but an indescribable combination of emphasis and gesticulation.[34]

Indeed, to his colleagues, Harris looked like a senator. The Tennessean's "appearance was pleasing and impressive. Above the middle height, his figure was well proportioned and compact." His eyes "were piercing and full of intelligence," and "his features . . . strong and framed to express and portray every feeling and sentiment of his mind and soul."[35]

As impressive a picture of a senator that the old governor made, there were some who found Harris's appearance and mannerisms amusing on occasion. Among the bald-headed senators featured in one newspaper article, Harris was likened unto a Chinese Mandarin. His bald pate had no fuzz on the top, and but a fringe of white around the side; his "fierce white mustache is waxed so stiffly that it stands straight out from his nose." Harris's mustache appears to have been an object of fascination for the press, as it was once described the "most remarkable mustache in congress." "It is a long, stiff, curling iron-gray mustache and looks at different times like a rapier, a claymore and a battleax."[36]

On other occasions, Harris's aggressive reactions were the source of amusement. Mistakenly identified by the chair during one session as "the Senator from Kansas," Harris "fairly roared with his deep voice: 'The senator from where?'" On another occasion, the Senate was debating a resolution to give a brick model of the battleship *Illinois* to that state. Harris, doubtless napping, although hopefully without the high tenor snore, awoke to understand the government was giving away a battleship, and protested that it might very well be needed one day. In re-

34. *Cong. Record,* 55th Cong., 1st Sess., 1898, 3175.

35. Ibid., 3176.

36. "Bald-Headed Senators," *Dunkirk* (N.Y.) *Observer Journal,* April 4, 1888; "Hirsute Adornment," *Davenport* (Iowa) *Daily Leader,* January 7, 1895.

buttal, it was pointed out to him that the brick ship would be worthless for coastal defense. "For once in his life Senator Harris blushed to the roots of the very few hairs which he has on the top of his head. The old warhorse was visibly disconcerted when he sat down."[37]

Even admirers thought that Harris could have an "irascible temper." A minor spat over a procedural matter arose with Senator John H. Mitchell of Oregon, who had, as a young man, changed his name. Mitchell protested that Harris had reacted in an ungentlemanly manner to him. Harris snidely retorted that while he might be ungentlemanly, he was not dishonorable, as he had the same name he "bore in his youth." Each senator had to be led to separate cloakrooms to head off a physical confrontation. On another occasion, two East Tennessee Republicans were riding in a Pullman car to Washington, talking of national and state politics. A "tall old man" dressed in night clothes came in to get a drink and overheard them talking of the Tennessee Democrats in Congress, to the effect that Bate was too old and "Senator Harris was a worn-out old Confederate soldier, who had no especial qualification for a place in the Senate." Suddenly, the old man "poured out invective" on the Republicans in general and those from Tennessee in particular. Astonished, the two Republicans asked: "And who are you that you feel called upon to defend the Democrats of Tennessee?" The old man replied: "I am Isham G. Harris, by Jupiter, and if these windows were big enough I would pitch both of you out into the blackness of night." Fortunately, apologies were made, libations were poured, and all was smoothed over.[38]

While Harris was successful in his reelection bid in 1888, Grover Cleveland was not, and in a campaign that made an issue of the tariff, Benjamin Harrison was elected president. When Republicans won, they turned to William McKinley, future president and then chairman of the House Ways and Means Committee, to draft legislation. The resulting McKinley Tariff of 1890 was, depending on one's viewpoint, either famous or infamous for raising rates higher than they had ever been.[39] Harris voted against the McKinley Tariff, but in light of the Democrats'

37. "That Long Contest," *Lima* (Ohio) *Times-Democrat*, November 8, 1893 (Kansas); "Senator Harris' Funny Blunder," *Fitchburg* (Mass.) *Sentinel*, November 7, 1893 (Illinois).

38. McKellar, *Tennessee Senators*, 404 (temper); "The Daily Scrap," *Atlanta Constitution*, February 6, 1895; "Stories of the Day," *Bristol* (Pa.) *Bucks County Gazette*, March 5, 1896 (Mitchell); "Chats of Visitors to the Capital," *Washington Post*, March 11, 1911 (Pullman car).

39. Homer E. Socolofsky and Allan B. Spetter, *The Presidency of Benjamin Harrison* (Lawrence: University Press of Kansas, 1987), 49–52.

weakness in the Congress after Harrison's victory, he and others of his party were willing to proceed on the tariff, reasoning that it could be lowered in the future when the political winds blew their way. In the meantime, consideration of the tariff meant that Congress did not have time to take up an elections bill proposed by Representative Henry Cabot Lodge of Massachusetts. Lodge's bill, known as the "Force Bill" in the South, was meant to guarantee the franchise to all voters, including the blacks, who in the main still were Republicans.[40]

Within a month of the McKinley Tariff's passage, however, disaster struck the Republicans in the midterm elections, causing Harris to gloat that he expected the "Democrats having a safe working majority in the next Congress, [but] I never anticipated such a Waterloo for the Republicans." Harris further opined that the Republicans would "intensify" their efforts to pass the Force Bill before the end of the 52nd Congress. After the short session started on December 1, 1890, the Democrats used every parliamentary trick at their disposal to delay consideration of the Force Bill, including proposing action on other legislation the Republicans desired in an effort to distract attention. It was the Democracy's intention to "resist the bill to the bitter end."[41]

Although later denied by both parties to the arrangement, the axiom that politics makes strange bedfellows soon proved to be the death-knell of the Force Bill. The makeup of the Senate changed dramatically in 1889 and 1890, as six new states were admitted to the Union, electing Republican senators who cared very little for the tariff and very much for silver coinage. Already, they had joined forces with the remainder of the Republican Party to pass in a partisan vote the Sherman Silver Purchase Act in July 1890, and returned the favor with support on the tariff. But these Western Republicans were willing to deal outside party lines. On January 5, 1891, the Senate was dealing with routine matters early in the afternoon when Senator George F. Hoar of Massachusetts moved to take up the elections bill. Senator James Z. George of Mississippi then resumed a speech he had started on the elections bill, when suddenly Senator William M. Stewart of Nevada moved to take up a silver coinage bill. Hoar protested, but Gorman argued

40. "No Holiday for Senators," *New York Times,* December 19, 1889; "M'Kinley Monstrosity," *Chattanooga Daily Times,* October 1, 1890; Looney, "Isham G. Harris," 30–32; Rhodes, *History of the United States From Hayes to McKinley,* 360–62.

41. "Fate of the Force Bill," *Washington Post,* November 7, 1890 (Waterloo); "Some Views of the Result," *New York Times,* November 7, 1890; "Force Bill Taken Up," *Washington Post,* December 3, 1890.; "The Force Bill," *Chattanooga Daily Times,* December 3, 1890; "Senatorial Caucus," *Chattanooga Daily Times,* December 4, 1890 (bitter end).

that the motion was not debatable. Presiding that day was Senator Green Harris of Tennessee, who ruled that "the Chair will entertain no proposition that amounts to or tends to debate, the question is: 'Will the Senate proceed to consider the bill to provide against a contraction of the currency?'" A vote was taken on the motion, which carried, shelving the Force Bill and confounding the Republicans, who were "utterly taken aback." Senator Henry M. Teller, Republican of Colorado, unconvincingly denied a deal with the Democrats, but nine days later, the Senate approved the free coinage of silver, although it failed to pass the House.[42]

Although Harris had earlier favored the Bland–Allison Act, a mild pro-silver measure passed in 1878, his first strident comments on behalf of silver currency date from after the Force Bill incident in 1891. In March, he let it be known that he thought free coinage of silver was second only to the tariff as an economic issue. In July, he opined Cleveland was the frontrunner for the Democratic nomination, and that he was sound on all issues but free silver. The senator also expressed the view that the people of Tennessee were pro-silver as well.[43]

By way of background, the United States had used silver coinage since the early days of the Republic, fixed at a certain ratio to gold. The fiscal demands of the Civil War effectively removed the government from the gold standard, as "greenbacks," paper money issued by fiat, were the primary currency in circulation. After the war, the Congress passed the Coinage Act of 1873, meant to retire the greenbacks and place the country back on the gold standard. Led by Senator John Sherman, opponents of silver coinage stealthily omitted a reference to silver coinage in the legislation, which was later termed by silver proponents as the "Crime of 1873." The resulting deflationary trend was unpopular in rural areas. Political agitation from that quarter and other interests opposing deflation led to

42. Socolofsky and Spetter, *The Presidency of Benjamin Harrison*, 57–60; Carl V. Harris, "Right Fork or Left Fork? The Section-Party Alignments of Southern Democrats in Congress, 1873–1897," *Journal of Southern History* 42 (1976): 471, 486; "The Coinage and Force," *Chattanooga Daily Times*, December 7, 1890; *Cong. Record*, 51st Cong., 2nd Sess., 1891, 910–12; "Knocked Out" and "Surprise Party," *Chattanooga Daily Times*, January 6, 1891; "Silver Free Coinage," *Chattanooga Daily Times*, January 7, 1891; Rhodes, *History of the United States From Hayes to McKinley*, 363–64. While many deemed the vote on January 5 the death of the Force Bill, Harris and his compatriots fought a tireless delaying action until January 26 to make sure that was the case. Watters, "Isham Green Harris," 184–85.

43. *Cong. Record*, 45th Cong., 1st Sess., 1877, 241; *Cong. Record*, 45th Cong., 2nd Sess., 1878, 1076, 1112; "The Issues," *Atlanta Constitution*, March 18, 1891; "A Talk With Senator Harris," *New York Times*, July 10, 1891.

the formation in 1876 of the relatively short-lived Greenback Party, and in 1878 of the Bland–Allison Act, which authorized the treasury to purchase a set amount of silver at market prices. The treasury then issued silver certificates, which were in reality fiat money, redeemable at the treasury for a set amount of silver, but also redeemable for gold. The result of the Crime of 1873 was more than two decades of political agitation that intensified in the early 1890s. That decade saw an unstable economic situation that included bank failures, a financial panic in 1893, and a near-disastrous run on the United States's gold reserves.[44]

Harris advocated a bimetallic monetary system, one that officially authorized the use of both silver and gold as money. As he expressed his early view, the silver issue was one of money supply. The more silver, the greater the money supply. If the money supply was contracted, the capitalists" money would purchase more. "Labor wants to increase the supply because it increases the price of labor and the products of labor." Harris was able to cite statistics to prove the capitalists' claims that gold would be driven out of the country with monetized silver was wrong. "Every consideration of propriety, justice and right demand the free and unlimited coinage of silver, and nothing but the greed and avarice of the capitalist opposes it."[45] Maintaining a surprisingly modern view, Harris on more than one occasion announced that money was "fiat," that is, it had value because the sovereign said it did. Since one of the touchstones of Harris's life was a unified Democratic Party marching behind the party standard, as will be seen below, there is some irony that his last major stand on the issue of silver was one that proved to be eminently divisive of the party.[46]

Back in Tennessee, a movement of disaffected farmers seized control of the Democratic Party in 1890. After 1880, farming had different appearances depending on the area of the state. In the hill country of the Upper Cumberland east of Nashville, for example, primarily white farmers owned their own farms and operated on a subsistence level, although the need to accumulate cash for certain necessary items or to pay taxes required some economic diversity. In the former

44. Milton Friedman, *Money Mischief: Episodes in Monetary History* (New York: Harcourt, Brace, Jovanovich, 1992), 53, 57–77, 117–18.

45. "Harris and Free Coinage," *Atlanta Constitution*, March 18, 1891.

46. Harris, "Right Fork or Left Fork? The Section-Party Alignments of Southern Democrats in Congress, 1873–1897," 484–88; Friedman, *Money Mischief*, 45, 54; "The Real People of Tennessee," *Atlanta Constitution*, July 17, 1896; "All Money is Fiat," *Atlanta Constitution*, October 7, 1894; "Senator Harris on the Senate," *Washington Post*, April 22, 1895.

plantation districts of West Tennessee, and to a lesser extent in the traditional farming areas of the other two sections of the state, the number of large farms had declined significantly from antebellum times, while small farms concomitantly had increased in number. The number of white-owned farms increased by one-half, while blacks only owned about 2 percent of total farm acreage, even though one-quarter of the farm labor in the state was black. A system of sharecropping and tenant farming developed, creating land and labor relationships that resembled slavery in many aspects, even for otherwise landless whites, as many sharecroppers could never get out of their indebtedness to property owners.[47]

Whether in debt or not, Tennessee farmers shared a number of problems with farmers across the nation in the late 1880s. Deflationary trends made farm debt more valuable in relation to falling farm prices. Issues that vexed Green Harris also bothered the farmers, including the high price of consumer goods from tariff-protected industries, railroad rates, and monetary policy that made credit difficult to obtain. Coupled with the unrelenting monotony of farm life of the day, farmers felt they were not given the respect they deserved. Eventually, many farmers joined organizations that coalesced in 1888 as the Tennessee Farmer's Alliance. A pet scheme of the movement was the subtreasury, a device whereby farmers could deposit certain nonperishable crops with the government as collateral for loans, thereby easing their credit concerns. At first nonpolitical, by the state election of 1890, the organization advanced its president, John P. Buchanan of Rutherford County, as a candidate for governor. The regular Democracy at first did not take Buchanan and the organized power of the Alliance seriously, but Buchanan won the nomination in 1890 over Josiah Patterson of Memphis, the Bourbons' candidate. Faced with the possibility of a party split giving the Republicans the election, the party regulars supported Buchanan, who was eventually elected.[48]

Buchanan was no extremist; indeed, the measures advocated by the Tennessee

47. Jeanette Keith, *Country People in the New South: Tennessee's Upper Cumberland* (Chapel Hill: University of North Carolina Press, 1995), 9–25; Bergeron, Ash, and Keith, *Tennesseans and Their History*, 202–4; McKenzie, *One South or Many*, 151–54, 156, 161–62; Robert Tracy McKenzie, "Freedmen and the Soil in the Upper South: The Reorganization of Tennessee Agriculture, 1865–1880," *Journal of Southern History* 59 (February 1993): 63, 69, 82; Hart, *Redeemers, Bourbons and Populists*, 115–16, 107–28.

48. Corlew, *Tennessee: A Short History*, 380–84; Hart, *Redeemers, Bourbons and Populists*, 142–54; Bergeron, Ash, and Keith, *Tennesseans and History*, 207–8; Connie L. Lester, *Up from the Mudsills of Hell: The Farmers' Alliance, Populism, and Progressive Agriculture in Tennessee, 1870–1915* (Athens: University of Georgia Press, 2006), 160–64, 168–69.

Farmer's Alliance were more conservative than those of the national movement. Buchanan lacked Bob Taylor's personal charm, and was unable to convince the party mainstream that the Alliance would not prove to be a dividing factor. While Buchanan, and indeed, the Tennessee Alliance leadership did not support the scheme, it was used as a focal point for attacks by mainstream Democrats, ranging from Bob Taylor to Senator Bate. At first, Harris did not think the Alliance had much staying power, and he predicted after the election in 1890 that it would disappear before the next election. By the next July, having been absent from Tennessee for a significant interval, Harris had to admit he was not sure he knew exactly what its strength was at that time. By October 1891, he felt sure enough to have a letter published in a Memphis newspaper reaffirming his support for the farmers, who Harris said suffered from class legislation such as the tariff policy more than any other group. But Harris did not see the subtreasury as a cure for their problems, as he deemed it not only unconstitutional but impractical. Likewise, the Alliance's proposals for land loans and government ownership of the railroads had similar problems. Harris closed by saying he was always "ready and anxious to relieve the farmer from all unjust burdens and to secure to him every advantage and encouragement within the scope of constitutional power, but I am not willing to attempt the usurpation of power not granted to Congress, or to enter that field of class legislation which is the most vicious and unjust of any that a government could adopt." The subtreasury was one of various factors that contributed to the Alliance's loss of influence. By the 1892 election, the Bourbons were able to place ex-Confederate Peter Turney in the governor's chair, and what was viewed as yet another threat to Democratic orthodoxy was vanquished.[49]

As the 1892 presidential election approached, Harris was unenthusiastic about the prospect of Grover Cleveland being the Democratic standard-bearer. Harris no doubt recognized Cleveland's strength, and stated the New Yorker was "able and honest man and sound on all Democratic doctrines save the one question of free silver." An article in the New York Times in March 1892 on the political situation in Tennessee termed the senator as "the ablest politician in Tennessee" and noted his political strength. Harris was reported to simply not like Cleveland, going back to the appointment of the Sky Blue mugwumps early in his previous ad-

49. Corlew, *Tennessee: A Short History*, 383–84; Hart, *Redeemers, Bourbons and Populists*, 155–69, 179–98; "The Kansas City Star thinks," *Chattanooga Daily Times*, November 26, 1890; "A Talk With Senator Harris," *New York Times*, July 10, 1891; "Blast from Harris," *Memphis Appeal-Avalanche*, October 4, 1891; Lester, *Up From the Mudsills of Hell*, 170–83.

ministration, but as a "practical" politician, would be for the "Democrat he regards as the strongest before the people."[50]

Harris protested that he was not hostile to Cleveland, and preferred him to
the other potential candidate, Senator David B. Hill of New York, but felt that
perhaps neither should run. Harris's antipathy to Cleveland was such that he was
conspicuously absent from a list of Tennesseans who were delegates to the Democratic convention in 1892. Bowing to political reality, Harris loyally campaigned
for the Democratic ticket, which, of course, included not only Cleveland, but the
Bourbon candidate for governor, Turney. Spending four weeks speaking across
the state, he predicted a Democratic sweep of Tennessee, with victories for Cleveland and Turney, and ignominious defeat for Buchanan, who was running as a
third-party candidate. When, in the end, the election resulted in a Democratic
victory, Harris presided over a mass meeting at Memphis celebrating Cleveland's
election.[51]

Even if Cleveland and Harris did not see eye to eye, their respective positions
required that they get along. At a short special session of the Senate in March
1893, Harris was elected president pro tempore, an expression of respect by his
colleagues that was viewed in Tennessee as "an honor well disposed." Harris was
"the recognized leader" of the Tennessee Democracy, and was appealed to as an
arbiter of Democratic legitimacy in other states as well. Therefore, when Harris
sent President Cleveland a memorandum on Tennessee affairs as guidance on patronage issues in Tennessee, Cleveland had to listen. The memorandum, dated
May 2, 1893, carefully explained how Federal offices in Tennessee were divided
among the sections, and, in the case of East Tennessee, among the three congressional districts. The Federal judicial district of East Tennessee, for example, was
entitled to an internal revenue collector, a U.S. marshal, and a U.S. attorney. Harris carefully analyzed why the men he recommended should be placed in each
spot. While Bate opposed James H. Bible of the 3rd District for U.S. attorney, Harris explained why Bible's appointment was important for keeping that congressional seat Democratic in normally Republican East Tennessee. Bible was extolled

50. "A Talk with Senator Harris."

51. "Settlement in Tennessee," *New York Times*, March 4, 1892; "Tennesseans at Chicago," *Memphis Commercial*, June 21, 1892; "Tennessee is Cleveland's," *New York Times*, October 5, 1892; "Senator
Harris is Sanguine," *Washington Post*, October 28, 1892; "Demonstration in Memphis," *Atlanta Constitution*, November 13, 1892.

as "an original, active and earnest Cleveland man." Another candidate was recommended "chiefly because he belongs to that class of old fashion hard shelled, strict construction democracy for which I have always fought."[52]

In the end, Harris's recommendations were largely followed, and Bible was appointed U.S. attorney, although the process seems to have taken a longer time than usual, perhaps in order to placate Bate. In his memorandum, Harris stated Bate was "chivalrous, as honest as any man in America and as true a democrat as lives he has the misfortune of subjecting the merit of all men to the single test of whether they have been uniformly his friends and supporters or his opponents. He never sees a fault in a friend or a virtue in an opponent." Bible himself had Harris's assurance from the start he would be appointed, relying on his understanding that "Senator Harris is frequently called into consultation with the President about Tennessee politics in particular and general matters of public import regarding the government. He continues to be the recognized leader of Tennessee democracy and is regarded as one of the foremost men in the United States senate."[53]

In June, Cleveland called for a special session of Congress to commence August 7, 1893, to repeal the Sherman Silver Purchase Act. The Treasury had a large supply of silver acquired pursuant to the provisions of the act, yet since the law allowed silver certificates to be redeemed in gold, the silver remained in the treasury, while the government's gold supply dwindled to what Cleveland considered a dangerous point. While Cleveland and the proponents of the gold standard blamed the silver purchases for the problem, Harris blamed "Wall Street and the capitalistic influences of the country" for the problem, and maintained that "a repeal of the Sherman act demonetizing silver by contracting the currency would be in accordance with the plans of the opulent." In a stopover in Chattanooga on his way to Washington in late July, Harris was interviewed while he refreshed him-

52. "The Nashville Banner says," *Memphis Appeal-Avalanche*, March 24, 1893; "Senator Harris is Sanguine," *Washington Post*, October 28, 1892; S. Thomas et al. to IGH, March 21, 1893, and IGH to G. Cleveland, May 2, 1893, Grover Cleveland Papers, LC.

53. "Jim Bible is Back," *Chattanooga News*, May 5, 1893; "Condon is Appointed," *Chattanooga News*, May 10, 1893; "Jim Bible At Last," *Chattanooga News*, September 21, 1893; "Two Are Tennesseans," *Chattanooga Daily Times*, September 22, 1893; IGH to G. Cleveland, May 2, 1893, Grover Cleveland Papers; "Jim Bible is Back," *Chattanooga News*, May 5, 1893 (Bible quote). Sadly, Bible died in office in June 1897 at age forty-two. "James H. Bible Dead," *Chattanooga Daily Times*, June 26, 1897.

self with coffee and milk, but was unwilling to predict what action the Congress would take, saying at least a hundred bills would be introduced on the issue.[54]

The House of Representatives passed the repeal within twenty days. But not for the last time, Cleveland's lack of tact hardened the hearts of those who were inclined to oppose him in any event. Unfortunately, those hearts were in the Senate, where Harris and other pro-silver senators began a filibuster on August 29. The impasse dragged on for weeks, until the pro-repeal majority split into three factions, one advocating cloture (a vote to limit debate), one proposing compromise, and one, led by Senator Voorhees on behalf of Cleveland, determined to last the filibuster out. Finally, Voorhees forced a continuous session of thirty straight hours, in which Harris labored mightily to hold the minority together, using his parliamentary skills and constant quorum calls.[55]

In the midst of the continuous session, Harris proposed a compromise, that silver purchases be continued to a limited extent and that all paper money under $10 be placed on a silver basis. Harris discussed his proposal with Gorman and others, but Cleveland would not agree. Senator Hill of New York then pushed cloture, but he could not get the support of the Republicans, who would want full debate when the inevitable struggle over the tariff came up next. Gorman tried his own compromise, but was rejected by Cleveland. Continuing to deny that the financial crisis was brought about by the silver purchases, on October 23, Harris told a reporter that unconditional repeal would never pass, and that "he would see the universe sink into the lower regions before he would allow this infamy to be forced upon the American people."[56]

Defying a president of one's own party was difficult, but Harris could rely on the support of the party rank and file at home. While commercial associations in Nashville and Memphis passed resolutions censuring Harris (and Bate, who also opposed repeal), citizens' meetings in both cities gathered in support. The majority of Tennessee voters favored silver, and the two senators knew that. In reporting on sentiment in Tennessee at this time, a reporter for the *Atlanta Constitution* wrote of Harris's influence: "For thirty odd years the name of Isham Harris

54. "Senator Harris," *Chattanooga News*, July 14, 1893; "Coffee and Milk," *Chattanooga News*, July 25, 1893.

55. Jeannette Paddock Nichols, "The Politics and Personalities of Silver Repeal in the United States Senate," *American Historical Review* 41 (October 1935): 26–34, 36–40.

56. Ibid., 41–48; "To the Finish," *Atlanta Constitution*, October 24, 1893; "What is a Panic," *Chattanooga News*, October 19, 1893.

has been a tower of strength and a token to conjure by in democratic circles." Only one man "has overborne him" in that interval, the long-departed Andrew Johnson. Harris was the "old man invincible" of the party in Tennessee.[57]

Strength in Tennessee only went so far. Within a day or two of expressing his willingness to condemn existence to the infernal regions, Harris, with his fellow silver Democrats, determined that holding out for a compromise would be useless. Harris went to Senator Fred T. Dubois of Idaho, and told him the filibuster would not continue, saying, "Dubois, I told you that we would stand by you until hell froze over. We have had another look at our hand and must lay down." No longer defiant, Harris said "I am all at sea, but believe the end of the fight is near. I will not be a party to obstructive tactics." With the filibuster at an end, the repeal passed the Senate at the end of October, with Harris again denying a deal with the pro-silver Republicans relative to the Force Bill. The Tennessean condemned the demonetization of silver for 70 million Americans on account of the "ideas or policies of foreign countries." A few weeks later, Harris warned that the fight for silver was not over. Indeed, there was some thought that the struggle had "left wounds that would never heal."[58]

Relations between Harris and Cleveland remained uneasy. Harris was invited with five other senators to the first state dinner of the season at the Executive Mansion, and Harris continued to advise the president on political appointments in Tennessee. Yet, while on the surface all appeared as it should, word came in late January 1894 that former Governor Porter, then the American minister to Chile, would resign. Cleveland's supporters in Tennessee were casting about to run someone against Harris, making first a strong effort at Governor Turney, and then Porter. Harris was not surprised, as he knew his views on silver had alienated the president. In the event, Porter did not become a serious candidate, but instead was nominated for a Federal judgeship later in 1894, but failed to win confirmation because of intense local opposition, even with Harris's ostensible support.[59]

57. "Up in Tennessee," *Atlanta Constitution*, October 22, 1893.

58. Nichols, "The Politics and Personalities of Silver Repeal in the United States Senate," 49–50; Arthur Wallace Dunn, *From Harrison to Harding: A Personal Narrative Covering a Third of a Century, 1888–1921* (New York: G. P. Putnam's Sons, 1922), 1:121; "How They Take It," *Atlanta Constitution*, October 25, 1893 ("at sea"); "Passes the Senate," *Atlanta Constitution*, October 31, 1893; "Senatorial Views," *Atlanta Constitution*, November 19, 1893; "Record of the Year," *Atlanta Constitution*, August 29, 1894 (wounds).

59. "Dined with the President," *New York Times*, January 5, 1894; IGH to Henry Thurber, Janu-

With the silver issue resolved, at least for a time, the next great matter was the McKinley Tariff. In January 1894, the House took up the issue of the tariff's demise, but features of the proposed change appeared to dissatisfy large segments of the body politic. Eastern interests opposed a possible income tax to replace the revenue that reform of the tariff would necessitate, Louisiana sugar interests opposed a reduction in the sugar schedule, and California congressmen wanted more protection for West Coast products. And, of course, the Republicans wanted the tariff left intact. Eventually, after much legislative fireworks, the House passed a tariff reform bill.[60]

The measure was then introduced in the Senate on February 2, and referred to the Finance Committee, of which Harris was a senior member. Initially, it was expected Senator Vorhees would steer the measure through the Senate, but his health began to fail. Deliberations in the Finance Committee revealed that the House version would not pass the Senate. On March 20, the full committee reported a bill with taxes on a few commodities, including sugar. In early April, Harris assumed leadership of shepherding the bill through the Senate. With his parliamentary skill, the "incisive and alert" Tennessean aggressively brushed aside Republican efforts to delay and obstruct the tariff debate. The problem, it turned out, was not with the Republicans, but with certain fellow Democrats, who were protecting economic interests in their home states. Harris kept the Senate going almost night and day in an effort to discourage filibustering. One day, while the aged Tennessean was catching a nap in the cloakroom, a quiet understanding was reached that allowed an early adjournment. Harris exclaimed: "The damned infernal buzzards! They adjourned the Senate on me while I was asleep!"[61]

The struggle took its toll on the aging Harris, whom Senator Matthew S. Quay of Pennsylvania accused of "growing more despotic every day." On one occasion

ary 26, 1894, IGH to Grover Cleveland, April 12, 1894, both in Grover Cleveland Papers, LC; "Minister Porter for the Senate," *Washington Post*, March 17, 1894; "Some Points on Politics," *Washington Post*, August 11, 1894; "Reject Mr. Porter for Judge," *New York Times*, August 18, 1894; "It is claimed," *Paris Post Intelligencer*, September 7, 1894; "In Hotel Lobbies," *Washington Post*, December 2, 1894; IGH to G. Cleveland, December 7, 1894, Grover Cleveland Papers.

60. "Record of the Year," *Atlanta Constitution*, August 29, 1894.

61. Looney, "Isham G. Harris," 53–54; "The change from Voorhees," *Nashville Banner*, April 6, 1894; "Washington Letter," *Warren* (Pa.) *Evening Democrat*, April 7, 1894; Lambert, *Arthur Pue Gorman*, 211–21; Dunn, *From Harrison to Harding*, 1:128.

in late May, the Senate was debating the resolution relating to the annexation of Hawaii when the time expired, and Harris insisted on resuming debate on the tariff. Republican Senator George F. Hoar of Massachusetts protested. Previously, Hoar had made a light-hearted comment that Harris was the "drum major" of the Democratic side. The tiring Harris was "stung"; if rested, he might have otherwise gotten the jest. When he realized Harris had taken the remark wrongly, Hoar stated that he had always held Harris "in the highest respect, not only for his kindness of heart, and his absolute integrity but his great intellectual capacity and clearness." Hoar deemed Harris the "undisputed master and superior" of parliamentary law in the Senate. "He addresses us on this side sometimes pretty roughly in tone and sometimes pretty roughly in substance, but I never supposed that anybody would make an appeal, either to his sense of justice or kindness of heart, unsuccessfully." Thus assuaged, the touched Harris expressed that "the kindest relations had always existed between Mr. Hoar and himself."[62]

Overcoming resistance in the Senate, Harris met with Cleveland on the morning of July 3, 1894, advising the president that the bill as it then stood, "without the dotting of an i or the crossing of a t," was the best that could be obtained. Cleveland made an effort to convince Harris changes should be made, but when Harris said it was impossible, Cleveland accepted the bill as it stood; "since delay was dangerous it was better to accept what he could obtain than to hazard all by striving for the impossible." Having obtained the president's grudging approval, Harris went back to the Senate, declaring that the tariff bill would pass that July 3, or there would be no Fourth of July for the U.S. Senate. The measure passed by a straight party vote.[63]

The bill then went to a conference committee with the House, where little, if any, progress was made. On July 17, Harris reported back to Cleveland, that the conference committee was nearing a deadlock. Unknown to the senators of his own party, on July 2 Cleveland wrote a scathing letter denouncing the Senate bill to Representative William L. Wilson, the floor manager in the House, sneering, "Every true Democrat and every sincere tariff reformer knows that this bill in its present form falls far short . . . our abandonment of the cause or the principles upon it rests means party perfidy and party dishonor." Cleveland was on the horns

62. *Cong. Record,* 53rd Cong., 2nd Sess., 1894, 4251, 5259, 5959; "Congress," Lowell (Mass.) *Daily Sun,* May 26, 1894.

63. Nevins, *Grover Cleveland,* 579; "Tariff Reform Victory," *Memphis Commercial Appeal,* July 4, 1894.

of a dilemma. It would be difficult to sign a bill he had so bitterly denounced on July 2, yet it would be just as bad to veto any type of tariff reform. Cleveland told Harris he would be satisfied with no duties on iron and coal, but Harris reiterated that change was impossible. The president, in the words of Senator James K. Jones of Arkansas, showed "his despair, contempt and inconsistency" by asking an "astounded" Harris if the Senate could be kept in session ten days after the date the House agreed to the Senate amendments.[64]

Finally, the conference committee gave up on July 18. The next day, doubtless with Cleveland's approval, Wilson had Cleveland's July 2 letter read in the House. As one Tennessee editor observed, it was "a remarkable act, of doubtful propriety and doubtful policy." Indeed, it was a massive political blunder, and it resulted in an acrimonious riposte from the senior members of Cleveland's own party in the Senate. On July 24, Senator Gorman rose to complain of the "infamous calumnies" heaped upon Senate Democrats, who had worked hard to save the country and keep the party in power. Cleveland's letter was "the most uncalled for, the most unwise, the most extraordinary communication," and ignored the constant lines of communication between the Senate and the executive branch. At one point, Gorman called on Harris as a witness, who descended from the chair and recounted that in his conversations with Cleveland, he had been led to conclude that the president favored passage of the Senate bill, not because he approved it, but because it was the best that could be secured. Gorman then resumed his attack, which was characterized by one writer as "the most remarkable anathema ever hurled at an occupant of the white house."[65]

With that heated rebuke, the bill headed back toward conference, but not without a bit of excitement. On July 27, Senator William D. Washburn of Minnesota moved that the Senate instruct its conferees to lower the proposed tariff on sugar. A point of order was raised in opposition to the amendment, and Harris, as presiding officer, ruled Washburn's motion out of order. The decision was appealed, and a motion was made to lay the proposed amendment on the table. Dramatically, each vote ended in a tie, as did the vote on the actual amendment itself. It was reported "there was a ring of jubilation in Harris's voice as he read

64. "Tangle on the Tariff," *Memphis Commercial Appeal*, July 17, 1894; Nevins, *Grover Cleveland*, 585; "Tariff Back on Track," *Memphis Commercial Appeal*, July 20, 1894.

65. "Give It Up in Despair," *Memphis Commercial Appeal*, July 19, 1894; "Cleveland to Wilson," *Memphis Commercial Appeal*, July 20, 1894; "An Exciting Day," *Nashville Banner*, July 23, 1894; "Attacked Cleveland," *Newark Daily Advocate*, July 24, 1894; "Gorman Tells All," *Washington Post*, July 24, 1894; Lambert, *Gorman*, 234; "Record of the Year," *Atlanta Constitution*, August 29, 1894.

the tabulation, and as soon as the resolution agreeing to a further conference was agreed to there was a scene of confusion and congratulation." Harris joined six other senators as conferees in a renewed effort to pass the bill.[66]

Eventually, a compromise was reached whereby the House would agree to pass the Senate Bill, as it was, and the Senate would agree to separate bills for free sugar, coal, iron ore, and barbed wire. The bill passed the House on August 13, although one Republican wag innocently asked if the president's letter should be read again. Cleveland let the bill become law without signature. Then, in accordance with the compromise, the House promptly passed bills for free sugar, iron ore, barbed wire, and coal. However, Harris, as the acting chair of the Senate Finance Committee, promptly received a letter from Secretary of Treasury John G. Carlisle, advising that further adjusting the tariff schedules, especially on sugar, would cause a deficit. The separate House bills withered away.[67]

The congressional session ended on August 28, 1894. The Senate had been in almost continuous session since December 1892, and much of that time was marked by intense struggle between a Democratic president and a significant number of senators of the same party. Harris had to turn his attention to matters at home, as his term was once again ending. While he made the comment at the first of 1894 that "he had never taken much delight in public life, and would much prefer to follow his profession of the law," there seems to have been no consideration that Harris would give up his seat after three full terms. Harris's stance in opposing Cleveland on the tariff seems to have caused some unrest in Tennessee, especially among the urban commercial classes, but there was no real threat from within the Democratic Party. If there was to be a threat, however remote, it would be from a fusion ticket between the Republicans and the waning Populist Party in Tennessee.[68]

After the "continuous strain" of "thirteen months of very hard work," Harris

66. *Cong. Record*, 52nd Cong., 2nd Sess. 1894, 7928–30; "Won By a Tie Vote," Newark (Ohio) *Daily Advocate*, July 28, 1894; "Had a Close Call," *Davenport Daily Leader*, July 29, 1894.

67. "Record of the Year," *Atlanta Constitution*, August 29, 1894; "Tariff Bill Passed," *Newark (Ohio) Daily Advocate*, August 14, 1894; "Would Make a Deficit," *New York Times*, August 16, 1894. An income tax was also passed as a part of the package, but was held unconstitutional by a decision of the Supreme Court the next year. *Pollock v. Farmers' Loan & Trust Co.*, 157 U.S. 429 (1895).

68. "Record for the Year"; "Personal Gossip," *New York Times*, January 7, 1894; "In East Tennessee," *Atlanta Constitution*, July 8, 1894; "Disgruntled Senators," *Nashville Banner*, July 21, 1894; "The Senate's Action," *Nashville Banner*, July 25, 1894; "Populism Not in Favor," *New York Times*, July 31, 1894; "Promised Support," *Nashville Banner*, April 16, 1894; "The Campaign Is Hot," *Washington Post*, October 29, 1894.

and Martha traveled to Texas. They stopped in West Tennessee for Harris to give a speech on the issues of the day. The senator noted the gross impracticalities of the Populist proposals, defended the effort on the tariff as the best result that could be obtained, denied that the Sugar Trust controlled the Senate by making due note of Secretary Carlisle's letter, celebrated the defeat of the force bill, and scoffed at the idea that the issue of silver coinage should be dictated by foreign economies. Philosophically, Harris stuck to his strict states' rights roots, stating, "the evil which most seriously threatens our form of government is found in the growing tendency to paternalism and centralization; the constantly increasing tendency of congress to take legislative jurisdiction and control of all subjects, however local and domestic in their character they may be, and the growing tendency of the people to appeal to congress for a remedy for all real or imaginary evils." Ironically using the phraseology of Abraham Lincoln, Harris attacked the Republicans as not seeking government by the people, of the people, and for the people, but for the capitalist class.[69]

It was a quick trip to Texas, although the break was beneficial. Called back to Washington on business in early October, Harris was noted to have improved in appearance, "looking hale and hearty after a good rest." By the end of October 1894, Harris returned to Tennessee and campaigned for the short remainder of the time in the smaller towns and rural districts of Middle and West Tennessee. The Republican/Fusion ticket was giving the Democrats some difficulty, and Harris joined other Democratic speakers in covering the state. The week before the election, Harris's age and exhaustion was demonstrated by a thief's ability to steal into his room in Bolivar while he was sleeping to steal the senator's watch.[70]

Nationally, the Republicans took advantage of the financial downturn, which they effectively laid at the door of the Democrats, to score a decisive win and gain effective control of both houses of Congress. In Tennessee, the election was

69. IGH to J. M. Dickinson, October 6, 1894, Jacob McGavock Dickinson Papers, TSLA; "Senator Harris Speaks," *Atlanta Constitution*, September 26, 1894; "Hon. Isham G. Harris," *Memphis Commercial Appeal*, September 24, 1894.

70. "Uncle Isham for Dave," *Memphis Commercial Appeal*, October 6, 1894; "In Hotel Lobbies," *Washington Post*, October 9, 1894; "Political Gossip," *Washington Post*, October 14, 1894; "Uncle Isham on the Stump," *Memphis Commercial Appeal*, October 18, 1894; IGH to J. M. Dickinson, October 6, 1894, Jacob McGavock Dickinson Papers; "He Believes in Organization," *Memphis Commercial Appeal*, October 26, 1894; "The Campaign Is Hot," *Washington Post*, October 29, 1894; "Stole His Watch," *Ft. Wayne Sentinel*, November 5, 1894.

close, and it appeared that the Republican candidate for governor, H. Clay Evans of Chattanooga, had won. But the Democrats held the legislature, and observers were able to conclude fairly early that Harris would have no problem in securing reelection. A Tennessean who was a former functionary in the House of Representatives told a Washington reporter, "Senator Harris has an invincible hold on the affections of the people of his State, and they regard him as a grand old man, who, having served them with distinguished credit for all these years, with intellectual vigor undiminished, is able to represent them still further in the national council. The sentiment in favor of his re-election is so strong as to be practically unanimous."[71]

In the interval between the November election and the convening of the General Assembly in January 1895, Harris returned to Washington to deal with the vacant judicial position in East Tennessee to which Porter had been nominated. When Porter's nomination was withdrawn, Cleveland nominated Charles D. Clark of Chattanooga for the post. Harris held up the confirmation when someone made an allegation that Clark's firm took an unethical fee. Clark's friends, including Harris's old opponent Judge David Key, rushed to his defense. While Harris was initially criticized for holding up the confirmation, it was later conceded there was little else he could have done. While Harris did not deem the claims against Clark to be valid, the episode delayed matters for some weeks. Finally, the charges were disproved and Clark's appointment confirmed.[72]

With the judgeship secured, in early January Harris traveled to Nashville and installed himself in Room No. 1 of the Maxwell House, where he received friends and supporters. Finally rested after the previous year's exertions, he was observed to be healthy and in good spirits. While a few stray Democratic candidates were named in the press, such as former General W. H. Jackson, the former senator's brother, and John L. T. Sneed, now a Memphis judge, no serious opposition came from within the party. Sneed said that even if he were inclined to run, Harris was a "steadfast friend" who had done him "many favors." There was a brief concern that the Republicans were attempting to interfere with the Democratic caucus

71. Richard E. Welch Jr., *The Presidencies of Grover Cleveland* (Lawrence: University Press of Kansas, 1988); "In Hotel Lobbies," *Washington Post*, November 20, 1894.

72. "Clark's Nomination Held Up," *Washington Post*, December 21, 1894; "An Outrage," *Chattanooga Daily Times*, December 21, 1894; "Those Charges," *Chattanooga Daily Times*; "Those Charges, *Chattanooga Daily Times*, December 23, 1894; "Judge Clark All Right," *Chattanooga Daily Times*, December 24, 1894; "Vindicated," *Chattanooga Daily Times*, January 22, 1895.

process, but the move turned out to be unsuccessful. The atmosphere as the General Assembly met was tense, as the gubernatorial election was still in the air. Republican Evans won the popular vote, but the Democrats retained control of the General Assembly. Under the state constitution, election contests were to be determined by laws established by the legislature. Eventually, the General Assembly formulated a process, and after taking much evidence, threw out 22,000 votes in Evans's favor and declared Turney reelected.[73]

In spite of this dispute, Harris was never in danger. With the Democrats in control, Harris was unanimously renominated by the party's joint legislative caucus. On January 22, 1895, Harris was reelected to his fourth term as senator, approximately doubling the vote of the Republican candidate, E. J. Sanford. No doubt anticipating Harris's reelection, his colleagues in the Senate once more elected him president pro tem on January 10. In Washington, Harris's reelection was again greeted with satisfaction, in gratitude for his "fidelity" to the needs of the people of the District of Columbia as the chairman of the Senate District Committee. Tennessee's senior senator returned to the capital and in February was honored at a reception at Page's Hotel, which included a huge bouquet of flowers from the vice president. "A quartet of male voices rendered some of the old Southern songs at intervals during the evening, a huge punch bowl was kept filled, and great good humor and pleasantry prevailed. The Senator had a gracious word for every one, and seemed thoroughly to enjoy the occasion."[74]

During the campaign, Harris predicted that silver would be an issue in the next session of Congress, as he doubted "congress will waste any time preparing a bill for the president to veto." Very little transpired in the last session of the 53rd Congress, but Harris and his pro-silver compatriots were not quiescent. Secure in the knowledge that the bulk of his constituents were pro-silver, in April Harris made statements to the press predicting that the Populists would probably hold the key to controlling the Senate in December, and reiterating his contention that

73. "For Governor," *Chattanooga Daily Times*, January 4, 1895; "Quiet Boom for Gen. Jackson," *Washington Post*, January 5, 1895; "Judge Sneed is Satisfied," *Memphis Commercial Appeal*, January 5, 1895; "Who Are They?" *Chattanooga Daily Times*, January 6, 1895; "Curious?" *Chattanooga Daily Times*, January 7, 1895; Eugene Lewis, "The Tennessee Gubernatorial Campaign and Election of 1894," *Tennessee Historical Quarterly* 13 (December 1954): 301–28; Hart, *Redeemers, Bourbons and Populists*, 211–15.

74. "Senator Harris Renominated," *Washington Post*, January 9, 1895; "Senator Harris Renominated," *New York Times*, January 8, 1895; "One Democrat," *Chattanooga Daily Times*, January 23, 1895; "Senator Harris Renominated," *Washington Post*, January 9, 1895; "Reception to Senator Harris," *Washington Post*, February 13, 1895.

silver would be money if the government said so, and that foreign traders would in any event treat it as a commodity, "just as your bale of cotton, hogshead of to-bacco or bushel of wheat."[75]

Interestingly, the scene of the struggle switched to Memphis, as the "sound money" forces had a meeting there in May, partly sponsored by Representative Josiah Patterson. Patterson was normally a Harris ally, but was in Cleveland's camp on the monetary issue. The bimetallists then arrived in the Bluff City in June. Harris was not a featured speaker, but did appear at the rostrum for a brief period to describe the purpose of the gathering. The delegates, Harris explained, were gathered for a non-partisan discussion on the future financial policy of the United States, and "no other question." Therefore, all attendees could participate without endangering their party allegiances. "It is a convention of bimetallists, and it understands bimetallism to mean the coinage of both gold and silver on the same terms and at the old ratio of 16 for 1, and the use of both as legal tender money of ultimate redemption, without regard to the financial policy of any other nationality on earth." The delegates heard a number of speakers in favor of silver, and departed, convinced of the educational value of the meeting.[76]

Back in Washington by August 1895, the silver Democrats met in a hotel room to plan for the 1896 campaign, as they recognized Cleveland's opposition made any further efforts in favor of silver useless while he remained president. While the *New York Times* sneered that the Memphis meeting was a fizzle, and that "white metal" was not needed for the restoration of good times, Harris and his al-lies were happy with the progress of matters, and Harris stated that he felt the ma-jority of Democrats were in favor of free silver, without regard to the policy of for-eign nations. Headquartered at Harris's house in Washington, the group, known as the Bimetallic Democratic National Committee, planned to simply seize con-trol of the Democratic Party in order to write a pro-silver platform for the 1896 elections.[77]

When the 54th Congress met in December 1895, it was suggested that Har-

75. "He Believes in Organization," *Memphis Commercial Appeal*, October 26, 1894; "They Favor Silver," *Atlanta Constitution*, April 21, 1895; "Senator Harris on the Senate," *Washington Post*, April 22, 1895; "Harris Interviews Himself," *New York Times*, April 22, 1895.

76. "Some Memphis Personalities," *Atlanta Constitution*, May 30, 1895; "Tomorrow the Conven-tion," *Memphis Commercial Appeal*, June 11, 1895; "Sixteen to One," *Memphis Commercial Appeal*, June 13, 1895; "Now for the Battle," *Memphis Commercial Appeal*, June 14, 1895.

77. "Interest in Free Coinage Disappearing," *New York Times*, August 13, 1895; "Outlook for 1896," *Atlanta Constitution*, August 22, 1895; "All on One Platform," *Washington Post*, June 29, 1896.

ris and his fellow Senate Democrats might join with the six Populist senators to control the Senate. Harris refused, refusing to compromise his party principles as a Democrat on the basis of the single issue of silver. Harris and his compatriots would simply endure the situation as they waited to outlast Cleveland. For his part, the president was dismayed by the Democratic Party's steady move toward a pro-silver position. Cleveland wrote a friend that he longed for the adjournment of Congress and the end of his term. He went on to state: "I honestly believe the present Congress is a menace to the good of the country if not its actual safety."[78]

That spring, Edward Ward Carmack, a Harris ally who previously was the editor of the *Memphis Commercial Appeal,* opposed Patterson for the Democratic nomination for the congressional district where Memphis lay. The bitter contest was an aspect of the struggle for the control of the party by the silver and gold forces. The local Democratic Committee split between the two factions, and each claimed to be the regular body. Harris's intimate friend, Colonel William H. Carroll, telegraphed the senator and requested that he come to Memphis to resolve the dispute. Harris complied, and presided over a crowded meeting that resolved the issue in favor of the pro-silver Carmack. Kenneth McKellar, then a young law partner of Carroll's and later a U.S. senator himself, recalled that "every one knew that any Convention presided over by Isham G. Harris was the regular Democratic Convention."[79]

The concerns of the present then gave way to preserving the memory of the past. In the late 1880s and early 1890s, a new wave of nationalism emerged that had as one of its phenomena a desire to honor the veterans of both sides of the Civil War. With the establishment of the Chickamauga and Chattanooga National Military Park and the Antietam National Battlefield in 1890, veterans of the Battle of Shiloh began agitating for the preservation of that battlefield as well. Harris was among the congressional supporters of that effort, and helped Bate shepherd it through the Senate in late 1894. In April 1896, Harris joined a succession of prominent visitors to the battlefield to assist in locating prominent features of the battlefield. Major D. W. Reed of the Shiloh National Military Park Commission asked the senator to help fix the location where Albert Sidney Johnston had

78. "Senate Reorganization," *Chattanooga Daily News,* January 1, 1896; "Senator Harris' Position," *Chattanooga Daily News,* January 2, 1896; Nevins, *Grover Cleveland,* 689–91; Cleveland to D. Dickinson, March 18, 1896, in *Letters of Grover Cleveland, 1850–1908,* ed. Allan Nevins (Boston: Houghton Mifflin, 1933), 432.

79. McKellar, *Tennessee Senators: As Seen by One of Their Successors,* 391–92.

fallen thirty-four years before. In the ride from the railroad station at Corinth to the battlefield, Harris declined to discuss any particulars with Reed, fearing that his dim memory of the events of thirty-four years before would be confused by opinions of others. He also admitted to Reed that "the whole subject of Shiloh is a bitter memory which I do not allow myself to talk about or think about when I can help it. I have never visited the field since the battle and would not now except at the urgent request of the friends of General Johnston."

When the senator and Reed arrived at Pittsburgh Landing, he declined the assistance of a number of friends and General Don Carlos Buell and left with Reed on horseback, asking him to conduct him to a point on the field on the right of the Confederate line with a small stream with very high banks. Reed took Harris to a place fitting that description, and in response to an inquiry noted that an 1862 camp site was nearby. Harris was satisfied that he was in the right location, telling Reed "everything is perfectly natural just as I remembered it," and fixed the location as where Johnston sat on a horse with his staff for a period putting troops in position. He then asked Reed to conduct him a half mile north, and recalled that at that point there was a large field on the left. He was taken to the corner of the Peach Orchard field, and after surveying the field, rode back to a large oak tree across the Hamburg–Savannah Road, and then down into a ravine to the rear. Harris fixed the spot of Johnston's wounding as near the oak tree, and the place where he had expired in the ravine, remarking, "I say emphatically, this is the place. I cannot be mistaken." The visit changed Harris's views toward preserving the field, as he remarked to Reed on the trip up from Corinth that he was not in sympathy with the efforts at that time to preserve the battlefields, preferring that there "might be no remembrance of it among the participants or their children." But after his visit, the senator stated, "I have changed my mind about your work here, and say that I am pleased with your plans and will take pleasure in doing anything I can, in Congress or out, to assist you in the work."[80]

In May 1896, the Democratic state convention nominated former Governor Robert Taylor for another term. The state platform was "strongly for free silver

80. Smith, *This Great Battlefield of Shiloh*, 17–30, 57, 60–62; D. W. Reed to Basil Duke, July 20, 1906, Series 1, Box 13, Folder 140, SNMPA. Harris's location of the site of Johnston's last minutes was challenged by Wiley Sword in his ground-breaking *Shiloh: Bloody April*, 443–46. But former Shiloh ranger and Shiloh historian Timothy B. Smith believes "there is little doubt Harris was correct in his positioning of the site." Timothy B. Smith, *The Untold Story of Shiloh: The Battle and the Battlefield* (Knoxville: University of Tennessee Press, 2006), 35–36.

and does not mention the administration." Harris was selected as one of the delegates at large to the national convention in Chicago, as Tennessee selected a free coinage delegation. A "goldbug" editor termed the senator as the "guiding spirit of the Tennessee mob." For his part, Harris would have agreed with the editor of the Bourbon *Chattanooga Daily News*, who bitingly remarked, "There are democrats and Cleveland democrats."[81]

Previously in 1895, Cleveland's concern over the government's gold reserves led to the sale of a series of government bonds. In February 1895, during a particularly dangerous run on the government's gold supply, Cleveland sold $65.1 million in bonds to a syndicate headed by J. P. Morgan. Morgan and his friends turned around and sold the bonds for a more than healthy profit. While Cleveland maintained to the end of his days that he had acted out of necessity for the good of the country, calls were made for a congressional investigation, and Harris was appointed to head a committee to investigate whether the true motivation for the sale was to enrich private interests. While a few hearings were held, Harris's intense interest in the coming campaign slowed the committee's work.[82]

After a trip to New York for bond hearings in mid-June, Harris went to Atlantic City, New Jersey, for a rest, and then returned to Washington for a series of meetings in preparation for the Democratic national convention in Chicago in July. While in New York, the senator fought off reporters seeking details of the silver Democrats' plans, including whether pro-silver Republicans and Populists would be included. It was expected by many that Harris would be tendered the permanent chairmanship of the convention, and that to cement the silver men's control, either he or Governor James S. Hogg of Texas would be named temporary chairman. On June 30, Harris and his confederates met in Chicago to organize for the convention.[83]

A reporter for the Associated Press observed that "not since 1860, when the Democratic party met in convention at Charleston and split on the subject of slav-

81. "The Tennessee Convention," *Washington Post*, May 8, 1896; "Partisan Bile," *Washington Post*, May 11, 1896; "Our Delegates at Large," *Chattanooga Daily News*, May 9, 1896; "Which Shall Prevail," *Chattanooga Daily News* November 7, 1895.

82. Brodsky, *Grover Cleveland*, 357–66; Nevins, *Grover Cleveland*, 664–66; *Cong. Record*, 54th Cong., 1st Sess., 1896, 4939; "Looking Into Bond Issue," *New York Times*, June 19, 1896; "All on One Platform," *Washington Post*, June 29, 1896; "The Bond Issue Investigation," *Washington Post*, July 17, 1896.

83. "All on One Platform," *Washington Post*, June 29, 1896; "Harris-Hogg," *Memphis Commercial Appeal*, July 1, 1896; "Bimetallic Conference," *The Daily* (Decatur, Ill.) *Review*, July 1, 1896.

ery has such irreconcilable difference of opinion existed in a great question . . . as now confronts the delegates" to the Chicago convention. The convention started as a struggle between the majority silverites and the pro-gold delegates, with leadership of the convention an important issue. Harris was not selected for either the temporary or the permanent chairmanship, although the latter was certainly expected. Politically, it was determined that because Senator John W. Daniel of Virginia was named temporary chairman, Harris, also a Southerner, should not be permanent chairman because of the appearance of sectionalism. Accordingly, it was given out that Harris was overcome by the jam of the crowd at the convention, and Senator Stephen M. White of California was named permanent chairman.[84]

Although appearances kept Harris in the background, it was barely so. He was recognized as a "heavyweight" and an "extremist" on the issue of silver, and "not a bit a compromiser," and "maddest of them all" over Cleveland's role in the repeal of the Sherman Silver Purchase Act. The silver issue was such to Harris that even though he was the crustiest of old Democrats, he was willing to consider the convention's naming of Republican Senator Edward Teller of Colorado as its candidate. In the end, thirty-six-year-old William Jennings Bryan, a former Nebraska congressman, gave his famed "Cross of Gold" speech, and became the nominee of the party, on a platform of silver coinage in a 16:1 ratio to gold.[85]

Harris had achieved his goal of making silver coinage the policy and platform of the Democratic Party, which was effectively the apogee of the silver agitation of the time. If they had won and gotten the chance to fix the silver to gold ratio at 16:1, Harris and his compatriots would have most likely inflicted severe economic damage to the exchange rate between the United States and its foreign trade partners, with significant adverse domestic consequences. An increase in the worldwide gold supply brought about by the use of a new extraction process that made South African gold economically viable brought about the very inflation the proponents of silver sought. A good policy for 1873 or 1879 was, by 1896, a bad one.[86]

---

84. "With Glittering Bait," *The Daily* (Decatur, Ill.) *Review*, July 4, 1896; "Silver Dick Leads," *Washington Post*, July 6, 1896; Louis W. Koenig, *Bryan: A Political Biography of William Jennings Bryan* (New York: G. P. Putnam's Sons, 1971), 186; "Why Senator Harris Declined," *Atlanta Constitution*, July 8, 1896.

85. "The Men Who Won the Silver Fight," *Atlanta Constitution*, July 5, 1896; "Teller," *Memphis Commercial Appeal*, July 4, 1896; "Bryan and Bland are Magic Names," *Memphis Commercial Appeal*, July 10, 1896.

86. Friedman, *Money Mischief*, 104–6, 116–25.

Bryan went about the country preaching the gospel of silver. The fatigued Harris returned to the capital "with the air of a man who had done a good job of work, and was minded to rest and let things run for a while." He planned to go to Tennessee and then to Texas. But, by October, Harris was back in Memphis to introduce Bryan as his swing through Tennessee took the candidate to the Bluff City. But the old senator's further participation in the campaign was hindered by a serious illness later in the month. In the end, McKinley won the election, 217 electoral votes to 176, and by 600,000 popular votes over Bryan. A "Gold Democrat" ticket of Civil War veterans John Palmer and Simon Bolivar Buckner finished a distant third. Waggishly, the *Washington Post* noted that it was confident that Harris's remarks on the election result "will run at the ratio of 16 cuss words to 1 of the other variety."[87]

With a lame duck administration in place, Harris knew little could be done before McKinley took office. When it was suggested after the election that the Senate should consider a tariff measure, Harris dismissed it as a waste of time since the Senate had not gotten any more pro-reduction since last time. The Tennessean felt that the Senate's time was better spent attending to several hundred judgments of the Court of Claims that required attention. Also requiring attention was a struggle with his former ally, Patterson, over patronage in Memphis. At issue was the appointment for postmaster at Memphis, where Harris's son was the assistant. Patterson as a gold man had the president's ear, but Harris had the power to hold up the appointment to force a compromise candidate. Patterson was bitter over his close loss to Carmack, and alleged fraud, resulting in a contest in the House, with Carmack narrowly prevailing.[88]

While the election results and the disputes with Patterson over patronage were doubtless upsetting, matters of a domestic nature also likely caused the aging senator some discomfort. Bad news relating to a public figure's family was con-

87. "Harris To Take a Rest," *Washington Post,* July 16, 1896; "Enthused Over Bryan," *Washington Post,* October 6, 1896; "Nominee Bryan Visits Tennessee," *Atlanta Constitution,* October 6, 1896; "Both Tennessee Senators Ill," *New York Times,* October 20, 1896; Ellis Paxson Oberholtzer, *A History of the United States Since the Civil War* (New York: Macmillan, 1937), 5:394, 400–402, 434, 436; "We Have Not Yet Heard," *Washington Post,* November 13, 1896.

88. "Secret for the Party," *Washington Post,* November 19, 1896; "Political Gossip," *Washington Post,* December 2, 1896; "Warm Contest for Postmaster," *Atlanta Constitution,* December 3, 1896; "Words by Patterson," *Atlanta Constitution,* December 13, 1896; Clyde J. Faries, "Carmack v. Patterson: The Genesis of a Political Feud," *Tennessee Historical Quarterly* 38 (Fall 1979): 332.

sidered as newsworthy in Harris's time as now, and in September, the newspaper published a report that Harris's son and private secretary Charles had been sued for divorce by his wife, Sallie A. Harris, who alleged "adultery on several occasions, giving the names, dates, and places." The couple had been "married in Memphis under the most favorable auspices in 1883," but had not lived together for more than two years. Divorce on the grounds of desertion was granted Sallie by default early in 1897, with custody of the couple's son and an award of alimony. This was the second episode of a scandalous nature in Harris's official "family" in as many years, as a previous secretary, B. C. Milliken, was indicted in 1895 for "burgularlously entering the bed–chamber of a young lady and attempting to chloroform her." To that point, Milliken had "always been regarded as an excellent gentleman." It was likely that the young lady rejected his advances, and the speculation was that it "set him crazy, [or] perhaps he was drunk."[89]

As the year turned to 1897, the infirmities of age finally began to catch up with the Harris family. After his serious illness in 1878, Harris suffered from various ailments as he aged: cholera in 1879, a mild case of malaria in 1883, "chronic neuralgia" in the early 1890s, "nervous prostration" subsequent to the 1894 adjournment, the "grippe" just before the silver convention in 1895, and a serious illness in October 1896, probably from pain in his eye. The opiates that he was administered because of that pain made it difficult for the senator to eat, and he was dangerously weakened. He was not completely recovered in mid-January 1897, when word came that Martha was seriously ill at home in Paris and might not recover. Martha had not lived in Washington with the senator for some years, as the climate disagreed with her. With son Edward, Harris traveled to Tennessee, the fatigue from the quick trip and the grippe confining Harris to his room even as his wife lay dying. Martha died on January 20, and the family took her body to Elmwood Cemetery in Memphis for burial, although the heartbroken senator was too sick to attend. At that time, Dr. R. D. Smartt of the First Methodist Church of Memphis consoled Harris and prayed for him.[90]

89. "Mrs. Harris Applies for a Divorce," *Washington Post*, September 27, 1896; "Senator Harris' Son Divorced," *New York Times*, January 28, 1897; "The Latest Sensation in Washington," *Cambridge* (Ohio) *Jeffersonian*, July 18, 1895.

90. "Personal," *Washington Post*, July 3, 1879; "Senator Harris' Sickness," *Washington Post*, October 22, 1883; Watters, "Isham Green Harris," 179; IGH to J. M. Dickinson, October 6, 1894, Jacob McGavock Dickinson Papers; "Tomorrow, the Convention," *Memphis Commercial Appeal*, June 11, 1895; "Both Tennessee Senators Ill," *New York Times*, October 20, 1896; "Once More He Rallies," *Nashville American*, July 7, 1897; "Senator Harris Summoned Home," *Washington Post*, January 17,

Upon his return to Washington, the condition in the senator's left eye that had been deteriorating for about two years required an operation, which gave him "great relief." It was speculated that a second operation might be necessary and that loss of sight in that eye was likely. Harris's health continued to decline, and he was absent from his desk in the Senate for a period of several weeks. A trip to Biloxi, Mississippi, seemed to restore his strength, and he was able to take his seat April 26, 1897, and his colleagues congratulated him on his recovery from illness. Early in the summer, Harris spent time in Atlantic City to see if the salt air would restore his health. But the aged senator began to sink, as an inflammation of the stomach kept him from keeping down any solid food. His last visit to the Senate was late in June, but he was unable to stay for long and had to be taken home by carriage. By July 6, it was feared that Harris only had a short time to live, but he rallied that day, to the extent that it was hoped that the senator might be removed out of the heat of Washington to a resort in Pennsylvania, as the trip back to Tennessee was considered too arduous. But the decision was made the next day that even a short trip to the Keystone State was too much for the patient to bear.[91]

Early on the morning of July 8, Harris seemed to rally one last time, but by noon, it was obvious that he was failing. The day before, he had predicted to a longtime friend, Representative Benton McMillan of Tennessee, that he would not last another two days. The senator lapsed into fits of unconsciousness, and only spoke once, declining medication that was offered by a nurse with the words, "No, I am tired." He peacefully expired shortly after 5:00 p.m., having been attended through the day by his son Edward and his wife, his longtime housekeeper, a nurse, and McMillan.[92]

Tributes of respect were paid from many quarters. Resolutions were passed by the Tennesseans in Washington, by Harris's "constituents" on the District of Columbia Board of Commissioners, and the Senate was adjourned to honor one of its most senior members, with Senator Bate making the formal announcement of

1897; "Senator Harris' Wife Dying," *Washington Post*, January 20, 1897; "Senator Harris' Wife Dead," *Washington Post*, January 21, 1897.

91. "Senator Harris's Failing Eye," *New York Times*, February 5, 1897; "Short Session of Congress," *New York Times*, April 27, 1897; "Senator Harris Dead," *Washington Post*, July 9, 1897; "Once More He Rallies," *Nashville American*, July 7, 1897, "Spirit of A Great Man Goes Across the River," *Nashville American*, July 9, 1897; "A Slight Improvement," *Memphis Commercial Appeal*, July 8, 1897.

92. "Spirit of a Great Man Goes Across the River"; "Senator Harris Dead"; "End of an Eventful Life," *Memphis Commercial Appeal*, July 9, 1897.

his colleague's death. Harris's body lay in state in the Marble Room at the Capitol, and a funeral tribute was paid in the Senate Chamber. Then, with a delegation of senators and congressmen, the body, with Harris's family, was transported from Washington, through Louisville, to Nashville, where the body lay in state in the Capitol. On July 13, the body was taken to Memphis, accompanied not only by the delegation from Washington, but by Governor Taylor and a number of state officials. The funeral services were held at the First Methodist Church, where the senator's body was flanked by an honor guard of former Confederate soldiers; at least one floral arrangement bore the symbols of both sides in the war. Harris was the subject of impressive eulogies, with Dr. Smartt expressing the opinion that Harris had a conversion experience as a result of Martha's death and died a Christian, and longtime family friend Rev. W. F. Hamner paying a short tribute. Finally, close to sundown, Green Harris was laid to rest next to Martha, Eugene, and little George at Elmwood Cemetery, with a company of Confederate Veterans doing last honors.[93]

Tributes to the dead senator were paid in newspaper editorials, at special memorial exercises in Memphis in November 1897, and in the halls of Congress in March 1898. Harris's humble beginnings, enterprise as a young merchant, and prowess at the law were extolled. His colleagues in the Senate fondly recalled aspects of his character, force of intellect, parliamentary expertise, and tact and deference in debate. Harris's long years of public service through momentous times and his firm convictions in the correctness of his course were deemed remarkable. Harris was also marked as a man of courage, not only on the battlefields of 1861–65, but also in the pursuit of his political convictions. His hometown *Memphis Commercial Appeal* summed up: "The secret of his success lay in his inexhaustible fund of sound, common sense, his earnestness, his sincerity, his integrity and his unyielding loyalty to friends and fidelity to duty."[94]

The touchstone of Harris's life was the rule of the Democratic Party, in its pur-

93. "Shadows Were Dense," *Memphis Commercial Appeal*, July 10, 1897; "Honors for the Dead," *Memphis Commercial Appeal*, July 11, 1897; "The Harris Funeral Train," *Nashville American*, July 12, 1897; "Lies At Rest in Elmwood," *Memphis Commercial Appeal*, July 14, 1897. An observer of the Senate obsequies was appalled by the inappropriate dress of some of the attendees. "Little Regard to Proprieties," *Washington Post*, July 14, 1897.

94. "Isham G. Harris," *Memphis Commercial Appeal*, July 9, 1897; "The Dead Senator," *Nashville American*, July 9, 1897; "Isham G. Harris," *Atlanta Constitution*, July 10, 1897; "Taylor's Tribute to Harris," *New York Times*, November 28, 1897; *Cong Record*, 55th Cong., 1st Sess., 1898, 3169–78.

est Jacksonian form, which he deemed in the best interests of his state and his nation. Party unity meant power, and in the Tennessee of Harris's time, only disunity could bring the party's opponents, whether Whigs or Republicans, to power. His untiring dedication to the Democracy first brought him to statewide power in 1857, and it enabled him to regain that power in 1877 and cement it in later years. To the Tennesseans of his time, he was the consummate Democrat and the ultimate arbiter of party regularity.

His contemporaries recognized Harris's zeal for a strict construction of the U.S. Constitution. To Harris, that meant the Federal government should stay out of what was traditionally the states' arena, whether that meant property in slaves, federal support for education, or internal improvements. An editorial at the time of his death noted that "as a statesman his talents were more conspicuous for what he prevented others from doing than for what he himself accomplished. His policy was one of negation, and he stood as a bulwark against the licentiousness and demoralizing tendencies of the times."[95] While this may have been true as a general statement, Harris the senator showed a willingness to use the Federal government's power with boldness and imagination where he thought it authorized by the Constitution. Although his strenuous efforts to use the authority of the Federal government to fight epidemic disease proved to be less than totally effective, his willingness to look beyond purely local regulation to address a national problem demonstrated an excellent lawyer's keen appreciation for the power allowed the Federal government by the U.S. Constitution. And while Harris's solution to the monetary issues of the day was better suited for the preceding decade, his concept of money as being nothing more or less than government fiat is commensurate with modern theory.

The great irony of Harris's life is that his zeal in 1861 for a strict construction of the U.S. Constitution's protection of property in slaves caused him to trample on the Tennessee Constitution in order to align the Volunteer State with the Confederacy. In the course of the Southern revolution, no state had a more energetic helmsman than did Tennessee. Harris's largely successful efforts to mobilize the military force of the state, to arm it, to equip it, and to provide for military manufactures to sustain it showed his traits of boldness, his iron will, and his utter dedication to the Confederate cause. In large part, what Harris could do as governor, he did. What could not be done was left to the Confederate government, and its

95. "Isham G. Harris," *Memphis Commercial Appeal*, July 9, 1897.

failings, added to the inherent geographic weakness of Tennessee's position, led to the loss of Nashville and large segments of the state in 1862.

From Shiloh until the final bitterness of Forrest's surrender in May 1865, Harris fought for the Confederacy's survival as long and as hard as any of its soldiers. His constitutional duties to the state of Tennessee prevented him from joining the army, "but he was in fact its inseparable companion from beginning to end, and heard its first reveille and its last tattoo." Every interval of the war saw Harris working for the Confederate cause, by raising troops, by encouraging the Tennesseans in the army, and by service in the field. His colleague, Senator William B. Bate, a Confederate general, stated that Harris "highly prized" his sobriquet as the "War Governor of Tennessee." Bate eulogized that Harris served "the Army of Tennessee, under all its commanders . . . through all the years of the war, exerting every effort to mitigate the hardships of the soldiers, to supply the necessities of their daily life, and sharing with them the sunshine and storm, the heat and the cold, the joy of victory and the sting of defeat."[96]

Nathan Bedford Forrest was truly correct when he termed Harris a "fighting governor." In peace and war, Harris unflinchingly pursued the course charted by his party and the Constitution, and went to battle for his principles, whether they were threatened by the Wilmot Proviso, Union military conquest, Federal tariff policy, or the state debt controversy, with boldness, courage, and the exercise of a keen intellect. When, at the end of his long life, his friends and foes gathered to eulogize him, his longtime opponent in the U.S. Senate, Senator George Hoar of Massachusetts, summed Harris up in an admirably succinct fashion, observing that his departed colleague was "faithful to the truth as he saw it, to duty as he understood it; to constitutional liberty as he conceived it."[97]

96. *Cong Record*, 55th Cong., 1st Sess., 1898, 3171.

97. *Cong. Record*, 55th Cong., 1st Sess., 1898, 3173. In part, Hoar's comment became the title of a short article on Harris's life in the *Franklin County Historical Review*, which concluded with the same line. See Adkins, "Isham G. Harris: Faithful to Truth as He Saw It," 103.

BIBLIOGRAPHY

PRIMARY SOURCES

MANUSCRIPTS

Duke University, Durham, North Carolina
    Perkins Library
        Charles Todd Quintard Papers
Library of Congress, Washington, D.C.
    Beriah Magoffin Letters
    George Washington Campbell Papers
    Gideon Johnson Pillow Letters
    Grover Cleveland Papers
    Isham G. Harris Papers
Museum of the Confederacy, Richmond, Virginia
    Eleanor S. Brockenbrough Library
        Fort Donelson/Lloyd Tilghman Files
Tennessee State Library and Archives, Nashville
    Claybrooke–Overton Papers
    Duncan Brown Cooper Papers
    Isham G. Harris Papers
    Jacob McGavock Dickinson Papers
    James D. Porter Papers
Tulane University, New Orleans, Louisiana
    Louisiana Historical Association Collection
        Jefferson Davis Papers
University of Georgia, Athens
    Stone Family Papers
        Correspondence of Robert G. Stone
University of North Carolina, Chapel Hill
    Southern Historical Collection, Wilson Library
        Gale–Polk Papers

Harding and Jackson Family Papers
Jason Niles Papers
John Perkins Papers
Kenneth Rayner Papers
Marcus Joseph Wright Papers
William W. Mackall Papers
University of Tennessee Special Collections Library, Knoxville
Oliver P. Temple Papers
Ramsey Family Papers
William B. Bate Letter
William G. Brownlow Papers
Western Reserve Historical Society, Cleveland, Ohio
William P. Palmer Collection of Bragg Papers
Alexander P. Stewart Letter

NEWSPAPERS

Amherst (N.H.) Farmer's Cabinet
Athens (Ga.) Southern Banner
Athens (Ga.) Southern Watchman
Athens (Ohio) Messenger
Athens (Tenn.) Post
Atlanta Constitution
Atlanta Southern Confederacy
Bangor Daily Whig and Courier
Bristol (Pa.) Bucks County Gazette
Brownlow's Knoxville Whig and Rebel Ventilator
Cambridge (Ohio) Jeffersonian
Chattanooga Daily Rebel
Chattanooga Daily Times
Chattanooga News
Clarksville Jeffersonian
Clarksville Semi-Weekly Tobacco Leaf
Daily Columbus Enquirer
Daily (Washington, D.C.) National Intelligencer
Daily (Columbia) South Carolinian

Dallas Weekly Herald
Davenport (Iowa) *Daily Leader*
Decatur (Ill.) *Republican*
Dunkirk (N.Y.) *Observer Journal*
Fayetteville Observer
Fitchburg (Mass.) *Sentinel*
Flake's Bulletin (Galveston)
Ft. Wayne Sentinel
Franklin Review and Journal
Galveston Daily News
Georgia (Macon) *Weekly Telegraph*
Hagerstown (Md.) *Herald and Torch*
Houston Tri-Weekly Telegraph
Idaho Tri-Weekly Statesman
Knoxville Daily Chronicle
Knoxville Daily Tribune
Knoxville Daily Register
Knoxville Weekly Age
Knoxville Weekly Whig and Chronicle
Knoxville Whig
Lima (Ohio) *Times-Democrat*
Lincoln Evening News
Lowell (Mass.) *Daily Sun*
Macon Daily Telegraph
Memphis Commercial Appeal
Memphis Daily Appeal
Memphis Daily Avalanche
Memphis Evening Post
Memphis Weekly Bulletin
Milwaukee Daily Sentinel
Montgomery (Ala.) *Weekly Advertiser*
Nashville American
Nashville Banner
Nashville Daily American
Nashville Daily Gazette
Nashville Patriot

Nashville Union and American
New York Herald
New York Times
Newark (Ohio) *Daily Advocate*
Paris Intelligencer
Paris Post Intelligencer
Paris Weekly Intelligencer
Philadelphia Inquirer
Savannah Daily News and Herald
Stevens Point (Wis.) *Journal*
The Parisian
Warren (Pa.) *Evening Democrat*
Washington Post
Weekly (Macon) *Georgia Telegraph*
Williamsport (Pa.) *Daily Gazette and Bulletin*
Winchester Daily Bulletin

GOVERNMENT PUBLICATIONS AND RECORDS

County Clerk's Office Records, Callahan County, Texas
State of Tennessee
    House Journal, 1877
    House Journal Appendix, 1870–71
    Public Acts of the State of Tennessee
    Senate Journal, 1847
    Tennessee Reports
U.S. Department of the Interior
    Censuses for 1859, 1860, and 1900
    Shiloh National Military Park Archives
        Series 1, Box 13, Folder 140
        Isham G. Harris letter
        D. W. Reed letter
U.S. Government
    Congressional Records
        Congressional Globe. 1849–53. Washington, D.C.
        Congressional Record. 1877–98. Washington, D.C.

Memorial Addresses on the Life and Character of Isham G. Harris Delivered in the Senate and House of Representatives. Washington, D.C.: Government Printing Office, 1898.

U.S. Code

U.S. *House Journal*

U.S. Public Laws

U.S. Senate, *The Executive Documents Printed by Order of the Senate of the United States for the Second Session of the Forty-Third Congress, 1874–75 and the Special Session of the Senate in March, 1875.* Washington, D.C.: Government Printing Office, 1875. Ex. Doc. No. 12.

U.S. Senate, U.S. Serial Set
   Document No. 234, 58th Congress, 2nd Session
      Journal of the Confederate Congress
National Archives and Record Administration
   Record Group 94
      Records of the Adjutant General's Office, 1780s–1917
      Case Files of Applications for Former Confederates for Presidential Pardons, M-1003
   Record Group 109
      Compiled Service Records of Confederate General and Staff Officers and Non-Regimental Enlisted Men, M-331
U.S. Reports
   U.S. State Department. *Papers Relating to Foreign Affairs Accompanying the Annual Message of the President to the First Session, Thirty-Ninth Congress, 1865,* Part III. Washington, D.C.: Government Printing Office, 1866.
   U.S. War Department. *War of the Rebellion: A Compilation of the Official Records of the Union and Confederate Armies.* 128 vols. Washington, D.C., 1880–1901.

COLLECTED WORKS WRITTEN BY CONTEMPORARIES AND
PARTICIPANTS, PUBLISHED PRIMARY SOURCES, MEMOIRS,
AND UNIT HISTORIES

"An Interesting Batch of Telegrams." *Confederate Veteran* 2 (April 1894): 110.
Buell, Don Carlos. "East Tennessee and the Campaign of Perryville." In *Battles and Leaders of the Civil War.* Ed. Robert Underwood Johnson and Clarence Clough Buel. Reprint, New York: Thomas Youseloff, 1956.

Chalmers, James R. "Forrest and His Campaigns." *Southern Historical Society Papers* 7 (October 1879): 449.

Cheatham, Benjamin F. "The Lost Opportunity at Spring Hill, Tenn.—General Cheatham's Reply to General Hood." *Southern Historical Society Papers* 9 (October, November, and December 1881): 524.

Chester, William W., ed. "The Diary of Captain Elisha Tompkin Hollis, CSA." *West Tennessee Historical Society's Papers* 39 (December 1985): 83.

Claiborne, John M. "Several Errors Corrected." *Confederate Veteran* 6 (August 1898): 374.

Clark, Champ. *My Quarter Century of American Politics*. 2 vols. New York: Harper and Brothers, 1920.

Coffman, Edward M, ed. "Memoirs of Hyland B. Lyon, Brigadier General, C.S.A." *Tennessee Historical Quarterly* 18 (March 1959): 35.

Cox, Jacob D. *Atlanta*. New York: Charles Scribner's Sons, 1892.

Crist, Lynda Lasswell, Mary Seaton Dix, Kenneth H. Williams, Peggy L. Dillard, and Barbara J. Rozek, eds. *The Papers of Jefferson Davis*, 12 vols. to date. Baton Rouge: Louisiana State University Press, 1971–2008.

Cullom, Shelby M. *Fifty Years of Public Service*. Chicago: A. C. McClurg & Co., 1911.

Cutler, Wayne. ed., *Correspondence of James K. Polk*, 8 vols. Knoxville: University of Tennessee Press, 1993.

Davis, Jefferson. *The Rise and Fall of the Confederate Government*. New York: D. Appleton & Co., 1881.

Dunn, Arthur Wallace. *From Harrison to Harding: A Personal Narrative Covering a Third of a Century, 1888–1921*. 2 vols. New York: G. P. Putnam's Sons, 1922.

Edwards Annual Director to the Inhabitants, Institutions, Incorporated Companies, Manufacturing Establishments, Business Firms, etc., etc. in the City of Memphis for 1869. New Orleans: Southern Publishing Company, 1869.

Edwards, Mary Virginia Plattenburg. *John N. Edwards: biography, memoirs, reminiscences and recollections; his brilliant career as soldier, author, and journalist; choice collection of his most notable and interesting newspaper articles, together with some unpublished poems and many private letters. Also a reprint of Shelby's expedition to Mexico, an unwritten leaf of the war*. Kansas City: J. Edwards, 1889.

Franklin, Ann York, comp. *The Civil War Diaries of Capt. Alfred Tyler Fielder, 12th Tennessee Regiment Infantry, Company B, 1861–1865*. n.p., 1996.

Garrett, Jill K., ed. *Confederate Diary of Robert D. Smith*. Columbia, Tenn.: Captain James Madison Sparkman Chapter, UDC, 1997.

Garrett, Jill K., and Marise P. Lightfoot, eds. "Excerpts from the Diary of James W. Matthews." In *The Civil War in Maury County, Tennessee*. Columbia, Tenn.: Privately published, 1966.

"Gov. Harris at the Close of the War." *Confederate Veteran* 5 (August 1897): 402.

Gower, Herschel, and Jack Allen, eds. *Pen and Sword: The Life and Journals of Randal W. McGavock*. Nashville: Tennessee Historical Commission, 1959.

Graf, Leroy P., Ralph W. Haskins, Patricia P. Clark, and Paul H. Bergeron, eds. *The Papers of Andrew Johnson*. 16 vols. Knoxville: University of Tennessee Press, 1967–2000.

Halstead, Murat. *Caucuses of 1860. A History of the National Political Conventions of the Current Presidential Campaign: Being a Complete Record of the Business of all the Conventions: with Sketches of Distinguished Men in Attendance Upon Them, and Descriptions of the Most Characteristic Scenes and Memorable Events*. Columbus: Follett, Foster and Company, 1860.

Hamer, Marguerite Bartlett. "The Presidential Campaign of 1860 in Tennessee." *East Tennessee Historical Society Publications* 3 (January 1931): 9.

Hamer, Philip M., ed. *Tennessee: A History 1673–1932*. 4 vols. New York: American Historical Society, 1933.

Hewett, Janet B., Noah A. Trudeau, and Bryce A. Suderow, eds. *Supplement to the Official Records of the Union and Confederate Armies*. 100 vols. Wilmington, N.C.: Broadfoot Publishing Company, 1994–2001.

Hilliard, Henry Washington. *Politics and Pen Pictures at Home and Abroad*. New York: G. P. Putnam's Sons, 1892.

Hoobler, James A., ed. "The Civil War Diary of Louisa Brown Pearl." *Tennessee Historical Quarterly* 38 (Fall 1979): 308.

Hood, John Bell. *Advance and Retreat*. New Orleans: Beauregard, 1879.

Johnson, Robert U., and Clarence C. Buel, eds. *Battles and Leaders of the Civil War*. New York: The Century Co., 1881.

Johnson, William Preston. *The Life of Gen. Albert Sidney Johnston*. New York: D. Appleton & Co., 1879.

Jones, Terry L., ed. *Campbell Brown's Civil War: With Ewell and the Army of Northern Virginia*. Baton Rouge: Louisiana State University Press, 2001.

Jordan, Thomas. "Notes of a Confederate Staff Officer at Shiloh." *The Century Illustrated Monthly Magazine* 29 (November 1884–April 1885): 629.

Kean, Robert Garlick Hill. *Inside the Confederate Government: The Diary of Robert Garlick Hill Kean, Head of the Bureau of War.* Ed. Edward Younger. New York: Oxford University Press, 1957.

Law, J. G. "Diary of Rev. J. G. Law." *Southern Historical Society Papers* 12 (May 1884): 215.

Liddell, St. John Richardson. *Liddell's Record.* Ed. Nathaniel Cheairs Hughes Jr. 1985. Reprint, Baton Rouge: Louisiana State University Press, 1997.

Lindsley, John Berrian, ed. *The Military Annals of Tennessee: Confederate.* 2 vols. Nashville, J. M. Lindsley, 1886.

Manigault, Arthur Middleton. *A Carolinian Goes to War.* Ed. R. Lockwood Tower. Columbia: University of South Carolina Press, 1983.

McKee, J. Miller. "The Evacuation of Nashville. The Panic that Succeeded the Fall of Fort Donelson—Incidents Connected with the Surrender of the City." *The Annals of the Army of Tennessee and Early Western History.* Ed. Edwin L. Drake. Nashville: A. D. Haynes, 1878.

McKellar, Kenneth. *Tennessee's Senators: As Seen by One of Their Successors.* Kingsport: Southern Publishers, 1942.

McMurry, W. J. *History of the Twentieth Tennessee Regiment Volunteer Infantry, C.S.A.* Nashville: The Publication Committee, 1904.

Moore, Frank. *The Rebellion Record; A Diary of American Events.* 11 vols. New York: G. P. Putnam, 1864.

Nevins, Allan. *Letters of Grover Cleveland, 1850–1908.* Boston: Houghton Mifflin, 1933.

Polk, William M. *Leonidas Polk, Bishop and General.* 2 vols. New York: Longmans, Green & Co., 1915.

Quintard, Charles Todd. *Doctor Quintard, Chaplain C. S. A. and Second Bishop of Tennessee.* Ed. Sam Davis Elliott. Baton Rouge: Louisiana State University Press, 2003.

Ramsey, J. G. M. *Dr. J. G. M. Ramsey: Autobiography and Letters.* Ed. William B. Hesseltine. 1954. Reprint, Knoxville: University of Tennessee Press, 2002.

Ridley, Bromfield L. *Battles and Sketches of the Army of Tennessee.* 1906. Reprint, Dayton: Morningside Bookshop, 1995.

Roman, Alfred. *The Military Operations of General Beauregard in the War Between the States, 1861–1865.* 2 vols. New York: Harper & Brooks, 1883.

Rowland, Dunbar, ed. *Jefferson Davis, Constitutionalist: His Letters, Papers and Speeches.* 10 vols. Jackson: Mississippi Department of Archives and History, 1923.

Savage, John H. *The Life of John H. Savage: Citizen, Soldier, Lawyer, Congressman, Before the War Begun and Prosecuted by the Abolitionists of the Northern States to Reduce the Descendants of the Rebels of 1776, who Defeated the Armies of the King of England and gained Independence for the United States, Down to the Level of the Negro Race.* Nashville: John H. Savage, 1903.

———. *The Life and Public Services of Andrew Johnson, Seventeenth President of the United States, Including his State Papers, Speeches and Addresses.* New York: Derby & Miller, 1866.

Schroeder, Seaton. *The Fall of Maximilian's Empire as Seen from a United States Gunboat.* New York: G. P. Putnam's Sons, 1887.

Shanks, W. F. G. "A Political Romance." *Putnam's Magazine* 16 (April 1869): 428.

Stewart, Alexander P. "The Army of Tennessee: A Sketch." In *Military Annals of Tennessee: Confederate.* Ed. John Berrien Lindsley. 1886. Reprint, 2 vols. Wilmington, N.C.: Broadfoot, 1995.

Sykes, E. T. "Error in the Harris–Adair Article." *Confederate Veteran* 5 (September 1897): 453.

———. "A Correction Explained—Gov. I. G. Harris." *Confederate Veteran* 6 (November 1898): 525.

Taylor, John M. "Twenty-Seventh Tennessee Infantry." In *Military Annals of Tennessee: Confederate.* Ed. John Berrien Lindsley. 1886. Reprint, 2 vols. Wilmington, N.C.: Broadfoot, 1995.

Taylor, Richard. *Destruction and Reconstruction: Personal Experiences of the Late War.* New York: D. Appleton & Co., 1879.

Temple, Oliver P. *East Tennessee and the Civil War.* 1899. Reprint. Freeport, N.Y.: Books for Libraries Press, 1971.

———. *Notable Men of Tennessee from 1833 to 1875: Their Times and Contemporaries.* New York: Cosmopolitan Press, 1912.

Thorndike, Rachel Sherman, ed. *The Sherman Letters: Correspondence Between General and Senator Sherman From 1837 to 1891.* New York: Charles Scribner's Sons, 1894.

Watterson, Henry. *"Marse Henry": An Autobiography.* 2 vols. New York: George H. Doran, 1919.

White, Mrs. D. Giraud. *A Southern Girl in '61: The War-Time Memories of a Confederate Senator's Daughter.* New York: Doubleday, Page & Co., 1905.

Works Projects Administration. *Transcription of the County Archives of Tennessee: Minutes of the County Court of Henry County, 1836–1849.* 2 parts. Nashville: Tennessee Historical Records Survey, 1942.

Worsham, W. J. *The Old Nineteenth Tennessee Regiment, June, 1861–April, 1865.* Knoxville: Paragon Printing, 1902.

Wright, Marcus J. "Thirty-Eighth Tennessee Infantry." In *Military Annals of Tennessee: Confederate.* Ed. John Berrien Lindsley. 1886. Reprint, 2 vols. Wilmington, N.C.: Broadfoot, 1995.

———. *Diary of Brigadier-General Marcus J. Wright, C. S. A., April 12, 1861–February 26, 1863,* n.p. 193?.

Young, J. P. *The Seventh Tennessee Cavalry: A History.* 1890. Reprint, Dayton, Ohio: Morningside, 1976.

———. "Hood's Failure at Spring Hill." *Confederate Veteran* 16 (January 1908): 25.

SECONDARY SOURCES

Abshire, David M. *The South Rejects a Prophet: The Life of Senator D. M. Key, 1824–1900.* New York: Frederick A. Praeger, 1967.

Adkins, Gilbert R. "Isham G. Harris: Faithful to Truth as He Saw It." *Franklin County Historical Review* 16, no. 2 (1985): 103.

Alexander, Thomas B. "Neither Peace Nor War: Conditions in Tennessee in 1865." *East Tennessee Historical Society Publications* 21 (1949): 32.

Andrews, William J. "In the Days of the Past." In *Maury County, Tennessee Historical Sketches.* Ed. Jill K. Garrett. Columbia, Tenn.: Privately published, 1967.

Ash, Stephen V. *Middle Tennessee Society Transformed, 1860–1870: War and Peace in the Upper South.* Baton Rouge: Louisiana State University Press, 1988.

———. "Sharks in an Angry Sea: Civilian Resistance and Guerilla Warfare in Occupied Middle Tennessee, 1862–1865." *Tennessee Historical Quarterly* 45 (Fall 1986): 217.

———. *When the Yankees Came: Conflict and Chaos in the Occupied South, 1861–1865.* Chapel Hill: University of North Carolina Press, 1995.

Atkins, Jonathan M. *Parties, Politics, and Sectional Conflict in Tennessee, 1832–1862.* Knoxville: University of Tennessee Press, 1997.

———. "Politicians, Parties, and Slavery: The Second Party System and the Decision for Disunion in Tennessee." *Tennessee Historical Quarterly* 55 (Spring 1996): 20.

Bailey, Anne J. *The Chessboard of War: Sherman and Hood in the Autumn Campaign of 1864.* Lincoln: University of Nebraska Press, 2000.

Baker, Thomas Harrison. *The Memphis Commercial Appeal: The History of a Southern Newspaper.* Baton Rouge: Louisiana State University Press, 1971.

Ball, Clyde L. "The Public Career of Colonel A. S. Colyar, 1870–1877." *Tennessee Historical Quarterly* 12 (October 1953): 213.

Baumgardner, James L. "Abraham Lincoln, Andrew Johnson, and the Federal Patronage: An Attempt to Save Tennessee for the Union?" *East Tennessee Historical Society Publications* 45 (1973): 51.

Beach, Ursula Smith. *Along the Warito or a History of Montgomery County, Tennessee.* Nashville: McQuiddy Press, 1964.

Bearss, E. C. "The Construction of Fort Henry and Fort Donelson," *West Tennessee Historical Society Papers* 21 (1967): 24.

———. "The Fall of Fort Henry." *West Tennessee Historical Society Papers* 17 (1963): 85.

Belissary, Constantine G. "The Rise of Industry and the Industrial Spirit in Tennessee, 1865–1885." *Journal of Southern History* 19 (May 1943): 193.

Bergeron, Paul H. *Antebellum Politics in Tennessee.* Lexington: University Press of Kentucky, 1982.

Bergeron, Paul H., Stephen V. Ash, and Jeanette Keith. *Tennesseans and Their History.* Knoxville: University of Tennessee Press, 1999.

Blankinship, Gary. "Colonel Fielding Hurst and the Hurst Nation." *West Tennessee Historical Society Papers* 34 (1980): 71.

Bratton, Madison. "The Unionist Junket of the Legislatures of Tennessee and Kentucky in January, 1860." *East Tennessee Historical Society Publications* 7 (1935): 64.

Brodsky, Alyn. *Grover Cleveland: A Study in Character.* New York: St. Martin's, 2000.

Bryan, Charles F., Jr. "A Gathering of Tories: The East Tennessee Convention of 1861." *Tennessee Historical Quarterly* 39 (February 1980): 27.

Bryan, Wilhemus Bogart. *A History of the National Capital from its Foundation through the Period of the Adoption of the Organic Act.* 2 vols. New York: Macmillan Company, 1914–16.

Butler, William. *Mexico in Transition: From the Power of Political Romanism to Civil and Religious Liberty.* 2nd ed. rev. New York: Hunt & Eaton, 1892.

Caldwell, Joshua W. *Studies in the Constitutional History of Tennessee.* 2nd ed. Cincinnati: Robert W. Clarke & Co., 1907.

———. *Sketches of the Bench and Bar of Tennessee.* Knoxville: Ogden Bros., 1898.

Campbell, Mary E. R. *The Attitude of Tennesseans Toward the Union.* New York: Vantage, 1961.

Capers, Gerald M., Jr. *The Biography of a River Town, Memphis: Its Heroic Age.* 1939. Reprint, New Orleans: Gerald M. Capers, 1966.

Cardin, W. Thomas. "History of Pisgah." In *Flournoy Rivers' Manuscripts and History of Pisgah*. Comp. Clara M. Parker and Edward Jackson White. Pulaski, Tenn.: n.p., n.d.

Carter, Arthur B. *The Tarnished Cavalier: Major General Earl Van Dorn, C. S. A.* Knoxville: University of Tennessee Press, 1999.

Cartwright, Joseph H. *The Triumph of Jim Crow: Tennessee Race Relations in the 1880's*. Knoxville: University of Tennessee Press, 1976.

Channing, Steven A. *Crisis of Fear: Secession in South Carolina*. New York: Norton, 1974.

Cimprich, John. *Slavery's End in Tennessee, 1861–1865*. Tuscaloosa: University of Alabama Press, 1985.

———. *Fort Pillow, A Civil War Massacre, and Public Memory*. Baton Rouge: Louisiana State University Press, 2005.

Clark, Blanche Henry. *The Tennessee Yeomen, 1840–1860*. Nashville: Vanderbilt University Press, 1942.

Clark, Pat B. *The History of Clarksville and Old Red River County*. Dallas: Mathis, Van Nort & Co., 1936.

Connelly, Thomas L. *Army of the Heartland*. Baton Rouge: Louisiana State University Press, 1967.

———. *Autumn of Glory*. Baton Rouge: Louisiana State University Press, 1971.

Connelly, Thomas L., and Barbara L. Bellows. *God and General Longstreet: The Lost Cause and the Southern Mind*. Baton Rouge: Louisiana State University Press, 1982.

Cooling, Benjamin Franklin. *Forts Henry and Donelson: The Key to the Confederate Heartland*. Knoxville: University of Tennessee Press, 1987.

———. *Fort Donelson's Legacy: War and Society in Kentucky and Tennessee, 1862–1863*. Knoxville: University of Tennessee Press, 1997.

Corlew, Robert E. *Tennessee: A Short History*. 2nd ed. Knoxville: University of Tennessee Press, 1990.

Coulter, E. Merton. *William G. Brownlow: Fighting Parson of the Southern Highlands*. 1937. Reprint, Knoxville: University of Tennessee Press, 1999.

Cozzens, Peter. *No Better Place to Die: The Battle of Stones River*. Urbana: University of Illinois Press, 1990.

———. *The Darkest Days of the War: The Battles of Iuka and Corinth*. Chapel Hill: University of North Carolina Press, 1997.

Cribbs, Lennie Austin. "The Memphis Chinese Labor Convention, 1869." *West Tennessee Historical Society Papers* 37 (1983): 74.

Crofts, Daniel W. *Reluctant Confederates: Upper South Unionists in the Secession Crisis.* Chapel Hill: University of North Carolina Press, 1989.

Cunningham, O. Edward. *Shiloh and the Western Campaign of 1862.* Ed. Gary D. Joiner and Timothy B. Smith. New York: Savas Beatie, 2007.

Daniel, Larry. *Shiloh: The Battle That Changed the Civil War.* New York: Simon & Schuster, 1997.

———. *Days of Glory: The Army of the Cumberland, 1861–1865.* Baton Rouge: Louisiana State University Press, 2004.

———. "In Defense of Governor Isham G. Harris." *North & South* 7 (May 2004): 74.

Davis, John Henry. "Two Martyrs of the Yellow Fever Epidemic of 1878." *West Tennessee Historical Society Papers* 26 (1972): 20.

Davis, William C. *An Honorable Defeat: The Last Days of the Confederate Government.* New York: Harcourt, 2001.

Dew, Charles B. *Apostles of Disunion: Southern Secession Commissioners and the Causes of the Civil War.* Charlottesville: University Press of Virginia, 2001.

Drake, James Vaulx. *Life of General Robert Hatton.* Nashville: Marshall & Bruce, 1867.

Dunn, Durwood. *An Abolitionist in the Appalachian South: Ezekiel Birdseye on Slavery, Capitalism, and Separate Statehood in East Tennessee, 1841–1846.* Knoxville: University of Tennessee Press, 1997.

Durham, Walter T. *Nashville, The Occupied City: The First Seventeen Months— February 16, 1862, to June 30, 1863.* Nashville: Tennessee Historical Society, 1985.

Eicher, David J. *The Longest Night: A Military History of the Civil War.* New York: Simon & Schuster, 2001.

Eller, Ronald D. *Miners, Millhands and Mountaineers: Industrialization of the Appalachian South, 1880–1930.* Knoxville: University of Tennessee Press, 1982.

Elliott, Sam D. *Soldier of Tennessee: General Alexander P. Stewart and the Civil War in the West.* Baton Rouge: Louisiana State University Press, 1999.

Ellis, John H. "Disease and the Destiny of a City: The 1878 Yellow Fever Epidemic in Memphis." *West Tennessee Historical Society Papers* 28 (1974): 75.

Engle, Stephen D. *Struggle for the Heartland: The Campaigns from Fort Henry to Corinth.* Lincoln: University of Nebraska Press, 2001.

Eyal, Yontan. "Trade and Improvements: Young America and the Transformation of the Democratic Party." *Civil War History* 51 (September 2005): 245.

Faires, Clyde J. "Carmack v. Patterson: The Genesis of a Political Feud." *Tennessee Historical Quarterly* 38 (Fall 1979): 332.

Feistman, Eugene. "Radical Disenfranchisement and the Restoration of Tennessee, 1865–1866." *Tennessee Historical Quarterly* 12 (June 1953): 135.

Fisher, Noel C. *War at Every Door: Partisan Politics and Guerrilla Violence in East Tennessee, 1860–1869.* Chapel Hill: University of North Carolina Press, 1997.

———. "'Prepare Them For My Coming': General William T. Sherman, Total War, and Pacification in West Tennessee." *Tennessee Historical Quarterly* 51 (Summer 1992): 75.

Ford, Lacy K. *Origins of Southern Radicalism: The South Carolina Upcountry, 1800–1860.* New York: Oxford University Press, 1988.

Foster, Buck T. *Sherman's Mississippi Campaign.* Tuscaloosa: University of Alabama Press, 2006.

Foster, Gaines M. *Ghosts of the Confederacy: Defeat, the Lost Cause, and the Emergence of the New South, 1865 to 1913.* New York: Oxford University Press, 1987.

Franklin, John Hope. *The Militant South, 1800–1861.* Cambridge, Mass.: Belknap Press, 1956.

Friedman, Milton. *Money Mischief: Episodes in Monetary History.* New York: Harcourt Brace Jovanovich, 1992.

"Gen. Albert Sidney Johnston." *Confederate Veteran* 3 (March 1895): 81.

Grant, C. L. "The Public Career of Cave Johnson." *Tennessee Historical Quarterly* 10 (1951): 195.

Groce, W. Todd. *Mountain Rebels: East Tennessee Confederates and the Civil War, 1860–1870.* Knoxville: University of Tennessee Press, 1999.

Hamer, Marguerite Bartlett. "The Presidential Campaign of 1860 in Tennessee." *East Tennessee Historical Society Publications* 3 (January 1931): 9.

Harris, Carl V. "Right Fork or Left Fork? The Section-Party Alignments of Southern Democrats in Congress, 1873–1897." *Journal of Southern History* 42 (1976): 471.

Harris, Robert E., comp. *From Essex England to the Sunny Southern U.S.A.: A Harris Family Journey.* Tucker, Ga.: Robert E. Harris, 1994.

Hart, Roger L. *Redeemers, Bourbons and Populists: Tennessee, 1870–1896.* Baton Rouge: Louisiana State University Press, 1975.

Hattaway, Herman, and Archer Jones. *How the North Won: A Military History of the Civil War.* Urbana: University of Illinois Press, 1983, 1991.

Headley, P. C. *Public Men of To-Day: Being Biographies of the President and Vice-*

President of the United States, Each Member of the Cabinet, the United States Senators and the Members of the House of Representatives of the Forty-Seventh Congress, the Chief Justice and the Justices of the Supreme Court, and of the Governors of the Several States. Hartford: S. S. Scranton, 1882.

Henry, J. Milton. "The Revolution in Tennessee, February, 1861 to June, 1861." *Tennessee Historical Quarterly* 18 (June 1959): 99.

Henry, Robert Selph. *"First With the Most" Forrest.* 1944. Reprint, Wilmington, N.C.: Broadfoot Publishing, 1987.

Hopkins, Anne H., and William Lyons. *Tennessee Votes, 1799–1976.* Knoxville: University of Tennessee Bureau of Public Administration, 1978.

Horn, Stanley F. *The Army of Tennessee,* 1941. Reprint, Wilmington, N.C.: Broadfoot Publishers, 1987.

———. "Isham G. Harris in the Pre-War Years." *Tennessee Historical Quarterly* 19 (1960): 195.

Hubbard, Charles M. *The Burden of Confederate Diplomacy.* Knoxville: University of Tennessee Press, 1998.

Hudspeth, Harvey Gresham. "Seven Days in Nashville: Politics, the State Debt, and the Making of a United States Senator; January 19–26, 1881." *West Tennessee Historical Society Papers* 52 (1998): 81.

Hughes, Nathaniel C., Jr. *The Battle of Belmont: Grant Strikes South.* Chapel Hill: University of North Carolina Press, 1991.

———. *General William J. Hardee: Old Reliable.* Baton Rouge: Louisiana State University Press, 1965.

Hughes, Nathaniel C., Jr., Connie Walton Moretti, and James Michael Browne. *Brigadier General Tyree H. Bell, C.S.A.: Forrest's Fighting Lieutenant.* Knoxville: University of Tennessee Press, 2004.

Hughes, Nathaniel C., Jr., and Roy P. Stonsifer. *The Life and Wars of Gideon J. Pillow.* Chapel Hill: University of North Carolina Press, 1993.

Jacobs, Dillard. "Outfitting the Provisional Army of Tennessee: A Report on New Source Materials." *Tennessee Historical Quarterly* 40 (Fall 1981): 257.

Jennings, Thelma. "Tennessee and the Nashville Conventions of 1850." *Tennessee Historical Quarterly* 30 (Spring 1971): 70.

Johnson, E. McLeod. *A History of Henry County, Tennessee: Descriptive, Pictorial Reproductions of Old Papers and Manuscripts.* Vol. 1. n.p., 1958.

Jones, Robert B. *Tennessee at the Crossroads: The State Debt Controversy 1870–1883.* Knoxville: University of Tennessee Press, 1977.

Jones, Robert B., and Mark E. Byrnes. "'Rebels Never Forgive': Former President Johnson and the Senate Election of 1869." *Tennessee Historical Quarterly* 66 (Fall 2007): 250.

Karabell, Zachary. *Chester Alan Arthur.* New York: Times Books, 2004.

Keating, J. M. *History of the City of Memphis and Shelby County, Tennessee.* 2 vols. Syracuse, N.Y.: D. Mason & Co., 1888.

Keith, Jeanette. *Country People in the New South: Tennessee's Upper Cumberland.* Chapel Hill: University of North Carolina Press, 1995.

Koenig, Louis W. *Bryan: A Political Biography of William Jennings Bryan.* New York: G. P. Putnam's Sons, 1971.

Lambert, John R. *Arthur Pue Gorman.* Baton Rouge: Louisiana State University Press, 1953.

Lamon, Lester C. *Blacks in Tennessee, 1791–1970.* Knoxville: University of Tennessee Press, 1981.

Lester, Connie. *Up From the Mudsills of Hell: The Farmer's Alliance, Populism, and Progressive Agriculture in Tennessee, 1870–1915.* Athens: University of Georgia Press, 2006.

Lewis, Eugene. "The Tennessee Gubernatorial Campaign and Election of 1894." *Tennessee Historical Quarterly* 13 (December 1954): 301.

Losson, Christopher. *Tennessee's Forgotten Warriors: Frank Cheatham and His Confederate Division.* Knoxville: University of Tennessee Press, 1989.

Lovett, Bobby L. "Memphis Riots: White Reaction to Blacks in Memphis, May 1865–July 1866." *Tennessee Historical Quarterly* 38 (Spring 1979): 9.

Lufkin, Charles L. "Secession and Coercion in Tennessee, the Spring of 1861." *Tennessee Historical Quarterly* 50 (Summer 1991): 98.

Madden, David. "Unionist Resistance to Confederate Occupation: The Bridge Burners of East Tennessee." *East Tennessee Historical Society Publications* 52–53 (1980–81): 22.

Maness, Lonnie. "Henry Emerson Etheridge and the Gubernatorial Election of 1867: A Study in Futility." *West Tennessee Historical Society Papers* 47 (1993): 38.

Martin, Asa Earl. "Anti-Slavery Activities of the Methodist Episcopal Church in Tennessee." *Tennessee Historical Magazine* 2 (1916): 98–109.

McBride, Robert M., and Dan M. Robison. *Biographical Directory of the Tennessee General Assembly.* 6 vols. Nashville: Tennessee State Library and Archives and Tennessee Historical Commission, 1979–91.

McDonough, James Lee. *Nashville: The Western Confederacy's Last Gamble.* Knoxville: University of Tennessee Press, 2004.

McKee, James W., Jr. "Felix K. Zollicoffer: Confederate Defender of East Tennessee, Part I." *East Tennessee Historical Society Publications* 43 (1971): 34.

———. "Felix K. Zollicoffer: Confederate Defender of East Tennessee, Part II." *East Tennessee Historical Society Publications* 44 (1972): 17.

McKenzie, Robert Tracy. *One South or Many?: Plantation Belt and Upcountry in Civil War-era Tennessee.* Cambridge and New York: Cambridge University Press, 1984.

———. "Freedmen and the Soil in the Upper South: The Reorganization of Tennessee Agriculture, 1865–1880." *Journal of Southern History* 59 (February 1993): 63.

———. "Prudent Silence and Strict Neutrality: The Parameters of Unionism in Parson Brownlow's Knoxville, 1860–1863." In *Enemies of the Country: New Perspectives on Unionists in the Civil War South.* Athens: University of Georgia Press, 2001.

McMurry, Richard M. *Atlanta 1864: Last Chance for the Confederacy.* Lincoln: University of Nebraska Press, 2000.

———. "The Mackall Journal and Its Antecedents." *Civil War History* 20 (December 1974): 311.

McPherson, James M. *Battle Cry of Freedom: The Civil War Era.* New York: Oxford University Press, 1988.

McWhiney, Grady. *Braxton Bragg and Confederate Defeat.* Vol. 1. Tuscaloosa: University of Alabama Press, 1969, 1991.

Miscamble, Wilson D. "Andrew Johnson and the Election of William G. ('Parson') Brownlow as Governor of Tennessee." *Tennessee Historical Quarterly* 37 (Fall 1978): 308.

Mooney, Chase C. "Some Institutional and Statistical Aspects of Slavery in Tennessee." *Tennessee Historical Quarterly* 1 (September 1942): 195.

———. "The Question of Slavery and the Free Negro in the Tennessee Constitutional Convention of 1834." *Journal of Southern History* 12 (November 1946): 487.

Moran, Nathan K. "'No Alternative Left': State and County Government in Northwest Tennessee During the Union Invasion, January–June, 1862." *West Tennessee Historical Society Papers* 46 (1992): 13.

———. "Military Government and Divided Loyalties: The Union Occupation of

Northwest Tennessee, June 1862–August 1862." *West Tennessee Historical Society Papers* 48 (1994): 91.

Myers, Raymond E. *The Zollie Tree.* Louisville: The Filston Club Press, 1964.

Nevins, Allan. *Grover Cleveland: A Study in Courage.* New York: Dodd, Mead & Co., 1933.

Nichols, Jeannette Paddock. "The Politics and Personalities of Silver Repeal in the United States Senate." *American Historical Review* 41 (October 1935): 26.

Oberholzer, Ellis Paxon. *A History of the United States Since the Civil War.* 5 vols. New York: Macmillan, 1937.

Parks, Joseph. *General Leonidas Polk, C.S.A.: The Fighting Bishop.* Baton Rouge: Louisiana State University Press, 1962.

———. *John Bell of Tennessee.* Baton Rouge: Louisiana State University Press, 1950.

Patton, James W. "The Progress of Emancipation in Tennessee, 1796–1860." *Journal of Negro History* 17 (January 1932): 67.

Phillips, Paul David. "Education of Blacks in Tennessee During Reconstruction, 1865–1870." *Tennessee Historical Quarterly* 46 (Summer 1987): 98.

Rable, George C. *But There Was No Peace: The Rule of Violence in the Politics of Reconstruction.* Athens: University of Georgia Press, 1984.

Randall, J. G., and David Donald. *The Civil War and Reconstruction.* Lexington, Mass.: D. C. Heath, 1969.

Rehnquist, William H. *Centennial Crisis: The Disputed Election of 1876.* New York: Knopf, 2004.

Rhodes, James Ford. *History of the United States from Hayes to McKinley, 1877–1896.* New York: Macmillan, 1919.

Rister, Carl Coke. "Carlota, A Confederate Colony in Mexico." *Journal of Southern History* 11 (February 1945): 33.

Robison, Daniel M. "Governor Robert L. Taylor and the Blair Educational Bill in Tennessee." *Tennessee Historical Magazine,* Series II, vol. II (October 1931): 28.

———. "The Political Background of Tennessee's War of the Roses." *East Tennessee Historical Society Publications* 5 (1933): 125.

Rothman, David J. *Politics and Power: The United States Senate 1869–1901.* New York: Atheneum, 1969.

Schlesinger, Arthur M., Jr. *The Age of Jackson.* Boston: Little, Brown, & Co., 1953.

Schroeder-Lein, Glenna R. *Confederate Hospitals on the Move: Samuel H. Stout and the Army of Tennessee.* Columbia: University of South Carolina Press, 1994.

Schweikart, Larry. "Tennessee Banks in the Antebellum Period, Part II." *Tennessee Historical Quarterly* 45 (1986): 199.

Schouler, James. *History of the United States of America Under the Constitution.* 7 vols. Cambridge, Mass.: Harvard University Press, 1894–1913.

Seawright, Sandy. "Ten 'Greatest Tennesseans'—A Reappraisal." *Tennessee Historical Quarterly* 35 (Summer 1976): 222.

Severance, Ben H. *Tennessee's Radical Army: The State Guard and Its Role in Reconstruction.* Knoxville: University of Tennessee Press, 2005.

Shaler, Nathaniel S. *Kentucky: A Pioneer Commonwealth.* Boston: Houghton, Mifflin & Co., 1885.

Shapiro, Karin A. *A New South Rebellion: The Battle Against Convict Labor in the Tennessee Coalfields, 1871–1896.* Chapel Hill: University of North Carolina Press, 1998.

Sikes, Lewright B. "Gustavus Adolphus Henry: Champion of Lost Causes." *Tennessee Historical Quarterly* 50 (Fall 1991): 173.

Simpson, Brooks D. *The Reconstruction Presidents.* Lawrence: University Press of Kansas, 1998.

Smith, Timothy B. *This Great Battlefield of Shiloh.* Knoxville: University of Tennessee Press, 2004.

———. *The Untold Story of Shiloh: The Battle and the Battlefield.* Knoxville: University of Tennessee Press, 2006.

Snodgrass, Charles Albert. *The History of Freemasonry in Tennessee, 1789–1943.* Nashville, Ambrose Printing Company, 1944.

Socolofsky, Homer E., and Allan B. Spetter. *The Presidency of Benjamin Harrison.* Lawrence: University Press of Kansas, 1987.

Souissant, St. George L. "Tennessee, the Compromise of 1850, and the Nashville Convention." *Tennessee Historical Magazine* 4 (December 1918): 215.

Speer, William S. *Sketches of Prominent Tennesseans.* Nashville: Albert B. Tavel, 1888.

Sword, Wiley. *Shiloh: Bloody April.* 1974. Reprint, Dayton, Ohio: Morningside Bookshop, 1988.

———. *The Confederacy's Last Hurrah: Spring Hill, Franklin, and Nashville.* Lawrence: University Press of Kansas, 1992.

Taylor, Alrutheus A. *The Negro in Tennessee, 1865–1880.* Washington, D.C.: Associated Publishers, 1941.

Tennessee Civil War Centennial Commission. *Tennesseans in the Civil War.* 2 vols. Nashville: n.p., 1964.

Tilley, Bette B. "The Sprit of Improvement: Reformism and Slavery in West Tennessee." *West Tennessee Historical Society Papers* 28 (1974): 25.

Trefousse, Hans L. *Andrew Johnson: A Biography.* New York: W. W. Norton & Co., 1989.

Trelease, Allen W. *White Terror: The Ku Klux Klan Conspiracy and Southern Reconstruction.* New York: Harper & Row, 1971.

Twain, Mark. *Life on the Mississippi.* New York: Harper Brothers, 1905.

Van Dyke, Roger Raymond. "Antebellum Henry County." *West Tennessee Historical Society Papers* 33 (1979): 48.

Walther, Eric H. *The Fire-Eaters.* Baton Rouge: Louisiana State University Press, 1972.

Ward, Andrew. *River Run Red: The Fort Pillow Massacre in the American Civil War.* New York: Viking, 2005.

Warner, Ezra. *Generals in Gray.* Baton Rouge: Louisiana State University Press, 1959.

Welch, Robert E., Jr. *The Presidencies of Grover Cleveland.* Lawrence: University Press of Kansas, 1988.

Whitley, Edith Rucker. *Tennessee Genealogical Records: Henry County "Old Time Stuff."* n.p., 1968.

White, Robert Hiram. *Messages of the Governors of Tennessee.* 11 vols. to date. Nashville: The Tennessee Historical Commission, 1952–.

———. *Development of the Tennessee State Educational Organization, 1796–1929.* Kingsport, Tenn.: Southern Publishers, 1929.

Williams, Frank B. "The Pan-Electric Telephone Controversy." *Tennessee Historical Quarterly* 2 (June 1943): 144.

Williams, T. Harry. *P. G. T. Beauregard: Napoleon in Gray.* 1955. Reprint, Baton Rouge: Louisiana State University Press, 1995.

Wills, Brian Steel. *A Battle from the Start: The Life of Nathan Bedford Forrest.* New York: HarperCollins, 1992.

Winters, Donald L. *Tennessee Farming, Tennessee Farmers: Antebellum Agriculture in the Upper South.* Knoxville: University of Tennessee Press, 1995.

Woodworth, Steven E. *Six Armies in Tennessee: The Chickamauga and Chattanooga Campaigns*. Lincoln: University of Nebraska Press, 1998.

——. *Jefferson Davis and His Generals: The Failure of Confederate Command in the West*. Lawrence: University Press of Kansas, 1990.

——. "'The Indeterminate Quantities': Jefferson Davis, Leonidas Polk, and the End of Kentucky Neutrality, September, 1861." *Civil War History* 38 (December 1992): 289.

Wyeth, John Allen. *The Life of Lieutenant-General Nathan Bedford Forrest*. New York: Harper and Brothers, 1899.

Yearns, W. Buck, ed. *The Confederate Governors*. Athens: University of Georgia Press, 1985.

Young, J. P. *Standard History of Memphis, Tennessee*. Knoxville: H. W. Crew, 1912.

UNPUBLISHED WORKS

Bryan, Charles F., Jr. "The Civil War in East Tennessee: A Social, Political and Economic Study." Ph.D. dissertation. University of Tennessee, 1978.

Jones, Paul W. and Joyce E. *Major Edward Travis*, 1993.

Looney, John Thomas. "Isham G. Harris of Tennessee: Bourbon Senator, 1877–1897." M.A. thesis. University of Tennessee, 1970.

McLeary, Ila. "The Life of Isham G. Harris." M.A. thesis. University of Tennessee, 1930.

Moran, Nathan K. "Isham Harris and Confederate State Government in Tennessee." Ph.D. dissertation. University of Memphis, 1999.

Partin, Robert Love. "The Administration of Isham G. Harris." M.A. thesis. Peabody College, 1928.

Tayloe, Stephanie Routon. *The Henry County, Tennessee Ancestor Series: Men of Distinction*, Vol. 1. n.d.

Watters, George Wayne. "Isham Green Harris, Civil War Governor and Senator from Tennessee, 1818–1897." Ph.D. dissertation, Florida State University, 1977.

INDEX